Non-State Regulatory Regimes

Myriam Senn

Non-State Regulatory Regimes

Understanding Institutional Transformation

Springer

PD Dr. Myriam Senn, LL.M.

ISBN 978-3-642-14973-3 e-ISBN 978-3-642-14974-0
DOI 10.1007/978-3-642-14974-0
Springer Heidelberg Dordrecht London New York

Library of Congress Control Number: 2010938123

Cover design: WMX Design GmbH, Heidelberg, Germany

Printed on acid-free paper

Springer is part of Springer Science+Business Media (www.springer.com)

Preface

This book grew out of an attempt to gain a better understanding of the conceptual basis of self-regulation. Like most books, the original intention evolved and was quickly replaced by a broader scope of investigation. The decision was to approach forms of ordering different from state regulation or non-state regulatory regimes. Then, it rapidly became evident that traditional methodological and analytical legal paths were not sufficient to explain the emergence and subsistence of forms of regulation that are either not originated in the state (non-state) or either that propose an alternative to state regulation. The optic had to be enlarged. The interplay of state regulation, non-state, and private regulation can best be studied when departing from public policy approaches. In comparison to other books on regulatory issues, this is also the most innovative element of this book. Public policy allows understanding the emergence of regulatory regimes and explaining how they coalesce and how they form a working system. As such, the book is a cross-disciplinary study.

Concentrating on structural issues about regulatory regimes, the book draws extensively on examples from the financial sector. It reflects my background in that sector. At the same time, it is a predestined sector for the purpose of this book, because not least following the 2007–2009 financial crisis one witnesses the emergence of a number of institutional arrangements and regulatory regimes both at the national and at the international or global levels.

The ideas underlying this book have been discussed in a range of fora. I am grateful to all those who have contributed in a variety of ways to the completion of this book and who have made comments and suggestions at various points of the development of the book. I would like to mention in particular:

A stay at the ESRC Centre for the Analysis of Risk and Regulation (CARR) of the London School and Economics and Political Science, that proved to be very valuable. I would like to thank Bridget Hutter, Michael Power, and Julia Black.

The Collegium Budapest Institute for Advanced Study offered an enriching research atmosphere and was a source of inspiration. The exchanges with colleagues and fellows were motivating. I am particularly grateful to Imre Kondor and Philippe C. Schmitter for their support and constructive discussions.

My participation in the Eurocores research program on The Evolution of Cooperation and Trading of the European Science Foundation (TECT), in particular in the group focusing on the Dynamic Complexity of Cooperation-Based Self-Organizing Commercial Networks in the First Global Age (1400–1800) proved to be fruitful as well. I am very indebted to Jack Owen and Rüdiger Klein for inviting me to participate in that multi-disciplinary research project for it gave me important insights to develop the concept of my own book.

I would also like to thank especially the reviewers of my "habilitation thesis" at the University of St.Gallen, Michael Blair QC, Peter Nobel and Rolf H. Weber.

This study was supported by a research grant of the Swiss National Science Foundation, which I thankfully acknowledge at this place.

Last but not least, I would like to express my appreciation and thanks to Mark Kyburz for his language proofreading of the manuscript, to Lukas Jaroch for his help along specific legal issues, Sadri Saieb for his very efficient assistance in providing research material, Anita Stauffacher for technical support, to Anke Seyfried for her professional advice, and finally to Gnanamanni Umamaheswari for overseeing the production of the book with care.

July 2010 Myriam Senn

Contents

List of Figures

Table of Legislation

Switzerland

Agreement on the Swiss banks' code of conduct with regard to the exercise of due diligence (CDB 08) from SwissBanking, Swiss Bankers Association, of 7 April 2008

Circular of the Swiss Financial Market Supervisory Authority (FINMA) on Self-regulation recognised as a minimum standard of 20 November 2008, FINMA-Circ. 08/10 (Self-regulation as a miminum standard)

Code of Conduct of the Swiss Funds Industry of 30 March, 2009

Code of Obligations of 30 March 1911 (CO) SR 220

Directive on Information Relating to Corporate Governance (Corporate Governance Directive, DCG) of 29 October 2008 (Entry into force on 1 July 2009) SIX Swiss Exchange, with Annex

Federal Act on Auditors' Authorization and Supervision of 16 December 2005 (Auditors Act, AA) SR 221.302

Federal Act on Cartels and Other Restraints of Competition (Cartel Act, LCart) of 6 October 1995, SR 251

Federal Act on Certification Services in the Domain of the Electronic Signature (Law on the Electronic Signature, SCSE) or 19 December 2003, SR 943.03

Federal Act on Collective Investment Schemes (Collective Investment Schemes Act, CISA) of 23 June, 2006, SR 951.31

Federal Act on the Federal Financial Market Supervisory Authority (FINMA) of 22 June, 2007 (Law on the Supervisory Authority, FINMASA) SR 956.1

Federal Act on Money Laundering of 10 October 1997 (FAML) SR 955.0

Federal Act on Securities Exchanges and Securities Trading (Securities Exchange Act, SESTA) of March 24, 1995, SR 954.1

Federal Constitution of the Swiss Confederation of 18 April 1999, SR 101

Federal Ordinance on Banks and Savings Banks of 17 May 1972 (Banking Ordinance, BO) SR 952.02

Gesetz betreffend die Gewerbe der Effektensensale und Börsenagenten of 2nd December 1883 (Law on securities trading and brokers)

Listing Rules of the SIX Swiss Exchange of 21 April 2010

Ordinance on Securities Exchanges and Securities Trading of 2 December 1996 (Exchange Ordinance, SESTO) SR 954.11

Rules of Procedure, SIX Swiss Exchange, 11/06

Swiss Code of Best Practice for Corporate Governance, economiesuisse of 2002

United Kingdom

Companies Act 2006

Financial Services and Markets Act 2000, 2000 Chapter 8

Letter of the FSA dated 10 April 2006, FSA, Reviewing our Money Laundering Regime PS06/1 (FSA, 2006)

Chapter 9, Continuing obligations, FSA Handbook, Release 100, April 2010

The Takeover Code, The City Code on Takeovers and Mergers (The Code)

United States

Credit Rating Agency Reform Act of 2006, Public Law No. 109-291, September 29, 2006, amending the Securities Exchange Act of 1934, 109th Congress

Sarbanes-Oxley Act of 2002 – H.R. 3763, Public Law 107-204, 107th Congress

Securities Act of 1933, Release No. 8222 / April 25, 2003, Securities Exchange Act of 1934, Release No. 47745 / April 25, 2003, Order Regarding Section 103(a)(3)(B) of the Sarbanes-Oxley Act of 2002

International

Basle II: International Convergence of Capital Measurement and Capital Standards: A Revised Framework – Comprehensive Version, June 2006, Basel Committee on Banking Supervision (Revised May 2008)

Charter of the United Nations

Code of Conduct Fundamentals for Credit Rating Agencies (May 2008) IOSCO

Council Regulation (EC) No 1/2003 of 16 December 2002 on the implementation of the rules on competition laid down in articles 81 and 82 of the Treaty; OJ L 1/1, 04/01/2003, 1–25

Directive 2004/25/EC of the European Parliament and of the Council of 21 April 2004 on takeover bids, OJ L 142, 30/04/2004, 12–23

Regulation (EC) No 1060/2009 of the European Parliament and of the Council of 16 September 2009 on Credit Rating Agencies; Credit Rating Agency Reform Act of 2007, September 29, 2006, Pub. L. No. 109–291 (2006)

Statute of the International Court of Justice

Core Principles for Effective Banking Supervision, October 2006, Basel Committee on Banking Supervision

The UN Global Compact launched by the United Nations in 2000

The United Nations Norms on the Responsibilities of Transnational Corporations and other Business Enterprises of 2003

Vienna Convention on the Law of Treaties 1969 (VCLT)

Table of Cases

Swiss Federal High Court

Case – BGE 99 Ib 104 of 4 May 1973
Case – BGE 105 Ib 348 of 25 October 1979
Case – BGE 109 Ib 146 of 3 June 1983
Case – BGE 116 Ib 331 of 11 December 1990
Case – BGE 117 II 315 of 15 August 1991
Case – BGE 125 IV 139 of 30 April 1999

Other cases

Case of the S.S. 'Wimbledon', P.C.I.J. Series A., No. 1 (1923) 23-24 (Permanent Court of International Justice)

Case concerning the United States Diplomatic and Consular Staff in Tehran (United States of America v. Iran) I.C.J. Reports 1980 (International Court of Justice)

Case No ARB/01/13, Decision of the Tribunal on Objections to Jurisdiction of 6 August 2003, Société Générale de Surveillance S.A. (SGS) v Islamic Republic of Pakistan, International Centre for Settlement of Investment Disputes

Case No ARB/02/6, Decision of the Tribunal on Objections to Jurisdiction of 29 January 2004, Société Générale de Surveillance S.A. (SGS) v Republic of the Philippines, International Centre for the Settlement of Investment Disputes

Tribunal de Grande Instance de Paris, Ordonnance de référé, 22 mai 2000, UEJF et Licra c/ Yahoo! Inc. et Yahoo France; Tribunal de Grande Instance de Paris, Ordonnance de référé du 11 août 2000, UEJF et al. c/ Yahoo! Inc. et Yahoo France; Tribunal de Grande Instance de Paris, Ordonnance de référé du 20 novembre 2000, UEJF et al. c/ Yahoo! Inc. et Yahoo France

Abbreviations

AIMA	Alternative Investment Management Association
BCBS	Basel Committee on Banking Supervision
BYBIL	British Year Book of International Law
CBA	Cost-Benefit Analysis
CDB	Agreement on the Swiss banks' code of conduct with regard to the exercise of due diligence
CGFS	Committee on the Global Financial System
Circ.	Circular
CRA	Credit Rating Agency
DNS	Domain Name System
DSU	Dispute Settlement Understanding
ECAI	External Credit Assessment Institution
ECE	Economic Commission for Europe
ECGI	European Corporate Governance Institute
ECOSOC	Economic and Social Council of the United Nations
EFTA	European Free Trade Association
et al.	et alii, and others
etc.	et cetera
EU	European Union
FAML	Federal Act on Money Laundering of 10 October 1997, SR 955.0
FAO	Food and Agriculture Organization
FINMA	Swiss Financial Market Supervisory Authority
FINMASA	Federal Act on the Swiss Financial Market Supervisory Authority (Financial Markets Supervision Act) of 22 June 2007, SR 956.1
FNRA	Financial Industry Regulatory Authority
FSA	Financial Services Authority
FSAP	Financial Sector Assessment Program
FSB	Financial Stability Board
FSF	Financial Stability Forum
G7	Group of Seven

G20	Group of Twenty
GAPP	Generally Accepted Principles and Practices of 11 October 2008
GATT	General Agreement on Tariffs and Trade
IAB	Internet Architecture Board
IAEA	International Atomic Energy Agency
IAIS	International Association of Insurance Supervisors
IANA	Internet Assigned Numbers Authority
IASB	International Accounting Standards Board
IASC	International Accounting Standards Committee
IATA	International Air Transport Association
IBM	International Business Machines
ICANN	Internet Corporation for Assigned Names and Numbers
ICAO	International Civil Aviation Organization
ICC	International Chamber of Commerce
ICCA	International Council of Chemical Associations
ICGN	International Corporate Governance Network
ICJ	International Court of Justice
ICTY	International Criminal Tribunal for the former Yugoslavia
IEC	International Electrotechnical Commission
IESG	Internet Engineering Steering Group
IETF	Internet Engineering Task Force
IFRS	International Financial Reporting Standards
IGO	Inter-governmental organizations
IIF	Institute of International Finance
ILC	International Law Commission
ILO	International Labour Organization
IMF	International Monetary Fund
IMO	International Maritime Organization
Inc	Incorporated
IOSCO	International Organization of Securities Commissions
IRSG	Internet Research Steering Group
IRTF	Internet Research Task Force
ISA	International Federation of the National Standardizing Associations
ISDA	International Swaps and Derivatives Association
ISLA	International Securities Lending Association
ISO	International Organization for Standardization
ISOC	Internet Society
IT	Information technology
ITU	International Telecommunications Union
IWG-SWF	International Working Group of Sovereign Wealth Funds
JMLSG	Joint Money Laundering Steering Group
LMA	Loan Market Association
MNC	multinational corporation
MOU	Memorandum of Understanding

NASD	National Association of Securities Dealers, Inc.
NGA	Non-governmental association
NGO	Non-governmental organization
NPM	New Public Management
NRSRO	Nationally Recognized Statistical Rating Organizations
NYSE	New York Stock Exchange
OECD	Organization for Economic Cooperation and Development
PCAOB	Public Company Accounting Oversight Board
PIG	Public interest group
RFC-Editor	Request for Comments – Editor
RIA	Regulatory Impact Analysis
RMP	Risk Management Plan
SBA	Swiss Bankers Association
SEC	Securities and Exchange Commission
SESTA	Federal on Securities Exchange and Securities Trading of 24 March 1995 (SR 954.1)
SESTO	Ordinance on Securities Exchanges and Securities Trading of 2 December 1996 (SR 954.11)
SFA	Swiss Funds Association
SGS	Société Générale de Surveillance
S&P	Standard & Poor's Corporation
SR	Systematische Sammlung des Bundesrechts
SRA	Self-regulatory association
SRO	Self-regulatory organization
SWF	Sovereign Wealth Fund
UDRP	Uniform Domain Name Dispute Resolution Policy
UK	United Kingdom
UN	United Nations
Uncitral	UN Commission on International Trade Law
Unctad	United Nations Conference on Trade and Development
UNEP	United Nations Environmental Programme
UNRISD	United Nations Research Institute for Social Development
UNSCC	United Nations Standards Coordinating Committee
US	United States
VCLT	Vienna Convention on the Law of Treaties between States and International Organizations or between International Organizations, 1986
VOC	Vereenigde Oostindische Compagnie
W3C	World Wide Web Consortium
WIPO	World Intellectual Property Organization
WSC	World Standards Cooperation
WTO	World Trade Organization

Introduction

This study explores the understanding of the concept of regulation. The purpose is to approach forms of ordering different from state regulation or non-state regulatory regimes. The main premise lies in the recognition that regulation does not only mean state regulation or the product of a state activity as legitimated authority. On the contrary, it is based on the assumption that regulation is also a domain of civil society. Regulation occurs in many spheres. Diverse regulatory regimes can be encountered. They lead to a fragmentation of regulation whereas the phenomenon of globalization adds to that process. Not surprisingly, we are now experiencing a considerable growth in academic studies on regulation in a range of fields: international relations, political science, law, sociology, or also economics. International organizations such as the OECD and other authorities analyze the process of regulation and may submit proposals for 'better regulation' or alternatives to regulation that may represent adequate forms of governance.

Non-state regulatory regimes raise a number of issues. Addressing and delineating these issues poses diverse challenges. The regimes are concretized by alternative forms of regulation. In practice, these forms of regulation are more common than seems initially apparent. They may appear in a number of forms, and play an important role in fields such as the financial and securities markets, the press and media, the pharmaceutical industry, the professions, or digitization, to mention a few. Hence, this study is an essay to outline the concept underlying these regimes. It will explore their various aspects, using a multifocal lens. As will be discussed, it is mainly an institutional issue. Non-state, autonomous regulatory regimes or alternative forms of regulation are driven by diverse, often private forces. The presence of epistemic communities, networks and private associations, or non-governmental, self-regulatory organizations as distinctive systems of interest representation taken in relation to the state is examined as steps leading to the substantiation and formalisation of the emergence of these regimes.

Seizing and defining the concept of regulation necessitates an interdisciplinary approach. It includes legal, political, international relations', economic, and sociological perspectives. The theoretical construct used as the backbone of the study consists in the discussion of the theoretical foundations and concrete examples, the analysis, and evaluation. Methodologically, the point of departure is an enlarged

M. Senn, *Non-State Regulatory Regimes*,
DOI 10.1007/978-3-642-14974-0_1,

definition of regulation. This study begins with setting the framework of traditional state regulation and then opens the field to private, alternative forms of regulation. The framework of state regulation revolves around the debate on whether and how to regulate as well as possibilities to negotiate the forms of regulation among the groups of interest concerned. It will lead the way to the possible emergence of alternatives to regulation and autonomous regulatory regimes. In that regard, the inclusion of the process of globalization is important. It appears to be essential to take the transnational aspects of regulation into account. Regulation is no longer only national or international, but largely subject to and dependent on global developments. Regulatory practices of national governments or regulatory agencies shaping national regulatory frameworks have striven to be inclusive of not only national but also multiple, international interests in the ways in which the rules of governance constitutive of transnational markets are shaped. At the same time, transnational regulation is emerging and constitutes non-state, autonomous regulatory regimes. It is based on global epistemic communities and networks that might set standards and define regulation efficiently. Thus, relationships between the factors shaping these regulatory forms are sought and their characteristics are examined.

This study draws extensively – although not only – on the regulatory developments within the financial markets. Financial markets have always made extensive use of alternative and also private regulatory solutions. Financial services are a prominent case of the emergence of non-state autonomous regulatory regimes. They also play a determining role in relation to the process of globalization and the constitution of epistemic communities and networks. Another reason for focusing on financial markets is that they are a most foundational domain.

The first chapter deals with the concept of state regulation. Its goal is to set the scene to introduce the core of the topic. Departing from the concept of state regulation assuming the form of classic command and control regulation, it first explores the rationales underlying it. Then, the impact of public policy issues and the debate on whether and how to regulate are discussed. The public theories underlying regulation are briefly cited and the role of the institutions involved in the process of regulation is examined. Based on these elements, the concept of regulation is broadened through the elaboration of the decentred analysis of regulation. It is no more understood solely in the sense of a state activity. A meta-regulatory approach is possible. Fragmentation and legal pluralism are the hallmark of regulation. Within that enlarged framework, autonomous regimes and alternative forms of regulation will appear.

The second chapter represents the core of the theoretical part of the study. Its objective is to seize the characteristics leading to the emergence of autonomous regulatory regimes. Contrary to what is generally admitted, these forms of regulation are common. They correspond to distinctive, modern systems of interest representation. This chapter approaches the basics of these regulatory regimes. It first discusses how alternative forms of regulation interact within the existing state regulatory framework. A distinction is made between the possible inclusion of these regimes in state regulatory concepts and the opposite, their emergence from civil society. The next characteristic considered is the functional and historical dimension. It is important to understand the emergence, development, and persistence of these autonomous regimes in the course of time. The core of the chapter concentrates on institutional structure. It is argued that the source of alternative forms of regulation is the theory of interest. Regulatory regimes always emerge from collective action. Individuals form epistemic communities to reach their objectives. Following the formalization of their relationship in the form of an association, these regimes acquire another quality. Different aspects of institutional structures of these regimes are discussed, taking into account the political currents of corporatism, liberalism, and pluralism.

Chapter three is devoted to the identification of cases or concrete examples representing alternative forms of regulation, non-state, hybrid, or private autonomous regimes. This chapter aims to provide an overview of possible forms of regulatory governance. It distinguishes the following categories of cases: Self-regulation, a firm's own regulation, co-regulation, coercive self-regulation, self-contained regimes, and global networks. The emergence, the underlying institutional arrangements, and the characteristics of the cases chosen are studied. Their contest should illustrate the theoretical foundations of the previous chapter and enrich the analysis undertaken in the next one.

The fourth chapter is the analysis. It attempts to cast some light on the concept of alternative forms of regulation and non-state, autonomous regulatory regimes. It also tries to show that non-state regimes are the result of a fragmentation of regulation and at the same time of a need for standardization. The components leading to fragmentation and standardization are examined in detail. The interplay of the state and civil society approach is explored. The process of transformation, which characterizes the development of these forms of regulation, is discussed at length, including aspects of cooperation, auto-constitutionalism, and effectiveness or impact of the regimes. Finally, the nature of these regulatory regimes is debated.

The focus of the fifth chapter is the evaluation. Regulation is evaluated as an institutional issue that should be adapted to the sectors and activities it regulates. The concept can be summarized as an issue of governance and of shifting the balance between the following key institutions: the state and the market actors within civil society, and their representative organizations.

Chapter 1
On Regulation

Abstract The chapter deals with the concept of state regulation. Its goal is to set the scene to introduce the core of the topic. Departing from the concept of state regulation assuming the form of classic command and control regulation, it first explores the rationales underlying it. Then, the impact of public policy issues and the debate on whether and how to regulate are discussed. The public theories underlying regulation are briefly cited and the role of the institutions involved in the process of regulation is examined. Based on these elements, the concept of regulation is broadened through the elaboration of the decentred analysis of regulation. It is no more understood solely in the sense of a state activity. A meta-regulatory approach is possible. Fragmentation and legal pluralism are the hallmark of regulation. Within that enlarged framework, autonomous regimes and alternative forms of regulation will appear.

This chapter defines a conceptual framework and introduces the core issues discussed in this study. It departs from the traditional understanding of the concept of regulation as the result of state activity. It proceeds by indicating some of its particular features and then enlarges the approach to discuss the concept of regulation in a broad sense, as distinct from the traditional notion.

In classical terms, regulation is constituted by statutes. The state intervenes through traditional command and control regulation, which means that the standards imposed are backed by criminal sanctions.[1] The involvement of the state is a key characteristic of regulation. The state is responsible for the rule-making and enforcement process and it can take sanctions. In a democratic state, its authority is accepted and recognized by the individuals.

This chapter, however, presumes that regulation is not only a product of state activity, but also of civil society, based on the efforts of individuals and private markets actors. In that regard, a basic assumption is that regulation in the traditional sense of state activity is just one form of normative ordering among others. Much more, regulation is understood as a form of governance, whose appearance can vary

[1] See for instance: Ogus A., Regulation: Legal Form and Economic Theory, 2004, 5.

M. Senn, *Non-State Regulatory Regimes*,
DOI 10.1007/978-3-642-14974-0_2,

greatly.[2] Regulation is not discussed as a static set of unmovable rules, but on the contrary as a dynamic one. It evolves both over the course of time and depending on the policy issues at stake as well as technological and societal developments. Regulatory alternatives, lying outside the authoritative state regulatory regime, belong to the broadened concept of regulation. This is even more important considering that the process of globalization gives rise to the emergence of different, non-state, private autonomous regulatory regimes characterizing that broadened concept. Thus, this chapter tries to pave the way, identify regulatory structures, their functioning, interactions and weaknesses, leading to the emergence of non-state regulation, not least with regard to the current process of globalization. It focuses on procedures of regulation and the structural framework involved rather than the substantive aspects of regulation. Hence, regulation itself is the object of study; a regulatory perspective is applied.

Methodologically, this chapter attempts to determine a configuration of regulation. A multifocal regulatory lens is applied. Besides the discussion of possible rationales for regulation, the role of public policy issues is analysed, not least because regulation is always the result of negotiations. It can take numerous different forms and the degree of a possible state intervention can vary depending on the concrete situation. Then, theories of regulation are examined; they are relevant insofar as they represent underlying currents of regulatory activities. Characteristics of regulation such as those within the decentred analysis of regulation are discussed too. They are important to establish a link to non-state regulation. Within the next step, the focus is placed on a new understanding of regulation, on meta-regulation. This new understanding appears to be a logical consequence of former developments, in particular the recognition that states are not omnicompetent as far as their capacities to take measures are concerned. They can also make errors.[3] Meta-regulation is a hallmark of future developments insofar as it contributes to seize regulation as a form of governance. Following that broadening of the understanding of the concept of regulation, this chapter explores various usages of regulation and considers a framework illustrating its occurrence in a broader sense, that is, as a marketplace. Regulatory pluralism replaces state regulation. Various kinds of regulation can be distinguished, each with its own distinctive and non-generalizable features. Such a perspective results in considering alternatives to regulation in the form of non-state regulation. Regulation is the product of the activities of transnational networks and the process of regulating takes place beyond governmental institutions. Finally, an operational definition of regulation as resulting from negotiations among individuals or with the state is suggested.

---

[2] Parker C., Scott C., Lacey N., and Braithwaite J., Regulating Law, 2004, 2–3, 288.

[3] Grabosky P., Using Non-Governmental Resources to Foster Regulatory Compliance, 1995, 527; Parker, Scott, Lacey, and Braithwaite, supra note 2, 6–7.

1 Rationales for Regulation

In practice, regulation affects nearly every aspect of daily life. Human behaviour is determined by regulation in a number of different situations. When driving a car as well as when walking down a street as pedestrians, we are subject to rules. For instance, a car driver is obliged to drive either on the right or the left-hand side depending on the regulation introduced by a particular country; similarly, pedestrians are not allowed to cross the road when the traffic lights are red. Industrial production is subject to regulation, too, in that products have to satisfy criteria fixed by the regulator in order to minimize risks before they can be used commercially, as may be the case with electrical products. As a last example, in the environmental sphere a lot of different measures are in place to regulate the use of chemical waste by factories. Such measures may take the form of taxes or, depending on the case, subsidies. They may also require the introduction of practical measures like the filtering and cleaning of water. Regulation reflects our understanding of economic and societal phenomena and the application of public policy. It permeates society as well as its economic organization.

There are many rationales for regulating. It is significant that individuals and markets expect the state to intervene with regulatory measures as soon as a market failure is perceived. There is a sense that something has gone wrong, and a sense of crisis arises.[4] An alleged inability of a market or sector to manage its structural problems will suffice to justify a regulatory intervention. Then, there is the general underlying assumption that an intervention by means of the introduction of rules by the state works as a corrective. Traditionally, the idea that regulation is used as a remedy to repeal market failures is prevalent. Regulation also plays an important role of coordination, which is particularly incisive in relation to economic activity. The central issues of economic activity are: who is allowed to produce what, where, how, in which quantity, and to distribute and consume it. Should the whole production process be left to the private economy, should the state take governance measures enabling it to determine this process, or should a blended solution or a cooperative model involving the private economy and the state be chosen? These measures cover the structural aspects of regulation. They are opposed to the subjective and political motives of policy-makers leading to the choice and introduction of substantive regulatory measures. Baldwin and Cave as well as Breyer, for instance, discuss a whole range of rationales for regulation.[5] Selected examples of rationales are examined below: externalities, information asymmetries, monopolistic situations, public service, and technological developments.

---

[4] Hancher L. and Moran M., Organizing Regulatory Space, 1989, 284.

[5] Baldwin R. and Cave M., Understanding Regulation, Theory, Strategy, and Practice, 1999, 9–17, 34 et seqq.; Breyer S., Regulation and Its Reform, 1982, 15 et seqq.

1.1 Externalities

Externalities or spillovers are a well-known rationale for regulating. Thus, if the prices of determined goods are not regulated, they will not reflect the true costs of production in the narrow sense of just producing a good, but in the broad sense of the costs incurred for society. For example, this may be the case in relation to environmental matters. The production of goods is often linked to a certain grade of pollution. Product prices, however, do not contain the costs due to the damages caused by the use of polluting materials. Insofar as manufacturers concerned will not take measures on their own initiative, the rationale for the state in order to eliminate the polluting factor will be to introduce rules prohibiting such pollution by forcing manufacturers to internalize the externalities by statute. In that case, regulation takes the form of precise, often technical rules, allowing for clear-cut application to a determined product or production process.[6] It is an efficient way of solving the issue at the national level.

1.2 Information Asymmetries

A second rationale lies in information asymmetries. This rationale is not limited to a definite sector of the economy, but can justify a regulatory measure in many different sectors. In the financial services sector, for example, information is treated as a good. Information asymmetries are frowned upon. They are current, however, which is not least a result of the technological developments and internationalization of financial transactions. Thus, financial services regulation always seeks to ensure the highest possible transparency in due time. It is generally admitted that it is an adequate measure to eliminate possible information asymmetries. Transparent markets should be entirely efficient. Although regulatory measures may contribute to diminish information discrepancies, they may still not be sufficient to ensure the efficiency of these markets. They are also limited to the national territory and do not meet the challenges of the globalization of financial markets.

Another sector where information asymmetries are used as a rationale justifying regulatory measures concerns the information allowing consumers to evaluate competitive products before buying them. Consumers must be in a position to objectively evaluate alternative products. However, furnishing information on products increases production costs and producers are reluctant to provide the necessary information. Prima facie, producers do not have any incentives to publish detailed information or they may just publish a minimum of information, which may not be sufficient to judge the quality of a product. To disseminate detailed information, producers have to invest money because the correct labeling and description of products as well as the simultaneous eulogizing of their qualities is not an easy task.

6 Baldwin and Cave, supra note 5, 11–12; Breyer, supra note 5, 23–26.

In particular, subjective perception, which can have a determining influence on choice, is also involved. One consequence of both this producers' attitude and the necessity to protect consumers is the introduction of rules requiring that detailed and accurate information be made accessible to consumers. Of course, this solution does not apply to all situations. In the case of highly competitive markets, for instance, it cannot be excluded that firms take adequate measures themselves.[7]

1.3 Monopolistic Situations

Yet another rationale is constituted by monopolistic situations. Cases of monopolies and natural monopolies are characterized by the following three facts: (1) There is only one producer and seller for an entire industry or market. (2) Consumers do not have any alternatives. (3) Barriers restrict entry to the market by others or third firms; exit would be difficult or may not make sense. In these cases, there is no competition and the firm dominating the market can abuse its power. Through the curtailing of production, it is possible to raise prices above the marginal costs, which will be discriminatory. As a result, income will be transferred from consumers to producers. A usual method to eliminate monopolistic situations is through the enforcement of antitrust or competition statutes. The aim of these statutes is to guarantee that the operations within a sector or industry are competitive.[8]

1.4 Public Service

A fourth rationale involves justifying the continuity and availability of (public) services. In this case, there is the assumption that it is in the public interest to guarantee as well as protect a minimal level of service considered socially desirable and essential for a specific sector. A typical case is the provision of transport services in remote regions. In mountainous villages, for instance, the demand for public transport varies during the course of a year. Demand is cyclical and hence discontinuous: it is very high in winter owning to the influx of tourists; it will be very low in spring and autumn (and there may even be no demand at all or only by a few locals); and in summer it will be moderate. Under such circumstances, it may be difficult to guarantee a determined level of continuity and the availability of the service at all times. The costs of ensuring continuity when there is only a very limited demand will be extremely high or even prohibitive and the fixed costs will add to that situation. The goal of regulation under such circumstances will hence be to ensure that services are sustained at all times. A pricing regulation will calculate and set prices so that all costs are covered. In other words, peak-period users will

---

7 Baldwin and Cave, supra note 5, 12; Breyer, supra note 5, 26–28.

8 Baldwin and Cave, supra note 5, 13.

subsidize periods in which demand is low. This entails a cross-subsidized service, which can be regarded as inefficient and unfair. However, this issue largely depends on the goods or services to be protected. For example, if water is concerned, it will be generally admitted that water has to be available at any time. It is a minimal standard and possible regulatory solutions, which some may consider unjustified, will have to be accepted anyway, not least due to a lack of alternatives.[9]

1.5 Technological Developments

A fifth rationale concerns technological developments. In the field of communication, the process of digitization, that is, the rise of the internet has called for intensive cooperation and coordination and the rapid definition of regulatory standards. In this field, a key challenge is to design regulatory solutions applicable at a global scale. Specific national rules would be of very limited use without coordination with other countries. The technical possibilities to develop worldwide applications required appropriate regulatory solutions. Due to this situation, traditional state regulation could not have coped with the challenges of digitization. Other forms of regulatory solutions have had to be worked out. Prompt and flexible regulatory measures based on expert knowledge and applicable worldwide have had to be taken. Private initiative and the constitution of networks have proved to be successful. A whole body of rules or an autonomous law of the internet constitutes a private regulatory regime frequently designed as global law without the state[10] or with marginal state involvement. The regulatory solution is a mixed or private one. It is widely respected because it represents the most efficient and workable possibility to regulate this particular field due to its specificities whilst ensuring a minimal grade of coordination.

This list of rationales is not at all exhaustive. Many other rationales exist, such as windfall profits, rationalization, scarcity, and rationing.[11] As the case of technological developments shows, the rationales for regulation also evolve in the course of time. New rationales may emerge depending on the issue at stake. The examples just discussed show that the application of alternatives to state regulation is either possible or may be necessary because global solutions may be needed. Different rationales may suggest different state remedies to a concrete situation and they also allow scope for private alternative. Design choices have to be made.

---

[9] Ibid. 12–13; Harrison J. L., Morgan T. D., Verkuil P. R., Regulation and Deregulation, Cases and Materials, 2004, 176 et seqq.

[10] Fischer-Lescano A. and Teubner G., Fragmentierung des Weltrechts: Vernetzung globaler Regimes statt etatistischer Rechtseinheit, 2007, 45–48; Berman P. S., Globalization of Jurisdiction, 2002, 311 et seqq., 371; Michaels R., The Re-Statement of Non-State Law: The State, Choice of Law, and the Challenge from Global Legal Pluralism, 2005, 1209–1259.

[11] See Baldwin and Cave, supra note 5, 11–16; Breyer, supra note 5, 15–35; Harrison, Morgan, Verkuil, supra note 9, 121 et seqq.

2 The Impact of (Public) Policy Issues

Of course, no state can function without discipline and – as the most severe measure and interference of the state – the power to penalize offenders. When considering markets, their weakness is that the unregulated interaction of self-interested parties may fail to produce certain collective goods that are a necessary precondition for an effective functioning of the market. In such cases, the rational behaviour may be to subject the market participants to some form of authority and control.[12] Authority and the power to define order is an expression of state authority. It is the product of public policy. Public policy encompasses a complex set of issues. In practice, a broad range of options and tools exist to achieve government policy objectives. A public policy measure does not only consist in choosing between an action by private market forces or a state intervention in the form of the introduction of rules. Public policy can mean government activity or also inactivity. It often takes the form of interstitial measures adopted by specialized bodies. Public policy in the broad sense is a policy that governs conduct in the public sphere or in the public interest whereas the influence of private interest groups is determining.[13] However, opting for a public policy measure is not an easy task, not least because the choice and introduction of a wrong or inferior policy instrument may have negative or suboptimal effects on the competitive force of a sector, its economic performance, or some of its other aspects. Thus, the right policy should be introduced and implemented.

In practice, there are numerous public policy issues, such as in relation to financial markets, energy, other economic matters, health, education, the environment, transport, or also the issue of terrorism. Public policy issues are not fixed and stable, but subject to evolution. New issues may arise at any time. They are determined by public interest and a sense that specific questions need to be addressed publicly.

2.1 *Regulatory Cycle*

To illustrate how public policy issues may emerge and lead to the introduction of regulatory solutions, a look at a traditional regulatory cycle may be useful.

---

[12] Along the same lines, see Streeck W. and Schmitter P. C., Community, market, state – and associations? The prospective contribution of interest governance to social order, 1985, 23.

[13] Baldwin and Cave, supra note 5, 19–21; Breyer, supra note 5, 71 et seqq.; Harrison, Morgan, Verkuil, supra note 9, 3 et seqq.; see also: Kaul I. and Mendoza R. U., Advancing the Concept of Public Goods, 2003, 78–111.

2.2 Phase 1: Free Market

In the first phase, the free market dominates and a public policy issue has not yet emerged or been identified as such. It is an ideal case of a free market economy, which operates without any intervention from the state or third parties. It can be interpreted in the sense that neither individuals nor the mass publics feel that the issue needs to be addressed.

2.3 Phase 2: Market Failure

The second phase represents a typical case, which can be subsumed under the idea of a market failure. Market failure should be understood in the sense of a superordinate concept. It means that there is a general recognition that an issue or a process cannot be left to its own devices anymore. A market failure gives rise to a policy issue. There is a recognizable need to intervene with governance measures, which admittedly should represent a corrective action and bring about a better solution.[14] This is the case after a financial crisis, for instance the 2007–2009 financial crisis. A situation or a market may then be sensed to be inadequately or insufficiently organized, or not or wrongly regulated. Gaps are identified within the market framework. Thus, it is generally expected that (even urgent) state intervention will produce the right solution. It should improve a situation and, in the case of financial markets, also provide investors with more security. However this is not an easy task, as the discussion and search for adequate responses to the said crisis impressively shows.[15]

2.4 Phase 3: Government Regulation

The third phase of the cycle is characterized by a governmental intervention in the form of the introduction of a regulatory measure to redress a situation. In practice, following public pressure, the usual, first response by governments to perceived policy issues is to regulate. The introduction of a regulation is assumed to represent a valid as well as justifiable solution whilst serving as a corrective to a market failure. Regulation is a consequence of that failure. Public debate does not concentrate on the question whether to regulate or not. On the contrary, public debate just

---

[14] Shapiro S. A. and Tomain J. P., Regulatory Law and Policy, Cases and Materials, 2003, 27–28.

[15] Declaration of the Summit on Financial Markets and the World Economy of the G20, 15 November 2008; see also: G-20, Communiqué, Meeting of Ministers and Governors, Sao Paulo, Brazil, 8–9 November 2008; Letter of the International Monetary Fund and FSF, November 13, 2008; see also Chapter 5, point 2 A Process of Transformation into Private Regulation.

concentrates on the kind of regulatory measures to be introduced. There is an unspoken sense that to regulate is the right thing to do. There is a general expectation that a regulation will solve an issue and governments may even be urged to take measures. However, it is exactly at this stage that different options should be considered before choosing the traditional way of introducing a new or adapting an existing regulation. Various options and alternatives, also private or non-regulatory ones, should be evaluated as they may offer the possibility to achieve objectives more efficiently depending on the case at stake. They may produce optimal solutions. Moreover, the aspects of the regulatory impact of a measure and cost–benefit considerations should also be taken into account.[16] In fact, it should be essential to first evaluate different regulatory as well as non-regulatory options, not least with regard to the significant implications a solution can have on competition or the economic performance of a sector.

An example illustrating this phase is the so-called 'dot.com-crisis' that began in 2000 and led to huge losses on the securities markets. Following the crisis, it appeared to be urgent to take measures. Pursuing the aim to protect investors by improving the accuracy and reliability of corporate disclosures made pursuant to securities laws, and for other purposes,[17] the United States passed the Sarbanes–Oxley Act very quickly.[18] This act not only introduced new rules, but it also established the Public Company Accounting Oversight Board or PCAOB, a new federal authority. The PCAOB is responsible for overseeing the audits of public companies subject to the federal securities laws of the United States. Its duties are described as follows:

> 'Under the Act, the PCAOB's duties include the establishment of auditing, quality control, ethics, independence and other standards relating to public company audits. In connection with this standard-setting responsibility, Section 103(a)(3)(B) of the Act provides that the PCAOB may adopt 'any portion of any statement of auditing standards or other professional standards that the [PCAOB] determines satisfy the requirements of [the Act] and that were proposed by 1 or more professional groups of accountants' as initial or transitional standards, to the extent the PCAOB determines necessary. . . .'[19]

The above passage of this new Act is an example of the introduction of a massive amount of regulatory measures after a crisis, that is, a recognized market failure. In this case, there was a general consent among the industry, politicians, and individuals that radical measures should be adopted. Opposition was weak. The introduction of the Act not only brought about a huge wave of regulation, but the state also took over the direct supervision of auditing, a previously unsupervised area. It created a new institution in the form of a specialized independent state agency in

---

16 Baldwin and Cave, supra note 5, 86–95; see also Chapter 4, point 2 Standardization, 2.3 Gradual Transformation, 2.3.2 Impact.

17 Introductory part of the Sarbanes-Oxley Act of 2002.

18 Sarbanes-Oxley Act of 2002 – H.R. 3763, Public Law 107-204, 107th Congress.

19 Securities Act of 1933, Release No 8222/April 25, 2003, Securities Exchange Act of 1934, Release No 47745/April 25, 2003, Order Regarding Section 103(a)(3)(B) of the Sarbanes-Oxley Act of 2002.

charge of auditing companies and secondary rules. The Act has impacted the accounting profession in many ways, dramatically influencing and changing its status. It applies to publicly held companies and their audit firms. It has an influence not only on the working manner of accounting firms, but also on the individual auditors in charge of auditing publicly held companies. Moreover, the state did not only delegate enforcement and supervising powers to the newly created agency, the PCAOB, but also rule-making powers.[20] Not least due to the increasing globalization of the financial markets and the international character of the crisis have several other countries also adopted a similar model of supervising the accounting profession or are still in the process of introducing corresponding measures using the Sarbanes–Oxley Act as a basis.

In fact, the example shows a response that is common to a number of policy issues. It is even typical as far as the general assumption is concerned that a state intervention should bring the right and adequate solution to a policy problem. The state just passes rules and alternatives to regulation are not even explored. The state appears as a kind of guarantor, effecting security with command and control measures. This attitude is generally accepted, but it entails the danger of taking exaggerated measures and creating further difficulties. As the implementation of the Sarbanes–Oxley Act shows, it causes problems and unjustifiable costs to a number of companies, which are far higher than first expected. The Act is described as a 'colossal failure, poorly conceived and hastily enacted during a regulatory panic.' Some already claim that it should be repealed. Others would like to see the constitutionality of the PCAOB and of the Act challenged in a court case. Moreover, its critics are not just limited to one country and its implementation causes problems to international businesses, too.[21]

Thus, due to the different impulses accompanying and shaping a regulatory process, a regulatory solution may prove to be inadequate in the long run. In particular, when urgent regulatory actions are taken, there may be a lack of thoroughly analysing a situation. This leads to wrong regulatory decisions. It may either result in too severe, mistaken, or non-adapted regulation. It may fail to induce

---

[20] By way of an excursus, it is worth taking the following remark into account: This example is also characteristic of another development, namely the emergence of new institutions taking the form of the creation of independent regulators or autonomous administrative agencies with regulatory powers. The use of this kind of institution has mushroomed since the 1980s and is still developing. However, it does not mean that it represents an adequate solution to public policy issues. These institutions are often hastily constructed and the consequences are not analysed. Although they offer some virtues as far as their independence, expertise, and flexibility is concerned, they also present some drawbacks: They may contribute to the fragmentation of governmental policies, there is still a risk of capture, and a balance between accountability and independency has to be found. They might not be appropriate in the longer term. See OECD Reviews of Regulatory Reform, Regulatory Polices in OECD Countries, From Interventionism to Regulatory Governance, 2002, 91–97.

[21] Butler H. N. and Ribstein L. E., The Sarbanes-Oxley Debacle: What We've Learned; How to Fix It (2006); Regulating Business, The trial of Sarbanes-Oxley, The Economist, April 22nd 2006, 59–60.

compliance and enforcement will be unsatisfactory. Lessons should be drawn from such experiences. The way that regulators or rule-makers might behave needs to be examined and possible approaches to policy analysis explored.

From a political point of view, the whole situation can be described as follows: Governments may have – not least depending on the prevailing political views at a specific point in time – a large number of motives for introducing regulations. The justification of a governmental regulatory intervention lies in the public interest criterion. However, the definition and delimitation of this criterion is regularly conceptualized, instrumentalized, and adapted to the needs of the government concerned to justify the measures taken.[22] On the markets, it is basically considered that any increase in regulation should be avoided. There is a prima facie general assumption that overregulated markets and new rules potentially damage economic activity. Regulation appears to be notably unpopular. Private market actors are characterized by an adverse attitude towards any governmental activity. However, their attitude is adapted to the state of the economy and of the sector they belong to. As soon as problems arise or a crisis occurs, there is a shift of opinion and such actors immediately call for more regulation to resolve the problems and overcome the crisis. At that point, they may even reproach the authorities not to have intervened or taken adequate measures earlier or at the right moment. The need for some statutory backing or support is not questioned. This is due not least to the notion of the coercive and curative force of governmental regulation among private market actors. The state should take severe measures as soon as possible and introduce a regulation, which is generally considered to be the right solution. In practice, whole waves of regulatory measures can then be identified.

2.5 Phase 4: Regulatory Failure

The fourth phase is the phase of regulatory failure. The recognition that regulatory measures were a failure occurs in the course of time, with the enforcement of rules and in relation to new developments. As just discussed, the introduction of a regulation following a crisis leads to a tendency to overreact with regulatory measures. The public policy response is exaggerated, too expensive, and inadequate. It may even be downright wrongheaded and create new problems. Overfastidious regulation will result in risks being overestimated, which in turn damages private businesses. A balance needs to be struck. Regulation always applies to dynamic processes. Not only does the attitude of markets actors evolve continuously, but technological and other external influences also change. Regulation is no longer seen as a remedy to former market failures. The parameters it defined are not the right ones anymore. Public opinion shifts. Gradually, there is a sense and

---

[22] Baldwin and Cave, supra note 5, 9, with further references; see also: McCrudden C., Regulation and Deregulation: An Introduction, 1999, 3–14.

recognition that an existing regulation is no longer adequate and the markets are hence considered to be overregulated. Individuals, economic associations, and other market actors begin to complain about the regulation in question and finally demand its abolition. In the end, politicians calling for less regulation and deregulation take the stage.

Hence, at this stage of a regulatory cycle, regulation is seen as a hindrance to economic development and the cause for unsatisfactory, insufficient, or even bad results. Inefficiencies are attributed to regulation. Regulation itself is seen as a reason for market failure. However, this failure is not the old one anymore, which entailed the introduction of the contested regulation. On the contrary, the 'new' market failure is due precisely to that regulation. One explanation for this state of affairs may be that one particularity of regulation is that rules are always introduced on an ex post basis and not ex ante. They should both represent a corrective to a former situation and be generally applicable at the same time. However, they are reactive measures only and do not take future developments sufficiently into account.

2.6 *Phase 5: Regulatory Reform*

The fifth phase follows a general call for regulatory reform. This situation itself can represent a public policy issue. 'Too much red tape' is a well-known complaint of individuals, businesses, and other market actors. Statutes and rules represent important constraints. Authorization procedures for permits, licenses, and other administrative requirements employed to control and supervise measures are complex and cumbersome and generate avoidable regulatory burdens. Administrative regulatory measures often impede innovation and create unnecessary barriers, which will ultimately have a negative impact on economic development. In fact, the role of regulation should be to support business and competition and ensure free market access. The call for less regulation or 'smart tape' is then taken over by politicians, who advocate administrative reform and a simplification of rules. This view is also shared by self-regulatory organizations (SROs), like the IIF for instance, when it advocates that: 'There should be a continuing impact assessment process with regular reviews of existing regulations. The review process should recommend remedial actions taken when a regulation has ceased to perform its intended function effectively. The IIF perceives that a number of regulations currently in place are not viewed as highly effective even by the regulators charged with administering them.'[23]

---

[23] OECD, From Red Tape to Smart Tape, Administrative Simplification in OECD Countries (2003) 3, 8; OECD Reviews of Regulatory Reform, supra note 20, 57–65; Institute of International Finance, Proposal for a Strategic Dialogue on Effective Regulation (December 2006) 13–14.

In that regard, however, it should not be overlooked that measuring and evaluating the impact of regulatory solutions is not an easy task. Many countries make efforts to address regulatory inflation and attempt to diminish administrative and other burdens. On its side, the OECD has produced considerable work in analysing administrative simplifications procedures in a range of countries. Its main conclusions are that each country adopts another strategy to simplify its rules and the consequent administrative charges. The focus is generally placed on cost–benefit considerations and finally on the fact that IT-driven mechanisms are becoming more important.[24] However, administrative processes are lengthy and their outcome is uncertain. At the same time, the recognition of regulatory failures offers opportunities to private market actors to develop alternative solutions among each other.

2.7 Phase 6: Deregulation

The end of the regulatory cycle, the sixth phase, is the phase of deregulation. There is then the feeling that deregulation is the only right solution to a regulatory issue. Based on negotiations, a change of approach and regulatory regime occurs. The next generation of rules, which should represent liberalisation, is defined and introduced. Once more, however a whole range of policy options may exist. These may prove to be better adapted to an issue at stake than the introduction of different, lighter regulatory measures. The challenge of crafting a new mode of governance should not be overlooked, not least because it should be orientated towards the future and promote innovation. The options may represent alternatives or new ways, as distinct from traditional command and control regulatory strategies. They should lead to a more effective and efficient achievement of a government policy than in the case of an approach based on command and control regulation only; also, they should have positive effects on the economy and competition as well as increase the overall performance of a sector.[25] Thus, as far as the next generation of regulation is concerned, various strategies should be evaluated and the instruments devised should be selected among a wide range of options.

[24] OECD, From Red Tape to Smart Tape, supra note 23, 65–70.

[25] Harrison, Morgan, Verkuil, supra note 9, 3 et seqq.; OECD Reviews of Regulatory Reform, supra note 20, 51–57.

2.8 Contribution of the OECD

As already stated, the OECD has been examining regulation for several years. It has emphasized the importance of a range of options when considering how to deal with a policy issue.[26] In 1995, it began to study the significance, direction, and means of reform in regulatory regimes in member countries. Its 'Recommendations of the Council of the OECD on Improving the Quality of Government Regulation' were the first-ever international statement on regulatory principles common to member countries. Then, in 1997, it produced a 'Report to Ministers on Regulatory Reform'. Its Recommendations for Regulatory Reform provided the basis for review of reform efforts in member countries conducted both in sectoral and policy areas.[27] Twenty reviews of member countries have been completed since and the review of Russia, the first of a non-member country, was completed in 2005. The concept of regulatory quality, which was at the core of the report, has largely supported horizontal regulatory reform work.[28]

In 1997, the OECD also enacted its first policy recommendations for regulatory reform and principles. However, the concept of regulatory reform has evolved since, owing to the fact that regulation is a dynamic concept and that countries have adopted new objectives and changed their working methods. They now adjust their methods to the prevailing policy environment at a given point in time. While measures were taken to reduce the scale of government in the 1990s, the focus is now placed on a pro-active approach. Regulation should be more responsive. Hence, with regard to the commitment of introducing and implementing better regulation, the OECD has formulated seven principles, redefined and adopted by the OECD Council in 2005. These 'Guiding Principles for Regulatory Quality and Performance' are:

1. Adopt at the political level broad programmes of regulatory reform that establish clear objectives and frameworks for implementation.
2. Assess impacts and review regulations systematically to ensure that they meet their intended objectives efficiently and effectively in a changing and complex economic and social environment.
3. Ensure that regulations, regulatory institutions charged with implementation, and regulatory processes are transparent and non-discriminatory.
4. Review and strengthen where necessary the scope, effectiveness and enforcement of competition policy.

---

26 OECD Reviews of Regulatory Reform, supra note 20, 51–57.

27 See OECD, Policy Principles, http://www.oecd.org/document/38/0,2340,en_2649_201185_2753254_1_1_1_1,00.html. Accessed 30 October 2009.

28 See OECD, Policy Principles, http://www.oecd.org/document/38/0,2340,en_2649_201185_2753254_1_1_1_1,00.html. Accessed 30 October 2009.

5. Design economic regulations in all sectors to stimulate competition and efficiency, and eliminate them except where clear evidence demonstrates that they are the best way to serve broad public interests.
6. Eliminate unnecessary regulatory barriers to trade and investment through continued liberalisation and enhance the consideration and better integration of market openness throughout the regulatory process, thus strengthening economic efficiency and competitiveness.
7. Identify important linkages with other policy objectives and develop policies to achieve those objectives in ways that support reform.[29]

Regulation represents a strategy and a consistent strategy should be developed and implemented. The regulatory measures should be carefully planned and prepared also at times when there is no direct necessity to take immediate and perhaps not fully mature actions. To find the best solution to an issue, alternatives to regulation as well as regulatory alternatives should be studied and evaluated. Regulation should not be an isolated activity, least of all considering the costs involved.

Thus, the OECD has studied the question of options to be considered when dealing with policy issues. It has established a OECD Checklist for regulatory decision-making. Its application should help find out whether a regulatory measure represents the best solution to a policy issue. The checklist states that:

> 'Regulators should carry out, early in the regulatory process, an informed comparison of a variety of regulatory and non-regulatory policy instruments, considering relevant issues such as costs, benefits, distributional effects and administrative requirements.'

However, the challenge is to ensure this occurs in practice.[30]

The OECD has also defined a selection of regulatory quality tools. These have been adopted and should be used in almost all OECD countries by now. They are: regulatory impact analysis (RIA), administrative simplification, transparency and communication, alternatives to regulation, and the issue of compliance and enforcement.[31] These tools serve to assess a measure. They are largely based on the participation of the parties concerned, should ensure the most adequate choice of a measure, and contribute to diminishing the risk of introducing wrong measures. Hence, the OECD has developed a 'State of Play' for regulatory policy, which presents a picture of the emergence of a regulatory policy agenda covering various aspects of regulation: government policies and rule-making tools, dynamics aspects of regulatory quality, regulatory institutions, policy successes and failures, the evaluation of policies and communication. It recognizes that regulatory policy is a central element of the wider business of government and an integral part of its

---

[29] OECD Guiding Principles for Regulatory Quality and Performance, 2005.

[30] See Alternatives to Regulation, OECD, http://www.oecd.org/document/34/0,2340,en_2649_37421_35260706_1_1_1_37421,00.html. Accessed 30 October 2009.

[31] OECD Policy tools for regulatory quality assurance, http://www.oecd.org/document/15/0,2340,en_2649_201185_35217551_1_1_1_1,00.html. Accessed 30 October 2009.

overall management capacities.[32] In comparison to the holistic and convincing approach of the OECD, Baldwin and Cave focus on the rules. They have identified five criteria to assess regulatory measures, instruments or activities, or to determine 'good regulation'. They are: legislative mandate, accountability or control, due process or fairness, expertise, and efficiency.[33]

The work of the OECD coincides with the regulatory initiatives of some countries like the Guidelines for Financial Market Regulation published by the responsible Swiss authorities in 2005, which define the requirements for a reasonable, cost-conscious and effective regulation of the financial markets.[34] These efforts are entirely justified as the regulatory issue needs to be addressed systematically. Current debate also shows that state regulation represents merely one possible public policy issue among others. State regulation is an incomplete solution as far as its application remains local. In particular, it cannot deal adequately with the challenges of globalization. International law too suffers from weaknesses similar to state regulation and cannot always cope with the challenges of globalization in a satisfactory way. Hence, there is room for alternative forms of regulation. Global regulatory solutions are often needed. They regularly take the form of non-state, private or hybrid autonomous regulatory regimes. These regimes abound.

3 Public Theories of Regulation

3.1 Background

Regulation represents concrete measures or orders applying to individuals or firms. It is defined on a case-by-case basis. Various currents can be made out that underlie and shape regulation. These currents or theories should contribute to explaining and justifying regulatory measures. Within these currents, regulation is conceived as a large subset of governance, whereby governance is to be understood as a wider set of control activities than those adopted by a government. It is not limited to the state. In relation to governmental activities, governance is linked to political theories and should be the expression of the values or moral criteria according to which regulatory choices and institutions are properly assessed.[35] They should be

---

[32] OECD Reviews of Regulatory Reform, supra note 20, 30–31, 100–109.

[33] Baldwin and Cave, supra note 5, 76–85, 77.

[34] Guidelines for Financial Market Regulation, Federal Finance Administration FFA, Swiss Federal Banking Commission, Swiss Federal Office of Private Insurance FOPI, Guidelines for Financial Market Regulation, September 2005, http://www.efd.admin.ch/dokumentation/grundlagenpapiere/00818/index.html?lang=en. Accessed 30 October 2009.

[35] Braithwaite J., Regulatory Capitalism, How it works, ideas for making it work better, 2008; Braithwaite J., Neoliberalism or Regulatory Capitalism, 2005; Chapter 4, point 2 Standardization, 2.4 Nature of Autonomous Regulatory Regimes.

applied for the benefit of the state. In an ideal case, moreover, governments should be in a position to justify their regulatory choices and policies in terms of normative theory. Although it may be difficult to attribute a regulation or a regulatory regime merely to a specific theory, because it is developed and shaped in the course of time and subject to various influences, different theoretical trends can be made out.

It is not the purpose of this study to analyse and evaluate these theories. Instead, selected theories representing basic trends are presented and discussed in brief since these serve to set the frame and contribute to a better understanding of the concept of regulation. Various approaches can be chosen to pinpoint these theories. They could be described from an historical point of view, covering the main currents of thought: seventeenth-century mercantilism, eighteenth-century liberalism, contemporary nineteenth and twentieth-century liberalism, the twentieth-century welfare and social state, neoliberalism since the 1970s, and finally regulatory capitalism.[36] These categories are well-known. Another approach could consist in considering these theories according to their authors. However, as only broad currents are considered here and an integral view is applied, an author-based approach would be too narrow. While the works of individual authors are extremely worthy, they often develop theories only applicable to specific fields.

Moreover, the goal is not to identify these theories as convincing dogmas to explain regulation. On the contrary, they represent influences on the development of rules and are hence useful to understand ongoing change. When a theory dominates at a certain point in time, this does not mean that it will be applied systematically and that it will be possible to attribute regulation solely to that theory or school of thought. Reality is more complex. Regulation does not depend on one factor only, but on different ones. In practice, overlaps and combinations of motives are inevitable. However, these theories and schools of thought contribute to explain and justify regulation and the rationales underlying it. This is not least recognizable because regulation is being studied increasingly as well as taught and researched independently as a topic as such. A lot of issues related to regulation are still open and a whole research agenda can be drawn up. A prominent example, broadly discussed at present, is the concept of risk-based regulation.[37] In fact, there is a real need to develop regulation as an independent scholarly subject. Scholars as well as practitioners should be more aware of the significance of the different theories underlying regulation and possess the necessary skills when dealing with regulatory issues.

3.2 *Proceduralist Theory*

First, the proceduralist theory of regulation focuses on procedures (nomen est omen). This theory concentrates on the way regulatory agencies reach their

[36] Braithwaite, Neoliberalism, supra note 35, 1–37.

[37] See, for example, Hutter B. M., The Attractions of Risk-based Regulation: accounting for the emergence of risk ideas in regulation, 2005, 1–14.

decisions. It is not a uniform theory. In practice, it is rather a movement drawing on different currents and theories, which deal with specific elements of a procedure or questions of instrumental issues. The basic view underpinning this theory is that it is a response to neoclassicist theory. John Rawls is probably its most influential theorist. According to his view of morality, each person is equally entitled to extensive basic liberties, which are compatible with a similar liberty for others.[38] These considerations are based on a collective view, which may be difficult to concretize in practice. The main critique advanced by Rawls and others is that regulators and regulatory agencies should not pursue economic efficiency as an end in itself. The theory is the result of a governmental procedure that should be orientated at being beneficial to individuals in general. In fact, from a practical point of view, it characterizes the role of governmental agencies in comparison to the possible participation of individuals or the public. However, it should not be discounted that the results of applying the procedural approach may ultimately not correspond to expectations at all.

3.3 *Welfarist Theory*

The welfarist theory of regulation or the theory based on welfare economics is considered to be an outgrowth of the fundamental debate that began with Adam Smith. According to this theory, the principal human motive is self-interest (1), the invisible hand of competition automatically transforms the self-interest of many into the common good (2), and the best government policy is that policy which governs least (3). It is influenced by neoclassical theory. Welfare economics is based on the idea of the welfare of individuals rather than society. Individuals constitute the basis for the measurement of welfare; they indicate whether there is a state of welfare or not. Thus, welfare economics uses techniques belonging to microeconomics, but the results are applicable to macroeconomics. Its goal is the maximization of social welfare and overall well-being. This should be understood in the sense of utilitarianism. Utilitarianist philosophy argues that the right action or policy is that which leads to the realization of the greatest happiness or the greatest happiness for the greatest number of individuals.[39] The view developed in the model of utilitarian decision making has become a major element in the liberal conception of state policy objectives. Finally, the movement of Law and Economics or the Economic Analysis of Law is also based on the concept of wealth maximization, which should be reached through the application of the criterion of efficiency.

---

[38] Rawls J., A Theory of Justice, 1999, 3, 15 et seqq.; see also Mathis K., Effizienz statt Gerechtigkeit, Auf der Suche nach den philosophischen Grundlagen der Ökonomischen Analyse des Rechts, 2004, 126 et seqq.

[39] As first developed by Jeremy Bentham. See Bentham J., An Introduction to the Principles of Morals and Legislation, 1996; see also Mathis, supra note 38, 110 et seqq.; Fletcher G. P., Basic Concepts of Legal Thought, 1996, 144–146.

Efficiency is the core of this movement. It should dominate legal thought and be applied to legal justice cases. According to Posner, there is

> 'The idea that law should attempt to promote and facilitate competitive markets and to simulate their results in situations in which market-transaction costs are prohibitive – the idea that I call 'wealth maximization' – . . .'[40]

3.4 *Neoclassical Theory*

On its side, the neoclassical theory of regulation is also based on the normative premises of welfare economics, meaning individual welfare and not the welfare of society. The focus is placed on efficiency in the Kaldor–Hicks sense and also on a subjective, preference-based view of the individuals and other actors concerned.[41] Efficiency is not considered to possess moral significance. However, it is assumed that it may contribute to welfare, although it represents an untenable moral foundation for the practice of regulation. In the broad sense, neoclassical theory belongs to the school of liberalism, and can be subsumed to neoliberalism in particular. As aptly suggested by Foucault, the basic principle of liberalism can be described as: "On gouverne toujours trop" or at least, according to him, 'it should always be presumed that we govern too much.' Thus, the neoliberalist approach is based on the idea of non-intervention by the state and opposes regulatory measures as inefficient.[42]

3.5 *Regulatory Capitalism*

A new current following the phase of neoliberalism is described as 'regulatory capitalism'. Its main representatives are Braithwaite and Levi-Faur. According to this theory, the corporatisation of the world is conceived both as a product of regulation and is the key driver of regulatory growth. The result is a world of

---

40 Posner R. A., Overcoming Law, 1995, 403 et seq.; see also Mathis, supra note 38, 142.

41 The Kaldor-Hicks criterion is used to evaluate regulatory choices, policies, or institutions. Accordingly, a change of situation corresponds to an improvement when the winners value their gains higher than the losers value their losses, that is, where compensation occurs. The criterion or model forms an underlying rationale for the cost-benefit analysis. See Hicks J. R., The Foundations of Welfare Economics, 1939, 696 et seqq.; Kaldor N., Welfare Propositions of Economics and Interpersonal Comparisons of Utility, 1939, 549; Harrison, Morgan, Verkuil, supra note 9, 422 et seqq.; Mathis, supra note 38, 50 et seqq.; Fletcher, supra note 39, 155–162; to the cost-benefit analysis, see among different studies: Sen A. K., The Discipline of Cost-Benefit Analysis, 2000, 931–952. See also: Adler M. D., Beyond Efficiency and Procedure: A Welfarist Theory of Regulation, Fall, 2000, 241–338, with further references.

42 "We always govern too much.", Foucault M., Naissance de la biopolitique, Cours au Collège de France (1978–1979), 2004, 22–25, 324.

more governance of all kinds with non-state regulation growing even more rapidly. The era is no more an era of regulatory nation-states, but of regulatory capitalism. It is 'one of the knowledge economy and of pluralistic networked governance.'[43] On their side, Boyer and Saillard attempt to develop a mode of regulation taking into account different institutional frameworks, such as the macroeconomics regime in the case of growth and crisis.[44] However, with the shift that can be observed and that is taking place towards the development of networks and their production of self-regulatory measures, the idea and role of regulation is changing. It is not linked to market irregularities anymore; instead, it is a medium or tool complementing business developments. Regulation is conceived as a mode of governance.

3.6 Other Theories

Apart from the last theory discussed, all other theories focus on the role played by the state. They are state centred. On their side, these new theoretical currents are beginning to develop an understanding of regulation that is not limited to the state anymore. Regulation is discussed in a broad sense. The process of globalization and the changing parameters accompanying it have to be taken into account. Regulation appears to be a form of governance resulting from the activities of epistemic communities and networks. However, a general theory of globalization and a theory explaining the emergence of non-state autonomous regimes and regulation are still missing.

4 Institutions

A study of regulation would not be complete without examining the regulatory institutions. Institutions play a crucial role. They determine what the rules are and assume responsibility for their implementation. Indeed, regulation is an institutional issue. The question here is which institutions are involved in the process of regulation and which roles do they play. As will be discussed later in Chap. 4, although institutions may be involved both in the process of determining state regulation and non-state regulation, their role may differ in each case.[45]

---

[43] Braithwaite, Regulatory Capitalism, supra note 35, 1 et seqq., 138; Braithwaite, Neoliberalism, supra note 35, 1–37, with reference to Jordana J. and Levi-Faur D., The Politics of Regulation: Examining Regulatory Institutions and Instruments in the Governance Age, 2004; Levi-Faur D., The Global Diffusion of Regulatory Capitalism, 2005, 598, 12–32.

[44] Boyer R. and Saillard Y., Théorie de la régulation, l'état des savoirs, 2002.

[45] OECD Reviews of Regulatory Reform, supra note 20, 85–88, 103; on the concept of institution, see Chapter 2, point 3 Institutional Structure, 3.7 Networks as Regulatory Institutions: From Autonomous Regulatory Regimes to Meta-regulation; Chapter 4, point 1 Fragmentation, 1.4 Institutional Transformation; Chapter 5, point 1 A Process of Institutional Transformation.

4.1 State Institutions

Regulation in the traditional sense of state regulation is based on the role of the state as the legitimated institution to determine what regulation is and enforce it. The state is understood in the sense of a community of individuals in a delimited territory, based on a democratic constitution. It is an authority with sovereign competences, responsible for the delimitation of regulation.[46] Regulation is a tool of the state. It can be understood as a deliberate form of state influence. It is determined by public interest and is universally valid. It is equally applicable and binding for all individuals. The regulatory functions are a state monopoly. For example, the Swiss Constitution of 1999 stipulates in articles 164 and 178 a (quasi-) monopoly or legislative monopoly of the state to define legislation.[47] Article 164, Legislation, reads as follows:

1. All significant provisions that establish binding legal rule must be enacted in the form of a federal act. These include in particular fundamental provisions on:
   (a) The exercise of political rights
   (b) The restrictions of constitutional rights
   (c) The rights and obligations of persons
   (d) Those liable to pay tax as well as the subject matter and assessment of taxes and duties
   (e) The duties and services of the Confederation
   (f) The obligations of the Cantons in relation to the implementation and enforcement of federal law
   (g) The organization and the procedure of the federal authorities
2. Legislative powers may be delegated by federal act unless this is prohibited by the Federal Constitution

and article 178, Federal Administration, reads as follows:

1. The Federal Council shall be in charge of the Federal Administration. It shall ensure that it is organized appropriately and that it fulfils its duties effectively.
2. The Federal Administration shall be organized into Departments; each Department shall be headed by a member of the Federal Council.
3. Administrative tasks may by law be delegated to public or private organizations, entities or persons that do not form part of the Federal Administration.

The prevailing concept is the centred understanding of the system of regulation. A single legislator is responsible for the process of regulation; that is, basically defining and implementing the rules.[48] Moreover, within a state monopoly, some

---

[46] Marti A., Selbstregulierung anstelle staatlicher Gesetzgebung?, 2000, 565, with further references.

[47] Federal Constitution of the Swiss Confederation of 18 April 1999, SR 101; Marti, supra note 46, 569–570.

[48] Marti, supra note 46, 565; see also Errass C., Kooperative Rechtssetzung, 2010, 182 et seqq.

openings towards other forms of regulation are possible. In federal states, local authorities are also empowered with rule-making functions and the monopoly is epitomized by the power to delegate and the principle of subsidiarity.[49] In the case of the Swiss Constitution, it is foreseen that it is possible to delegate legislative competences with regard to secondary measures by way of statute. However, according to prevalent opinion, this matter of fact should be expressly stated in the Constitution. According to article 32 paragraph 3 of the old Constitution of 1874, it was possible to delegate secondary legislative competences in the field of economic administrative law based on the principle that the economy had to be involved in the implementation of rules. Article 178 paragraph 3 of the new Constitution now applies to all fields of the administration. Individuals as well as private organizations can participate in the legislative process, but delegation is limited to administrative duties or tasks. As a result, the participation of private bodies in the regulatory process has become even more precarious. However, the objective was first to ensure and open the regulatory process to the participation of individuals and private organizations. In the case of the economy, their broader participation as well as the exchange of interactions should be guaranteed anyway. The rules on the economic activity lay down principles according to which the Confederation, the Cantons, and the economy are together responsible and shall contribute to the welfare and the economic security of the population.[50]

The rules regarding the delegation of regulatory competences to private organizations or individuals may differ from country to country. As a study of the OECD observes, most countries believe that strong central oversight bodies close to the centre of the government are essential to progress at the administrative level. However, it is noteworthy that some small countries with traditions of cooperation and consensus prefer more decentralized solutions.[51] In such cases, various institutions belonging to the state can exercise a regulatory function. They can be considered hierarchically: parliament, state departments, municipalities, and local authorities like cantons, courts and tribunals, independent regulatory agencies, external advisory bodies, and possibly self-regulatory organizations subject to state supervision.[52] Their status can vary and each may have different competences and exercise different regulatory duties. They will act in their way, depending on their attributions, specific responsibilities, roles, and strategies. Binding and prescriptive rules are defined by parliament. It has the capacity to impose direct duties or obligations and monitor their enforcement. Last, in the case of a court, the rulings issued should lead to the enforcement of the rules thereupon. Courts have comprehensive enforcement powers. The focus will be placed on the fairness of the

---

49 OECD Reviews of Regulatory Reform, supra note 20, 72.

50 Article 94 paragraph 2 of the Constitution; Botschaft des Bundesrates, BBl 1997 I 295, 408–409; Marti, supra note 46, 569–570; Rhinow R., Wirtschafts-, Sozial- und Arbeitsverfassung, 2000, 166.

51 OECD Reviews of Regulatory Reform, supra note 20, 86.

52 Baldwin and Cave, supra note 5, 63 et seqq.; OECD Reviews of Regulatory Reform, supra note 20, 84.

judgments or rulings as far as the application of rules is concerned. Practically, courts are in charge of enforcing the policy laid down by the state.[53]

4.2 *Private Institutions*

Besides the state-defined regulation, there may be room for private regulation. Self-regulatory organizations may either operate independently, based on their own initiative or they may cooperate with the state and fulfil some delegated tasks. Depending on the sector concerned, they may be very active and play a determining role. They may constitute private autonomous regimes. With regard to the process of globalization, a number of such regimes is now flourishing and thus non-state regulation. They are managed by self-regulatory organizations or constituted by networks at the global level. These transnational networks can give rise to different forms of non-state regulation.

Another facet with regard to the institutions involved in the regulatory process and that adds to an understanding of the intricacies of interplays between state and non-state regulation concerns the alternative possibility of the application of a non-state regulation in the public sector by private institutions.[54] This aspect has long been ignored. However, it has attracted more attention and has experienced a kind of revival with the debate regarding the role and regulation of rating agencies and their supervision by the state, although they are now largely discredited. Rating agencies are private business institutions operating on the market. Besides the fact that their activity, that is, the establishment and publication of ratings, is closely watched and adhered to by the business and especially the financial community worldwide, the fact that regulators make use of these ratings accounts for their unique position. Ratings are standards adopted by state regulation. Their use is integrated in the regulation and declared binding by the state for third parties. Insofar, the case of the rating agencies represented a paradox as long as they were not regulated entities.[55] It was a case of regulating the regulator by private market actors. However, it also indicates that private institutions – also commercial ones –, regulators or non-governmental organizations de facto can have the power and authority to decisively influence or determine the regulation of public sector authorities.

Hence, as far as institutions are concerned, they are not limited to state institutions alone. There is still room for private institutions. Moreover, state regulatory regimes (both at the national and international levels) cannot always cope with the

---

53 OECD Reviews of Regulatory Reform, supra note 20, 84–88.

54 See the very good contribution of Scott C., Private Regulation of the Public Sector: A Neglected Facet of Contemporary Governance, March 2002, 56–76.

55 Schwarcz S., Private Ordering of Public Markets: The Rating Agency Paradox, 2002, Issue 1. See also Chapter 3, point 1.2. Credit rating agencies.

challenges of globalization. The rise of private and non-state autonomous regimes developing at the global level represents a third order beyond the scope of the institutions traditionally forming part of state processes.

5 Decentred Analysis of Regulation

Based on the characteristics of regulation discussed above, the concept of regulation in the traditional sense appears insufficient to explain the emergence of private regulation, that is, alternative forms of regulation. Indeed, they lead to a decentring of the state regulatory concept. Decentred analysis of regulation may be useful to expand the understanding of the concept of regulation and identify alternative forms of regulatory action. Such analysis encompasses dealing with issues ranging from the role of the state and the regulatory design to the more fundamental questions of the understanding of regulation. It offers the possibility to enlarge the concept of state regulation to cover other forms of regulation.

In the traditional sense, the notion of regulation understood as originating from the state is centred on the state. It is a form of command and control exercised by the state. The involvement of the state takes the form of authoritative measures. Regulation is an outflow of state activity and the product of public policy measures, as stated. An important aspect of the delimitation of the concept of regulation is constituted by the relationship between the state and the individuals or market actors within the economy. However, it is not possible to cope with all issues satisfactorily, based on this narrow understanding of the concept of regulation. Depending on the issue, different regulatory measures are needed and will be more adequate. Thus, the concept of regulation should be regarded as a concept that is not limited to the centralized activities of a government. Much more, it represents a governance measure that can be differentiated from the web of concepts in which it is located. The approach to regulation is thus broadened and decentred from the state.

5.1 Decentred Approach

With decentred perspectives, it is possible to embrace the concept of regulation from a multifaceted approach. A comprehensive understanding of the concept of regulation and its interactions within the environment is possible. Regulation encompasses a far wider set of techniques and instruments.[56] The concept of regulation is enlarged and regulation can assume various forms depending on the area considered. It is determined by the regulatory needs and the characteristics of an area. Regulation is no more based on the idea of the 'regulatory state'. When enlarging the concept of regulation by choosing the path of decentred

[56] Black J., Critical Reflections on Regulation, 2002, 4, with further references.

understandings of regulation, that idea is replaced by the concept of the 'regulatory society'. The latter constitutes the source of the emergence of autonomous regulatory regimes and alternative forms of regulation.[57]

Decentralization is not a determined policy concept. There is no single form of decentred regulation. On the contrary, it can take a variety of forms and can cover different policy experiments. Decentred perspectives are rooted in systems theory. Decentralization consists in opening the legislative process. It focuses on the fact that regulation can appear in a number of different contexts and take different forms. It is often meant to improve the use of strictly centred procedures, which may not be satisfactory or adapted to concrete situations or fail to deliver the expected results. At the same time, it is assumed that the approach is orientated towards the market or market-based. A better involvement of the private actors should be possible. Measures should be based on their initiative too. The concept of decentring regulation implies that the state does not have the monopoly on shaping and determining regulation. The regulatory functions are dispersed or fragmented among different market actors. Decentralized approaches offer flexibility; solutions based on decentralization can be rapidly adapted to the characteristics and needs of an area at different levels. A decentred understanding of regulation enables an integral view of what regulation is. The limits of regulation become fluid. However, the criteria applied to define the concept of decentred regulation have to be determined. The foundations characterising regulation as the product of a governmental activity are not applicable anymore. Conceiving regulation in terms of a decentred perspective is a difficult task. It depends on numerous elements departing from the nature of the relationship between state and society as well as within a society upon which traditional conceptualizations of regulation are construed. Here, the decentred approach to regulation will include the following criteria: fragmentation of knowledge, of power, and of control, complexity, coordination and cooperation, ungovernability, self-regulation, or alternative regulatory forms defined by autonomous regulatory regimes and globalization. Although, they are derived from or may be similar to Foucauldian notions, they should not be understood strictly in that sense here.[58]

5.2 *Fragmentation of Knowledge, Power, and Control*

Fragmentation[59] of knowledge, of power, and of control constitutes an element of the concept of decentralization because the regulatory functions are not

[57] Majone G., The Rise of the Regulatory State in Europe, July 1994; Black, supra note 56, 1.

[58] Black J., Decentring Regulation: Understanding the Role of Regulation and Self-Regulation in a 'Post-regulatory' World, November 2001, 105 et seqq.; Black, supra note 56, 1–7; Senn M., Decentralisation of Economic Law – An Oxymoron?, October 2005, 442 with further references, 443–453.

[59] Basically, the term 'fragmentation' is used in this study. Instead of fragmentation, 'delegation' may be used, but this needs to be understood as an authoritative decision that transfers

concentrated anymore; on the contrary, they are distributed among the different actors concerned. Hence, this undoing of a centralized system or the existence of a decentralized system of governance results in fragmentation, which is an innate part and characteristic of decentralization. However, the degree of fragmentation can vary within a function or an element considered. It may depend on the level of control still held by a centre in a model. In relation to regulation, the determining elements of knowledge, power, and control are not centralized anymore but fragmented or may even be dispersed. The state and other private actors all fulfil their own specialized functions, but they may not master the whole regulatory process each on their own. Fragmentation implies that there is an information asymmetry between the regulators and the regulatees or a fragmentation of knowledge, which adds to diversity. Furthermore, regulation should be understood in a broad sense in relation to fragmentation or also dispersion. It is not produced by the state only, but by a whole range of market actors. As a consequence, the central authority of the state is basically weakened. Hence, fragmentation results in a distribution of power that implies that there is scope for the initiative of private market actors or individuals and the emergence of autonomous regimes and alternative forms of regulation.

5.3 Complexity

Fragmentation consequently leads to an emphasis on complexity. Complexity belongs to the concept of decentralization because it implies that the centre is weakened and loses, at least in part, its meaning and function while other entities – such as networks or self-regulatory organizations – emerge. These entities may then assume some agreed regulatory responsibilities and functions. A system is constituted, albeit not a simple, single-centred system, but one comprising a lot of ramifications. Thus, it represents a complex system narrowly linked to, or even dependent on, the concept of decentralization. There are many interactions, which can simultaneously develop their own dynamics. This increases the complexity of a system, already made complex by different actors and other specific factors, which can determine and influence its working. Networks of interdependencies and references to factors, subjects, and contexts are constituted; these are intra-organizational as well as external networks. Theoretically, intra-organizational relations

policy-making authority away from established, representative organs to a non-majoritarian institution, whether public or private. Thus, the definition implies that it is largely used as a policy method, which should not always be the case with fragmentation. See Thatcher M. and Stone Sweet A., Theory and Practice of Delegation to Non-Majoritarian Institutions, January 2002, 1, 3; Thatcher M., Delegation to Independent Regulatory Agencies: Pressures, Functions and Contextual Mediation, January 2002, 125, 125–131; Shapiro M., Judicial Delegation Doctrines: The US, Britain, and France, January 2002, 173, 173–175; Senn, supra note 58, 444–445.

consist in the linkages existing between one (mother) organization and its sub-organizations. These organizations are not considered to be autonomous but interdependent. Although the processes and tasks are similar to those of external networks, the question of the integration of these sub-organizations in the main organization is much more important. This is underpinned by the fact that it is not possible to retire from an organization without leaving the whole system. In addition, the working of the network is linked to a hierarchical structure among the institutions and actors concerned, which constitutes a key element of that network. The working of a whole network or organization depends on their interactions and readiness to cooperate with each other. As the roles and functions of the different institutions and individuals are predetermined by the rules governing an area, they are intertwined. Once more, it is not possible to quit a sub-organization only: one must leave the whole organization. External networks are characterized by the fact that they represent horizontal systems, which result in a horizontal cooperation occurring between the organizations concerned. These organizations can act autonomously, but they may (voluntarily) cooperate as they are dependent on each other to some degree and pursue similar interests. Consequently, there is also a possibility to quit a network and continue to act autonomously.[60] These kinds of networks may be encountered both among public or private groups of interests.

5.4 *Coordination and Cooperation*

The criteria of fragmentation and complexity both result from the fact that decentred understandings of regulation encompass a whole range of interactions among the state and private actors as well as individuals and private organizations. To work, these interactions have to be coordinated. Decentred governance is narrowly linked to the question of coordination and cooperation among the different individuals and market actors concerned. Coordination is probably the most important characteristic of regimes of decentred governance and may be considered to constitute the core of their existence. It is an inherent part of decentralization and emanates from the sheer existence of a decentred system. Decentred systems are constituted by a multitude of centres, which have to work together to ensure the functioning of the system as a whole. Consequently, these centres must coordinate their activities. In fact, decentralization represents a dichotomy between autonomy and integration, and good and effective coordination constitutes a pivotal precondition for their functioning. Practically, it is necessary to organize the exchange of information among the individuals and market actors concerned and ensure their broad integration into the respective rule-making and enforcement processes. In particular, decentred models are characterized by interdependencies among the

[60] Willke H., Systemtheorie III: Steuerungstheorie, 1998, 112–125; Black, supra note 58, 107–108; Senn, supra note 58, 446–447, with further references.

individuals and market actors, each playing a determined role. They should work together, on the one hand, and hence, also constitute a reliable basis for the market actors, on the other. Depending on the degree of centred and decentred governance introduced or applied in a model or area, different interdependencies can be created or emerge and the kind of interactions among individuals and market actors can differ depending on the situation. Multi-way processes of cooperation or interactions can take place as a whole range of activities, functions, and experiences may need to be coordinated. The actors involved constitute a network among themselves. They are interdependent and willing to interact and cooperate. Moreover, within a transnational network, there are no territorial limits. Interactions will extend well beyond national borders. Within these regimes, it is assumed that there are many reasons for reciprocal interests and interactions among the actors concerned. These interactions and linkages, which can occur at different levels, again indicate that the regimes are immanently complex. An important motivating reason for coordination and cohesion concerns the advantages arising for the participants from their interactions. Coordination and cohesion also involve risks, however, such as the risk of conflicts of interest. In addition, it should not be overlooked that the interdependencies themselves may also lead to a subtle dynamic of dependencies and independencies, which characterises decentralization as such and may represent another challenge to be managed. It should also not be forgotten that coordination represents a genuine contradiction and sets limits to the autonomy and the responsibilities of the different individuals and market actors concerned.[61]

5.5 *Ungovernability*

The criterion of ungovernability is linked to the autonomy of individuals, market actors, and networks within decentred regimes. It means that these regimes are mainly self-regulated. There is no intervention or governance emanating from the state. Regulation represents the 'conduct of conduct'.[62] However, decentred systems of regulation are not stable, but dynamic. Individuals can continue to develop relations and standards among themselves or act in their own way in the absence of state intervention. Thus, the ensuing introduction of a state regulation may well produce unintended outcomes, because the emergent networks will have developed their own regulatory solutions first. There is an inherent ungovernability of the actors, networks and regimes concerned, and a state regulatory strategy will have to take into account the existing (private) regulatory standards. Then, the attitude of the regulatees towards compliance with rules may have a determining influence on the enforcement of state rules. Although, due to their autonomy, they will, to an

61 Black, supra note 58, 109–110; Senn, supra note 58, 449–451, with further references.

62 Black, supra note 56, 4, with reference to Foucault.

extent, be insusceptible to the introduction of external (state) regulation in a first phase, its enforcement will lead to changes in their behaviour. However, to implement measures, a minimal consensus among these individuals and market actors is necessary. A further characteristic of ungovernability is that no single actor will dominate the regulatory process unilaterally, which is owing to the interdependencies among actors.[63]

5.6 *Self-regulation*

Finally, decentralization raises an issue of self-regulation as an alternative form of regulation and non-state, private autonomous regime, as it implies that more diversity, or a greater variety of institutions and bodies, may contribute to the shaping of a determined governance model. This is because powers are fragmented and attributed to national and international authorities, private market actors, or other bodies playing definite roles. Depending on the model, decentralization may represent a combination of national, governmental, non-governmental, international, or private actors organized in different ways according to the circumstances. One consequence of this greater diversity is that these actors may develop themselves and act autonomously or exercise their functions in their respective fields in the absence of intervention. In other words, there is room for different kinds of regulations and for self-regulation and non-state autonomous regulatory regimes. Such scope is linked to the possibility of the actors acting on their own due to decentralization. Private regulatory regimes and self-regulation represent a further regulatory ramification in a decentralized system, which is characterized by their reliance on the initiative of the private actors or networks concerned. In fact, these may not be entirely autonomous insofar as their autonomy may be limited by existing state regulation and perhaps supervision.[64]

5.7 *Globalization*

The picture would not be complete without taking into account the phenomenon of globalization. The concept of decentred regulation travels well within the idea of globalization, which is characterized by the emergence of all kind of autonomous regimes based on the activities of transnational networks, which abut on the existing (UN-) international organizations. These networks are generated by epistemic agreements among individuals or groups of interest. They are the source of autonomous regulatory regimes. Similarly to decentralized processes, globalized

[63] Black, supra note 58, 111; Black, supra note 56, 4–5.

[64] Black, supra note 58, 112–114; Senn, supra note 58, 452, with further references.

processes are complex and based on innumerable interconnections among the individuals, epistemic communities, and networks concerned. There is no determined or fixed shape for autonomous regimes emerging in the context of globalization. These globalized regimes are dynamic, can develop on a continuous basis, and are adaptable to the prevailing circumstances. Moreover, it is not least through the process of globalization that the strategic significance of regulation as a form of decentralized governance together with the recognition of the role of non-state regulation is increasing in a number of countries. Decentred regulation is not the sole result or the consequence of globalization, although it can very well be identified in relation to, or as constituting a part of, that process.

6 Meta-regulation

Within both institutions and academia a debate has been launched regarding the phenomenon of meta-regulation or the regulation of regulation, or the regulation of law. Meta-regulation recognizes the limitations of the state to deal with complex issues. It studies the interplay of legal or state and other forms of regulation. The role of meta-regulation is to focus on procedures rather than on the determination and prescription of behaviour through rules and, as a consequence, on enforcement and sanctioning questions. There is a reflection on the activity of regulating and not on regulating individual actions, concrete situations or cases. Meta-regulation implies conceiving the regulatory framework or its structure. The interactions of regulation as state regulation and other forms of non-state regulation or normative ordering are studied. In addition, within meta-regulation the focus is placed on institutions and processes.[65] Various regimes of regulation can be distinguished. They influence each other, and are distinguished from each other by the fact that their role is to regulate different matters each in their own way, that is, with their own instruments and methods. They can be considered as representing an array of various regulatory instruments and methods. Thus, one should now ask how these various tools operate, what their influence or regulatory impact is in practice, and to which extent they contribute to realizing the values they should represent. Another aspect concerns the extent of their contribution to the monitoring and enforcement of regulatory or other standards. The various forms of regulation may compete among each other as far as their effectiveness and impact are concerned. It is also possible that the real impact of a regulatory solution may prove to be inadequate or quite different from the intended effects. Through the analysis and evaluation of these forms of state and non-state regulation and their impact, the most adequate regulatory form or strategy to be applied to a concrete situation should be

[65] Morgan B., The Economization of Politics: Meta-Regulation as a Form of Nonjudicial Legality, 2003, 489 et seqq.; Parker C., The Open Corporation, Effective Self-regulation and Democracy, 2002, 245 et seqq.

identified.[66] As such, meta-regulation consists in a method that should serve to analyse the existing regulatory framework and configure it.

From a methodological point of view, the meta-regulatory approach raises questions in relation to determining possible ways to compare different forms of state and non-state or private regulation. Should an economic, historical, or technical approach be applied? There is still no consensus regarding the premises under which different forms of regulation can be compared or, according to Paterson and Teubner, structurally coupled.[67] Different ways exist, depending on the goal of a comparison, the techniques employed to examine it, the environment, and the expectations of the market. By the same token, it is useful to consider the concept of regulation as a regulation that can occur in many spheres or also as a concept pertaining to a regulatory space that could somehow be compared to geographical sites in which regulatory regimes exercise their influence. There is state and non-state or private regulation emerging from civil society and which can take the form of a whole range of regulatory regimes. This is an important aspect to explore the concept of meta-regulation because the spheres or spaces where the principles and standards applied in one sector are concretized and achieve their effects are often effectively sealed off from those applying to other sectors.[68] Meta-regulation concentrates on these interactions or the absence of interactions. The meta-regulatory approach differs from Teubner's regulatory trilemma, whose first aim is to concentrate on the problem of inadequate structural coupling of politics, law, and societal life. This situation is due to the fact that these sectors are both more autonomous and more interdependent at the same time.[69] According to Teubner, any regulatory intervention attempting to change a specific form of behaviour or the societal order should be assessed under the following aspects: (1) is the regulatory measure relevant or effective, that is, will individuals comply with it; (2) does it produce integrating effects on societal life, that is, is it responsive to existing norms and values; and (3) does it produce an integrating effect on regulatory law itself, that is, is it coherent with other rules? Thus, the focus is placed on effectiveness, responsiveness, and coherence. Teubner's approach is rooted in systems theory. However in the case of meta-regulation, according to Grabosky – who first construed the phenomenon of meta-regulation –, Braithwaite and Parker, it is not necessary to rely

66 Parker, Scott, Lacey, and Braithwaite, supra note 2, 6–7; see also Morgan, supra note 65, 489–490.

67 Paterson J. and Teubner G., Changing Maps: Empirical Legal Autopoiesis, 1999, 451, 457; Parker, Scott, Lacey, and Braithwaite, supra note 2, 7.

68 Hancher and Moran, supra note 4, 276 et seqq.; Scott C., Analysing Regulatory Space: Fragmented Resources and Institutional Design, Summer 2001, 329; Parker, Scott, Lacey, and Braithwaite, supra note 2, 285, Black J., Law and Regulation: The Case of Finance, 2004, 33–59.

69 Teubner G., Juridification: Concepts, Aspects, Limits, Solution, 1987, 408; see also: Parker, Scott, Lacey, and Braithwaite, supra note 2, 10, 287.

on systems theory to discover that it leads to more responsive and more effective results than command and control regulation.[70]

As already stated, meta-regulation is used to configure regulation. It entails different policy implications, and should contribute to realizing these. It is best suited to deal with complex issues. It is based on the recognition that many regulatory instruments do not bring about the right impact or fail when applied. In that regard, meta-regulation is considered to be a possible way out of the assumption or even recognition that governments are limited and not omnicompetent as far as their possibilities to take measures are concerned.[71] Meta-regulation takes into account the increased individual awareness according to which the whole process of regulation should be thought of more thoroughly and regulatory measures should be analysed in-depth. Regulation should be defined only on the basis of the results of this approach. Another possibility is due to a sense that the regulatory approach and role of states is changing. The state is attributed a steering role, no longer a rowing one.[72] This conception offers more scope and analytical alternatives for the study and development of non-state and private forms of regulation emerging from civil society as well as for the debate about the interactions between these forms of regulation. Thus, the state adopts a meta-regulatory approach. It concentrates more on monitoring the regulatory process than on regulating. One example of this monitoring is the empowering of private associations or SROs representing groups of interest to self-regulate their respective sector. In the context of meta-regulation, it could be described as the regulation of self-regulation by the state. As another example, the state may also concentrate on the management of risks and hence attempt to adapt risk management systems based on a meta-regulatory approach. Its most important contribution to the regulatory process is probably to define frameworks of rules best adapted to concrete situations and ensure their implementation.[73]

Meta-regulation is narrowly linked to public policy issues. It should contribute to managing the interactions among the different aspects accompanying the introduction of regulatory measures, like political, economic, or others. As such, it can be qualified as a way of systematizing regulatory policy. Morgan characterizes meta-regulation as an instance of nonjudicial legality rooted in the increasing legalization of politics and the reliance on nonjudicial mechanisms of accountability. It is also a form of reflexive regulation. It should strengthen internal reflection on regulation and self-control. An important function of meta-regulation is to find ways to empower civil society or its institutions, such as SROs or other associations or groups of interest, in order to develop private regulatory solutions or private autonomous regimes whilst rendering these accountable. It should also give rise to

[70] Parker, Scott, Lacey, and Braithwaite, supra note 2, 287; Grabosky, supra note 3, 527–550; see also on criticisms of command and control: Parker, supra note 65, 8–12.

[71] Grabosky, supra note 3, 527; Parker, Scott, Lacey, and Braithwaite, supra note 2, 6–7.

[72] Parker, Scott, Lacey, and Braithwaite, supra note 2, 7, 288.

[73] Ibid. 10–12.

the creation of new regulatory instruments, measures, or methods and hence foster regulatory pluralism. The interactions of the institutions that will then assume responsibility for regulatory activities could be construed as institutional meta-regulation. This form of meta-regulation means the regulation of one institution by another or the shaping of the regulatory activities of one institution as a result of the regulatory activities developed by another institution. Auditing companies are a practical example of institutions. Such companies can be conceived as meta-regulators with the capacity to steer the self-regulatory capacities of public sector organizations, for example with regard to financial controls.[74] Insofar, similarly to the concept of decentred regulation, meta-regulation is a concept that travels well at the global level. It is not limited to national borders but applies to processes based on a functional approach.

7 Regulation as a Marketplace

Following the discussion of decentred regulation and meta-regulation, this section considers complex interactions among different regulatory orders and conceptualizes these in terms of regulatory pluralism or interlegality.[75] As already stated, regulation can appear in relation to a number of issues and assume a number of forms either as state or non-state regulation. When the focus is placed on the forms and processes of regulation, it rapidly becomes clear that regulation constitutes a market. It is a marketplace. It is possible to distinguish between those who demand and those who supply regulation. In the economy, from manufacturing or the telecommunications sectors over the financial markets to the transport and energy sectors, there are different kinds of regulatory orders. Moreover, various sectors of world society have developed a global law on their own through their networks, as stated. This occurs in relative insulation from the state, official international politics, and international public law.[76]

The concept of regulation is complex and contemporary regulation is multidimensional. Besides the fact that regulation evolves and may vary with regard to form and content, its origins and also the range of its applications as well as the perspective chosen to define rules and analyse them indicate the multi-faceted nature of the topic.[77] Regulation belongs to the concept of regulatory space,

---

[74] Morgan, supra note 65, 491–492, 509–614; Parker, Scott, Lacey, and Braithwaite, supra note 2, 6–12, 269 et seqq.

[75] de Sousa Santos B., Toward a New Legal Common Sense, Law, Globalization, and Emancipation, 2004.

[76] Giddens A., The Consequences of Modernity, 1990, 70; Teubner G., Global Bukowina: Legal Pluralism in the World Society, 2006, 3–28.

[77] A multitude of methods exist and can be applied depending on the question to be resolved and the objectives pursued. For an example of the complexity of methods, see the excellent contribution of: Örücü E., The Enigma of Comparative Law, Variations on a Theme for the Twenty-First Century, 2004.

regulatory arena, or regulatory market. This regulatory space must be organized. It encompasses a range of regulatory issues and can be considered in terms of different approaches. National, supranational and international peculiarities, historical timing, organizational structure, interdependences including epistemic communities and networks can be taken into account to organize this space. Multiple regulatory solutions or processes emerge, and as such legal pluralism.[78]

At the level of the state, regulatory markets cover the role and interactions of different governmental institutions at different levels, such as in a federal state: the municipal level, the level of the cantons or states, and the federal level. These institutions will all be equipped with different powers and capacities. Moreover, there will also be a whole range of independent authorities, agencies, and organizations acting on the basis of powers delegated by the state. There will also be scope for private initiative and other bodies not belonging to the state at the same time. These participants in the regulatory process may be non-governmental, industry associations, international bodies, or interest groups and networks. Altogether, they will constitute a whole range of markets or sub-markets with alternating roles of the state and private economy.

As a marketplace, competition among regulatory places or regimes is possible. It can take place at the national, regional, or global level. It is not limited to state regulation, but also encompasses non-state regulation. Through the lens of competition among regulatory markets, the question of the choice of the optimal regulation becomes acute. Interest groups or networks looking for a regulatory solution may be confronted with questions of regulatory shopping and the search for good, effective, or responsive regulation among a range of regulatory regimes.[79] Moreover, regulatory issues are largely influenced by politics, and depend on concrete circumstances and the constellation of market forces. An important factor in relation to regulatory shopping is the cost of regulation. Here again, the study of the potential costs of a measure, cost–benefit analysis, often determines the choice of a specific regulatory solution. Thus, the existence of regulatory markets and competition among these markets may decisively lead to an improvement of regulatory solutions adopted under a range of aspects.

Chairman Alan Greenspan illustrated the working of these regulatory markets as follows:

> 'Migration of activity from government-regulated to privately regulated markets sends a signal to government regulators that the many transactors believe the costs of regulation exceed the benefits. When such a migration occurs, government regulators should consider carefully whether less regulation or different regulation would provide a better cost-benefit tradeoff without compromising public policy objectives.'
>
> Chairman Alan Greenspan, remarks at the Financial Conference of the Federal Reserve Bank of Atlanta, Coral Gables, Florida (Feb. 21, 1997).

---

[78] Hancher and Moran, supra note 4, 276 et seqq.; Merry S. E., Legal Pluralism, 1988, 869–896; Griffiths J., What is Legal Pluralism?, 1986, 1–55; Teubner, supra note 76, 14.

[79] Ayres I. and Braithwaite J., Responsive Regulation, Transcending the Deregulation Debate, 1992, 4 et seqq.

The regulatory marketplace experiences even more diversity with the process of globalization. This dimension adds to the plurality of regulation. The emergence of epistemic communities and transnational (both governmental and private) networks,[80] not least in the wake of the globalization of business, entails a whole range of alternative regulatory forms. Apart from the coercive power of orders such as the UN Charter or the rules of supranational organizations such as the European Union for instance, autonomous, often private, regulatory regimes abound. They may compete with other similar regulatory regimes or with state regulation. In particular, they represent efficient forms of regulation and are not only introduced where the state or international organizations cannot cope with a situation, but also in cases in which they are judged to be adequate and competitive. As a result, a shift from state regulation towards an increasing role of autonomous regulatory regimes is possible. The rules enacted by these networks add to regulatory pluralism. They constitute a new form of transnational regulation.

8 Alternatives to Regulation

Regulation is not the sole policy instrument that can be used to solve policy issues within the state. On the contrary, there are many non-regulatory alternatives, that is, either alternatives in the form of a secondary impact of regulation, where the focus is not placed on regulation, or alternatives to regulation in the form of measures of a different, non-regulatory type. Here, both are discussed insofar as they represent alternatives to classical state regulation based on command and control measures. In comparison to state regulation, they may represent either substitutes, complements, or alternative forms of implementation of state regulation.[81] They are discussed as regulatory alternatives because the focus is placed on the objectives and possibilities to influence behaviour based on the measures adopted although it is not excluded that their basis may be found in a regulatory measure or a statute. On their side, regulatory strategies first concentrate on regulatory techniques and the choice of the appropriate regulatory method.[82] The goal of the following brief presentation of alternatives is to add a further facet to the concept of regulation discussed in this chapter. The presentation is not exhaustive; it is based on analyses prepared by the OECD and discusses the most important types only: economic

---

[80] Sajó A., Transnational Networks and Constitutionalism, 2006, 209–225; Senn, supra note 58, 461–463.

[81] OECD Reviews of Regulatory Reform, supra note 20, 51 seq., 135 seq.; Breyer, supra note 5, 156.

[82] OECD Reviews of Regulatory Reform, supra note 20, 135; Baldwin and Cave, supra note 5, 34–57; Breyer, supra note 5, 156; on the strategies, see hereinafter Chapter 2, point 1 Embedding Autonomous Regulatory Regimes.

instruments, information and education campaigns, performance-based regulation, process based regulation, co-regulation, guidelines, and voluntary approaches.[83] In practice, however, numerous other alternatives can be distinguished. New alternatives can develop on a continuous basis depending on the circumstances and issues.

8.1 Economic Instruments

The first alternative is the use of economic instruments. These instruments are applied in an array of situations and various usable instruments are at the disposal of governments to achieve their policy objectives. These can take the form of taxes, subsidies, authorization requirements, tradeable permits, and so forth. The use of these instruments is very efficient in practice because they are directly applicable and offer the possibility to correct or adjust a situation without distortion. They can be used either to initiate a pursued behaviour or on the contrary to prevent an undesirable behaviour. Another advantage of the use of economic instruments it that the economy can achieve its policy goals at very low costs. A further advantage lies in the fact that these instruments can indirectly play a role of market incentives insofar as they reward innovations and technical changes adopted by individuals or industries in connection with the achievement of these objectives.[84] As far as the form of this alternative is concerned, it may either accompany regulation or constitute part of it. In the case of taxes, for example, a specific form of conduct can be encouraged through the possibility of obtaining special deductions or credits. On the contrary, a tax may be imposed to deter an undesirable conduct, as in the case of an industry polluting water or the environment. However, different outcomes are possible. While most individuals or firms might adapt their conduct or respectively their production, for example through installing antipolluting equipments, others will continue to pay taxes. Formally, the taxes do not substitute regulation. They may be implemented provided there is a constitutional or statutory provision or they may take the form of statutes themselves.[85] On its side, the case of tradeable permits represents a market-based approach. A limited number of rights to engage in a specific form of conduct is established and then traded on a market. Those willing to pay most for a privilege will buy up the rights and the state or the regulator who initially established and allocated the rights will be able to control them. It does not know at which price the rights will finally be traded. Practical experiences show that the use of these permits causes numerous problems.[86]

---

83 OECD Reviews of Regulatory Reform, supra note 20, 135–142.

84 Ibid. 137–139, with examples based on the experiences of various countries; Breyer, supra note 5, 156 seq.

85 Breyer, supra note 5, 164–171.

86 Ibid. 171–174; Baldwin and Cave, supra note 5, 47–48.

8.2 Information and Education Campaigns

The second alternative are information and education campaigns. According to the OECD, this is the most widely used alternative approach to regulation in OECD member countries.[87] This approach addresses information asymmetries within determined markets or in relation to determined topics. The aim of these campaigns is to empower individuals with sufficient information to both inform them thoroughly about a product, a project, and so forth whilst enhancing their choices or also effecting a change of behaviour. Such campaigns often represent attempts of moral suasion by governments. However, they may be largely suggestive and motivated by government or state interests. In practice, this kind of campaign will first be used when a change of behaviour is expected or considered to bring about substantial externality effects. It should then enable individuals and consumers to make informed choices and avoid risks as far as possible. There are numerous examples to illustrate the use of this instrument, such as government anti-smoking campaigns to mention a very well-known instance, or education initiatives for investors launched by supervisory authorities of financial markets to improve their knowledge and awareness of financial risks.[88]

8.3 Performance-based Regulation

The third alternative – performance-based regulation – focuses on the objective of a government with regard to a determined policy issue and not on the means to achieve it. As a consequence, the individuals, businesses, or industries affected are required to adopt measures to reach the objectives or the outcomes set. In practice, the enforcement of performance-based regulation by individuals, industries, or market sectors should be conducted in a way that distinguishes the individual characteristics, capabilities, and performance of these actors to create clear incentives for appropriate conduct and equally clear disincentives for inappropriate conduct. They will comply with a given statute when they realize the objectives set. Government involvement is possible but it is not essential. A great virtue of this alternative lies in the fact that the individuals, businesses, or sectors concerned will choose the economically most advantageous, cheap, and efficient way to attain their goal. At the same time, this manner of proceeding will enhance innovations and promote the adoption of new technologies. However, a possible drawback of this alternative may be the costs of the measures to be taken. These are not always foreseeable and calculable in advance. They often represent a higher burden for small businesses than for large companies. This alternative also implies a greater

---

87 OECD Reviews of Regulatory Reform, supra note 20, 139.

88 OECD Reviews of Regulatory Reform, supra note 20, 139–140, with examples; Baldwin R., Why Rules Don't Work, 1990, 326–328.

responsibility of the private economy to develop appropriate implementation strategies and in such cases governmental guidelines or safe harbours may be welcome. However, these guidelines should not become mandatory regulation and undermine the alternative of performance-based regulation itself, as this offers room for individual initiative. In such cases, a balance should be found. From a formal point of view, one advantage of this alternative is that written regulation can be simplified because it merely describes the objectives to be reached and no fastidious regulatory details have to be worked out. Performance-based regulation is narrowly linked to management-based regulation as will be discussed in Chap. 4.[89]

8.4 *Process-based Regulation*

A fourth alternative, similar to performance-based regulation, is process-based regulation. Again, this approach places the emphasis on the initiative of individuals, industries and businesses whereas it is based on cooperation between the public and private sectors. They form partnerships and often assure a balance between public and private interests. Process-based regulation regularly applies in relation to privatization processes. This form of regulation requires the development of processes with the aim to ensure a systematic approach to identifying, assessing, controlling and minimizing risks. This alternative is characterized by the assumption that producers or service providers will choose and, if necessary, develop low-cost solutions themselves to manage risks, provided they have the right incentives. In the case of financial institutions for instance, they will rely on their own internal models, risk management or control processes validated and verified by their responsible supervisory authorities. These solutions are more effective than a direct government intervention because in practice there are often multiple risks and producers or service providers are in a better position to understand, apprehend, and take adequate measures, not least due to their expertise.[90]

8.5 *Other Approaches*

In its Reviews on Regulatory Reform,[91] the OECD discusses three more regulatory alternatives to regulation: co-regulation, guidelines, and voluntary approaches. These are not presented as such here for the following reasons:

---

89 OECD Reviews of Regulatory Reform, supra note 20, 135–136; Coglianese C., Nash J., and Olmstead T., Performance-Based Regulation: Prospects and Limitations in Health, Safety and Environmental Protection, December 2002.

90 OECD Reviews of Regulatory Reform, supra note 20, 136–137, with examples; Padoa-Schioppa T., Regulating Finance – Balancing Freedom and Risk, 2004, 41–42, 46–48.

91 OECD Reviews of Regulatory Reform, supra note 20, 137–142.

- Co-regulation is based on a cooperation between the state and individuals or groups of interest. These actors agree to jointly implement rules or a policy. Co-regulation usually consists in part of industry-association self-regulation together with some government oversight or ratification.[92] It thus represents a hybrid form of regulation. There is a blend between an authoritative and a voluntary regulatory approach. As part of an authoritative approach, co-regulation encompasses the existence of state regulation. As part of a voluntary approach, co-regulation may be subsumed under self-regulation. The sector or industry concerned may also issue secondary rules or supervise the implementation of rules.[93] Thus, co-regulation is neither an alternative to regulation nor an optional form of attaining defined policy objectives. It should rather be classified as a regulatory technique based on private measures adopted to implement a statute.
- Guidelines correspond to the promulgation of non-binding recommendations. They may be quasi-regulatory guidelines when promulgated by a government or regulatory agency. Guidelines may also represent a kind of information campaign wherein the state or a government sets out processes, provides explanations and interpretations to government policies, or praises a behaviour, such as in the case of conflicts of interest. They may be recommendations published by supervisory agencies to warn consumers for instance.[94] As such, they represent a technical instrument accompanying information campaigns. They are addressed to individuals, groups of interest, or networks. Guidelines may also be used to provide interpretation of regulations. They can be encountered in all kinds of situations and represent a flexible instrument for practitioners.[95] They do not qualify as rules. On the contrary, they may at the most epitomize a form of soft law. They may also be enacted by private organizations and, for example, be declared mandatory for the members of the said organization. Guidelines are thus considered to represent a kind of mild form of codes of conduct or a regulatory technique rather than an alternative.
- Voluntary approaches belong to self-regulation. They are arrangements initiated by private industry, businesses, associations, or networks. They adopt self-imposed requirements among themselves, and these may exceed, complement the prevailing regulatory requirements, or endure state regulation. Often, such approaches have been developed in the course of time and adapted to the characteristics of their field of application. In such cases, governments will be reluctant to intervene. These approaches could also be classified as regulatory alternatives as far as they represent a non-governmental form of attaining objectives although these may be the same as the state objectives. They may

---

92 Ayres and Braithwaite, supra note 79, 102.

93 OECD Reviews of Regulatory Reform, supra note 20, 137; see also Chapter 3, point 3 Co-Regulation.

94 http://www.moneymadeclear.fsa.gov.uk/. Accessed 30 October 2009.

95 OECD Reviews of Regulatory Reform, supra note 20, 140; Chapter 3, point 1 Self-Regulation and point 3 Co-regulation.

take the form of codes of conduct, voluntary agreements, or other measures and they also fragment the state regulatory order. In the case of state involvement or a specific state regulation, the enforcement of (penal) sanctions will be endorsed by governments. However, it is considered here that voluntary approaches rather represent a regulatory technique where the involvement of the state is non-determining prima facie.[96]

9 Definition of Regulation

The roles and functions of regulation are both complex and the term has already been defined in many different ways. When dealing with the concept and nature of regulation, the prima facie assumption is linked to the idea of statutory regulation as the product of governmental activity based on the public interest criterion. However, it appears to be difficult to find a universally recognized definition of regulation. There is no general agreement as to what regulation is and there is confusion. The notion of regulation is basically linked to the idea of a form of authority whereas at first glance the question of the legitimacy of the rules is not primary. According to the dictionary, the term 'regulation' means:

> The act of regulating, or the state of being regulated. Also, an instance of this. [...]
>
> A rule prescribed for the management of some matter, or for the regulating of conduct; a governing precept or direction; a standing rule. [...]
>
> That is prescribed by, or in accordance with, a regulation or regulations; such as is required or insisted on under some regulation; hence, regular, usual, ordinary, common.[97]

and 'to regulate' means:

> To control, govern, or direct by rule or regulations; to subject to guidance or restrictions; to adapt to circumstances or surroundings. [...]
>
> To make regulations.
>
> To exhibit regulation.[98]

The definition is interesting for this study because it does not imply a participation of the state as the sole institution in a position to decree regulation. However, the term 'regulation' is defined using precisely the same word. Another definition of regulation is provided by the OECD. According to the OECD, 'regulation' means:

> The full range of legal instruments by which governing institutions, at all levels of government, impose obligations or constraints on private sector behaviour. Constitutions,

---

96 OECD Reviews of Regulatory Reform, supra note 20, 140–142, with examples; hereinafter Chapter 3, point 1 Self-Regulation.

97 The Oxford English Dictionary, Volume XIII, 1991, 525.

98 Ibid. 524.

parliamentary laws, subordinate legislation, decrees, orders, norms, licences, plans, codes and even some forms of administrative guidance can all be considered as regulation.[99]

This definition illustrates an understanding of 'regulation' in a traditional, narrow sense insofar as it represents an activity centred on the state. Such state-centredness is the main attribute of regulation in this view. Although different institutions within the state can enact regulation, they all belong to that institution.

According to Baldwin and Cave, the word regulation comprises different meanings[100]: First, regulation can be understood to represent a specific set of commands. It includes the idea of a sovereign and a subject and there is an attitude of obedience and submission. It is then also designed as coercive regulation. Its coercive character is expressed by the addressees' recognition that the rules are binding.[101] A second feature of regulation is its deliberate state influence. Regulation is still centred on the state but it has a broader meaning. It includes all state actions that may shape or influence industrial or societal behaviour and not only the rules.[102] A whole range of actions or modes of influence can be subsumed under regulation. A third feature of regulation is its expression of morality within society or in other words of the generally accepted or conventional morality standards within a group. As a moral force, it is not necessary to have a state-derived form of regulation. In that case, regulation is understood to exercise a form of societal control or influence in practice and the mechanisms affecting behaviour are deemed regulatory.[103] Regulation can then be understood to represent an activity of attempting to influence, determine, or control the behaviour of others.

Selznick's classic definition of regulation as sustained and focused control exercised by a public agency over activities that are societally valued is often cited with approval. However, the exclusive focus on public agencies, common within American studies of regulation, is problematic when so much regulatory activity is decentred within the state. It ignores that many regulatory regimes do not focus on a public agency.[104]

When attempting to define regulation, it should not be ignored that virtually every activity and every business is affected by regulation in some way. Regulation appears in a number of forms. According to Harrison, Morgan, Verkuil, the word regulation does not describe a simple, straightforward phenomenon. The following characteristics of regulation stand out: Regulation is both direct and indirect;

[99] OECD, Recommendation of the Council of the OECD on Improving the Quality of Government Regulation; The OECD Report on Regulatory Reform: Synthesis Report, 1997.

[100] Baldwin and Cave, supra note 5, 1–2, with further references.

[101] In that sense, see also: Hart H.L.A., The Concept of Law, 1997, 55 et seq., 56–57, with the elaboration of the notion of the 'internal aspect of rules' as opposed to social rules. In particular, it is observed that feelings are not sufficient to explain the adherence to binding rules.

[102] Baldwin and Cave, supra note 5, 2.

[103] Hart, supra note 101, 169.

[104] Selznick P., Focusing Organisational Research on Regulation, 1985, 363; Baldwin and Cave, supra note 5, 2; Scott C., Privatization and Regulatory Regimes, 2006, 653.

regulation is both pervasive and partial; regulation is imposed by both the state and federal authorities; and regulation is neither static nor permanent.[105]

On their side, Hancher and Moran consider that regulation and in particular economic regulation should be understood as 'a process of intermediation and bargaining between large and powerful organizations spanning what are conventionally termed the public and private domains of decision-making.'[106]

These different definitions of the word regulation show that there is no generally recognized concept.[107] It varies depending on the point of view. In the examples cited, the definition is narrow and not sufficient to capture the entire concept adequately. This study takes into account that the traditional understanding of the legal state according to which it is deemed necessary to also regulate a rule of law (that is, appear in a substantial procedure) is no more self-evident. The adoption of a broader definition of regulation is necessary. The idea of legality plays an important role within a regulatory regime where it is premised upon acting in accordance with a set of norms. In that regard, Hutter is certainly right to state that following the recognition of the limits of public law approaches to regulation, attention is now turned to alternative methods and sources of regulation. Contemporary regulation implies a broadening conceptualization of regulation. It is no longer understood as an exclusive domain of the state, and a role of non-state actors in regulation is now widely acknowledged.[108]

In this study, the term regulation is understood as a dynamic concept. It is not a defined mode of activity that only pertains to a state legal system. It can appear in different orders and the conceptualization ascribed to regulation depends on the concrete circumstances as well as on the perception of what an order or a regulation is. It can also be a form of governance. In particular, the decentred view of regulation opens perspectives for different forms of regulation while the idea of state regulation remains limited to specific, fixed forms of regulation.

10 Conclusion

This chapter has discussed various aspects of regulation. Its main objective has been to delineate the regulatory landscape within which non-state, autonomous regulatory regimes or alternatives to regulation may emerge. The concept of regulation has been delimited through adopting a reversed funnel. Starting out from the discussion of the motivations to regulate, the background of regulation and the

---

[105] Harrison, Morgan, Verkuil, supra note 9, 3–4.

[106] Hancher and Moran, supra note 4, 272.

[107] See also Breyer, supra note 5, 4; Bartelt G., Regulatorische Marktinterventionen – Ansätze zu einer Theorie regulatorischer Marktintervention als Grundlage zur Beurteilung ihrer Effizienz, 1989, 6–13.

[108] Hutter B. M., The Role of Non-State Actors in Regulation, April 2006, 2; Hutter B. M., Regulation and Risk: Occupational Health and Safety on the Railways, 2001.

public policy issues were then considered to establish the link between regulation and politics. The next step concentrated on the theories of regulation. With the discussion of aspects of the decentred analysis of regulation, the approach to regulation was enlarged and meta-regulation introduced the discussion of regulation as a process. Based on these aspects, regulation as a market place was described. The concept of regulation was then extended to the alternatives to regulation, opening the window to other, third types of measures. A further step consisted in the study of the institutions involved in the process of regulation. Finally, a tentative definition of regulation was offered. Overall, this chapter serves as a background for the discussion of non-state, autonomous regulatory regimes. The mechanisms and limitations of state regulation have been discussed. At the same time, it also indicated that there are openings for non-state, alternative regulatory regimes. It will be useful to identify and establish links to a possible embedding of non-state, autonomous regulatory regimes in relation to state regulation.

Chapter 2
An Approach to Autonomous Regulatory Regimes

Abstract The chapter represents the core of the theoretical part of the study. Its objective is to seize the characteristics leading to the emergence of autonomous regulatory regimes. These alternative forms of regulation are common. They correspond to distinctive, modern systems of interest representation. The chapter approaches the basics of these regulatory regimes. It first discusses how alternative forms of regulation interact within the existing state regulatory framework. A distinction is made between the possible inclusion of these regimes in state regulatory concepts and the opposite, their emergence from civil society. The next characteristic considered is the functional and historical dimension. The core of the chapter concentrates on institutional structure. It is argued that the source of alternative forms of regulation is the theory of interest. Regulatory regimes always emerge from collective action. With the formalization of the relationships these regimes acquire another quality. Thus, different aspects of institutional structures of these regimes are discussed.

The first chapter discussed the regulatory framework and departed from the traditional point of view, that is, state regulation. It set a frame that might contextualize other forms of normative ordering or such used regularly when examining the nature of non-state, autonomous regulatory regimes. Based on state regulation, the goal was to better understand possible rationales that may lead to the emergence of non-state, autonomous regimes. This chapter focuses on the conceptualization of these regimes as well as the initial discussion of their mode of operation.

The attempt to comprehend the concept of alternative forms of regulation, self-regulation, or autonomous regulatory regimes is not new. A number of studies already exist. These are worthy contributions to the discussion and often deal with specific aspects.[1] However, as Berman formulates, one of the most important tasks of international law remains

[1] P. S. Berman, The Globalization of Jurisdiction (2002) 324; see also as cited in A. Fischer-Lescano and G. Teubner, Fragmentierung des Weltrechts: Vernetzung globaler Regimes statt etatistischer Rechtseinheit (2007) 46. Some studies are for instance: A. Ogus, Rethinking Self-Regulation (Spring 1995) 97–108; J. Black, Constitutionalising Self-Regulation (1996) 24–55; A. C. Page, Self-Regulation: The Constitutional Dimension (March 1986) 141–167; M. Koskenniemi, Fragmentation of International

DOI 10.1007/978-3-642-14974-0_3, © Springer-Verlag Berlin Heidelberg 2011

'recognizing and evaluating non-state jurisdictional assertions that bind sub-, supra-, or transnational communities. Such non-state jurisdictional assertions include a wide range of entities, from official transnational and international regulatory and adjudicative bodies, to non-governmental quasi-legal tribunals, to private standard-setting or regulatory organizations.'

Indeed, capturing the genuine nature of these forms of regulation is a difficult task. Such difficulty is partly due to the meshing of centralized and decentralized regulatory solutions, state and non-state as well as statutory and self-regulatory elements, negotiations and scientific approaches. It is also a challenge to overcome the divide, not least because these alternative regimes are the product of non-linear dynamics.[2] It is a subtle and complex concept.

Methodologically, the process of conceptualizing alternative forms of regulation can be visualized through the image of a chain. Where the first chapter sought to embrace characteristics determining state regulation, this chapter concentrates on core features of private and non-state forms of regulation as they appear when originating from the background of civil society. A sequential process is applied. Some general hypotheses are set forth to explain the probable context of their emergence, evolution, and persistence. As a result, they are conceptualized explicitly as a multi-facetted, iterative, evolutionary, and continuous process. To develop the concept, identify its structure, and discuss its appearance either as an autonomous regime or in relation to a state regulatory regime, approach is devoted to specific aspects, each contributing to explain these forms of regulation. It also produces a conceptual chain.

Within that chain, two main sources of contemporary, alternative forms of regulation are identified and differentiated: the state source and the civil society source. While the state source is characterized by a delegation of regulatory competences from the state authority to private actors, the civil society source corresponds to a sectoral and functional, often historically motivated development of alternative forms of regulation. To effect the passage from one source to the other, the state approach is first narrowed by focusing on the public policy debate and regulatory strategies. Then, the core of the passage to the civil society optics is accomplished through a decentred analysis of regulation. The next point examines the historical or evolutive aspects of these regulatory regimes, including the temporal and sectoral ones. This matters since various self-regulatory rules and structures that finally led to the constitution of modern private autonomous regimes can be traced to the medieval ages while others are contemporary sectoral ones.[3] The institutional structure of these forms of regulation is then explored, forming the core of the whole chapter. Institutions are the most important feature, contributing to the

Law: Difficulties Arising from the Diversification and Expansion of International Law (2006); B. de Sousa Santos, Toward a New Common Sense: Law, Science and Politics in the Age of the Paradigmatic Transition (1995) 114 et seq.

[2] J. Braithwaite and P. Drahos, Global Business Regulation (2000) 23–24; A. Fischer-Lescano and G. Teubner, Regime-Kollisionen, Zur Fragmentierung des globalen Rechts (2006) 128.

[3] For a basic study, see A. Black, Guild & State (2003).

explanation of the emergence and persistence of autonomous regulatory regimes. The approach adopted here is multisequential. Sequences leading from the theory of interest to legal pluralism and networks as regulatory institutions are analyzed as a continuous and iterative process of transformation and evolution, all characterizing their appearance.

1 Embedding Autonomous Regulatory Regimes

To approach forms of normative ordering different from state regulation, or non-state autonomous regimes, it is necessary to take into account that they cannot merely be included in a linear concept of regulation. Traditional conceptions of regulation are inadequate to capture the complexity of these regulatory forms or, as it appears, non-state regulation. Moreover, as already stated, the approach is characterized by a dichotomy between regulatory regimes emerging from the state on the one hand, and from civil society on the other. Alternative forms of regulation can be the product of state regulation as a form of regulation resulting from a delegation by the state. These are then the result of public policy choices or can be classified as the outcome of political and legal decisions. They represent non-spontaneous regimes, that is, steered regulation. They can also emerge from civil society, arising from an evolutive development from societal norms to private autonomous regulatory regimes. These bodies of rules constitute regimes abiding by their own logic and dynamics. Some can be described as spontaneous global law, as discussed by Teubner, which have their roots at the periphery of the state legal regime within the optic of a state-centred perspective.[4]

1.1 Traditional State Approach

Within the inherent dichotomy of the sources of alternative forms of regulation, the state approach allows for capturing part of the complexity of the concept of alternative forms of regulation. Hereinafter, the focus is on two aspects connected to the emergence of this form of regulation and that exercise a major influence on its possible appearance: the public policy debate and state (regulatory) strategies.

From the point of view of the state, alternatives forms of regulation, non-state and self-regulatory measures belong to the public policy debate on whether to regulate or not. They have a political capacity and may exert an impact in relation to other existing forms of governmental activities and administrative structures.

---

[4] G. Teubner, Global Private Regimes: Neo-Spontaneous Law and Dual Constitution of Autonomous Sectors? (2004) 71–87. On the concept of civil society, see: M. Foucault, Naissance de la biopolitique (2004), Leçon du 4 avril 1979, 295–320; A. Ferguson, An Essay on the History of Civil Society (1767) http://www.constitution.org/af/civil.htm (last visited 15 December 2009), Part first, Section I; see also: M. Kaldor, Global Civil Society, An Answer to War (2003).

They are based primarily on state delegation. Delegation means an authoritative decision that transfers policy-making authority away from established, representative organs to a non-majoritarian institution, whether public or private. Defined thus, delegation is largely used as a policy method.[5] The opposite of a delegation of state powers is the concept of the subsidiarity of state intervention. In this case, an existing alternative form of regulation, non-state or self-regulatory solution can subsist as a regime as long as it is not replaced by state regulation.

The discussion of state (regulatory) strategies shows that diverse regulatory and non-regulatory strategies can be distinguished. The goal of that passage is to better understand the delimitation of private and non-state autonomous regulatory regimes from other forms of state strategies that should determine behaviour. As will be discussed, within that framework, alternative forms of regulation and in particular self-regulation themselves constitute a strategy, based on civil society playing an active role.

1.1.1 Public Policy Debate

The public policy debate is about choosing policies to be applied in the public sphere in pursuit of the public good. Besides the evolutive view, according to which themes and issues prevail at a certain point in time and constitute public policy issues, many other criteria can exercise a decisive influence on the definition of issues and lead to the question of the choice of the policy instrument to be applied. Within that debate, a crucial question when a public policy issue arises, resides in the decision whether the issue at stake should be regulated or not. A range of strategies should be evaluated first, independently from the fact that the result can be either a state or a private solution. In fact, the debate often implicitly considers two opposed regulatory alternatives: the imposition of industry-wide regulation by the state or allowing unconstrained markets to determine the allocation of scarce resources themselves. Thus, the argument concentrates on the requirements or claims of power, that is, the decision to opt for either a solution based on governmental intervention or private initiative.[6]

Should a regulation already exist, the question is thus whether it should be replaced, abolished, or adapted to new circumstances to render it more adequate and efficient. Depending on the interests in the matter, different points of view can be taken into account and may prompt controversial debate. In particular, criteria justifying a regulatory solution will have to be evaluated. In case the debate results in the conclusion that no regulation is needed to find a solution to a policy issue, it

[5] On the concept of delegation, see Chapter 1, point 5 Decentred Analysis of Regulation, n 59.

[6] I. Ayres and J. Braithwaite, Responsive Regulation, Transcending the Deregulation Debate (1992) 133. For a broader discussion of public policy, see: M. Moran, M. Rein and R. E. Goodin, The Oxford Handbook of Public Policy (2006).

should then be necessary to follow Montesquieu's maxim: 'When it is not necessary to enact a law, it is necessary not to enact any law.'[7]

Once it is generally admitted that a regulation is needed and a decision has been taken to regulate, a host of questions arises: who should regulate, what should be regulated, and how (in both formal and substantive terms).[8] In this respect, it should first be mentioned that within the debate about the choice of regulatory form, this occurs against the background of the leading idea in a democratic state, which is that all exercise of power should take into account the principles of liberty, fairness and good administration.[9]

The analysis of public policy issues is insofar important in relation to non-state, alternative forms of regulation as it allows for focusing on pivotal factors influencing a policy decision as well as justifying the choice of a form of regulation. However, public policy is an extremely complex, subtle, and rich process. Policies are based on a blend of economic, legal, and public management principles. There is no single unified doctrine. The relevant literature shows that not only the term but also its meaning differs according to the author.[10] Hood, for example, covers three conventional strands employed in the public policy literature to analyze governmental instruments: the interests or ideas approach, the institutional approach based on state organization, and the institution-free approach based on the tool kit used.[11] Harrison, Morgan, Verkuil try to simplify the approach to public policy and suggest addressing the issues from three equivalent perspectives, not least to help preserve the richness of the debate: public interest, public administration, and public choice.[12] In fact, both Hood's and Harrison, Morgan, Verkuil's approaches are similar and useful, because they cover the main aspects of public policy. Their categorizations are adopted below with a view to better describe the situation and role of the state as a regulator. At the same time, its limited scope of intervention should also become apparent, such as possible causes for autonomous regulatory regimes emerging from the public policy debate.

---

[7] 'Lorsqu'une loi n'est pas nécessaire, il est nécessaire de ne pas faire de loi.', attributed to C. L. de Secondat, Baron de La Brède et de Montesquieu, De l'esprit des lois (1748).

[8] S. A. Shapiro and J. P. Tomain, Regulatory Law and Policy: Cases and Materials (2003) 73 et seqq.

[9] For instance, Black, supra note 1, 29, with further references.

[10] For instance, Ayres and Braithwaite, supra note 6, 133 seq.; see also G. Majone, The Rise of the Regulatory State in Europe (July 1994) 77 seq.; Moran, Rein and Goodin, supra note 6; OECD Reviews of Regulatory Reform, Regulatory Polices in OECD Countries, From Interventionism to Regulatory Governance (2002) 28; J. Freeman, The Private Role in Public Governance (June 2000) 543–675.

[11] C. Hood, The tools of government in the information age (2006) 470–471.

[12] J. L. Harrison, T. D. Morgan, P. R. Verkuil, Regulation and Deregulation, Cases and Materials (2004) 19.

Public Interest

Public interest is decisive when selecting a form of intervention. According to Hood, the key question is which political, ideological, scientific, or other processes lead to the choice of a policy instrument in the public interest.[13] Public interest can adopt many different meanings and there is no general consensus on what public interest is.[14] Baldwin and Cave distinguish between public interest theories, interest group theories, private interest theories, and institutional theories. While they consider that public interest theories centre on the idea that those seeking to institute or develop regulation do so in pursuit of public interest related objectives rather than group, sector, or individual self-interests,[15] other versions of interest theories attempt to cast some light on the behaviour leading to policy choices or regulatory solutions. These theories often base their approach on economics. Economic rationalism is generally seen as a leading motivation for the choice of policy measures.[16] Harrison, Morgan, Verkuil define the path of public interest analysis as concentrating on the application of economic theory alone. From an economic point of view, the efficiency[17] of the measures taken is important. In reality, however, markets are imperfect and present disparities. There are market failures. Based on the assumption that state intervention should provide some benefit, the point is the possible and adequate use of public resources and powers to improve economic outcomes. Emphasis will hence be placed on identifying distributive goals and how they should be realized.[18] In particular, when attempting to intervene in a market, different forces, each representing another interest, clash. Two considerations arise here: firstly, numerous interests, possibly constituting specific groups of interest, exist; and secondly, the power of the interests represented will have a determining influence on the outcome of a debate.

A distinction should be made as far as state interests are concerned. Their representatives argue that in order to preserve or save public interest, state regulation is necessary. In other words, state regulation should aim at covering public interest. With regard to the political process, this argument represents a rationale justifying the introduction of a state regulation while other forms of regulation

---

[13] Hood, supra note 11, 470.

[14] For a discussion of the concept with a focus on its democratic credentials, see M. Feintuck, 'The Public Interest' in Regulation (2004).

[15] R. Baldwin and M. Cave, Understanding Regulation, Theory, Strategy, and Practice (1999) 18–20.

[16] Ibid. 26, who consider it an expression of ideas.

[17] A discussion of this term lies beyond the scope of this passage as much as an indepth consideration of the abundant literature on efficiency. For the purpose of this study, it is assumed that efficiency applies to competitive markets, which should adjust the supply and demand for goods.

It should be noticed, however, that some authors claim that 'As efficiency becomes the objective, it tends to replace or function as a stand-in for the public interest.', S. Sassen, Territory, Authority, Rights, From Medieval to Global Assemblages (2006) 196.

[18] Harrison, Morgan, Verkuil, supra note 12, 19–32.

should be avoided. According to this point of view, another possibility would be to tolerate other forms of regulation as far as they take into account the interests of the public and the responsible organizations are not allowed to solely promote specific group interests. Hence, the state may take measures to prevent self-regulatory organizations (SROs) from adopting private or self-regulatory measures solely in their members' interest. These SROs should then be made generally responsible towards the public.[19] On their side, the interested autonomous groups or SROs involved in the political process may exercise a determining influence.[20] Such groups constitute a form of self-management, control their members, and have to represent their interests, although they should not be limited to solely pursue their own interests.[21] Their possibilities to be active and exercise influence as well as the attention afforded them will largely be based on the prevailing notion of democracy and its practice within a state as well as on hegemonic forces. Depending on the interplay of these forces, different rule-making and rule-enforcement priorities and scenarios will be made out. Thus, the approach does not only represent a choice between governmental or non-governmental or state and non-state and private regulation. On the contrary, it is also part of a choice among different regulatory possibilities to either exercise or renounce governmental influence. Traditionally, however, the focus is first on statutory regulation as the product of state activity, as legitimized by public interest.

If private interests dominate and a general rule is not needed, but a specialized one would be sufficient, which should apply to determined cases or groups, a policy decision might favour the introduction of private, non-state regulation. The choice of that regulatory form will be based on the rationales exercising a determining influence and the expectations about the envisaged behaviour. The choice may be reinforced by the adequacy and efficiency of measures already taken by individuals or the economy on an informal basis. Based on the experiences made, it should then be possible to convince the public and the regulator that state intervention is not needed.

Yet another view of the public interest theory lies in the assumption that those who attempt regulation to solve a policy issue are considered to be disinterested expert regulators acting as agents in the public interest. However, this theory is not easily applicable in practice. There is not only no consensus on the notion of public interest, but the independency and disinterestedness of the regulatory experts is also questioned. The problem of capture should not be ignored and expert regulators are not always efficient.[22]

---

[19] For more details, see W. Streeck and P. C. Schmitter, Community, market, state – and associations? The prospective contribution of interest governance to social order (1985) 1–29.

[20] Ibid. 1–4; Black, supra note 1, 30, with further references.

[21] Streeck and Schmitter, supra note 19, 1–2.; Black, supra note 1, 30, with further references. See also for an American view: F. I. Michelman, Foreword: Traces of Self-Government (1986); C. R. Sunstein, After the Rights Revolution: Reconceiving the Regulatory State (1990).

[22] Baldwin and Cave, supra note 15, 22–25; G. J. Stigler, The Theory of Economic Regulation (Spring 1971) 3 seq.

Finally, in relation to public interest, it should also be taken into account that the role of the state as a regulator is characterized by recurrent, continuous processes of regulation and deregulation. Depending on the prevailing political power, the role of governments as regulators changes. While some governments have a bias towards less intrusive forms of policy instruments, others do not. In some countries, proper waves of privatisation of whole industries or sectors can be made out. The main goal of such privatisation is to promote private initiative. Privatisation can also result from the fact that it represents a discharge for a state. The concessions accorded to private companies through statute to conduct and assume determined tasks or the delegation of supervisory functions to private bodies are cases in point. On the contrary, waves of nationalisation and re-delegating responsibilities to the state can be identified, in particular following crises. Hybrid forms can be encountered, too. Narrowly linked to these debates is the significance given to self-regulation as an alternative form of regulation. Based on a delegation by the state, it may attract more attention or experience a revival with some political forces. It is then a popular policy approach whether driven by a government philosophy to have minimal involvement in the structuring of the private sector or because it is adopted as an efficient method of regulation. On the contrary, it may be replaced by governmental regulatory solutions when other forces dominate.

Public Administration

The public administration approach recognizes that regulatory measures are necessary to solve problems within society. However, there is an inherent duality within every such measure taken: there is a need to intervene and protect private market actors whilst every such measure has the potential to either improve or damage economic development. Administration is considered to be a burden in any case. In the course of time, practices become irrelevant and cumbersome, and generate unnecessary charges, so-called ‘red tape’. There is then a call to restore common sense. The public administration approach concentrates on the search for ways out of government ‘red tape’, and a simplification of governmental activities in order to act more effectively.[23] The aim is to reduce the number and complexity of government formalities and paperwork. For instance, possibilities to simplify the granting of licenses and permits by the state, introduce other tools, delegate some functions (that is, create room for alternative solutions), and so forth, are studied and evaluated. In the long run, it would be better to set an appropriate regulatory course or determine a framework for the development of regulation with general implementation goals. On its side, the OECD already analyzed this situation in the mid-1980s. It has reviewed the policies and commonly used tools in OECD countries as part of the efforts undertaken to systematically address administrative burdens in

[23] Harrison, Morgan, Verkuil, supra note 12, 32–34; Ayres and Braithwaite, supra note 6, 4–5.

response to regulatory inflation and the increasing complexity of public administration.[24]

This discussion has been ongoing in a range of countries for several years. It concentrates on technical and organizational aspects, including the idea that management techniques and practices drawn from the private sector should be transferred to the public sector, that is, governmental bodies and administration. It is generally admitted that public administration and the implementation of public programmes does not work in practice, and that these are poorly managed and fail to satisfy individual expectations. A well-known form of this critique is New Public Management (NPM). NPM emerged in the late 1970s from the neo-liberal movement, the development of information technology, and the use of management consulting firms to introduce reforms. It is constituted by a set of techniques and practices epitomizing administrative doctrines dominating public administration reforms. Best practices should be developed. The goal is not to suppress regulation or change the institutions concerned but to render the functioning of governmental bodies more efficient.[25]

With regard to public administration, Hood focuses on the forms of organization or institutions at the disposal of the state to exercise its role. There may be public corporations, independent or private sector contractors, and various forms of public-private partnership. This does not exclude opting for new, ad-hoc public-private institutional forms, and leaves room for the adoption and introduction of non-state or alternative forms of regulation, in particular when there is the promise of more efficient solutions. As such, these forms of regulation are one policy issue among others within that debate,[26] and the approach could actually be broadened.

To analyze a situation under the public administration approach, regulatory solutions should be evaluated before opting for the right remedies. Two well-known methods are generally used to assess regulation[27]: cost-benefit testing or cost-benefit analysis (CBA) and regulatory impact analysis (RIA). CBA takes into account that regulation is costly. The intrinsic costs of regulation, however, should be compensated by future gains in efficiency obtained following the introduction of a new regulation. Hence, a governmental measure should only be adopted when

[24] From Red Tape to Smart Tape, Administrative Simplification in OECD Countries, OECD publication, 14–15, 65; see also OECD Reviews of Regulatory Reform, supra note 10, 57–65; Harrison, Morgan, Verkuil, supra note 12, 32–34 and: S. Breyer, Regulation and Its Reform (1982) on the resulting 'mismatch' between an economic problem and the type of regulatory process used to address it.

[25] For a basic reference, see: D. Osborne and T. Gaebler, Reinventing Government, Reading (1992). See also, for example, M. Power, The Audit Society, Rituals of Verification (2002) 43–44; C. Parker, The Open Corporation, Effective Self-regulation and Democracy (2002) 13–17; Harrison, Morgan, Verkuil, supra note 12, 32–34.

[26] Hood, supra note 11, 470, with further references.

[27] The OECD mentions the following regulatory quality tools used in OECD countries to assess regulatory measures: regulatory impact analysis, assessment of regulatory alternatives, consultation with affected parties, plain language drafting requirements, evaluation of the results of regulatory programmes. See OECD Reviews of Regulatory Reform, supra note 10, 31.

a superior outcome is guaranteed. However, how analysis and evaluation should be conducted is very controversial. Many methods of cost-benefit testing of regulation have been developed. Indeed, cost-benefit analysis consists in evaluating regulatory measures, but the assessment of potential regulatory effects cannot always be quantified. It is part of a risk assessment system that seeks to identify the problem and the harm involved, estimates the risk associated with the harm, identifies regulatory options, evaluates the impact of the options on the risk, places a monetary value on expected benefits of each option, compares the costs with the benefits, and identifies any important issues of equity or other considerations.[28] This risk assessment system is combined with appraisals. However, there is no consensus on the way appraisals should be conducted. The methods used are imperfect and it is difficult to estimate non-efficiency values like accountability or expertise.[29] However, CBA is regularly used in practice – one of the motives may be because there are no better or more reliable methods – to submit rules and regulatory programmes to critical examination and to introduce corrective measures if judged necessary.

The goal of the second method, RIA, is to foster efficiency. RIA estimates the quality of regulation in function of the cost-effectiveness of its results or impact. It is based on the assumption that policy issues involve trade-offs between different uses of resources. The effects on innovation, trade, and competition should be taken into account. RIA attempts to embrace dynamic effects. It should apply before a regulatory measure or statute is passed and serves as a benchmark to decide whether a regulatory measure should be adopted and implemented.[30] RIA belongs to a trend towards more empirically based regulation. However, it does not replace political accountability, as is sometimes implied.

Public Choice

The third perspective, public choice, is based on the assumption that individuals or groups act in their own interest to maximize their welfare. They will take decisions based on political motives in their favour. Public Choice Theory or New Political Economy, an economic theory developed by James A. Buchanan, analyses how the collective process of decision-taking by politicians, governments, and individuals takes place under economic aspects and how far self-interest and non-economic forces influence politicians and governments. Such comparative analysis studies the working of institutions. The concept of a political system as an exchange process for the achievement of mutual advantages is applied. The state is considered to be

---

28 Baldwin and Cave, supra note 15, 88; Harrison, Morgan, Verkuil, supra note 12, 422 et seqq.

29 Baldwin and Cave, supra note 15, 88–95; Harrison, Morgan, Verkuil, supra note 12, 422 et seqq.; E. A. Posner, Law and Social Norms (2000) 184–202.

30 Baldwin and Cave, supra note 15, 86–87, with reference to the Executive Order 12291 issued by President Ronald Reagan in 1981, which continues to this day, consolidated under the Executive Order 12866. On the RIA, see also OECD Reviews of Regulatory Reform, supra note 10, 44–51.

a specific market where different groups meet to take collective decisions. Hood describes the situation in a similar way when governments gather information and attempt to influence citizens' behaviour when they come into contact with them.[31] Consequently, it is admitted that governments, too, can make errors or act in the wrong way. They should not only be considered to represent a corrective for wrong or false developments on the markets, and neither do they always act in the public interest. Indeed, they are often not directly concerned by the measures they take and, contrary to the groups of interests directly concerned, they might not be motivated either. Thus, a purely public sphere is also illusory. Moreover, state employees depend on their own, specific interests or the interests of the groups they represent. As a result, there is a problem of capture within the public choice approach, a problem of regulatory capture. For example, the interests of an industry may receive too much weight within a regulatory process. As groups of interest, industries are often very well organized; they can submit their concerns, conduct very effective lobbying, and exercise a lot of pressure. They can be very influential when striving to protect their own interests and adopt a position to absorb the costs of an adequate regulation representing transaction costs to them.[32] As a result, industries will often prevail with sustaining their interests. Unlike the general public that is not organized at all, and may remain less influential and unable to secure a majority when decisions are taken.[33] However, although it is difficult to speak with one voice or to achieve unanimity in practice, decisions based on the majority are basically considered to be fair.

This theory is criticized. Amartya Sen claims that it is often applied in a simplified form and that governments are only self-interested entities. He even argues that the theory is absurd. Furthermore, interest groups are influential bodies that may merely exacerbate the adoption of inefficient measures under certain circumstances. This will be negative for the general public and can be interpreted as representing a failure of a state system. In this perspective, the political process becomes primarily a way of cooperating to achieve mutual advantages. It is in no way a means for redistributing resources among individuals. Hence, a regulatory solution introduced on the basis of these premises may well be inadequate and even create new problems in the course of its implementation.[34] The governmental process is also lengthy and it is difficult to cope with new developments through adaptations of state regulation. This will leave room for non-state, private initiative and alternative forms of regulation are generated. A prominent example is the

---

[31] C. Hood, The Tools of Government (1983); Hood, supra note 11, 471.

[32] On the problem of capture, see Ayres and Braithwaite, supra note 6; Harrison, Morgan, Verkuil, supra note 12, 36–37; see also Stigler, supra note 22, 3–9; R. A. Posner, Theories of Economic Regulation (Autumn 1974) 335 seq. On the pubic sphere, see Freeman, supra note 10, 564–565.

[33] For a comprehensive discussion, see J. M. Buchanan and G. Tullock, The Calculus of Consent (1962).

[34] M. Olson, The Logic of Collective Action: Public Goods and the Theory of Groups (1965); A. K. Sen, Collective Choice and Social Welfare (1970); Stigler, supra note 22, 10–17. See also Ayres and Braithwaite, supra note 6, 133 seq.

development of regulatory regimes in the field of information and communication technology (lex cybertoria), partly due to the fact that public administration and public policy have neglected or underestimated the extent to which information and communication technology alter not only the way that states work, but the functioning of society as a whole.[35] These technologies bear the stamp of globalization; states and international organizations of states are no longer the adequate excipients to regulate these fields. 'Contemporary cyber-technology is transforming both the instrumentalities and the issues faced by contemporary government in important ways.'[36] This gives rise to a decentralization of power and control in society, and opens the door to the emergence of non-state regulatory regimes.

To summarize the public policy debate in relation to non-state, autonomous regulatory regimes or alternative forms of regulation, (state) regulation is the product of an appreciation and weighting of different interests at a determined point in time. The debate can take place in the course of lively interactions among interested groups and can be largely mapped by the search for efficient solutions. It encompasses the study of a range of solutions and also covers non-state regulation. In addition, depending on the dominating powers, the organization and efficiency of the groups of interest concerned, waves of non-state or self-regulatory measures or alternative forms of regulation are recognizable insofar as this kind of regulation can be slaughtered by some regimes and then experiences a revival with other regimes as an alternative to state regulation.

1.1.2 State (Regulatory) Strategies

After discussing how public policy may apply to opt whether to regulate or not, this point focuses on possible state regulatory strategies. Once a decision in favour of a regulatory measure has been taken, the next step is to choose the right regulatory strategy to implement a measure and reach the desired goal. Different strategies can be considered. In fact, states or governments can choose between a whole range of possible approaches. States should evaluate which regulatory strategy – including alternative forms of regulation – is most adequate and efficient with regard to an issue or a concrete situation. In particular, it should not be overlooked that the introduction of a suboptimal or wrong strategy or the choice of an inadequate regulatory instrument may produce negative consequences or even just lead to the opposed result. Indeed, with regard to the economic performance or productivity of a sector or its competitiveness, the choice of the strategy is crucial, because as Baldwin and Cave have correctly stated:

---

[35] Hood, supra note 11, 472; for a broader discussion, see Chapter 3, point 6 Global Networks, 6.1 Digital Networks.

[36] Hood, supra note 11, 476.

> 'A regulatory system will be difficult to justify – no matter how well it seems to be performing – if critics can argue that a different strategy would more effectively achieve relevant objectives.' [37]

Thus, particular attention should be paid to the choice of the right strategy. Strategies depend on the instruments at the disposal of a government to handle a policy issue. No state can exist without powers to take measures, powers to discipline, and powers to sanction those who do not respect the order or contravene that order. If necessary, these powers should be used to influence economic or other policy issues.[38] In the literature, a number of regulatory strategies are analyzed, including non-governmental ones.[39] Here, the basic strategies adopted are briefly discussed: imperative forms of regulation; motivating or incentive-based measures; disclosure measures; direct intervention by the state and self-regulation; and other possible regulatory strategies. These are important not least due to their impact in practice. They can be used to define derived strategies or their ramifications. Again, the discussion of these strategies should contribute to better understanding the rationales possibly leading to the choice of non-state or alternative forms of regulation.

Imperative Forms of Regulation

Imperative forms of regulation, that is, command and control regulation represent traditional, classical state regulation taking the form of statutes. They imply a sovereign control or governance over societal developments undergoing commands and prohibitions or being realized through imperative control. States are equipped with rule-making and enforcement powers. They enact prescriptive laws or statutes, which can either compel action or not. They set standards that must be observed. These standards are backed by criminal sanctions to ensure their enforcement.[40] However, the specification or delimitation of adequate standards is a difficult task and as far as technical aspects are concerned, the right benchmarks should be set. In particular, the measures taken should guarantee the attainment of the desired impact. This should be possible based on the availability of the correct information. Beside these aspects, the burden of opposed political forces representing contrary opinions should not be ignored. It may require a lot of persuasion. For many,

---

[37] Baldwin and Cave, supra note 15, 34.

[38] Ibid. 34.

[39] For example, Baldwin and Cave, supra note 15, 34 seq.; Breyer, supra note 24, 156 seq.; Ayres and Braithwaite, supra note 6, 133 seq.; Securities and Exchange Commission, 17 CFR PART 240 – Release No. 34-50700; File No. S7-40-04, Concept Release Concerning Self-Regulation, March 8, 2005, point V. Alternative Regulatory Approaches (SEC Concept Release); see also OECD Reviews of Regulatory Reform, supra note 10, 135–142, Regulatory Alternatives; P. N. Grabosky, Using Non-Governmental Resources to Foster Regulatory Compliance (October 1995) 529.

[40] Ayres and Braithwaite, supra note 6, 38–40; Baldwin and Cave, supra note 15, 35; A. I. Ogus, Regulation: Legal Form and Economic Theory (2004) 5.

command and control regulation also embodies the core understanding of regulation. As such, it denotes all that can be bad about regulation, like poorly targeted rules, rigidity, ossification, under- or over-enforcement, and unintended consequences.[41]

As far as the proper rules are concerned, the rule-making function regards the state in its role as defining basic standards. Diverse instances can subsequently be entrusted with passing the detailed rules following a delegation of powers. The respective competences will be laid down in the statute. The whole process constitutes a top-down approach. While the government in its role as regulator delimits the broad aims and the regulatory framework, the other (subordinate) instances and supervisors orient themselves towards the practical measures to be taken in concrete cases for statute enforcement.[42] On its side, the enforcement of standards defined thus may be difficult and costly. Based on the statute, the focus is on concretizing goals, attaining envisaged targets, and delimiting the detailed measures necessary to reach them. Governmental intervention as such may no longer be central. On the contrary, as stated, there may be broad delegation to agencies and market forces may remain influential with regard to implementing measures.[43] An entire infrastructure may have to be built to control and supervise implementation and observance of rules.[44] This is the case, for instance, in relation to the licensing and supervision of financial institutes. Based on authorization, the institute will have to observe all the detailed rules governing its operations. It will have to respect organizational requirements on a continuous basis, establish internal control procedures and fulfil all the legal duties. Measures to be taken must also be adapted to actual circumstances as well as managed. In such cases, it is typical that the first article of the statute sets the broad objective as a form of programme. For example, the first article of the Swiss Federal Act on Collective Investment Schemes reads as follows:

> The purpose of this Act is to protect investors . . .[45]

or, Part One of the British Financial Services and Markets Act 2000, 'The Regulator' asserts that the regulatory objectives are:

> [. . .]
> 3. Market confidence: (1) The market confidence objective is: maintaining confidence in the financial system. [. . .]
> 4. Public awareness: (1) The public awareness objective is: promoting public understanding of the financial system. [. . .]
> 5. The protection of consumers: (1) The protection of consumers objective is: securing the appropriate degree of protection for consumers. [. . .]

---

41 J. Black, Critical Reflections on Regulation (2002) 2.

42 Ibid. 2; R. Baldwin, Rules and Government (1996) 164 seq.

43 Chapter 1, point 7 Regulation as a Market Place; OECD Reviews of Regulatory Reform, supra note 10, 135–136.

44 For more details, see: Baldwin, supra note 42, 142 seq.

45 Federal Act on Collective Investment Schemes (Collective Investment Schemes Act, CISA) of 23rd June 2006, SR 951.31.

6. The reduction of financial crime: (1) The reduction of financial crime objective is: reducing the extent to which it is possible for a business carried on-
   (a) By a regulated person, or
   (b) In contravention of the general prohibition
   to be used for a purpose connected with financial crime.[46]

Based on the programmatic article, the steps leading to its attainment have to be enumerated. It is expected that the result is less dense regulation. In particular, individuals and businesses may dispose of a certain margin to decide which measures are appropriate, adopting these based on their own initiative. For instance, based on the statute, the Federal Act on Collective Investment Schemes, the Swiss Funds Association SFA defined a Code of conduct applying to the fund industry. It should maintain and promote the standing of the Swiss fund industry and guarantee uniform adherence to the spirit of the statute and its objective.[47]

In other sectors, such as the environment, a factory could be required to reduce the grade of water contamination by statute. It would be free to choose the measures insofar as they lead to reaching the defined goal. In that case, it would not be subject to any sanctions. However, the implementation of this strategy may be too onerous for small businesses and they may a priori prefer state intervention by way of directives.

The strength of this strategy lies in the fact that the defined standards are mandatory and must be respected. They determine correct behaviour and allow for imposing sanctions in case of non-observance. Such procedure is often used in practice. However, the adequacy and also the impact of a specific regulation are initially unknown. A weakness of this strategy is the danger of capture between the state in its role as a rule-making authority and the interested regulated individuals or industries. In particular, they have to cooperate at different levels: economic, political, and institutional. However, they may also pursue similar goals. Another weakness of this strategy is that it may result in overregulation due to the expertise of the interested groups. A tendency to regulate many details cannot be denied. It could weaken the competitiveness of the industry concerned as a result.[48]

Incentives Systems

With incentives systems, the state exercises its influence indirectly, for example through the imposition of taxes. Measures based on taxes should lead individuals, businesses, or potential defaulters to adopt an adequate attitude and act in the public interest. The foundation of this regime is the motivation of the market actors concerned whereas different measures are conceivable, like positive or negative

---

[46] Financial Services and Markets Act 2000, 2000 Chapter 8.

[47] CISA, supra note 45; Code of Conduct: http://www.sfa.ch/index.php?site=2&page=1 (last visited 15 December 2009).

[48] Baldwin and Cave, supra note 15, 36 et seq.

taxes. For example, the producer, causer, or originator of an undesired state – such as air pollution in the environmental field – is obliged to pay taxes failing compliance with the requisite standards. This can represent a very high burden, as the tax can be prohibitive and constitute a sanction. As a consequence, the polluter will be expected to take adequate measures to avoid paying that tax. Another incentive can, on the contrary, consist in having some individuals or businesses pay fewer taxes or obtain financial support in case they adopt measures to correct a situation, such as when they are able to diminish the grade of air pollution.

Incentives systems are based on economics. It is generally admitted that they contribute to rendering work and production cycles more efficient. They tax away the producer's excess profit and offer the possibility to redistribute it to consumers. Hence, the ends of regulation can be accomplished more directly.[49] The origins of the introduction of such systems or strategies are diverse. It can be governance by the state, which follows the principle that the responsible party is liable for the damages it causes. It may also be based on so-called understandings or agreements concluded between the state and the economy or industries resulting from negotiations between the state and the economic partners concerned, and replacing rules. In these cases, a consensus is reached when parties agree upon a solution, often a collective agreement model. Industry commits itself to take measures, thereby impeding a state intervention. Industry may have various motives. For example, it may have a decisive interest in taking efficient measures to either preserve its reputation, to reestablish it, or for some other reasons. These collective agreement models are normally declared to be generally binding by order of the state. They also apply to other actors within the economy who then have to adopt specific behaviour. Such a part-private approach to establishing norms through declaring agreements generally binding creates incentives insofar as the actors concerned actively participate in formulating agreements, obliging them to respect these agreements and reach the defined goals.[50]

Under this regime, the businesses or the economic sector concerned must react and introduce measures contributing to systematically control and reduce a risk or avoid an undesired effect. An advantage of this method is that the businesses take the initiative to intervene and develop adequate solutions that are not too costly or cost less than the taxes imposed by the state. It is an efficient type of solution.[51] Another advantage is that the necessity for the state to regulate or to intervene remains small. The foreseen sanctions motivate the regulatees or industries concerned to effectively implement the measures taken, hence gaining momentum. For the regulators, the danger of capture is reduced, because they are not involved in constant negotiations and exchanges of information with industry.[52] Moreover,

[49] Breyer, supra note 24, 164–171, 167.

[50] Baldwin and Cave, supra note 15, 41–43.

[51] Chapter 1, point 7 Regulation as a Marketplace; OECD Reviews of Regulatory Reform, supra note 10, 136–137.

[52] Baldwin and Cave, supra note 15, 42.

besides the fact that these systems do not require a lot of information, they are said to encourage industries to voluntarily reduce harmful conduct as much as possible.[53]

However, these regimes also present weaknesses. From the point of view of efficiency, they can result in a negligent way of acting to produce even more efficiently. This can negatively influence workers. Furthermore, it is not always possible to predict the impact of a measure actually designed to represent an incentive. For instance, in the environmental sector the fixing of a maximal allowed grade of water pollution to be observed can prompt different effects depending on the industry. The measures taken, and the resulting costs, can differ with the business concerned, production modes, or also other factors, such as the geographical situation, the products used, and so forth. The effect on each business will correlate with the profit derived within each production process, and for each unit produced. The results may not always be those expected, although the businesses concerned may act in an economically rational manner. In addition, the advantages may be exaggerated and not always fulfil the expectations of a sceptical public.[54]

Disclosure

Regulating information disclosure is common nowadays. The goal is not to govern or control markets or production processes. It is not an interventionist strategy and there is no direct action taken by the state. The strategy consists in regulation requiring the disclosure of particular information to a broader public. Disclosure is mandatory and the information must be correct and not misleading. The aim of disclosure measures is to help buyers and sellers or investors make better informed choices.[55] Information disclosure can be requested as well regarding specific products, such as consumer goods, or in relation to accounting and financial data. A wide range of disclosure rules can be distinguished whereas the disclosure strategy is particularly recommendable in the context of goods trading where small differences might exist and comparison should be possible.

In the field of economic law, in particular company and financial services law, there has been a huge wave of measures requiring the disclosure of financial data and other related information mainly since the mid-eighties. Such a development is based on the assumption that the efficiency of the financial markets can be reached provided measures ensuring transparency are taken. These should reduce information asymmetries. The rules on the disclosure of price sensitive information applied in the field of securities laws are an example. They require the disclosure and

53 Baldwin and Cave, supra note 15, 42; Chapter 1, point 8 Alternatives to Regulation, 8.4. Process-based Regulation.

54 Baldwin and Cave, supra note 15, 42–44; see also Breyer, supra note 24, 278–280; Ogus, supra note 40, 250–256.

55 Baldwin and Cave, supra note 15, 49; Breyer, supra note 24, 161–162.

publication of potential quote relevant data belonging to the field of activity of listed companies, and which may influence the price building process on the market. They also explain in detail how to proceed when disclosing this kind of information to avoid distorting fair price building.[56]

This regulatory strategy should improve the protection of the individual investors, and contribute to avoid market abuses. Based on the disclosed information, private market actors or individual investors should be in a position to judge and evaluate the information received. They should then be able to take decisions based on a reliable knowledge of the situation, in accordance with their preferences and their attitude towards risk. It is then their responsibility to make use of the information at their disposal in a sound way. Better information should also exercise a preventive effect, provided market participants are in a position to interpret it correctly. This is not always an easy task, because specialist knowledge may be necessary and there is a danger to either over – or underestimate the risks. In the case of the disclosure of financial information, knowledge of the workings of the financial markets and products is necessary. Wrong interpretations can have serious consequences.

In practice, information can be published and distributed by businesses themselves. However, an authority or an agency can be assigned the task to first check and correct it. The responsible authority may also disclose its own, additional information in the form of warnings or alerts, such as in cases where the information disclosed on a private basis might not sufficiently highlight potential risks. A weakness of the strategy lies in the costs accompanying the disclosure of information. These can be unreasonably high, such as with food safety where the preparation, publication, and scrutiny of the products may be a lengthy process and consumers may prefer to rely on the expert opinion of an authority. Finally, information quality must be guaranteed on a continuous basis, which is often difficult.[57]

Direct State Intervention

As a strategy, the state can choose to intervene directly. Stigler, for instance, distinguishes four policies that an economic sector or industry may expect to be applied directly by the state: a subsidy of money, control over entry by new rivals, policies affecting or hindering the production of substitutes and complementary products, and finally policies determining price-fixing.[58] In these cases, the state makes use of its own resources. For example, it may build an infrastructure, such as a factory, and place it at the disposal of private industry; alternatively, it could rent

[56] For instance, articles 49–56, 53 Listing Rules of the SIX Swiss Exchange of 21 April 2010; Listing Rules, Chapter 9 – Continuing obligations, for the United Kingdom.

[57] Baldwin and Cave, supra note 15, 49–50; Breyer, supra note 24, 162–164.

[58] Stigler, supra note 22, 3–6.

the buildings to private businesses. The state can also decide to distribute subsidies directly and exercise a decisive influence on determined economic activities. In this way, economic sectors or industries can be supported on a selective basis. With regard to its direct impact, this solution may prove to be very useful when the focus is placed on determined industries, such as in difficult economic situations. In practice, other forms of direct intervention may be represented by taxes, the introduction of authorization requirements, permits, contracts, or concessions. The introduction of authorization requirements renders the control of a whole market possible.[59] Permits can be traded and the entry into a market as well as subsequent controls within that market are then governed by these permits insofar as a permit must be bought for the exercise of an activity. In that case, the state may allow buying or selling permits to enter a market among individuals or businesses, such as take-off and landing rights at airports.[60]

In theory, the use of these instruments is a priori a privileged governance mechanism of a state to control the development of economic situations and enforce policy goals. It is generally admitted that such instruments offer important gains in efficiency when compared with traditional forms of regulation. It is possible to rapidly attain the goals set. Direct intervention offers the advantage of supporting investments and encouraging them. It is in particular interesting for small businesses, which, depending on their commercial business environment, are not always in a position to invest sufficiently. Thus, they can reach their goals at moderate costs.[61] On its side, the state participates in the economic process and no longer solely takes a supervisory role. Moreover, it is possible to avoid difficulties usually accompanying the effective enforcement of rules.

In the case of subsidies, a weakness of the strategy lies in the fact that distributional issues may arise. The repartition of monies may cause problems in particular when prices are fixed and several businesses could be entitled to subsidies. Another disadvantage results from the fact that following the activism of the state, businesses may be less motivated to invest in the research and development of new methods. This could lead to a reduced propensity to innovate, such as when the state takes measures to protect the environment. Industries or businesses may then direct their activities to obtaining subsidies. On their side, tradeable permits require control to avoid abuse both by the businesses owning them and third businesses. Thus, such permits can lead to a distortion of the market in the absence of effective competition to buy or sell them. In such cases, competition rules and trade practices, like franchises or other agreements, should be enacted and provide for potential correction.[62]

---

59 Baldwin and Cave, supra note 15, 50–51; OECD Reviews of Regulatory Reform, supra note 10, 137–139.

60 These measures can also be classified as market-harnessing controls. See Baldwin and Cave, supra note 15, 46–47; see also Breyer, supra note 24, 171–174.

61 OECD Reviews of Regulatory Reform, supra note 10, 138.

62 Baldwin and Cave, supra note 15, 48–51.

Self-regulation

States may well act as self-regulators under certain circumstances. One of the newest and most blatant case regards the regulation of Sovereign Wealth Funds defined at the international level. It is constituted by the Generally Accepted Principles and Practices, GAPP or Santiago Principles, of 11 October 2008 adopted by the International Working Group of Sovereign Wealth Funds. Representing a joint policy response of states managing SWFs to increase the visibility of these funds as large investors, the regulatory character of the Principles is twofold. They are the result of a voluntary initiative by a group of states, for the purpose of 'self-regulating' themselves. At the same time, they are defined by states to control and justify their activities unfolded in private markets. By the same token, the accompanying creation of the International Forum of SWFs is also the result of a voluntary initiative of IWG-SWF members. Constituted by a Declaration, it has no international law statute. In these terms, this regime is unparalleled.

Usually however, when self-regulation is used as a state strategy, it constitutes not a pure but a hybrid form of self-regulation.[63] Such self-regulation results from a cooperation between the state and private business or representatives of civil society based on a regime of state delegation. Such cooperation is based on a participation of both the state and civil society whereas the extent of the self-regulatory solution depends on the delegation of legislative powers by the state. The state defines the framework and dictates the extent of that solution. Its involvement can take different forms and degrees. In practice, diverse constellations or models of cooperation can be encountered, including coercive or supervised self-regulation, as will be discussed in the next chapter.

Basically, self-regulation lies in the hands of organized interest groups, associations or SROs with a field of activity in an economic sector or a regulated industry. These groups, associations or SROs are responsible for the introduction of self-regulatory measures and their implementation vis-à-vis their members. According to the degree of voluntariness, regulation and the requirements of order adopted autonomously by an association can take diverse degrees of bindingness, such as codices, agreements, or others. They may be in a position to impose sanctions, based on their own initiative, depending on an agreement with their members. An important characteristic of this form of self-regulation is the pro-active attitude of the associations or SROs concerned. Often, measures will be adopted to prevent state intervention or state interference. Self-regulation is then a constraint, a consequence of state pressure.[64]

The repartition of the regulatory functions between the state and an industry or its associations or SROs can be represented by diverse interactions, where each

[63] On possible forms of self-regulation, see Ogus, supra note 1, 97–108; Ayres and Braithwaite, supra note 6; see also Chapter 3; G. De Minico, A Hard Look at Self-Regulation in the UK (2006) 183–211.

[64] OECD Reviews of Regulatory Reform, supra note 10, 140–141.

party enacts proper rules and takes appropriate measures, complementing each other. In practice, it often takes the form of state-approved rules of conduct. The associations or SROs are then responsible for rules implementation. Their members are motivated to act self-responsively.[65]

With regard to firms, the model of enforced self-regulation as defined by Ayres and Braithwaite involves negotiations between the state and individual firms so as to establish regulations particular to each firm.[66] The degree of state governance can vary from case to case. Self-regulation approved by the state will then replace the strategy of direct control by the state through imperative forms of regulation, based on statutes.[67]

Self-regulation can also be understood to represent a form of frontline regulation, encompassing rules directly applicable, including rules of conduct or directives.[68] A key advantage of this form of regulation is its flexibility.[69] It is designed by professional experts and well adapted to the characteristics of the sector or industry concerned. Changes can be introduced rapidly. Self-regulation reinforces the cohesion among the members of an industry or group and it is recognized as helping avoid the problems of implementation and legitimacy, which are encountered in the context of state intervention,[70] although this view is contested by various authors. Hence, governments often hesitate to intervene directly, in particular when an industry is well-organized on account of its own (self-)regulation. However, self-regulation also presents severe weaknesses. SROs are often influenced and dominated by a few important businesses or groups tending to protect their own interests and exercise a dominating influence. In addition, self-regulatory organizations often do not operate in a transparent way and the enforcement of self-regulatory measures may not be satisfactory due to the problem of capture. As a result, depending on the circumstances, it may be difficult to justify the relative autonomy, which characterizes self-regulation.[71]

---

[65] Ibid. 137; on possible models of interactions, see SEC Concept Release, supra note 39, V. Alternative Regulatory Approaches, discussing eight possible regulatory approaches; see also Chapter 3; see also R. Baldwin, Why Rules Don't Work (1990) 321–337.

[66] Ayres and Braithwaite, supra note 6, 116–117; Baldwin and Cave, supra note 15, 133; Chapter 3, point 2 Firm Own Regulation.

[67] Ayres and Braithwaite, supra note 6, 38–40, for a presentation of a Pyramid of Regulatory Strategies.

[68] Baldwin and Cave, supra note 15, 39–40.

[69] Ayres and Braithwaite, supra note 6, 101 seq. and 110 et seqq. for a broad discussion of the advantages and disadvantages of self-regulation.

[70] Streeck and Schmitter, supra note 19, 1 seq., 22–25. For a detailed discussion of legitimacy, see hereinafter, point 3 Institutional Structure, and Chapter 4, point 2 Standardization, 2.4 Nature of Autonomous Regulatory Regimes, 2.4.2 Legitimacy and Accountability.

[71] M. Priest, The Privatization of Regulation: Five Models of Self-Regulation (1997) 268–274, with further references.

Other (Regulatory) Strategies

The list of strategies discussed above is not exhaustive. Only basic strategies have been presented in brief. These merely provide an overview and a sense of the framework within which autonomous regulatory regimes and alternatives to regulation may emerge. Ramifications of these strategies are possible. In practice, strategies can be developed on an ad hoc basis, in accordance with a concrete situation and the prospect of their successful enforcement. Other strategies can constitute attaining objectives set via regulatory measures, such as rights and liabilities applying to determined industries. Guidelines and directives of an authority or private organization can also serve to enforce governmental measures. These can provide explanations or indicate how to behave, for instance in case of conflicting interests. Further strategies can assume the form of public compensation or insurance schemes. Typical examples are workers receiving indemnities from their employers due to potential health damages. At the same time, they create incentives for employers to adopt preemptive measures.[72]

Moreover, the regulatory developments in a regulated industry, such as the banking and financial markets sector, can illustrate the choice of strategies. In relation with the underlying discussion regarding a state of inadequately, under- or over-regulated financial markets, it appears to be essential to opt for alternative regulatory strategies. In particular, one issue consists in studying how far the formation of adequately protective structures for individual claims on the one hand, and collective concerns on the other, could be left to market forces. The protagonists of regulatory measures argue that the aims of modern banking and financial markets laws are to ensure the protection of individual investors and the good working of financial markets. This is considered sufficient to justify regulatory measures. On their side, economists base their thoughts on the disparity of information among market actors. They opine that these disparities are sufficient to justify the introduction of rules. In such cases, a close strategic solution could consist in the introduction of disclosure regulation to counterbalance these disparities. However, considered on the whole, banking and financial markets regulation represents a complex set of specialized norms or risk-based regulation, whose first aim is the recognition, definition, and coverage of risks through adequate measures to protect investors. Different strategies, also hybrid strategies, apply depending on the risk to be regulated. Furthermore, in this particular field, the historical point of view should not be ignored. Since the first banking acts were passed in 1934 in different countries, risk-based regulation has developed, not least due to the fact that it is a dynamic, complex, and ever-changing industry. Justified by the objective of protecting the investors as well as seizing and controlling risks through regulation, it has become a huge regulatory domain. Ad hoc regulatory strategies have been introduced on a continuous basis, and depending on the situation. However,

[72] Baldwin and Cave, supra note 15, 53–55.

the development of this regulation can be compared to a Sisyphean task.[73] Following crises, different matters and risks are identified, leading to the enactment of regulations corresponding to remedial measures. Such realignment represents a never-ending task, as the 2007–2009 financial crisis impressively shows, once more. In this changing environment, supervised collaborative regulatory regimes may appear to be a working alternative.

1.2 From State to Civil Society Approach: A Decentred Perspective

As already stated, the sources of autonomous regulatory regimes and alternative forms of regulation are twofold. An inherent feature of the concept is its dichotomy of sources. After discussing the traditional state approach to regulation, the focus is now placed on the emergence of these regimes from civil society.[74] However, how is it possible to move from the first (that is, state) approach to the other? Is there a transition? How are these orders linked? To realize the passage from one regime to the other, it is necessary to break the frame of the traditional state order. The most adequate analytical instrument to reach this goal when departing from state regulation is to broaden the view based on the decentred analysis of regulation. The first chapter has discussed features of the decentred analysis of regulation in relation to state regulation and focused on the following criteria: fragmentation of knowledge, power and control, complexity, the criterion of coordination and cooperation among different individuals and market actors, the criterion of ungovernability and autonomy of market actors, and finally the issue of self-regulation and globalization.[75] Within the decentred analysis of regulation, self-regulation as a private autonomous regime is generally examined and discussed in relation to state regulation as the result of state delegation. This traditional understanding of self-regulation is stereotypical and the concept as such is not questioned. As a form of regulation, it can be included in the decentred analysis of regulation insofar as state regulation

---

[73] On that development see for instance: T. Padoa-Schioppa, Regulating Finance: Balancing Freedom and Risk (2004); R. McCormick, Legal Risk in the Financial Markets (2006) 95 et seqq., 140 et seqq.; see also: B. A. Simmons, The Legalization of International Monetary Affairs (Summer 2000) 573–602; J. Black, The development of risk-based regulation in financial services: just 'modelling through'? (2005) 156–180; see also: R. Friedland and R. R. Alford, Bringing Society Back In: Symbols, Practices, and Institutional Contradictions (1991) 232–263.

[74] For a discussion of regulatory regimes, see C. Scott, Privatization and Regulatory Regimes (2006), 651 et seqq. See also the approach developed by B. Kingsbury, N. Kirsch, & R. B. Stewart, The Emergence of Global Administrative Law, in: Law and Contemporary Problems (Summer/Autumn 2005) 15–61, 42–52; B. Kingsbury, N. Kirsch, R. B. Stewart, & J. B. Wiener, Foreword: Global Governance as Administration – National and Transnational Approaches to Global Administrative Law (Summer/Autumn 2005) 1–13, focusing on the emergence of global administrative law.

[75] Chapter 1, point 5 Decentred Analysis of Regulation.

is considered within a centred perspective, that is, from inside the state, and there is a connection between self-regulation and the state in its role as a central, leading regulator, hence leaving room for private autonomous (that is, self-regulatory regimes) through a delegation of some of its legislative powers.

However, self-regulation also represents a form of non-state regulation produced by autonomous regulatory regimes emerging from civil society. While regulation in the traditional sense is centred towards the state in its role as a regulator, private autonomous regimes cannot be subsumed under that regulatory framework as such. Originally, they are not linked to the state at all. They are genuine to decentred regimes. Thus, distinction is necessary. Private autonomous regimes or self-regulation are understood in a broad sense, as independent regimes emerging from private initiative within civil society. They appear in other spheres than the state or on its periphery. Instead of being centred, the approach including these regimes is multi-centred. The concept of the regulatory state could be replaced by the concept of 'regulatory society', which becomes apparent when the focus is placed on these regimes. This approach also takes into account that private autonomous regimes represent a non-static, but evolving and dynamic concept. In practice, it is possible to encounter many institutional arrangements qualifying as private autonomous regimes. It is not a concept that travels well when analyzed as part of a centred system of state regulation. As forms of regulation, these regimes should be linked to the sphere of the state insofar as they complete it. They are autonomous.

Self-regulatory solutions pertaining to private autonomous regimes, as encountered nowadays, are a new form of self-regulation. Such self-regulation is no longer of the kind that arose from secular evolution. New self-regulation appears at the global level. It is oriented towards different issues, mostly economic, scientific, and technological. It does not encompass moral and legal views, but corresponds to a functional and sectoral approach. This development was already predicted by Jenks in the 1950s and Luhmann in the 1970s. Luhmann attributed this development to the transformation from normative – morality, law – to cognitive expectations – the economy, science, technology. He argued that transformation had to occur during the transition from nationally organized societies to a global society.[76] Indeed, there is now a number of (global) regimes, which adds to the fragmentation of law.[77] These autonomous regimes are heterarchical and not homogenous. As will be discussed in Chap. 4, there are not only private autonomous regimes, but also

[76] W. C. Jenks, The Conflict of Law-Making Treaties (1953) 403, as cited in Koskenniemi, supra note 1, 10; N. Luhmann, Die Weltgesellschaft, as translated and cited by A. Fischer-Lescano and G. Teubner, Regime-collisions: The vain search for legal unity in the fragmentation of global law (Summer 2004) 1000.

[77] Ogus, supra note 1, 98–100; Page, supra note 1, 144–148; P. Cane, Self Regulation and Judicial Review (1987) 324–328; Koskenniemi, supra note 1; Fischer-Lescano and Teubner, supra note 1; Fischer-Lescano and Teubner, supra note 2, 7–9; A.-M. Slaughter, Global Government Networks, Global Information Agencies, and Disaggregated Democracy (2001) 36–38.

non-state autonomous regimes. Instead of centralization, a decentred, polycentric system of rules is emerging.

1.3 Civil Society Approach

Civil society is the second source of regulation. Within this source, non-state, private autonomous regimes are considered to represent proper, independent, and autonomous regulatory regimes or alternative forms of regulation. They constitute bodies of rules with societal roots. Such a process corresponds to the creation and development of norms, standards or rules by individuals and associations on the periphery or outside a state regulatory framework. However, it appears to be a complex task to identify these regimes first, on account of the somewhat unusual and non-uniform process of creation of standards and rules within civil society. In particular, traditional conceptions of sovereignty and the procedures applied to define legal, state rules are inadequate to capture the complexity of the emergence of these regimes, not least because the process of formalization of their rules is uncoordinated and obscure; it is effectively informal. A methodology applying outside the state framework has to be set up. The norms that will finally emerge develop to form standards and private autonomous or self-regulatory rules in the course of an original, individual, often arduous, and non-linear or uneven process. The passage from private standards to rules proceeds from a micro- to a macro-level. The example of commercial usages is predestined to illustrate this process. Departing from informal, isolated trading activities, the lex mercatoria constitutes a whole body of rules nowadays.

The origins of self-regulation can be traced back to medieval times. It has long been considered an issue to be resolved at the national level. On their side, autonomous regulatory regimes emerge not only at the national or regional level, but their appearance is also typical in connection with the phenomenon of globalization. In effect, they epitomize it. Global both non-state and private regulatory regimes flourish in different fields. The strategic importance of these regimes as a medium of governance increases continuously and they influence developments in many countries. This is largely due to the fact that national state regulatory concepts and regulatory concepts applied by international organizations have not been efficient enough with regard to the process of globalization and the necessity to develop global rules in a reasonable time and manner. Epistemic communities and global networks are in the process of having a standing as institutions defining applicable standards and rules. The example of the regulation of information and copyright law with regard to technological developments illustrates this point. Moreover, in the case of global regulatory regimes, the shape of regulation is not fixed. The regulatory solution is the result of a dynamic process of creating standards and rules and adapting to existing circumstances. These regimes lead to a fragmentation and dispersion of regulation or a 'global law without the state' as designed by Fischer-Lescano and Teubner when considered from the point of view of the state. It adds to the multidimensionality of regulatory regimes characterizing legal pluralism.[78]

In comparison to state regulation, the regulatory regimes emerging are alternative forms of regulation. They are the product of the activities of an epistemic community or network (or web of influence). They are self-sufficient as well as self-sustained. They are part of a participatory governance model, corresponding to the needs of their members. Their primary objective is to satisfy just these needs. Regulatory regimes can adopt different forms. The designation of these regimes as non-state regulation can be considered to constitute an umbrella concept. In particular, diverse arrangements – also such comprising state representatives, as will be discussed – can be subsumed or qualify as autonomous regulatory regimes or alternative forms of regulation. They are often based on contractual agreements. However, they do not follow a linear dynamic. On the contrary, they constitute a 'unitas multiplex' of autonomous regimes, which develops on the periphery of a state regulatory regime. At the same time, it should not be ignored that the process of crystallisation of an alternative regime also implies that there is a tendency towards the juridification of norms within which an approach to a state regulatory regime could be contemplated.[79]

This raises a question concerning the relationship between non-state autonomous regulatory regimes or alternative forms of regulation and customary law. Teubner argues that while customary law emerges from diffuse communication processes, the new non-state regimes are a typical product of societal differentiation. The rule-making function of both is different. Customary law takes shape in the long term out of informal processes of gradually repeated interactions. Alternative regulatory regimes, on the contrary, lead to the creation of self-regulation or specialized forms of explicit norm-making within functional subsystems. In comparison, this takes place in relative short periods of time. There is an idea of velocity.[80] This point of view is certainly correct. Non-state autonomous regulatory regimes are distinctive, precise, targeted regimes applying to specific, determined fields not or inadequately regulated before. These are linked to the process of globalization and technological issues and orientated towards efficiency.

---

[78] Fischer-Lescano and Teubner, supra note 1, 45; G. Teubner, Global Bukowina: Legal Pluralism in the World Society (2006) 3–28.

[79] Fischer-Lescano and Teubner, supra note 76, 1033; Scott, supra note 74, 654; see also in this sense: B. Z. Tamanaha, A General Jurisprudence of Law and Society (2001) 77 et seqq.

[80] Teubner, supra note 4, point III, 73 et seqq.; D. Held and A. Mc Grew, D. Goldblatt and J. Perraton, Global Transformations, Politics, Economics and Culture (2008) 14–28, 70–74; Sassen, supra note 17, 378–390, 384.

2 A Brief Evolutive View

As already stated, regulation is not static. It evolves in the course of time and can assume different forms depending on the environment. Its institutional structure may change, too. In that regard, the discussion of autonomous regulatory regimes leading to non-state regulation would not be complete without examining the evolutive aspects of their constitution. It is one of their significant features. Both the temporal and sectoral evolution of regulation are of interest.

2.1 Temporal Approach: Past and Present

The evolution of regulation presents a non-linear picture. It has long been a private activity. In particular, as Braithwaite and Drahos strikingly state, it should not be forgotten that 'State supremacy occupies only one century in a 2,000-year history.' Consequently, state regulation is a recent phenomenon.[81] The temporal evolution of regulation shows that while some legal orders and principles survived for centuries or almost a millennium, like Roman law, others only lasted for a short period of time. The development of law, in particular of the fundamentals of medieval business law, has been largely influenced by the shared identity of Christendom in Europe. It was the basis for the conceptual legal foundations corresponding to the recognition of principles in a first stage.[82] The foundations often found their expression in self-regulation. Self-regulation is an older, atavistic notion of private regulation. It is a well-known characteristic of archaic and medieval societies. It took the form of codes of conduct or usances and has been the precursor of future regulations and statutes.[83] A secular evolution can be retraced, although it experienced both phases of expansion and recessive ones. It marked the 'first global age' (1400–1800). The roots of self-regulation can be found in the traditional rules of medieval and early modern industries as well as mercantile, corporatist, and professional organizations or guilds. These developed customary practices that led to a certain standardization of their market and trading activities and contributed to develop their commercial transactions more efficiently.[84] Self-regulation has regularly emerged for reasons of proficiency, adequacy, and adaptation to practical needs. The associations, organizations, or guilds defined their own specific order

[81] Braithwaite and Drahos, supra note 2, 480; in this sense, see also: Berman, Globalization, supra note 1, 442–449.

[82] Braithwaite and Drahos, supra note 2, 3–6.

[83] Black, supra note 3, 6–10, 12–14; Braithwaite and Drahos, supra note 2, 145–146; O. von Gierke, Das Deutsche Genossenschaftsrecht (1954) Bd. I, 358 seq.

[84] Black, supra note 3, 6, 12–13; Braithwaite and Drahos, supra note 2, 45–47; see also the discussion by S. Deakin, The Return of The Guild? Network Relations in Historical Perspective (2009), 58–65.

and rules of conduct applicable to their members. These were subsequently enforced together with proprietary rights and duties. They also developed customs within their markets, introduced weights and measures, and judged the quality of merchandise. They contributed to the building of capitalist regulatory institutions in medieval Europe[85] and in many cases paved the way for future regulation.

Over time, these guilds or associations were subject to different currents. While their self-regulatory orders flourished with increasing trading activities in medieval Europe, they declined before the industrial revolution in England.[86] Their decline was mainly due to the rise of nation-states, which degraded them to solely voluntary, non-binding measures not stipulating any sanctions. The emergence of nation-states was followed by a codification of laws in many different fields. Important institutional and organizational foundations of regulation were defined in this period. However, the regulatory orders first shaped by these private associations did not disappear. The rules established by guilds or associations often marked the origin of the subsequent creation of entire bodies of (state) norms. In many cases, self-regulation has been the precursor of future state regulation, not least due to the role played by self-regulatory associations in developing basic conceptual foundations and basic principles of regulation in a first stage as well as the power they gained in the course of their centennial existence. Their influence and the self-regulatory orders they defined remain noticeable and significant. Such orders can still be recognized and encountered today in a number of fields, such as the professions for instance. These orders may determine the form of governance in relation to economic processes. Hybrid forms of these orders, that is, combined with state rules are often encountered, too.

Together with the development of the nation-state concept, regulation was territorially limited. However, the conception of territorially defined and limited regulation is not immovable. Regulatory spaces organized by states produce orders that are not universally valid. They present weaknesses. First, it may be difficult for them to cope with challenges at other levels, such as the transnational or global level, in a satisfactory way. Second, their motivation is bound to national and political interests and perhaps not efficient enough, while – depending on the issue at stake – other interests may dominate, such as economical or commercial business interests. Third, the technicalities of the matters to be regulated may call for other solutions than state-based regulation. Fourth, the proliferation of epistemic communities and NGOs leads to the systematic re-organization and representation of interests, hence favouring the development of non-state regulatory regimes not bound to state limits and formulating standards applicable at the global level. These emerge from the interactions within epistemic communities and result from a worldwide collaboration of groups of experts forming transnational networks.

[85] Braithwaite and Drahos, supra note 2, 4.

[86] Ibid. 46; Black, supra note 3, xxiii; see also M. Schulte Beerbühl and J. Vögele, Spinning the Commercial Web, International Trade, Merchants, and Commercial Cities, c. 1640–1939 Centuries. An Introduction (2004) 11–23.

A genuine feature of these communities and self-organized networks is to develop activities on an informal basis in a first stage. Initially, such endeavour consists in the exchange of information among experts. Later, relationships become more formalized and ultimately an order may be generated. These networks often deal with matters that are not regulated at all or covered by orders such as the coercive order of the UN and its organizations, or where new issues arise. They constitute a fora for regulatory debate that may lead to a broad governance discussion regarding possible regulatory measures. Based on the regulatory and policy discourse, normative frameworks are elaborated.

These alternative forms of regulation are typical of the process of globalization. Although transnational law was already examined in the 1950s and 1960s, the emergence of autonomous regulatory regimes has only been clearly perceived since the 1970s,[87] with the identification of new forms of global regulation (largely developing on a non-state and private basis). Such awareness was accompanied by the study of networks in international relations that began to break down the state into its constituent parts instead of dealing with it as a single unified actor. The legal focus then shifted to the private and non-state side of international legal relationships with an emphasis on multinational corporations.[88] Private regimes regarding international business transactions were studied. These regimes are not linked to systems of territorial sovereignty. Thus, this process is extremely conducive to self-regulation. All networks and not only government networks, as stated by Slaughter,[89] have a high propensity for self-regulation. They represent informal, unpoliticized ways of communication among their members in pursuit of similar interests and goals. Considering the pressures such networks are subject to in order to effect solutions for their members and act as safeguards, they have to be very efficient.[90] The emerging regimes epitomize a new form of self-regulation, one not limited territorially. It can shift from the local to the global level. It is becoming even more important as an alternative, global form of regulation. It is represented by rules or also a set of values and principles for common actions rather than formal regulation.[91]

Both in legal and political science, non-state actors have begun to be considered as a subject of international law and politics. The focus has no longer been solely on states. In the 1980s, attention shifted from the actors to the analysis of their legal and political interactions. Techniques and mechanisms of regulating and influencing regulatory issues and the behaviour of actors were studied. NGOs began to

---

87 Braithwaite and Drahos, supra note 2, 3–5; Slaughter, supra note 77, 4–9.

88 A.-M. Slaughter and D. Zaring, Networking Goes International: An Update (2006) 212–213, with further references.

89 A.-M. Slaughter, Sovereignty and Power in a Networked World Order (2004) 311–313; K. Raustiala, The Architecture of International Cooperation: Transgovernmental Networks and the Future of International Law (2002) point II.3.

90 B. M. Hutter, The Role of Non-State Actors in Regulation (May 2006) 11.

91 Harrison, Morgan, Verkuil, supra note 12, 494 et seqq.; see also R. L. Jepperson and J. W. Meyer, The Public Order and the Construction of Formal Organizations (1991) 204–231.

play a more important role and there was a move beyond international state organizations.[92]

2.2 *Sectoral Approach: Functional Differentiation*

As already stated, the evolution of self-regulation and alternative forms of regulation and the appearance of non-state autonomous regulatory regimes are linked to a shift from territorial to functional and sectoral regime affiliation. Diverse rationales may explain this development.

Regulation is an activity as such. It must be organized. It occurs in particular places and at particular times. It is dominated by organizations. The basis for defining, setting, and implementing regulation is an appropriate institutional arrangement. The institution must dispose of adequate resources, knowledge, and expertise to devise rules, monitor and police their enforcement.[93] Hence, it is an institutional issue. In the case of the institution of the state as the sole regulator, it is linked to the conception of territoriality. In the course of time however, regulatory practices of states and their regulatory agencies shaping national regulatory frameworks have striven to be inclusive of multiple – not only national, but also international – interests in ways the rules of governance constitutive of transnational markets are shaped and apply to diverse sectors. There has been a shift to a functional approach.

That shift from territorial to functional and also sectoral differentiation is narrowly linked to the substantive, practical issues at stake.[94] In particular, in the course of time, the pursuit of economic interests began to dominate. The institution of the state lost its influence and economically motivated regulation became standard. Efficient solutions had to be found. The issues to be dealt with became more complex whilst assuming a global character not least due to increased mobility, new means of communication, and the use of economies of scale at the global level, leading to the emergence of global markets. This situation leads to a breakdown of traditional state regulation. New regulatory solutions have to be found. Besides the dominating economic interest and the global orientation of regulatory issues, a third determining element conducive to the shift to a functional approach is the development of technology. Hence, the networks concerned are different from state political networks. They are mostly constituted by experts (who can be both governmental and private) directly interested in obtaining concrete results. These experts are not bound to the implementation of generally applicable (legal) principles like states, but instead cooperate with other individuals or interested

92 Slaughter and Zaring, supra note 88, 213–214.

93 L. Hancher and M. Moran, Organizing Regulatory Space (1989) 284–286.

94 Fischer-Lescano and Teubner, supra note 76, 1009; see also R. W. Scott and J. W. Meyer, The Organization of Societal Sectors: Propositions and Early Evidence (1991) 108–140.

groups to work out efficient solutions. The solutions developed are practical, ad hoc solutions. In fact, as Hancher and Moran state:

> 'One of the most striking features of regulatory debates is the growing extent to which they are expressed in languages of technical complexity and legal discourse often far removed from everyday lay political argument.'[95]

In practice, the emergence of these regimes is not limited. In the literature, various examples of autonomous regulatory regimes are discussed. The most prominent private regulatory regimes cited by a number of authors are the lex mercatoria or law merchant of the global economy and the lex cybertoria or law of the Internet. Other cases regard e-commerce, transnational taxation, transnational copyright, computer crime, human rights, global trade, or the lex constructionis, among others. They may be private or hybrid regimes. However, it should not be overlooked that the functional and sectoral approach does not only encompass contemporary developments. It is also the expression of a long term evolutionary process in a range of sectors. For example in the professions, self-regulatory regimes have always been significant and still constitute a strong part of the specific regulatory framework. Another typical example is the financial sector where self-regulation has a long tradition and there is now often room for transnational and transgovernmental network solutions, as will be discussed in the next chapter. As a result, these regimes work out solutions where the states or international organizations of states could not take action in a satisfactory way in a first place.[96] In comparison to how states work, the networks producing these regimes are efficient. Their formal, regulatory aspects are negligible while the actual impact of such regimes should not be underestimated.

3 Institutional Structure

Regulation is a matter of organizing regulatory space.[97] Its structure depends on the institutions operating within it, the role they exercise, and their respective powers. As such, the contest of non-state and private autonomous regulatory regimes is an institutional issue. Thus, this part explores how such regimes emerge, that is, how they are generated, discusses the accompanying prerequisites supporting their constitution and shows how the transformation process works. A conceptual chain of sequences is built to understand the specific structure of institutionalizing procedures, thereby rendering possible their very appearance and existence. The sequences are analytical and heuristic. The following sequences are examined: the theory of interest, collectivity, private regulation, state intervention, and non-state

95 Hancher and Moran, supra note 93, 294.

96 Fischer-Lescano and Teubner, supra note 76, 1010–1011; Berman, supra note 1, 327 et seqq.

97 Hancher and Moran, supra note 93, 277.

orders. Finally, the concept of transnational networks and networks as regulatory institutions is outlined.

3.1 *Theory of Interest: From Interest to Associability*

Within this study, the crucial element at the point of departure of the conceptual chain is interest since this determines the development of all further activities. The term 'interest' can be defined as:

> The relation of being objectively concerned in something, by having a right or title to, a claim upon, or a share in. [...]
>
> The relation of being concerned or affected in respect of advantage or detriment; esp. an advantageous relation of this kind. [...]
>
> A thing in which one has an interest or concern. [...]
>
> A business, cause, or principle, in which a number of persons are interested; the party interested in such a business or principle; a party having a common interest; a religious or political party, business connexion, etc. [...][98]

The origins of interests are societal. Human beings form the basis of the conceptual chain, and their primary motivation is to satisfy their own needs. At this stage, these needs forge themselves and are subject to a process of concretization. They convert into self-interests. With the passage from needs to interest, individuals become conscious, identify and define the interests at stake, and prepare to represent these towards the outside world. They will decide to pursue their own interests only if they judge that this is feasible, desirable, and likely to succeed. This attitude is linked to the recognition of similar interests by other individuals and there is a gradual formation of collective, often commercially motivated private interests to the mutual benefit of all participants. The group will displace the individual as the locus of self-interest.[99]

In fact, there exists a rich and profound debate on the concept of 'interest'. In the literature the term has been discussed and analyzed at length. As already stated in relation to the public policy debate, diverse theories of interest have been formulated. Interest is part of 'public interest theories of regulation', 'interest group theories', 'private interest theories', or the 'theory of interest politics', among others.[100] Hereinafter, the focus is on the institutional aspects of these theories.

Public interest theories are based on the assumption that those who seek to regulate act in the pursuit of public interest related objectives and not primarily in

---

[98] The Oxford English Dictionary, Volume VII (1991) 1099.

[99] T. Hobbes, Leviathan or the Matter, Forme and Power of a Commonwealth Ecclesiastical and Civil, Part I, Ch. 13, 14. For Hobbes, the State is grounded solely in the self-interest of the individual. See: A. Black, Individuals, Groups and States: A Comparative Overview (1996) 334.

[100] See 1 Embedding Autonomous Regulatory Regimes, 1.1 Traditional State Approach, 1.1.1 Public Policy Debate, Public Interest; Baldwin and Cave, supra note 15, 18–33.

the interest of groups, sectors, or individual self-interests.[101] According to these theories, economic markets are fragile and may operate inefficiently without any state intervention. They consider government intervention to be a response to a publicly recognized need to correct the way markets operate. Regulation is just a product or also an instrument. The expert regulators – as already stated in relation to the public policy debate – are considered to be independent and privately uninterested. Their duty is to transpose public interest into rules. Moreover, another assumption lies in the fact that government regulation is virtually costless. In reality, this is rarely the case. Neither is regulation costless, nor are expert regulators independent. While regulation – in particular in case wrong regulatory measures have been introduced – may be very expensive,[102] expert regulators live in a situation of an ongoing conflict of interest. There is a problem of capture. This is an important assumption of Stigler's theory of economic regulation. Stigler argues that, as a rule, regulation is acquired by industry as well as designed and operated primarily for its benefit. Besides the fact that they should have enough specialized knowledge, regulators may be corrupted and succumb to specific economic and political influences.[103] Posner is one of the main enemies of these theories and criticizes their lack of substantial empirical support.[104]

According to interest group theories, regulation is the result of interactions among different groups of interest on the one hand, and among these groups and the state in its role as regulator on the other hand. These groups reflect their own views and may be differently organized. Regulation is the product of negotiations taking place between the legislator and interest groups representing businesses or other affected parties. It emerges from a consensus reached on the basis of compromises between the legislator and the groups in question. Diverse versions of these theories exist, ranging from corporatism to pluralism. Within the corporatist approach, interest groups are first considered to act in partnership with the state. Regulation should then be the expression of all the represented interests. In the case of liberal pluralism, interest groups are considered to be competing against each other. They use their power to define what regulation is in their view.[105]

Then, private interest theories are motivated not by the public, but by private interests. Here, too, various ramifications of the theories can be subsumed under this category. Peltzman and Stigler have developed one important instance. They argue that there would be a regulatory market wherein the regulator would be captured by

---

101 Baldwin and Cave, supra note 15, 19.

102 Stigler, supra note 22, 10 seq. For a generalization of Stigler's view, see: S. Peltzman, Toward a More General Theory of Regulation (1976) 211–240, and also: S. Peltzman, The Economic Theory of Regulation after a Decade of Deregulation (1989) 1–41.

103 Stigler, supra note 22, 3 et seqq.; also: Peltzman (1976) supra note 102, 211–240; Peltzman (1989) supra note 102, 1–41; Baldwin and Cave, supra note 15, 20–21.

104 Posner, supra note 32, 335–358; Baldwin and Cave are critical too, supra note 15, 20–21.

105 Baldwin and Cave, supra note 15, 21, with further references. For an example of its application, see Geoffrey P. Miller, An Interest Group Theory of Central Bank Independence, in: Journal of Legal Studies, Volume 27, No. 2, 1998.

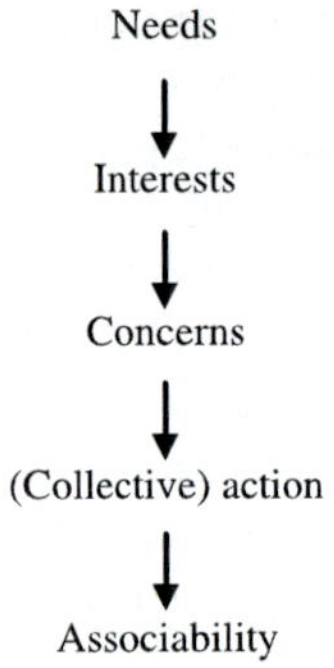

Fig. 2.1 Process of conversion within interest politics

industry, trying to achieve the most beneficial regulation for its business. This economic approach assumes that the parties involved are income maximizers. However, it presents weaknesses. It is not possible to explain a range of developments based on this approach. For example, deregulatory processes cannot be satisfactorily explained as the result of an attitude of industries implementing a regulation they first defined themselves. Peltzman himself recognizes that the main problem of this theory is its lacking account of the role played by institutional arrangements when regulation is defined.[106]

Within the theory of interest politics as formulated by Schmitter, interest is regarded both as a descriptive cause and as a motive for acting. 'Interest' is conceptualized as a multisequential, iterative, and continuous societal process. It is part of a chain leading from needs to interests to concerns to collective actions and finally to associability. Associability is characterized by the possibility of a voluntary collectivity. It implies interaction among members, and that these join forces to pursue similar interests. An important precondition for reaching this state of affairs is that the individuals involved are willing to develop a joint strategy. A process of collective representation and control takes shape. Within this chain, the passage from one sequence to the other depends on a dualistic process of theory or socially determined reflection and strategy or politically constrained choice. The process is one of value subtraction involved in the conversion of need into associative action.[107] In an ideal world, the theory of interest politics would result in the attainment of a good polity, meaning one in which all interests can be considered, pursued, and satisfied taking existing constraints into account (Fig. 2.1).[108]

Within this study, the concept of interest is understood in terms of its relation to being concerned with something by having a right or claim to it, or because it may result either in a direct advantage or disadvantage for oneself. In a first phase,

[106] Peltzman (1976) supra note 102, 211–240; Peltzman (1989) supra note 102, 1–41; Stigler, supra note 22, 10 seq.; Baldwin and Cave, supra note 15, 21–25.

[107] P. C. Schmitter, A Prolegomenon to a Theory of Interest Politics (2006) 300–304.

[108] Ibid. 298; with a similar figure.

interests are identified and defined. An interest implies the exercise of activities, which can be organized interest politics.[109] It is a motivation for acting, that is, a motivation justifying individual action. The pursuit of these interests leads to their transformation and concretization. With the formation and articulation of clearly defined individual concerns, the knowledge of these concerns crystallizes. Individuals become aware of their common concerns. They recognize that they are confronted with similar problems and pursue similar interests. They begin to influence each other and a collective consciousness forms to accompany the perception and formulation of individual interests. With the need to take action, they are no more represented by isolated individuals but by groups of experts or collectivities, and finally epistemic communities. Their concerns are gradually transformed into collective ones.[110] The members of these communities begin to consult each other on the measures to be taken, deciding on the strategic choice of adequate instruments to reach the objectives set. Together with their associability, they begin to organize themselves in order to pursue common interests and defend them efficiently. They formulate clearly defined aims. These groups finally constitute working systems or networks, whose sole aim is to satisfy the needs of their members.

3.2 Collectivity: From Associability to Association

The second sequence within the conceptual chain is characterized by a shift from associability towards a specification and formalization of the relationship of individuals' common interests. It consists in the link from associability to association, constituting a self-regulatory, private autonomous body. As the process of linking interests among individuals produces stronger ties and a collective consciousness emerges, the intention to adopt a determined structure arises. This sequence focuses on such (formal) association. Association means that there is a collectivity and an act of associating or a state of being associated. The term 'association' is defined as:

> The action of combining together for a common purpose; the condition of such combination; confederation, league. [. . .]
>
> A body of persons who have combined to execute a common purpose or advance a common cause; the whole organization which they form to effect their purpose; a society; [. . .][111]

Two aspects are distinguished: first, a formal one regarding the possible legal form of an association, that is its incorporation as defined by state regulation and its registration; and secondly, a substantive one concerning the subject matter of the association.

---

109 Ibid. 299.

110 Ibid. 302–303.

111 The Oxford English Dictionary, Volume I (1991) 718.

Formally, the association can adopt the form of a private partnership and be registered according to the statute of the home-country.[112] In case an association adopts a legal form, its internal relationships are formalized through establishing bylaws and the adoption of rules, defined on the basis of a consensus among its members. Membership is based on an agreement with the association. For the members, this means that they agree with the rules established, usually consisting in rules of conduct. Sanctions towards members are not excluded and may be part of the governing rules.

Within this study, different kinds of private associations are comprised under this term, all representing collectivities. In the following, its use should be understood as an overall term, which can stand for:

- Self-regulatory associations or organizations (SRAs or SROs)
- Non-governmental associations or organizations (NGAs or NGOs)
- Corporations, groups of corporations, and multinational corporations (MNCs)
- A sector association representing the interests of an entire industry, or
- Other forms of national and international or global private or non-state associations (possibly including networks)

Associations or SROs are constituted on a voluntary basis and find their roots in the willingness of their members to act together, protect their mutual interests, maintain standards among each other, and reach the same goals. Considered from an historical point of view, contemporary associations represent a new form of medieval associations or guilds of merchants or artisans. They are active in numerous domains.[113] They both characterize and represent the outcome of this stage of the transformation process. They emerge from civil society interactions in the form of a collectivity.

An association is a body of individuals or affiliated members who pursue common interests embodied in the form of the purpose of the association, such as trade, business, or professional interests. They form a community and the association or SRO is the result of their act of consorting or joining with others. They have strong ties among each other, are mutually dependent, and delegate their own capacity for interest theorizing and promotion to the association. Professionalization occurs. For an association to function properly, two basic conditions must be fulfilled with regard to its relationship with its members: power and authority.[114] It will dedicate itself to the representation of its members' interests, developing its expertise and pursuing its statutory goals. The form of the representation of interests by an association and its field of action are determined by its resources, its structure, and organization. Through creating an association, members loss their

---

[112] Black, supra note 3, 193–195, 221–230.

[113] For a basic introduction to guilds, see Black, supra note 3; J. Braithwaite and C. Parker, Conclusion, in: Regulating Law (2004) 273; see also for an interesting discussion of the situation in Japan: U. Schaede, Cooperative Capitalism: Self-Regulation, Trade Associations and the Antimonopoly Law in Japan (2000).

[114] Schmitter, supra note 107, 308–310.

autonomy as far as the interests represented by the association are concerned. The association or SRO is expected to engage in collective action on their behalf and represent their interests. Through its constitution, it acquires the power to affect its members' behaviour and opinion.[115] However, members have the possibility to express their views and cast votes. They formulate its policy. Although the association will finally exercise control over their behaviour, it will reflect its members' opinion. When identified through its guiding principle of interaction and allocation, Streeck and Schmitter would design an association or SRO as an 'organizational concertation'.[116] The link from associability to a collectivity or association is a matter of organizational degree.[117]

As stated, to represent collectivities, different types of associations or groups of individuals can be distinguished. Hutter observes that civil society embraces a broad range of actors and organizations of varying size, sophistication, and orientation, operating at local, national, or transnational levels.[118] Numerous and diverse associations or SROs can be encountered, and these can be organized and represented by a peak-organization. Among associations, NGOs are a fast growing sector. They are characterized by the following three elements: First, they are not established by a government nor by an intergovernmental agreement. Second, they are typically private institutions. Third, the concerns, purposes and objects of NGOs are, in contrast to their origins, of a public nature. While there were 176 international NGOs in 1909, by 1993, there were not less than 28,500, more than 90% occurred since 1970.[119] Fifty-seven new NGOs were accredited to the 1968 Tehran Conference on Human Rights as opposed to 831 to the Vienna Conference 25 years later. In Eastern Europe, over 100,000 NGOs are said to have emerged between 1988 and 1995.[120] They appear in many different fields, such as the professions, sports, the media, marketing, or financial services. In this respect, it is worth noting that Russia passed a statute on non-governmental organizations in December 2005. Based on this statute, the state can control the activities of these organizations.

---

[115] Ibid. 308–309.

[116] Streeck and Schmitter, supra note 19, 1–4.

[117] Within an industry, it is possible to encounter entire networks of self-regulatory associations, which may also require the respect of their respective rules reciprocally, that is, among themselves. See Black, supra note 1, 25, citing the example of company and financial services law in the UK. In the UK, the London Stock Exchange was first responsible for the Listing Rules. It also required the respect of the Code of Best Practice of the Cadbury Committee on the Financial Aspects of Corporate Governance and under the old order of the Act of 1986, the self-regulatory organizations required the respect the City Code on Takeovers and Mergers from their members.

[118] Hutter, supra note 90, 2–3, 7–11.

[119] To the definition: P. Macalister-Smith, Non-Governmental Organizations, Humanitarian Action and Human Rights (1995) 483; D. Thürer, The Emergence of Non-Governmental Organizations and Transnational Enterprises in International Law and the Changing Role of the State (1999) 43–45; to NGOs numbers: Braithwaite and Drahos, supra note 2, 499–500.

[120] To human rights numbers: C. Chinkin, Monism and Dualism: The Impact of Private Authority on the Dichotomy Between National and International Law (2007) 137, with further references; to Eastern Europe numbers: Hutter, supra note 90, 7, with further reference.

These have to register and are thoroughly regulated by the state. The rationales for the introduction of these rules are mainly political. Their main aim is to hinder the formation of revolutionary cells.[121] Such 'nationalizing' of associations has been criticized. On the other hand, the fact that NGOs are now formally recognized by the United Nations (UN) underlines their significance. Based on an initiative of the Economic and Social Council of the United Nations (ECOSOC), and according to article 71 of the Charter of the United Nations, a legal framework for the participation of NGOs in the work of the UN has been created. It paves the way for their greater integration in the international legal system. Article 71 authorizes the ECOSOC to consult the expertise of NGOs. With regard to the large number of NGOs and to make efficient use of their expertise, they have been divided into three categories: general, special, and roster according to determined criteria. Organizations belonging to the first category are concerned with most of the activities of the ECOSOC and its subsidiary bodies. They have the right to participate in meetings, produce oral and written statements and positions, and submit drafts for agreements or resolutions. Organizations belonging to the second category are assigned special competence with regard to determined fields of activities covered by ECOSOC. They have rights similar to NGOs belonging to the general category, but they are more limited and can only make occasional contributions. Organizations belonging to the last category have the lowest status. They can also participate in the activities of other UN organs. Altogether, NGOs are considered to be secondary subjects of international law.[122] Besides the UN organization, other bodies may have opened up their work to NGO participation. However this occurs in a very informal way, such as meetings of the Basel Committee on Banking Supervision with the Institute of International Finance or other industry representatives.[123]

A look at the regulatory activities of the OECD or the UNCTAD shows that SROs representing the economy as well as business enterprises or multinational companies are in a particularly advantageous position of force. In comparison to

---

[121] Russlands Duma verabschiedet NGO-Gesetz, Daumenschrauben für die Bürgergesellschaft, Neue Zürcher Zeitung (22 December 2005) 1; O. Yablokova, Amended NGO Bill Quickly Approved, Moscow Times (22 December 2005).

[122] Article 71 of the Charter of the United Nations states that:

> 'The Economic and Social Council may make suitable arrangements for consultation with non-governmental organizations which are concerned with matters within its competence. Such arrangements may be made with international organizations and, where appropriate, with national organizations after consultation with the Member of the United Nations concerned.'

Chinkin, supra note 120, 135–136, 143–144; R. Wedgwood, Legal Personality and the Role of Non-Governmental Organizations and Non-State Political Entities in the United Nations System (1999) 21–36; J. Delbrück, The Role of the United Nations in Dealing With Global Problems (1997) 277, 295; C. Baudenbacher, Globalisierung und Regionalisierung des Wirtschaftsrechts (2004) 12–14; U. Korkut, Participatory policy-making, participatory civil society: A key for dissolving elite rule in new democracies in the era of globalization (2007) 340–352; K. Martens, Examining the (Non-)Status of NGOs in International Law (2003) 1–24.

[123] According to information received from the BCBS.

consumer organizations, they are well organized, function efficiently, and have enough resources to defend their interests (that is, for lobbying). SROs can also play a role with regard to the enforcement of law through international courts. Two aspects must be distinguished here. The first aspect concerns the right of NGOs to lodge complaints while the second refers to their right to be admitted as parties and intervene. In relation to the WTO, for instance, only states have the right to complain. Individual persons and associations are not legitimated to complain. The question whether a SRO can present opinions in relation to cases to be decided is still not resolved. Until now, the WTO Appellate Body has decided that submissions by associations should be admitted when the SROs take the initiative to represent them.[124]

On its side, the institutional order of the state is characterized by the following key institutions: the state, the community, and the market. In a democracy, market forces should develop freely and the state institutions should contribute to determine the framework within which these forces flourish. Thus, there is room for the emergence of associations or SROs. These associations can be considered to represent a fourth power, as discussed in the neo-corporatist work of Streeck and Schmitter.[125] As such, they lead to a reshaping of the institutional order. They are powerful entities, empowered to act and influence decisions. Ayres and Braithwaite see the process of empowering what they design as public interest groups (PIGs), that is, associations and SROs as a tripartite one. According to them, tripartism means a regulatory policy that fosters the participation of SROs or associations in the regulatory process in three ways:

- It grants the PIG and all its members access to all the information that is available to the regulator.
- It gives the PIG a seat at the negotiating table with the firm and the agency when deals are negotiated.
- The policy grants the PIG the same standing to sue or prosecute under the regulatory statute as the regulator.[126]

Although the approach is far-reaching, its basic elements and direction are adequate to empower these entities. From an institutional point of view, these associations can hence be considered to operate as a kind of arbitrator within the state. They represent the interests of directly concerned market actors facing the institutional structure of the state, and community. The admission of SROs or associations as partners within a societal order implies a shift of the existing balance of forces. The classic state order is an order of relative subordination and privacy. With the associations, negotiations become more important and play a determining role within policy debates. In relation to the state, private interest groups, associations or SROs typically represent the professional interests of sectors or industries.

---

124 WTO Panel Report on United States Import Prohibition of Certain Shrimp and Shrimp Products, WT/DS 58/AB/R, 15 May 1998; Baudenbacher, supra note 122, 26–28.

125 Streeck and Schmitter, supra note 19, 1–29.

126 Ayres and Braithwaite, supra note 6, 56–58.

They have been conceptualized in a pluralist context as voluntary organizations focusing on the representation of interests.[127]

The policy idea behind associations is not the sole relevant aspect to understand what associations are and do. It is worth considering the approach of the general theory of politics. Within that theory, the corporatist approach can be used to explain the relationships behind or surrounding associations. Corporatism means a political system where part of the legislative power is delegated to civil assemblies representing economic, industrial, or other professional groups. In his seminal work, Schmitter defines corporatism as:

> '... a system of interest representation in which the constituent units are organised into a limited number of singular, compulsory, noncompetitive, hierarchically ordered and functionally differentiated categories, recognized or licensed (if not created) by the state and granted a deliberate representational monopoly within their respective categories in exchange for observing certain controls on their selection of leaders and articulation of demands and supports.'[128]

Corporatism does not regard the association as such. It links organized interest groups or SROs within civil society with the decisional structures of the state, because these influence the decision-making process. Nowadays, they are often understood as meaning the role of business corporations in relation to government decision-making, which must be attributed to their economic power and comparative advantage in relation to the general public or non-organized individuals. Corporatism can also be qualified as a form of capture insofar as it is dependent on groups of interests. It may be understood as state corporatism, which means that in autocratic states, organizations are used by the state solely to restrict public participation in the political decision-making process. As such, it has a pejorative connotation, not least because the powers of civil society are limited in such cases. China is a case in point, for instance, where there is often only one organization within a sector: 'All Chinese associations, of all types, need to be officially registered, and only one organization is recognized as the representative for each sectoral constituency.' Moreover, almost all these organizations are first instituted by the government, and membership can be declared obligatory.[129]

Another approach, the neo-corporatist one, advocates a mixed institutional order. Associations emerge as the result of multifaceted interactions between diverse institutional structures. Markets, community, state, and associations exercise countervailing power and equilibrium is reached. Neo-corporatism can thus also be seen as forming a process of bargaining between diverse forces, wherein the purely self-interested associations attempt to maximize their members' benefits. In practice, moreover, it is often argued that the interests of business enterprises dominate opinion-building within this approach. Direct citizen participation as

[127] Streeck and Schmitter, supra note 19, 18–20.

[128] P. C. Schmitter, Still the Century of Corporatism? (1974) 36:1, 86, 92–94.

[129] J. Unger and A. Chan, China, Corporatism, and the East Asian Model (January 1995) 29–53, and 39: citing the example of the organization of calligraphy connoisseurs.

such does not constitute part of the system. As Ayres and Braithwaite state, the emphasis on direct citizen participation in the regulatory game belongs rather to the republican tradition.[130] A typical example of the neo-corporatist process – albeit not within a state, but at the international level – is the International Labor Organization (ILO). It is the only organization of the United Nations that accomplishes its work based on a tripartite structure. Its three bodies are governments (two delegates), employers (one delegate), and workers (one delegate). These bodies shape ILO policies and programmes. The successful operation of the organization is based on a dialogue among the tripartite constituents at different levels and through its three main bodies. First, the annual International Labour Conference in June plays a central role. It establishes and adopts international labour standards and is a forum for discussion. There, employer and worker delegates can express themselves and vote according to instructions received from their respective organizations, which, however, may not be free from political influences. Second, the Governing Body is the executive council of the ILO. It takes decisions on ILO policy and establishes its programmes. It is represented by the same key of government, employer, and worker representatives. Third, the International Labour Office is the permanent secretariat of the organization.[131]

The republican approach as advocated by Ayres and Braithwaite places emphasis on direct citizen participation in the regulatory process. Under this approach, there is a multidimensional conception of an effectively working democracy. The approach basically deviates from the neo-corporatist one, where representation by associations is primarily restricted to organized groups like business or unions. It can be very local, due to the fact that micro-structures are seized and citizens are increasingly empowered by voting rights, voting options, and other opportunities to participate in the collective decision-making process.[132] It involves four basic commitments: (1) deliberation in government that shapes as well as balances interests; (2) political equality, which involves an organizational empowerment of disorganized constituencies; (3) universality, or debate, to reconcile competing views, as a regulative ideal; and (4) citizenship and community participation in public life.[133]

Pluralism is yet another institutional design. The concept emerged from the critique of legal centralism in the 1970s and 1980s. In particular, legal centralism disregarded societal reality as composed of a great diversity of orders. It is constituted of plural, heterogeneous, intersecting orders. Pluralism marks the origin of an understanding that legal orders transcend the state. Under pluralism, a great variety of groups should arise spontaneously. The groups, that is, associations or

---

130 Ayres and Braithwaite, supra note 6, 17; see also: Streeck and Schmitter, supra note 19, 1, 8–18; A. Cawson, ed., Organized Interests and the State (1985).

131 http://www.ilo.org/global/About_the_ILO/lang–en/index.htm (last visited 16 December 2009).

132 Ayres and Braithwaite, supra note 6, 17–18.

133 C. R. Sunstein, Beyond the Republican Revival (1988) 1539–1590; also as cited by Ayres and Braithwaite, supra note 6, 18.

SROs are endowed with different, asymmetrical powers. They have their own organizational structures and are unequal and heterogeneous. They may not be supported, recognized, or licensed by the state. Pluralism stands for a system with a large number of interest representations, hence permitting the coexistence of different interests.[134] Nor do they represent a monopoly within their categories. There can be a multiplicity of diverse communicative processes. Pluralism is also a symbol for diversity. It focuses on the individual preferences representing its basic concept of interest. Information gathering and opinion forming are important activities for most pluralist regimes. Pluralism is narrowly linked to liberalism, which means that the state should not intervene but remain weak. The basic underlying assumption is that the private market order should be strong. Individualism should not be limited or threatened. On the contrary, it should be promoted.[135] The constitution and development of activities through associations should not be restricted in any manner by the state. This is even more accentuated within neoliberalism. In a Foucauldian sense, neoliberalism denotes a programme rather than a reality. From an institutional point of view, it corresponds to a process of privatization and deregulation, including a deregulated international trade regime and a diminished public sphere.[136] The focus is on individualism rather than collective structures. Finally, the debate on pluralism is narrowly linked to a growing interest in questions regarding transnational and global regulatory regimes.

As a result (of these currents), it can be stated that the basic associative order is characterized by opposite influences: the free market economy and state governance. Admittedly, this order should be designed to represent the interests of sectoral networks within the economy, towards the state or other national organizations, or towards international organizations at the international level. In practice, political systems may tolerate, accept, or foster the emergence of associations or SROs. However, as discussed, a political system may also demote them. With regard to the general theory of politics, collectivities may be subsumed either under the categories of corporatism, neo-corporatism or pluralism, whereas least state influence will be encountered in the case of pluralism. The policy position of the state is a response to the possible behaviour of collectivities. In the case of the

[134] E. Gruner, Wirtschaftsverbände und Staat, Das Problem der wirtschaftlichen Interessenvertretung in historischer Sicht (1954) 1–27; E. Gruner, Der Einbau der organisierten Interessen in den Staat (1959) 59–79, 63; E. Gruner, Die Wirtschaftsverbände in der Demokratie, Vom Wachstum der Wirtschaftsorganisationen im schweizerischen Staat (1956).

[135] Schmitter, supra note 128, 95–96; Ayres and Braithwaite, supra note 6, 17–18; Teubner, supra note 78, 3–28. For an historical overview, see Black, supra note 99, 329–340; S. Roberts, After Government? On Representing Law Without the State (2005) 11–13; see also: M. Koskenniemi, Global Legal Pluralism: Multiple Regimes and Multiple Modes of Thought (March 2005) 1 et seqq.; S. E. Merry, Legal Pluralism (1988) 869–896; J. Griffiths, What is Legal Pluralism? (1986) 1–55; Fischer-Lescano and Teubner, supra note 2, 41–43; W. W. Burke-White, International Legal Pluralism (2004) 963–979.

[136] Foucault, supra note 4, 77 et seqq.; J. Braithwaite, Regulatory Capitalism, How it works, ideas for making it work better (2008) 1 et seqq.; J. Braithwaite, Neoliberalism or Regulatory Capitalism (October 2005) 3; Tamanaha, supra note 79, 115–117.

introduction of limitations to the constitutions of associations, its aim is to exercise a determining influence on their activities. However, despite a possible involvement or influence of the state, their original source is to be found in the societal periphery of the legal order.[137] Their source remains private or attributed to non-state approaches.

As far as the process of globalization is concerned, there is a shift from national regulation to global standards and rules defined by non-state regimes. These result from the activities of private and non-state bodies, that is, webs of influence, epistemic communities, and networks. In relation to this process, the states and international organizations of states are not in a position to influence the emergence and operations of these transnational associations or networks. On the contrary, they may be just the cause of the emergence of these associations. They may be undermined by politics and not dispose of the right instruments to respond to the challenges of a globalization of business. Indeed, they have not been able to capture the complexity of contemporary developments in a range of fields. States as well as international organizations of states have failed to develop generally applicable solutions to various global issues until now. Moreover, the delegation of competences by states to international organizations to enact rules presents weaknesses. There may be a loss of democratic opinion building and control of the regulatory measures introduced, which may be due to different factors like the size of the organization, the extent of the delegated powers, and intervention possibilities. Similarly to states, international organizations may lack the knowledge, contacts to core information providers, or motivation to adopt measures or the measures taken may not be enforced by the states in the end. As a result, the bureaucratic power of international institutions may be reinforced, but these remain in part inefficient. Instead, they offer room for new forms of interactions.

Epistemic communities and global networks have finally emerged. Formally, they may constitute associations. They define the standards and rules to be applied in their own sector. Such rules are private and self-regulatory or must be adopted by the states. These epistemic communities and networks possess expert knowledge. Their members are experts, professionals defending their particular business, technological, or scientific interests. They expect their representative association to act in their interests. Here, efficiency and interest maximization represent shared values, which become the aim of the standard-setting activities. In particular, this holds true in the field of economics and commercial transactions where businesses cannot wait for the enactment of state regulation and will instead determine the standards and rules governing their transactions. The measures taken by an association follow a logic different from that of state law. They are considered legitimate as far as the criteria of efficiency and interest maximization are fulfilled. Moreover, associations or networks are able to react in a flexible way, remaining credible as far as their achievements benefit their members. They can take adequate measures unlike cumbersome and sluggish states or international organizations bureaucracies,

137 A. Giddens, The Consequences of Modernity (1990) 70; Teubner, supra note 78, 3–4.

which cannot always compete with them. As a result, states and international organizations are currently losing influence while non-state and self-organized networks are becoming more influential.[138] The basis of global governance has changed.

3.3 Private Regulation: From Association to Self-regulation

Associations or SROs fulfil different functions: they clarify and conceptualize the interests of the group, define policies, coordinate their members' behaviour, prepare measures to be taken, organize activities, compile reports, represent interests vis-à-vis the general public and other bodies. They form proper systems of interest representation. Their work can rest on various criteria: the conditions to be fulfilled to guarantee the good functioning of a sector, professional accuracy, efficiency, acceptance, impact, confidence, low costs, and preservation of a private, non-state solution. An association or SRO may also dispose of some enforcement powers and may be in a position to take disciplinary measures or inflict sanctions on its members. However, it has no immediate jurisdiction over either individuals or natural or legal persons other than its members. In accordance with Ayres and Braithwaite's model of enforced self-regulation, it is argued that it is easier to secure convictions within an association, because the rules are more precise and less complex than in the case of state regulation. Although the problem of capture cannot be ignored,[139] the working of these disciplinary measures and sanctions will contribute to forge its credibility in the public. It is often motivated by the efforts made by an association to avoid state intervention and publicly demonstrate that it acts and exercises its powers effectively. Consequently, it may in part represent a form of constraint action. Nevertheless, informing the public about its goals and policy is very important and an association may assume the function of interest intermediation. It works in a market-oriented manner, driven by efficiency and representing a form of autonomous governance.[140]

As far as the regulatory capacity of associations or networks is concerned, it is not a clear-cut function. They are considered to be part of the process of defining and formalizing norms. Thus, the following questions arise: how do they generate these norms, what are these norms, values and principles, and which is their relation to other forms of regulation? When discussing norms defined by SROs or networks

---

[138] For example, see A. Sajó, Transnational Networks and Constitutionalism (2006) 223–224; Sassen, supra note 17, 197; A.-M. Slaughter, The Power and Legitimacy of Government Networks (2004) 6–7, using the word 'effectiveness'; A. M. Florini, Who does what? Collective action and the changing nature of authority (2000) 15–31.

[139] Ayres and Braithwaite, supra note 6, 12, 55–56; Priest, supra note 71, 257; see also Chapter 3, point 2 Firm Own Regulation, Concerning the Model of Enforced Self-Regulation.

[140] J. Delbrück, Exercising Public Authority Beyond the State: Transnational Democracy and/or Alternative Legitimation Strategies? (2003) 35.

and how they emerge, it must first be remembered that the classical hierarchy of state regulation is not applicable. Alternative forms of regulation and self-regulation pertain to non-hierarchical networks or regulatory regimes. A hierarchical process may be found within a network only as far as the internal procedure leading to the building of norms, standards and rules is considered. However, their internal relations are looser and less structured than in the case of state institutions. There is also no hierarchy between associations or networks.[141] They adopt individual forms in accordance with their field of action and objectives. Every network develops its own operative mechanisms. Different practices and steps can be distinguished, which, although they may be unintentional and do not occur consciously, can be understood as a methodology underpinning the formation of norms, standards and rules. At the global level, the process is enhanced by the notion of the sustainable development of the network and the use of the internet, which provides for a standardized foundation to communicate. In fact, at that level, the transnational aspect is of growing importance with regard to the operations of networks or SROs. These exercise an ever-growing influence both on the creation of law through regional and international organizations and as autonomous bodies defining global self-regulatory or non-state regulatory regimes of rules. They are in a position to operate successfully, unlike states.[142] In their seminal study on 'Global business regulation', Braithwaite and Drahos argue that effective and decent global regulation depends on the determination of individuals to engage with powerful agendas and decision-making bodies that would otherwise be dominated by concentrated economic interests. They also argue that global business regulation emerges from various epistemic communities. These communities have a shared understanding of regulation in any particular sphere that leads them not merely to advise, but to govern as well. In effect, the study suggests that the world is run by these communities. Indeed, it is a core issue of the phenomenon of globalization, whose impact still needs to be explored. However, it should not be ignored that global official institutions such as the organizations belonging to the UN and the IMF, the World Bank or the OECD also play an active role in developing new, global practices and rules.[143] The result is a dispersion of rules.

The creation of values, principles and norms following rationales different from the state legal process can be classified under the category of autonomous or self-regulatory measures. They can take the form of formal or informal consensus between members or with third parties, conventions, standardized agreements, routines contacts among the network's members or between networks or organizations, processes of standardization, assimilations of behaviour, etc. In fact, they

[141] Fischer-Lescano and Teubner, supra note 2, 10, 21, 48. On the discussion of norms, standards, and rules, see Chapter 4, point 2 Standardization, 2.3 Gradual Transformation, 2.3.1 From Standards to Rules, Transformation.

[142] In this sense, and in relation to constitutionalism, see: Sajó, supra note 138, 20–21.

[143] Braithwaite and Drahos, supra note 2, 6–10, 24–26; P. S. Berman, From International Law to Law and Globalization (2005) 485–556; P. M. Haas, Introduction: Epistemic Communities and International Policy Coordination (Winter 1992) 1–35.

constitute numerous modes of cooperation. They may refer to the internal relations and behavioural standards applying within a group, and external relations towards the public, government, media, other associations or sectors of activities, or also individuals.[144] In such cases, the central system of state regulation loses its significance in particular in relation to the regulation of determined topics or sectors, while regulation defined by autonomous regimes or networks takes shape, that is non-sate and self-regulation. A polycentric order emerges wherein the traditional state regulatory order is merely one order among others and the centralized system of state regulation is also influenced by global developments. This may be caused by regulatory agencies that are members and participate in the work of international organizations and networks, largely determining the future national rules when transposing the international order into their respective countries. It can also be the product of the adaptation of national rules to globally developed practices. Instead of a unity of rules, there is a plurality of rules. A functional approach dominates, which varies depending on the sector concerned.[145] On its side, the state legal system is ponderous and in the case of international solutions, the process may be more fastidious, as the example of the WTO impressively shows.

When departing from the state concept, the question of a link between self-regulation or non-state regulation and soft law arises first. Soft law is widely used to qualify a number of regulatory measures or tools, whereas the most common ones are the codes of conduct, guidelines, recommendations, directives, or the practices of businesses or Gentlemen's Agreements. It also applies to a number of situations. In a broad sense, soft law also means other forms of influences, as described in article 38 paragraph 1 litera d of the Statute of the International Court of Justice:

> 1. The Court, whose function is to decide in accordance with international law such disputes as are submitted to it, shall apply:
>
> ...
>
> d. subject to the provisions of Article 59, judicial decisions and the teachings of the most highly qualified publicists of the various nations, as subsidiary means for the determination of rules of law.[146]

Soft law was initially considered to belong to international law.[147] It still largely applies to that field. International organizations regularly take measures belonging to soft law, for example in the form of guidelines, codes of conduct, principles, or best practices. The UN-organizations, the OECD, the IMF or the World Bank too regularly publish recommendations for their member states. A cooperation with

---

144 Fischer-Lescano and Teubner, supra note 76, 1012–1014; Fischer-Lescano and Teubner, supra note 2, 48.

145 Fischer-Lescano and Teubner, supra note 76, 1005–1009.

146 http://www.icj-cij.org/documents/index.php?p1=4&p2=2&p3=0#CHAPTER_II (last visited 16 December 2009).

147 D. Thürer, Soft Law (2000) 452–460; D. Thürer, ‚Soft Law' – eine neue Form von Völkerrecht? (1985) 429–453; J. O'Brien, International Law (2001) 98–99.

these states as addressees of the measures may also take the form of standard agreements. These organizations do not qualify as regulators as such, but their work, the implementation of their programmes, policies, and recommendations also represent a kind of soft law. It is expected that the member states will observe or incorporate them into their legal regimes.[148]

The most important feature of soft law is its non-binding character. At the same time, there is a recognition that it should have a legal effect and be observed in practice, thus determining behaviour. The measures adopted have quasi-legal (state) regulatory character. However, soft law also means that in case of the non-observance of rules, the issue of enforcement arises. Formally, soft law does not belong to state regulation but represents a kind of private governance.

Another characteristic of soft law regards its relation to the possibility to submit rules to court. Courts have no obligation to observe and apply such rules similarly to binding, state regulation when issuing their rulings. Therefore, its impact is largely diminished due to the fact that its idiosyncratic enforcement and dispute-settlement mechanisms rely on the goodwill of the groups of interests and associations concerned. However, as soft law often takes the form of public codes of conduct or recommendations, the market expects a determined behaviour from these groups or associations. They should respect these codes. Consequently, members of these groups who would not take them into account would be excluded from their market or businesses or, in other words, be subject to de facto sanctioning. In addition, in the case of unilateral measures or declarations of international organizations or bodies, enforcement can be jeopardized, albeit that these measures may have an impact as far as the reputation of their addressees is concerned. For example, the G7-states exercise measures based on unilateralism, qualified as watchlisting or blacklisting, when they declare that certain countries are offshore financial centres and the said countries are not at all members of the group. In effect, this means that they cannot take position or complain before a court, although the declaration will damage their repute.[149]

Soft law can be considered as a pre-stage of state regulation. The concept of soft law is broadly used and appears under various forms. It is set by official bodies, although it does not represent state regulation as such. It is a kind of 'para-law', not least because it is also generally admitted that the principles of law can be applied

---

[148] http://www.oecd.org/document/28/0,3343,en_2649_34889_2397532_1_1_1_1,00.html (last visited 14 December 2009); Chapter 3, point 2 Firm Own Regulation; A. Boyle, Soft Law in International Law-Making (2006) 141–158; J. J. Kirton, M. J. Trebilcock, Introduction: Hard Choices and Soft Law in Sustainable Global Governance (2004) 3–29; N. Bayne, Hard and Soft Law in International Institutions: Complements, Not Alternatives (2004), 336–352. See also A. Kern, R. Dhumale, J. Eatwell, Global governance of financial systems, The International Regulation of Systemic Risk (2006) 143–153, discussing the case of the Basel Committee, and Slaughter, supra note 89, 298–300, discussing the case of the World Bank.

[149] Baudenbacher, supra note 122, 29–30; Chapter 4, point 1 Fragmentation, 1.4 Institutional Transformation, 1.4.3 Epistemic Communities and Transnational Networks; see also: J. Black and D. Rouch, The development of the global markets as rule-makers: engagement and legitimacy (May 2008) 224; Koskenniemi, supra note 1, 248; De Minico, supra note 63, 183–211.

by analogy. Its function is to supplement the state legal order. As such, it does not have any 'contra legem' but only 'praeter legem' effect. Soft law is more a law of values and principles than a law of structures and rules. Here, soft law is considered as an umbrella concept and self-regulation could then represent a sub- or pre-form of soft law – also from an intertemporal point of view – when departing from the perspective of the concept of state law.[150] Moreover, it should be taken into account that hybrid forms can also be encountered. For instance, this is the case when associations enact private codes of conduct, but must submit these to an authority for approval. They are then binding for the members of the association concerned. In such cases, they can be classified as soft law.[151]

To summarize, self-regulatory measures can take different shapes according to needs, legal space, and institutional possibilities. Self-regulation can be either the result of a strategy or part of it. It can also represent a form of governance and be enforced in different ways. In the course of time, it is possible that self-regulation as a private voluntary form of regulation loses its significance or may no longer prove to be an adequate solution. It will be replaced by a state regulation. Thus, a shift from one form of regulation to another is possible. De facto, already existing norms are rendered coercive through the stamp of the state.[152]

3.4 State Intervention: From Self-regulation to State Regulation

State intervention is briefly discussed here as part of the conceptual chain of autonomous regulatory regimes and alternative forms of regulation and because the temporal aspects are also taken into account. It constitutes a loop in the chain. Between the appearance of medieval (or old) self-regulation and contemporary (or new) forms of often global self-regulation, states and international organizations have often adopted measures in the course of time and directly or indirectly influenced existing (old) self-regulatory solutions. On the contrary, this is (still) not the case with regard to (new) self-regulation produced by networks.

---

[150] D. Thürer, The Role of Soft Law in the Actual Process of European Integration (1990) 133; Thürer, supra note 147, 443 seq.; L. Senden, Soft Law, Self-regulation and Co-regulation in European Law, Where Do They Meet? (January 2005) http://www.ejcl.org/91/abs91-3.html (last visited 11 December 2009); De Minico, supra note 63, 183–211; Teubner, supra note 78, 16; O'Brien, supra note 147, 98–99.

[151] In a ruling, the Swiss Supreme Court denied the recognition of the Agreement on the Swiss banks' code of conduct with regard to the exercise of due diligence (CDB 03) of the Swiss Bankers Association as binding rules. It declared that this Code of due diligence represented an 'instrument of the ethical self-regulation.' Case 125 IV 139, 144, of 30 April 1999.

[152] Fischer-Lescano and Teubner, supra note 76, 1012–1014; J. Black, Decentring Regulation: Understanding the Role of Regulation and Self-Regulation in a 'Post-Regulatory' World (2001) 103–105; Baldwin and Cave, supra note 15, 76 seq.

From the perspective of the state, the following questions emerge: How is a self-regulatory system influenced by a state intervention? Which relationship exists between a self-regulatory solution and a state legislative regime? How can it develop and persist in a regulatory state?

This sequence focuses on the state framework surrounding self-regulation, that is, the link to state regulation (apart from soft law, as just discussed). Self-regulation and state regulation represent two different normative orders. One is dictated and legitimised by the democratic state. Its inherent characteristic is the authority of the state with regard to the rules it defines, and which are adopted democratically. That state order applies to all citizens. On the contrary, self-regulation is a private order. Self-regulatory rules are defined and adopted on a voluntary basis by the members of an association or SRO. They will be binding and directly applicable. They might be capable of being imposed on third parties, in particular those entering into contact with that order. They constitute close regimes, not least at the global level, but it is not excluded that these private codes become standards for a sector.[153]

Self-regulation can be linked to a state system in an informal way at first. A self-regulatory solution may be submitted to pressures exercised either by states or the general public or other groups of interests. Thus, the responsible SRO will work out self-regulatory rules which will be able to stand up to possible criticisms.

Another form of interaction between self-regulation and a state regulatory regime is based on delegation. As already discussed, the state determines the extent and form of the self-regulatory solution.[154]

Cases of state intervention thus occur by application of the principle of subsidiarity. Subsidiarity is a key issue with regard to state intervention. The principle of subsidiarity implies that a central or higher authority should perform only those tasks that cannot be effectively managed at a local or another level. Hence, states should only intervene when the use of other forms of action or regulation are unsatisfactory or inadequate or when their definition and application would represent a failure. The principle of subsidiarity concerns the policy of task allocation. A functional approach applies. While some tasks are traditionally considered to genuinely belong to the state, others are first exercised by private market participants. In fact, there is potential for self-regulatory solutions, but evidence of regulatory failures indicates that a state cannot completely abdicate its responsibilities when a regulatory problem requires a response from the government.[155] Then, self-regulation is limited territorially, and concerns local rather than global self-regulation.

---

[153] Sajó, supra note 138, 11.

[154] See above, point 1 Embedding Autonomous Regulatory Regimes, 1.1 Traditional State Approach, 1.1.2 State (Regulatory) Strategies, Self-regulation, and the case discussed in Chapter 3, point 4 Coercive Self-regulation, 4.1 Delegated Self-regulation.

[155] Harrison, Morgan, Verkuil, supra note 12, 494–496.

3.5 Non-state Orders: From State Regulation to Legal Pluralism

The concept of state regulation as the sole order is based on a monist representation of the legal order. It is centered on the state. However, as stated, a variety of regulatory regimes emerge from civil society, following a process of so-called ‘functional differentiation’. The world is made of a plurality of interacting regimes. These lead to a fragmentation and dispersion of the legal order and decentralization away from the state, that is, polycentricity. They oppose monolithic state power and there is increased devolution and autonomy for non-state, private organizations or associations. These regimes are also reflected within the idea of power sharing. Different rationales can explain this phenomenon. One is the fact that there is no general legislative body in the international world, but specialized, international organizations represented by states. New organizations can be created at any time. Another rationale is the result of the development of the law itself. This accompanies the increasing specialisation of parts of society and its autonomisation. However, state law, as already stated, is not adapted and flexible enough to produce adequate solutions at the global level. It is also insufficient to resolve in an abstract way potential conflicts that may arise, such as between economic and environmental regimes or between human rights and diplomatic immunity. Yet another rationale for these developments is the deepening complexity of society and also of the needs for technical specialisation.[156] Thus, civil society may be in a better position to develop (ad hoc) regulatory solutions finally leading to a plurality of regimes. According to Koskenniemi, such plurality can be compared to the fact that there also are different sovereignties. Each regime has its own characteristics and mode of functioning. It constitutes a body of standards and rules regarding a particular subject matter and a specialized, ‘self-contained’, or non-state regime. Koskenniemi observes that such regimes do not necessarily depart from the state legal order.[157]

On their side, associations add to legal pluralism. In that regard, the role of business enterprises should be mentioned. In particular, besides SROs, MNCs also influence the activities of the state, such as when state agreements are concluded. MNCs as non-governmental actors represented by businesses or business associations are powerful. They can largely determine the development of law through regional and international institutions and bring their expert knowledge into discussion. Their influence on outcomes may also be informal, through lobbying or

---

[156] Koskenniemi, supra note 1, 249; Fischer-Lescano and Teubner, supra note 76, 1007–1008, with reference to Luhmann.

[157] Koskenniemi, supra note 1, 10–11, with reference to W. C. Jenks, The Conflict of Law-Making Treaties (1953) 403, in relation to the fragmentation of international law, and 247–249. See also: Conclusions of the work of the Study Group on the Fragmentation of International Law: Difficulties arising from the Diversification and Expansion of International Law, United Nations, 2006, n 11.

increased public pressure.[158] For example, the conclusion of bilateral and international agreements is very often motivated by economic rationales, such as the conclusion of the Paris Convention to the Agreement on Trade-Related Aspects of Intellectual Property Rights or the Berne Convention for the Protection of Literary and Artistic Works. Such agreements were not only motivated by the holder of a trademark right first, but rather commercial interests played a determining role.[159]

Thus, legal pluralism flourishes. As already discussed, its sources are manifold. In relation to the state, the resulting fragmentation can be caused through conflicting interpretations of general law. It can occur through the emergence of special statute as an exception to general law or it can represent a differentiation between types of special statute. Some note that there is an erosion of the state, which resides in the production processes, commercial dealings, and the unknown future of science.[160] The conceptual bonds between statute and government are loosened. States adopt an attitude of admitting or supporting hybrid, non-state or alternative regulatory measures in the form of plural, heterogeneous, intersecting normative orders.[161]

These non-state orders or 'regimes' can be conceptualized as follows:

> A manner, method, or system of rule or government; a system or institution having widespread influence or prevalence. Now freq. applied disparagingly to a particular government or administration.
>
> ...
>
> The set of conditions under which a system occurs or is maintained.[162]

or:

> 'sets of implicit or explicit principles, norms, rules, and decision-making procedures around which actors' expectations converge in a given area of international relations.'[163]

Further, the term 'regulatory regime' can be understood as

---

158 K. Nowrot, Legal Consequences of Globalization: The Status of Non-Governmental Organizations Under International Law (1999) 589–601.

159 Berne Convention for the Protection of Literary and Artistic Works of 9 September, 1886, Paris Act of 24 July 1971, as amended on 28 September 1979; Baudenbacher, supra note 122, 12–14.

160 Sajó, supra note 138, 11; K.-H. Ladeur, Towards a Legal Theory of Supranationality – The Viability of the Network Concept (March 1997) 33–54; see also: H. M. Riemer, Nicht Staatliche Normensysteme und andere Gesetze und ihr Verhältnis zum System der staatlichen Rechtsnormen – ein Überblick (2007) 114–122.

161 Koskenniemi, supra note 1, 30 et seqq.; Roberts, supra note 135, 12.

162 The Oxford English Dictionary, Volume XIII (1991) 508.

163 S. D. Krasner, Structural causes and regime consequences: regimes as intervening variables (Spring, 1982) 186; S. D. Krasner, International Regimes (1983) 2; S. Haggard and B. A. Simmons, Theories of International Regimes (Summer 1987) 493–496; Slaughter and Zaring, supra note 88, 214; D. Zaring, International Law by Other Means: The Twilight Existence of International Financial Regulatory Organizations (1998) 309–310; R. O. Keohane, The Demand for International Regimes (1983) 141, 151.

> 'the set of interrelated units which are engaged in joint problem solving to address a particular goal, its boundaries are defined by the definition of the problem being addressed, and it has some continuity over time'.[164]

While the first two definitions are broad, the third one is more restrictive, limiting the concept of regime only to a specific matter. In practice, that concept can apply to numerous circumstances. The proliferation of regimes raises the issue of the development of a theory of legal pluralism. These regimes constitute an institutional zone. In particular, they characterize the concept of pluralism and lead to decentralization,[165] the perception of epistemic communities, and transnational networks offering workable solutions to issues that matter to the parties involved, for instance technical standardization, professional rule production, intra-organizational regulation in multinational enterprises, contracting, and arbitration.[166] A theory of legal pluralism disregards an order based on state legal regimes and centred on the state, not least because these regimes ignore other, third regimes and the interrelationships between state law and the laws of other communities or networks. Legal pluralism can encompass all sorts of regulatory orders and recognizes them as operating under the label of regulation. There is a vast web of regulation or 'regulation in many rooms'.[167] According to Teubner, legal pluralism has a dynamic character, it can be defined as representing a multiplicity of diverse communicative processes in a given societal field that observes social action under the binary communicative code of legal and illegal. It no longer represents a set of conflicting societal norms.[168] These non-state orders represent specialized and autonomous spheres of action and interactions producing their own standards and rules. There may be a plethora of instruments tailored to situations to which they apply. While standards and rules may cover spheres of life that are traditionally classified as public, they do not represent positive law. The nature of these orders is not uniform. It will differ depending on the circumstances of a concrete case. They will not qualify as 'self-contained' regimes either, as discussed by Koskenniemi.[169]

---

164 J. Black, The decentred regulatory state? (2007) 263, with reference to C. Hood, H. Rothstein and R. Baldwin, The Government of Risk (2001) 9–17.

165 Black, supra note 152, 146. For a basic discussion of legal pluralism, see de Sousa Santos, supra note 1, 114 et seq.; also Sassen, supra note 17, 242–247; Koskenniemi, supra note 135, 1 et seqq.; Merry, supra note 135, 869–896; Griffiths, supra note 135, 1–55, according to whom legal pluralism just corresponds to a number of systems of 'social control'. Fischer-Lescano and Teubner, supra note 2, 41–43; Burke-White, supra note 135, 963–979.

166 G. Teubner, Foreword: Legal Regimes of Global Non-state Actors (2006) xiii.

167 B. Z. Tamanaha, A Non-Essentialist Version of Legal Pluralism (June 2000) 298; Koskenniemi, supra note 135, 1 et seqq.; Merry, supra note 135, 869–896; Griffiths, supra note 135, 1–55; Fischer-Lescano and Teubner, supra note 2, 41–43; Burke-White, supra note 135, 963–979.

168 The use of the concept of 'the binary code of legal and illegal' is based on N. Luhmann, The Coding of the Legal System, European Yearbook in the Sociology of Law, 1991/92, 145–146; Teubner, supra note 78, 14; Tamanaha, supra note 167, 306–307; Roberts, supra note 135, No 1, 19.

169 Koskenniemi, supra note 1, 10–11; Slaughter and Zaring, supra note 88, 215–218. On self-contained regimes, see also Chapter 3, point 5.

3.6 *Transnational Networks: From Legal Pluralism to Autonomous Regulatory Regimes*

Pluralism also encompasses non-state orders. The emergence of these orders is based on an epistemic value agreement among interested individuals, their members or groups. They operate primarily as epistemic communities. The term 'epistemic communities' is used as a comprehensive concept. Haas first defined this term:

> Epistemic communities are networks 'of professionals with recognized expertise and competence in a particular domain and an authoritative claim to policy-relevant knowledge within that domain or issue-area.'

They have a shared set of normative and principled beliefs, shared causal beliefs, shared notions of validity, and a common policy enterprise.[170] Another definition comes from Braithwaite and Drahos:

> Epistemic communities of actors: Large audiences of state, business and NGO actors who meet sporadically and share a common regulatory discourse based on shared knowledge, sometimes technical knowledge requiring professional training.[171]

Formally, epistemic communities also constitute the basis for further concretisations in the form of networks. In the course of time, these communities are involved in a process of specification as decisions-takers and as groups of experts within the public sphere. Networks can be understood as linked to this transformation process (and directed towards concretisation) and as focussed on the interests represented. They can be defined as:

> A piece of work having the form or construction of a net; a collection or arrangement (of some thing or things) resembling a net. [. . .]
>
> An interconnected chain or system of immaterial things. ... Also, a representation of interconnected events, processes, etc., used in the study of work efficiency. [. . .]
>
> An interconnected group of people; an organization.[172]

---

170 P. M. Haas, Introduction: epistemic communities and international policy coordination (Winter 1992) 3. See also: Slaughter and Zaring, supra note 88, 214–215; Braithwaite and Drahos, supra note 2, 501–504, with reference to Haas, they cite: 'Communities which 'are loose collections of knowledge-based experts who share certain attitudes and values and substantive knowledge, as well as ways of thinking about how to use that knowledge.', 501. For an example of a lack of value agreement and consequently little networking in the context of European privacy regulators, see F. Bignami, Transgovernmental Networks vs. Democracy: The Case of the European Information Privacy Network (2005), as cited by Sajó, supra note 138, 20.

171 Braithwaite and Drahos, supra note 2, 24. 'Epistemics is the scientific theory of study of the processes of knowledge', The Oxford English Dictionary, Volume V (1991) 338. On his side Giddens defines 'expert systems' as: 'systems of technical accomplishment or professional expertise that organise large areas of the material and social environments in which we live today.', Giddens, supra note 137, 27.

172 Oxford English Dictionary, Volume X (1991) 345–346.

or also as defined by Slaughter and Zaring:

> informal institutions linking actors across national boundaries and carrying on various aspects of global governance in new and informal ways.[173]

Hence, networks constitute a narrower notion of epistemic communities. They correspond to more elaborated and formalized entities. Both epistemic communities and self-governing networks are typical of the process of globalization. They travel well at the transnational level. They emerge spontaneously and can be governmental or private. A common feature is their basis, which is rooted in the collaboration among their members or interested groups and their inherent compliance with the issues they deal with.[174] Although networks may represent a higher grade of formalization than epistemic communities, both terms can also be used as synonyms. Contrary to state hierarchical structures, they are not monitored by a (mother) organization. They embody informal horizontal relationships. They add to the decentralization of regulation and contribute to the dismantling of the state. Regulatory networks also serve as the unifying framework for technical committees, epistemic communities, or webs of influence, for example in relation to the public sphere or the regulation of specialized matters, such as technology. They also are in a position to assume governmental decision-making functions.[175]

Besides such fundamental epistemic agreement among participants, the pursuance of mutual interests based on common principles is essential although it is not necessary to concur on all matters. However, like-minded participants in an epistemic community or group have a positive influence on the quality and worthiness of their network, while differences of opinion between the participants may risk undermining its integrity and credibility.[176] Participants should be interested in both working and exchanging ideas among each other and also with other networks. They act as responsible entities. The advantages they expect to gain from participating in a network work as a motivating, cohesive force. On the other side, they are

---

173 Slaughter and Zaring, supra note 88, 215.

In fact, a huge literature about networks exists. Originally, the concept was first developed in sociology and anthropology. Schulte Beerbühl, Vögele, supra note 86, 14, with further references.

174 Slaughter and Zaring, supra note 88, 215.

175 See Sajó, supra note 138, 2–3 and 5, with reference to K. Raustiala's definition of 'transgovernmental networks' as follows: 'Transgovernmentality refers to the involvement of specialized domestic officials who directly interact with each other, often with minimal supervision by foreign ministries. They are 'networks' because this cooperation is based on loosely-structured, peer-to-peer ties developed through frequent interaction rather than formal negotiation. Thus defined, the phrase 'transgovernmental networks' captures a strikingly wide array of contemporary cooperation', K. Raustiala, supra note 89, point I. Introduction, with further references.

176 Sajó, supra note 138, 1 et seq. 19–20; G. Majone, The European Commission: The Limits of Centralization and the Perils of Parliamentarization (July 2002) 383–388; A.-M. Slaughter, A New World Order (2004) 169; B. Hunt, The Timid Corporation, Why Business is Terrified of Taking Risk (2003) 125. See also the discussion in relation to global administrative law: B. Kingsbury, N. Kirsch, & R. B. Stewart, The Emergence of Global Administrative Law (Summer/Autumn 2005) 15–61, 21.

also dependent on each other to some degree, not least due to this situation.[177] Hence, for a transnational (regulatory) network to function properly, several conditions have to be satisfied besides the definition of common rules, communication lines, business principles, a high level of professionalism, a widely-shared (regulatory) philosophy, and a good deal of mutual trust. These conditions may be difficult to fulfil, but the very existence of a network should provide an environment favourable to the development of the requisite properties.[178]

Epistemic communities constituted by state representatives and transgovernmental networks can be encountered among national authorities within an area, for example in the course of their participation in the activities of international organizations. They can represent the state in working groups of these organizations, task forces or committees and participate in the formulation of policies and rules as well as exercise their influence. They may also take the initiative to constitute autonomous committees together, or in relation, with other networks. The emergence of these networks may be initiated by international organizations themselves, based on the votes of their members. In this case, these organizations will possess ultimate decision-making powers.[179]

In relation to globalization, the emergence of epistemic communities and transnational networks and their respective development of activities represent a paradox. While the process of globalization may be compared to a process of centralization and unification of regulation at the global level, epistemic communities and transnational networks lead to a functional fragmentation and diversification of regulatory regimes and finally a dismantling of the state. Governance networks operate in the vacuum of the international setting to which the sovereign nation state has merely limited access.[180]

The good functioning of these self-organized networks and their sustainability leads to the emergence of non-state, autonomous regulatory regimes. Their formation and crystallisation is recognizable due to their persistence. Regulation by non-state ordering is beyond the control of public power. It is a new kind of order, which may represent a serious challenge to traditional state regulation and constitutionalism. It is detached from the state order. It applies either to sectors that are not regulated by the state, where global solutions are needed, or typically with regard to the process of globalization, as the case of financial services discussed in the next chapter shows. Moreover, such globalizing networks change the dynamics of shaping public and private spheres considerably. They are increasingly capable of determining what remains in the public sphere. From a political point of view, transnational networks challenge the monopoly that the state exercises through its

---

177 H. Willke, Systemtheorie III: Steuerungstheorie (1998) 112–121.

178 G. Majone, The New European Agencies: Regulation by Information (1997) 262–275; Majone, supra note 176, 382–383; G. Majone, Delegation of Regulatory Powers in a Mixed Polity (September 2002) 336.

179 Sajó, supra note 138, 5.

180 Teubner, supra note 78, 3–28; Sassen, supra note 17, 242–247; Black, supra note 152, 146; Braithwaite and Drahos, supra note 2, 501–504; Sajó, supra note 138, 11–12.

administrative machinery. According to Sajó, this process is representative for the role of governance, which leads to private and non-state actors or SROs exercising a decisive influence on the public opinion or who might even play a role as a kind of public authority instead of politically accountable government agencies.[181] Networks are capable of replacing state law with their own norms. In many respects, they are also able to determine what is 'private', enabling self-regulation to remain beyond the reach of state intervention. They give rise to a law without the state. They are orders which subsist beside the state order[182] and – it should be added – international coercive orders.

3.7 Networks as Regulatory Institutions: From Autonomous Regulatory Regimes to Meta-regulation

To seize autonomous, non-state regulatory regimes and include them in a general concept of regulation, these regimes are now linked to the debate on meta-regulation. Meta-regulation studies the interplay and interactions of state regulation and other forms of regulation. It includes various forms of normative ordering.[183]

Meta-regulation finds its roots in public policy issues. It represents a way to systematize regulatory policies. Moreover, meta-regulation is important and should be widely used. It also contributes to the possibility of empowering civil society or its institutions. With meta-regulation, it is possible to consider alternative regulatory regimes as distinctive regulatory regimes whereas the normative order is based on values recognized by interested groups, networks or society, which define the parameters to be reached.[184]

Focusing on the phenomenon of regulation in a broad sense, in particular the procedures of regulation, meta-regulation contributes to an understanding of regulation as a new institutional issue or subject of investigation and not merely as a tool employed by the state to implement policy issues. Regulation becomes an institution. The term 'institution' is conceived as:

> The giving of form or order to a thing; orderly arrangement; regulation. The established order by which anything is regulated; system; constitution. [...]

---

[181] Sajó, supra note 138, 2–3, 10, with further references, in particular to J. N. Rosenau; E.-O. Czempiel, eds, Governance without Government: Order and Change in World Politics (2000). See also R.A.W. Rhodes, Understanding Governance, Policy Networks, Governance, Reflexivity and Accountability (2001) 46, 51–53; Roberts, supra note 135, 1–24, who designates these orders as essentially negotiated orders at either the local or global level.

[182] Sajó, supra note 138, 10; Slaughter, supra note 176, 167–169; Sassen, supra note 17, 242–247; Rhodes, supra note 181, with a focus on the British situation.

[183] See Chapter 1, point 6 Meta-Regulation.

[184] Tamanaha, supra note 79, 133 et seqq.

> An established law, custom, usage, practice, organization, or other element in the political or social life of a people; a regulative principle or convention subservient to the needs of an organized community or the general ends of civilization.
>
> An establishment, organization, or association, instituted for the promotion of some object, esp. one of public or general utility, religious, charitable, educational, etc. [...] as a literary reformatory, mission, or the like; as a literary and philosophical institution, a deaf and dumb institution, [...][185]

Institution can also be defined as:

> An institution is a system of rules, beliefs, norms, and organizations that together generate a regularity of (social) behavior.[186]

and in the field of international relations, most scholars have come to regard international institutions as sets of rules meant to govern international behavior or:

> sets of rules that stipulate the ways in which states should cooperate and compete with each other.[187]

With the substantiation of regulation, the phenomenon of regulation is explored in relation to itself, thus institutionalized as such. Processes and methods different from those used for state regulation are part of the discussion. The traditional concept of state regulation is enlarged. Regulation as an institution encompasses the notion of a form of organizing a regulatory space. Heuristically, it could be explained by the fact that alternative regimes form where the state fails. Various authors have already tried to delineate this development. For De Sousa Santos, there is a changing nature of state power in that the state is seen as 'expanding in the form of civil society', involving a 'dislocation of power from formal institutions to informal networks'. In Teubner's approach to reflexive law, law becomes 'a system for the co-ordination of action within and between semi-autonomous social sub-systems.' Hence, the state adopts more the function of 'steering rather than rowing.'[188]

The institutionalization of regulation through the path of meta-regulation, which includes other, alternative forms of regulation in the concept of regulation, is determined by a trend towards efficiency and interest maximization. This trend prevails in the debate on normative validity of alternative forms of regulation. The implementation of regulatory solutions is considered justified as long as it is efficient. Such solutions are generated by professional networks, which dispose of expert knowledge and are better positioned to take regulatory measures.

---

185 Oxford English Dictionary, Volume VII (1991) 1046–1047.

186 A. Greif, Institutions and the Path to the Modern Economy, Lessons from Medieval Trade (2006) 30.

187 B. A. Simmons and L. L. Martin, International Organizations and Institutions (2002) 194, with reference to J. J. Mearsheimer. The False Promise of International Institutions (1994/95) 5–49. See also W. W. Powell and P. J. DiMaggio, The New Institutionalism in Organizational Analysis (1991), 1–38.

188 As cited by Roberts, supra note 135, 4–5; Braithwaite and Parker, supra note 113, 288; see also: W. W. Powell, Expanding the Scope of Institutional Analysis (1991) 183–203.

Public interest and public power are influenced by competing networks, which should provide for fairness, accountability, and responsiveness.[189]

The emergence of epistemic communities and the process of their formalization towards networks, associations, or self-regulatory organizations enacting their own rules on an autonomous basis lead to the constitution of new (legal) institutions. This institution-building process takes place on a case by case basis, independently from the existing national and international legal system and institutional structures. Institutions are characterized by their individuality and may enter into conflict with existing legal rules and practices. At the same time, governance is becoming more prominent to the detriment of government. Following the erosion of the state institution, it forms itself as a cohesive force. Instead of politically accountable government agencies, private actors exercise public authority or at least have a decisive influence on public determination. Networks represent a mechanism of global governance.[190] However, contrary to the state, they do not have corresponding powers to ensure the implementation of the order.

3.8 *Summary of Sequences*

The institutional structure of autonomous regulatory regimes, that is, alternative forms of regulation, non-state and self-regulatory regimes has been discussed in terms of a sequential approach. Starting out from the theory of interest, a logical evolution of the institutional development can be drawn. It can be compared to a process of becoming conscious of issues or interests by individuals to the emergence of collectivities subsequently formalized as associations. Autonomous regulatory regimes are constituted and rule for their members. They constitute non-state orders that lead to legal pluralism. The concept takes the global dimension into account. Figure 2.2 illustrates such institutionalization:

4 Conclusion

This chapter has examined various aspects of the theoretical foundations of regulation as determined by autonomous regulatory regimes. First, this form of regulation was placed in relation to the traditional frame of state regulation. Secondly, the perspective was broadened, employing the decentred approach to regulation and including the civil society approach. Thirdly, the evolutive view of regulation was

[189] Sajó, supra note 138, 20–21; also Sassen, supra note 17, 196–197.

[190] Sajó, supra note 138, 10; Slaughter, supra note 176, 167–169; Sassen, supra note 17, 242–247; Rhodes, supra note 181, with a focus on the British situation, and 46–60, discussing different uses of governance, that is, in relation to networks, 51–52.

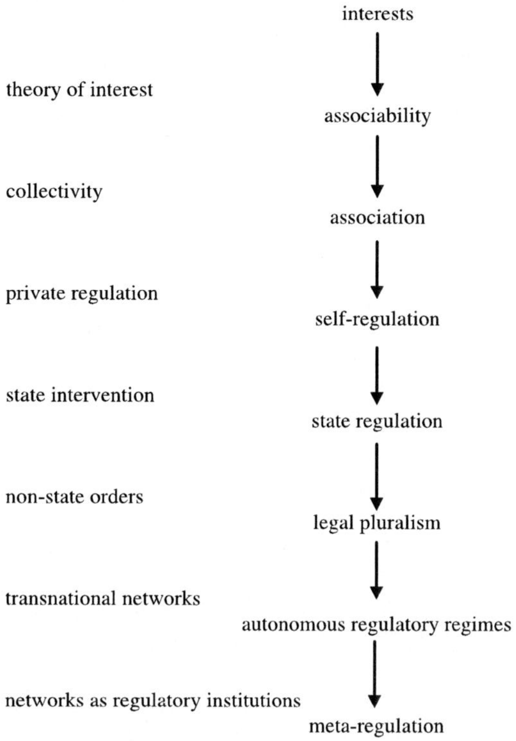

Fig. 2.2 Process of conversion of the institutional structure[191]

discussed under its temporal as well as its sectoral aspects. Finally, the institutional structure was focused on an attempt to comprehend the basis of the emergence of autonomous regulatory regimes. A sequential approach was applied, including interest, associability, association, private autonomous regimes, state regulation, legal pluralism, alternative forms of regulation, and meta-regulation.

[191] In comparison, Chapter 1, point 2.1 Regulatory Cycle, described the development of regulation focusing on and illustrating the role and steps of involvement of the state in regulatory matters.

Chapter 3
Case Studies

Abstract Chapter 3 is devoted to the identification of case studies or concrete examples representing alternative forms of regulation, non-state, hybrid, or private autonomous regimes. This chapter aims to provide an overview of possible forms of regulatory governance with examples taken mainly from the field of finance. Financial markets have always made extensive use of alternative and also private regulatory solutions. It distinguishes the following categories of cases: Self-regulation, a firm's own regulation, co-regulation, coercive self-regulation, self-contained regimes, and global networks. The emergence, the underlying institutional arrangements, and the characteristics of the case studies chosen are studied. Their contest should illustrate the theoretical foundations of the previous chapter and enrich the analysis undertaken in the next one.

The first two chapters have discussed the framework of regulation and an approach possibly leading to the emergence of autonomous regulatory regimes. The goal of this chapter is to identify and explore possible typologies of alternative forms of regulation or autonomous, non-state regulatory regimes based on concrete cases, each representing another form of regulatory governance. This is important with regard to the numerous regulatory arrangements that can be encountered, although the cases discussed are illustrative only and it is not purported to offer a complete account of possible regulatory arrangements. Diverse institutional structures are recognized, classified, and examined, but there is a focus on regimes of standards and rules situated on the border, periphery, or beyond regimes of state regulation. Such regimes may also formally be co-opted by the state or constitute themselves within the state regulatory framework. The classification as a typology should not be understood to represent a hierarchy. Based on the use of typologies, a simplified description of each case considered is possible. The contest of the case studies chosen should serve to illustrate the theoretical foundations of the previous chapter and enrich the analysis undertaken in the next one.

Methodologically, the focus is placed on selected aspects which are relevant with regard to the purpose of this study. Discussion concentrates on the historical development, underlying institutional arrangements, and main characteristics of the concrete cases chosen. These aspects are briefly examined. They are most adequate to understand the emergence and subsistence of the regimes. By contrast, discussion

M. Senn, *Non-State Regulatory Regimes*,
DOI 10.1007/978-3-642-14974-0_4, © Springer-Verlag Berlin Heidelberg 2011

does not focus on the specific regulatory techniques and tools; these may be written norms (legal and non-legal) and accompanying sanctions, economic or market-based instruments, social norms and corresponding sanctions, technologies and processes. Neither does it deal with questions of substantive law, but rather with the institutional and procedural aspects of the cases discussed. This contextual exclusion does not undermine the usefulness of the typologies adopted.[1]

The following typologies are identified: self-regulation, firm own regulation or enforced self-regulation, co-regulation, coercive self-regulation, self-contained regimes, and global networks. Several rationales may justify the choice of these typologies. First, they allow for covering and classifying various constellations of cases and mapping their institutional arrangements. Second, they take into account that there are multiple levels of state or also non-state involvement in reality and that the degree of statutory underpinning varies from case to case. In the UK a representative range of 54 schemes has been identified regarding government involvement in alternatives to state regulation in a study published in the year 2000.[2] While there is presumably no state participation in the case of a private autonomous regime, the case of coercive regulation is primarily determined by the state. Third, the choice of cases also results from an evaluation of already discussed forms of regulation in the literature.[3] Finally, the regimes discussed correspond to distinctive systems of interest representation.

1 Self-regulation

Self-regulation can embody various types of private authority. There is no participation of the state in the case of (pure) self-regulation. As a form of regulation based on the voluntariness of private market participants constituting private autonomous regimes, it applies to various circumstances in practice. It is typically encountered in relation to the regulation of new, often technological sectors. Nowadays, there is a proliferation of specialized types of private authority operating on a self-regulatory basis. They can play a role as important governance mechanisms whose authority is not entered by the state. There are multiple institutions that

---

[1] On the basic issue of how regulation can be exercised, see R. Baldwin and M. Cave, Understanding Regulation – Theory, Strategy, and Practice (1999); J. Black, Critical Reflections on Regulation (January 2002) 1–2.

[2] See: Alternatives to State Regulation, Better Regulation Task Force, July 2000, 6.

[3] For a discussion of other models, see, for instance, M. Priest, The Privatization of Regulation: Five Models of Self-Regulation (1997–1998) 233 et seqq., 239–240; or the model of 'enforced self-regulation' as developed by I. Ayres and J. Braithwaite, Responsive Regulation, Transcending the Deregulation Debate (1995); J. J. Boddewyn, Advertising self-regulation: organization structures in Belgium, Canada, France and the United Kingdom (1985) 30–43; P. S. Berman, The Globalization of Jurisdiction (2002) 311–529; A. Fischer-Lescano and G. Teubner, Regime-Kollisionen, Zur Fragmentierung des globalen Rechts (2006).

organize and ensure their own normative order. From a historical point of view, these regimes have often been the precursor of future state regulation. Sectors which were first solely regulated by the private economy have subsequently been regulated by the state, sometimes as the result of a secular evolution.[4] However, as the disparate cases discussed hereinafter indicate, it can be postulated, that pure forms of self-regulation hardly exist in reality. Most are hybrid forms, which can appear under various constellations.

The following case studies are briefly discussed hereinafter: commercial arbitration, credit rating agencies and voluntary codes of conduct.

1.1 Commercial Arbitration

1.1.1 Historical Aspects

Commercial arbitration corresponds to a private regulatory regime first constituted by an older system of regulation expanding into new economic sectors. It is part of the lex mercatoria or law merchant, whose roots lie in customary merchant practices. Their archetype can be traced back to the law of eleventh century traders and businessmen. Merchant and guild law first assumed the form of usances and influential codes of conduct. Such law formed a body of merchant customs encountered in important trading centres throughout Europe, such as the 'Custom Book of Milan' of 1216. Already at that time, the lex mercatoria was a spectacular example of transnational private ordering. The rules developed on a purely private basis and official rules only emerged over time.[5] The private lex mercatoria was then often transposed into official rules. One example is the French 'Ordonnance de Commerce' of 1673, which – contrary to a general assumption – was not dictated by the French Minister Colbert or by the Lawyer Savary. Rather, it merely transposed into official rules the existing lex mercatoria and customary merchant practices, applicable in Paris and Marseille at that time. This particular lex mercatoria had been modeled on the merchant practices of medieval Northern Italian cities.[6] Nowadays, the substantive part of the lex mercatoria is represented by codes together with the general conditions of business, commercial, or trade activities. It may take the form of agreements with choice of law or other standardized clauses, such as – for instance – in the documentation of the International Swaps and Derivatives Association

---

[4] S. Sassen, Territory, Authority, Rights, From Medieval to Global Assemblages (2006) 242–246 and 265–268.

[5] J. Braithwaite and P. Drahos, Global Business Regulation (2000) 46, 53; A. Black, Guild & State, European Political Thought from the Twelfth Century to the Present (2003) 14–16, 25–26, 36–38, 55–56.

[6] B. Straccha, De mercatura seu mercatore (1575), as cited by P. Böckli, Neun Regeln der 'Best Practice' für den Rückkauf nichtkotierter eigener Aktien (2001) 575–576.

(ISDA).[7] The 'contrat sans loi' may also refer to the lex mercatoria and then be adjudicated according to the rules of international private law.[8]

Arbitration concerns the procedural aspect of the lex mercatoria. The enforcement of the lex mercatoria is guaranteed by designated arbitral courts. In the course of time, arbitration has become increasingly common and continues to develop as a method of dispute resolution by private justice in the law of business transactions.[9] It represents a private regulatory form of rule enforcement taking place among private parties. Arbitrage services are offered by private agents or private tribunals. Nowadays, arbitration is largely a global phenomenon. The growing importance of this regime is marked by the increasing number of arbitration centres and arbitrators that have taken place since the 1990s. While there were 120 centres in 1991 and seven more in 1993, there were about 1,000 arbitrators in 1990 and twice as many in 1992. Various specialized institutions offer arbitrage services, including the International Chamber of Commerce in Paris (ICC), the London Court of International Commercial Arbitration, or the World Bank's International Center for the Settlement of Investment Disputes.[10] For instance, the goal of the ICC is to boost international trade and investments in the free transfer of goods and services as well as the free movement of capital. It has its own ICC International Court of Arbitration, which is experiencing increasing demand. While its arbitration consisted of 3,000 cases between 1923 and 1976, the Court has received new cases at a rate of more than 500 a year since 1999.[11]

1.1.2 Institutional Arrangements

Although some institutions symbolize the existence of an arbitral system, there is no rule as such defining what arbitration is and how it should be organized. Forms of arbitration are not limited as long as private parties agree to submit to the rulings of designated third-party judges. The private agents or tribunals offering arbitrage services as such constitute an institutional zone. The modern development of arbitration as a quasi self-regulatory body of rules is mainly a consequence of the globalization of the economy. In case of conflicts relating to the enforcement of

---

7 Braithwaite and Drahos, supra note 5, 542.

8 I. Schwander, Der contrat sans loi und das nichtstaatliche Recht im Internationalen Privatrecht (2006) 117–134.

9 L. R. Nottage, The Procedural Lex Mercatoria: The Past, Present and Future of International Commercial Arbitration (December 2006); M. Senn, Decentralisation of Economic Law – An Oxymoron?, in: Journal of Corporate Law Studies, no 2, October 2005, 435–437; H. G. Gharavi, The proper scope of arbitration in European Community competition law (Winter 1996) 185, 185–188; C. Baudenbacher and I. Higgins, Decentralisation of EC competition law enforcement and arbitration (Winter 2002) 1, 2–3.

10 Sassen, supra note 4, 242–247.

11 http://www.iccwbo.org/home/menu_what_is_icc.asp (last visited 21 November 2009); Braithwaite and Drahos, supra note 5, 492.

contractual agreements or other disputes, international arbitration is becoming even more important. Business relationships and exchanges across national borders, such as transnational mergers and acquisitions, are steadily increasing, regularly calling for ad-hoc solutions.[12] In this regard, arbitration is a flexible instrument, conducive to working out solutions for individual cases. It can be ideally adapted to the needs of private actors within the economy.

As a mechanism of dispute resolution, arbitration applies to private parties. These design and recognize their arbitrators themselves, and the latter will act as private judges and issue judgments based on negotiations with the parties concerned. In a broad sense, arbitration can include methods of arbitrage controlled by courts. It can be a process parallel to court proceedings or include various courts and out-of-court mechanisms such as mediation. A further possibility is the adoption of the rules of the UN Commission on International Trade Law (UNCITRAL), whose goal is to reduce or remove obstacles to the flow of international trade due to disparities in national laws.[13]

Beside the use of arbitration services in relation to business transactions, arbitration also plays an important role in other sectors. In European Union competition law, for instance, the decentralised enforcement of rules introduced with the Regulation of 2002[14] lets room for arbitration proceedings.[15] It also has a long tradition in relation to maritime and commodity disputes. It appears as an alternative form of regulation, that is, an independent and autonomous domain of regulation for conflict resolution employing forums other than courts. Within that regime, professional organizations like the ICC enjoy a strong position of power based on tradition, experience, and international repute and influence. It articulates norms and guidelines for its members to be used for arbitral matters.[16]

Arbitration leads to decentring with regard to the state. It is a private autonomous regulatory regime existing beyond territorial borders, and meeting the needs of the actors concerned. Hence, the state has no direct influence on these developments. This is not least due to the fact that the enforcement of state regulation may be a rigid and perhaps less efficient process not always adapted to commercial needs. It does not offer sufficient room for negotiations. Arbitrage represents an alternative to a national or supra-national legal regime. Moreover, it should be noticed that together with the increasing number of arbitration centres and arbitrators there is a sharpening of competition among them, necessitating even more efficient operation.

---

[12] Sassen, supra note 4, 245; H.-J. Mertens, Lex Mercatoria: A Self-applying System Beyond National Law? (2006) 31–35.

[13] http://www.uncitral.org/uncitral/en/about/origin.html (last visited 21 November 2009); Sassen, supra note 4, 243–244.

[14] Council Regulation (EC) No 1/2003 of 16 December 2002 on the implementation of the rules on competition laid down in articles 81 and 82 of the Treaty; OJ L 1/1, 04/01/2003, 1–25.

[15] Baudenbacher and Higgins, supra note 9, 15–17; Gharavi, supra note 9, 197–199; see also: Mertens, supra note 12, 39–40.

[16] Sassen, supra note 4, 243–245.

However, the state plays an institutional role to the extent that it supports private arbitration. This can occur by way of enforcement or by way of preventing the judicial system from being used as means of attacking an agreement to arbitrate and be bound by the result. State rules issued in that regard are governed by the Convention on the Recognition and Enforcement of Foreign Arbitral Awards, or New York Convention, adopted by the United Nations in 1958 and also take the Washington Convention relating to the settlement of investment disputes between states and citizens of other countries of 1965 into account.[17]

1.1.3 Characteristics

Arbitration consists of broad principles, whose application changes from case to case. Its normative substance is extremely indeterminate. As a form of regulation pertaining to the lex mercatoria, 'It is more a law of values and principles than a law of structures and rules.'[18] It is an economic regulation in pursuit of facilitating trade relationships.

Commercial arbitration is based solely on the voluntariness of the parties concerned. Arbitral regimes are based exclusively on the initiative of private actors. These choose their preferred centres, that is, those best meeting their needs. Thus, arbitration is orientated towards the interests of firms seeking international arbitration. It is a private justice system that is driven by private business interests. It operates in relative insulation from the state or, at the global level, from official international politics and international public law.[19] It represents a specific form of self-regulation. In particular, the assistance mechanisms, which have been introduced for national authorities and courts, have no equivalent with respect to arbitrators. Arbitrators are private actors. They are free from the constraints under which other authorities operate. They are not obliged to take precedents into account and are not concerned with the development of a coherent case law. Their approach is the same, irrespective of the area of law concerned. They are guided by the chances that the parties will reach an agreement in order to resolve a problem. They may also apply the specific rules designed by parties and ignore other national or supra-national rules.[20] This allows the parties to a dispute

---

[17] In Switzerland, for instance, the law applicable to arbitration belongs to the Federal Act on Private International Law while the UK produced the UK Arbitration Act 1996.

[18] G. Teubner, Global Bukowina: Legal Pluralism in the World Society (2006) 21, with further references; Mertens, supra note 12, 35–39. On the concept of principle, see Chapter 4, point 2 Standardization, 2.3 Gradual Transformation, 2.3.1 From Standards to Rules.

[19] A. Giddens, The Consequences of Modernity (1990) 70–78.

[20] A. Redfern and M. Hunter, Law and Practice of International Commercial Arbitration (1999); C. Hopfe, The Rise of International Commercial Arbitration and the Demise of Judicial Recourse: Whatever Happened to 'Public Policy'? (1998) 263; G. Born, International commercial arbitration in the United States: commentary and materials (1994); E. Cotran and A. Amissah, eds, Arbitration in Africa (1996); M. Pryles, Dispute Resolution in Asia, Hague (2002); J. Paulsson, International

to avoid being forced to submit the case to the courts of the other and maintain the secrecy of the process. They can make use of the expertise and technical knowledge of the members of arbitrage tribunals. These arbitrators are professionals specialized in their field and in a position to judge which measures and solutions are reasonable and best adapted to a concrete case. However, although arbitrators may be able to deal with complex issues in relation to the application of the rules, they are not specialized in dealing with public policy issues. Hence, there may be a risk that the interests of third parties and the public will not be sufficiently taken into account.

1.2 Credit Rating Agencies[21]

1.2.1 Historical Aspects

Credit rating agencies (CRAs) produce assessments providing an indication of the level of the credit or financial standing of a debtor or third companies, of issues, bond issues or of determined transactions regarding their capability to fulfil their commitments timely towards creditors. The history of rating agencies is the history of a few companies specialized in the establishment and provision of ratings: Standard & Poor's, that is, H.V. Poor's, published its first analysis in 1860. It was the precursor of modern stock reporting and analysis. The Standard Statistics Bureau was founded in 1906. Its role was to provide previously unavailable financial information on US companies. In 1916, it began to assign debt ratings to corporate bonds. It continued to develop its activities and in 1941 Poor's Publishing merged with Standard Statistics to form Standard & Poor's Corporation (S&P). In 1966, the company was acquired by The McGraw-Hill Companies, Inc.[22]

Moody's Investors Service was incorporated in 1914. It was first the company of John Moody, who published his inaugural Moody's Manual of Industrial and Miscellaneous Securities in 1900. It provided information and statistics on stocks and bonds of various bodies. In 1909, John Moodys returned to the market, but instead of collecting information on companies, he offered investors an analysis of securities values. Already in 1913, 'Moody's ratings' were a factor in the bond market. In 1924, Moody's ratings covered nearly the entire US bond market.

Handbook on Commercial Arbitration; A. J. van den Berg, The New York Arbitration Convention of 1958 (1994); Guide to ICC arbitration (1994); M. Rubino-Sammartano, International Arbitration Law and Practice (2001).

[21] Credit rating agencies have been chosen as a case study, because they first represented a strong case of self-regulation. However, as will be discussed, they have been gradually absorbed into state and international regulation.

[22] http://www.standardandpoors.com/about-sp/timeline/en/us/ (last visited 21 November 2009).

The activities of Moody's were extended to new products in the 1970s. It is now one of the leading rating agencies worldwide.[23]

Fitch Ratings was founded in 1913. It began its activities as a publisher of financial statistics. In 1924, it introduced its own nomenclature to meet the growing demand for independent analysis of financial securities. Since 1989, it has experienced dramatic growth and in the course of the 1990s, it grew in all areas and provided high quality analysis and research. It merged with IBCA Limited in 1997 and other companies in 2000. In 2006, it expanded its activities to the credit derivatives market. Fitch Ratings is now a global, full-service rating agency.[24]

The Canadian DBRS was founded in 1976. It is a full-service rating agency, privately owned and operated without affiliation to any financial institution. It has standing as a leading provider of timely, comprehensive, indepth credit analysis to the world's capital markets not least with regard to its extensive coverage of securitizations and structured finance transactions. It also offers industry analysis, rating reports, and ratings indices for issuers and investors throughout the world.[25]

Beside these well-known agencies operating both at the national and international level, a whole range of rating agencies have emerged in the course of time. They often cover small, specialized markets.

1.2.2 Institutional Arrangements

Rating agencies are specialized in the assessment and evaluation of issuers, issues, or other financial products. They are free in the assessment of the information they receive from the rated entities. However, their ratings will not be more reliable than the underlying information.[26]

From an institutional point of view, the global market for rating agencies first presented a particular situation. These agencies did not qualify as regulated entities by the state. What added to the peculiar situation of rating agencies is that their assessments were used by authorities to fulfil their supervisory duties, that is, assess the financial situation of entities they had licensed. In other words, they played a role as 'regulating the regulator'.

Indeed, ratings are still used for regulatory purposes. For example, in Switzerland, as in other countries, ratings are used to evaluate the capital adequacy requirements of supervised institutes. They are part of the regulatory process. While ratings are mostly used by regulators, they may also be of interest to courts. The Swiss Federal High Court has already taken position in a specific case by

---

[23] http://www.moodys.com/moodys/cust/AboutMoodys/AboutMoodys.aspx?topic=history (last visited 21 November 2009).

[24] http://www.fitchratings.com/corporate/aboutFitch.cfm?detail=3 (last visited 21 November 2009).

[25] http://www.dbrs.com/about (last visited 21 November 2009).

[26] S. L. Schwarcz, The Role of Rating Agencies in Global Market Regulation (2001) 299–301; R. Trigo Trindade and M. Senn, Control and Responsibility of Rating Agencies in Switzerland (2006) 141.

employing an assessment established by a rating agency. In the particular case, the former Credit Suisse Group was opposed to consolidating all the companies belonging to the group in order to save equity capital. It declined the decision of the supervisory authority defining the consolidation perimeter and filed an appeal with the Federal High Court. Credit Suisse argued that, indeed, rating agencies were not all defining and assessing the consolidation perimeter of Credit Suisse, Credit Suisse First Boston, and the other companies of the group in the same way. Thus, the delimitation of the perimeter was an issue of appreciation. As the ratings established by rating agencies had shown, it was possible to restrict the consolidation perimeter or – in other words – deny a duty of assistance in case of insolvency among the different companies of the group. Similarly, the Court could consider a restricted consolidation perimeter and conclude that there was no de facto duty of assistance among the different companies of the group. However, the Federal High Court rejected this point and argued, based on an assessment established by Moody's, that there were sound reasons for accrediting different ratings to the companies of the group or also delimiting the consolidation perimeter in different ways. This, however, could not exclude any duty of assistance among them, to which Moody's admitted. Hence, the Federal High Court concluded that a duty of assistance did indeed exist.[27]

The crisis accompanying the collapse of Enron and other business companies showed that their assessments could also be wrong, sparking a lively debate on their possible submission to state regulation and supervision. In the wake of Enron, the self-regulatory statute of the rating agencies has been questioned and an international debate has been launched. Among others, the International Organization of Securities Commissions (IOSCO) thoroughly analysed their situation first in 2004. In particular, it was unclear whether self-regulation and compliance with specific standards of quality were sufficient and could be left to the discretion of the industry or whether it was preferable to establish a mandatory legal framework.[28] IOSCO established a report and subsequently, after extensive consultation, it enacted rules of conduct applying to rating agencies. The high-level objectives of that code of conduct are: to ensure the quality and integrity of the rating process, to have independent rating agencies able to avoid conflicts of interest, and assume their responsibilities towards the investing public and issuers.[29] These recommendations

---

[27] Case 116 Ib 331 of 11 December 1990. See Consideration E.3.b); see also Moody's Bank Credit Report, Crédit Suisse, October 1989, 4 and Moody's Corporate Credit Report, CS First Boston, Inc., Financière Crédit Suisse – First Boston, April 1990; Trigo Trindade and Senn, supra note 26, 144.

[28] Report on the Activities of Credit Rating Agencies, Report of the Technical Committee of IOSCO (September 2003) and IOSCO Statement of Principles regarding the Activities of Credit Rating Agencies, Statement of the Technical Committee of IOSCO (September 2003). Beside IOSCO, other bodies established reports on specific issues related to the use of ratings, for instance the Committee on the Global Financial System (CGFS) published a report entitled 'The role of ratings in structured finance: issues and implications in 2005' (January 2005).

[29] Code of Conduct Fundamentals for Credit Rating Agencies (Revised May 2008); see also: A Review of Implementation of the IOSCO Code of Conduct Fundamentals for Credit Rating Agencies (March 2009).

correspond to a form of soft law. They are not formally binding, but rating agencies have first agreed to comply with them.

To date, rating agencies are under great pressure. Formally, they remain free to define their own rating process and methodology as well as their own nomenclature. De facto, their position on the market depends on two factors: their credibility and their reputation. These elements should exercise a self-disciplinary influence on their operations and market participants adhering to ratings remain determinant. Furthermore, competition with other agencies obliges agencies to maintain utmost performance. However, severe criticism continues to be levelled at their practices, not least following to the 2007–2009 financial crisis. IOSCO revised its code of conduct and the former Financial Stability Forum (FSF, now Financial Stability Board, FSB) urged its member bodies to explore outstanding issues related to the role of rating agencies in structured finance. The EU has introduced a Regulation in 2009 and in the US, with the introduction of the Credit Rating Agency Reform Act of 2006, the SEC received authority to register and oversee credit rating agencies or NRSROs. It can promulgate rules regarding public disclosure, recordkeeping and financial reporting, and substantive requirements to ensure that the agencies conduct their activities with integrity and impartiality. Later on, rules amendments, in particular addressing issues of transparency and potential conflicts of interest, have been adopted.[30]

On its side, the use of ratings prepared for the establishment of capital standards leads to a specific form of enrolment of the rating agencies in a regulatory regime. The introduction of the new capital adequacy framework commonly known as Capital Accord or 'Basel II', enacted by the Basel Committee on Banking Supervision (BCBS), defines a framework for the recognition of rating agencies or External Credit Assessment Institution (ECAI). The following criteria have to be fulfilled to merit recognition: rating objectivity, agency independence, international access to individual assessments and transparency, information disclosure, resources, and credibility.[31] National supervisors are responsible for determining whether a rating agency will be recognized in accordance with these criteria. However, they will not be supervised on a continuous basis. Subsequently, the supervisory authorities can use the assessments of these rating agencies for the evaluation of the capital requirements of banks and broker-dealers for supervisory matters.

---

[30] Regulation (EC) No 1060/2009 of the European Parliament and of the Council of 16 September 2009 on Credit Rating Agencies; Credit Rating Agency Reform Act of 2007, September 29, 2006, Pub. L. No. 109–291 (2006); 17 CFR Parts 240 and 249b Oversight of Credit Rating Agencies Registered as Nationally Recognized Statistical Rating Organizations; Final Rule, June 18, 2007; Amendments to Rules for Nationally Recognized Statistical Rating Organizations, Exchange Act Release No. 34-59342 (February 2, 2009) ("SEC Final Rule"), 16–31; J. C. Coffee, Gatekeepers, The Role of the Professions in Corporate Governance (2006) 283–314.

[31] International Convergence of Capital Measurement and Capital Standards, A Revised Framework, Basel Committee on Banking Supervision (BCBS), Bank for International Settlements (BIS) (June 2004, updated version of November 2005) 23–24.

1.2.3 Characteristics

The example of rating agencies has corresponded to a category of cases where private firms shape regulation by regulating other businesses, states, or international organizations. However, in this case, a phase of transformation of the regulatory status has just taken place. In practice, various other models exist for exercising influence and interacting with businesses, states, or international organizations. Other examples include the International Air Transport Association (IATA), which has determined the economic regulation of the civil aviation industry for decades, or the Société Générale de Surveillance (SGS), which provides inspection services in many countries and has taken over customs services in a range of developing countries. Insurance companies, too, can play an important role as business regulators.[32]

As far as the market for rating agencies is concerned, only a few international agencies cover a majority of the financial markets. That market is dominated by four agencies: S&P, Moody's, Fitch, and DBRS. They constitute an oligopoly. These agencies have a worldwide presence by now. They rate international companies and firms from a whole range of countries. According to the 'Report on the Activities of Credit Rating Agencies' of IOSCO, in some jurisdictions only the three largest international rating agencies – Moody's, S&P, and Fitch – are operative.[33] This situation raises questions in the field of competition law as well as in relation to equal opportunities issues and conditions prevailing for participation in the market.

At the national level, for example in Switzerland, the credit rating scene is small. Further to the operations of international agencies, there are also Swiss agencies covering the national market. These can be divided into two groups. The first is constituted by banks. They establish ratings for Swiss companies, governmental issues and municipalities, cities or cantons, which are primarily prepared for their own internal use. Although it is recognized that the ratings established by banks are professional and of good quality, it should not be overlooked that these entities are not entirely independent. In particular, the companies or issues rated are often their own clients, although banks may also rate entire business sectors, such as insurances, without regard to possible client status. The second group consists of a few minor, specialized agencies, operating locally and focusing on specific sectors or products. There are no restrictions for agencies willing to enter the market and there is room for newcomers. These agencies need not register or fulfil authorisation requirements, unless they require an ECAI-recognition. They may have difficulties to position themselves, not least because the local market is not very large. However, there has been no case of abuse of a dominant position by a rating agency

---

[32] Braithwaite and Drahos, supra note 5, 488–494; J. Benjamin, Financial Law (2007) 514–517.

[33] Report on the Activities of Credit Rating Agencies, IOSCO (September 2003) 6; Trigo Trindade and Senn, supra note 26, 145–146; Exclusion Zone: Regulators Promise a Belated Review of the Ratings Oligopoly, in: The Economist (February 8, 2003) 65.

so far, as prohibited by competition law.[34] To date, no intervention from the Competition Commission has been required. The risk of such an abuse is in effect neither very serious nor imminent. The international rating agencies and national companies operating in the country all have to defend their reputation and the objectivity of their ratings. They are therefore expected to take the necessary measures to avoid such a situation. As far as the US are concerned, for instance, ten rating agencies are designated NRSRO and many non-NRSRO agencies vigorously seek NRSRO recognition.[35] There is the assumption that the SEC – by recognizing certain rating agencies – has bestowed a competitive advantage on them.

1.3 Voluntary Codes of Conduct

1.3.1 Historical Aspects

The notion of a code of conduct is very broad. In practice, numerous forms of codes of conduct can be encountered, as defined by associations for their members. From a historical point of view, the first step leading to the elaboration of voluntary codes of conduct is informal. Usances or trade practices develop within an industry or within groups of interest and sector standards are defined in the course of time. For instance, guilds governed and supervised their own markets and introduced the practices, measures, and standards necessary for the development of their trading activities and quality assurance among each other. They determined the rules applying to their markets or set the governing behavioral standards.[36] With the organization of such groups and the constitution of associations, guidelines are defined and formal conventions or rules of conduct applying among association members are laid down. Codes are based on a consensus among members and determine the behaviour to be adopted. They may have been transmitted from generation to generation, as in the professions. The responsible associations act as standards-setting bodies for their sector. They articulate norms and guidelines for their members deemed acceptable to justify activities towards the public. They exercise de facto monopolies in defending their members' interests through the application of their codes of conduct.[37]

---

[34] Trigo Trindade and Senn, supra note 26, 138–140; Article 7 'Unlawful practices of enterprises having a dominant position' of the Federal Act on Cartels and Other Restraints of Competition (Cartel Act; LCart) of 6 October 1995 (text as of 23 March 2004) SR 251.

[35] Annual Report on Nationally Recognized Statistical Rating Organizations, As Required by Section 6 of the Credit Rating Agency Reform Act of 2006, U.S. Securities and Exchange Commission, June 2008, 1 et seqq.; Coffee, supra note 30, 304–306.

[36] Black, supra note 5, 76 et seqq.

[37] Regulating the professions, Taking care of their own, in: The Economist (December 18th 2004) 62–63.

For example, the Swiss banking industry represented by the Swiss Bankers Association (SBA) has already adopted a whole array of self-regulatory measures. It has established codes of conduct designed to safeguard the reputation of banks and strengthen the Swiss banking system from a competitive and service point of view. Codes of conduct of the SBA may also have been defined in close cooperation with the supervisory agency. As such, they represent forms of co-regulation. An important code of conduct introduced by the SBA and set forth on an entirely private and voluntary basis is the 'Agreement on the Swiss banks' code of conduct with regard to the exercise of due diligence' (CDB) regarding customers. It was first concluded between the Swiss National Bank, whose role was instrumental, the Swiss business banks, and the Swiss Bankers Association in the 1970s in response to a banking crisis resulting from violations of asset management directives.[38] It defines what constitutes good industry practice or ethically correct management of banking relationships. Since then, this Code has been revised and adapted every 5 years based on the experiences made. Its revisions mainly serve to confirm the use of the concept and may improve and refine it. It is a binding Code for the whole banking industry. Since 1987, the National Bank has ceased participation. Based on a consensus among its other partners, the Code has become an important standard applying to all banks in Switzerland. Its main goals are:

- To verify the identity of their contracting partners and, in cases of doubt, to obtain from their contracting partners a declaration as to the identity of the beneficial owner of the assets
- Not to provide any active assistance in the flight of capital
- Not to provide any active assistance in tax evasion and similar acts by providing incomplete or misleading attestations[39]

1.3.2 Institutional Arrangements

Private, voluntary codes of conduct are the product of the initiative of private interest groups or SROs. They determine the standards and impose these on their members. They are driven by the motivation of these groups or SROs to set standards in order to ensure a level playing field among their members as well as towards the public. They develop autonomous regimes of rules, administering and enforcing these among their members. In isolated cases, they will assume this role

---

[38] Agreement on the Swiss banks' code of conduct with regard to the exercise of due diligence (CDB 08) from SwissBanking, Swiss Bankers Association, of 7 April 2008; P. Nobel, Die neuen Standesregeln zur Sorgfaltspflicht der Banken (1987) 149 et seqq.; P. Nobel, Die Sorgfaltspflicht des Bankiers (1985) 222; Case 105 Ib 348 of 25 October 1979; Case 109 Ib 146 of 3 June 1983; see also: A. Abegg, Regulierung hybrider Netzwerke im Schnittpunkt von Wirtschaft und Politik (2006) 266–290.

[39] Agreement on the Swiss banks' code of conduct with regard to the exercise of due diligence (CDB 08); supra note 38, 7.

towards another group or community.[40] These rules are considered to be a hallmark of an association towards the public and state. However, it should not be ignored that these codes of conduct often correspond to constrained forms of regulation. They may have been elaborated to forestall or avoid state regulation or control. In these cases, they are likely to have adequate accountability and compliance mechanisms, sufficient to ensure their effective enforcement. They should guarantee for the credibility of the measures and the association's attitude towards third parties. They can then claim standing within a given sector without any direct state involvement. This attitude is typical of the press and advertising sectors, a number of professions, sports, or trade associations.[41] Cooperation between the state and private industry might also be possible. In such cases, codes of conduct serve as co-regulatory measures. They will be enacted by an industry-association based on negotiations or state approval of rules.

As far as the good functioning and rules observance are concerned, an association will assume the role of an arbitrator or supervisor. It is in a position to enforce rules on its members. It will dispose of an internal or possibly external arbitration panel to deal with cases of non-compliance. Sanctions can be foreseen for the case of the non-observance of rules. These can result in the extreme case of excluding a member from an association. However, the problem of capture cannot be ignored. Moreover, depending on an association's degree of organization, mediation mechanisms can be placed at the disposal of members. Such mechanisms may have an effect similar to an independent third-party mediation designed to resolve differences.

Individual firms, in particular multinational companies, can also develop rules of conduct on their own or within their industry. These rules can be used to justify their activities towards the external world. In particular, they demonstrate that the company or industry respects ethical rules and contribute to ensure its good reputation. The pharmaceutical industry is a case in point here. As far as the global chemical industry is concerned, Responsible Care is a voluntary transnational initiative or code of conduct.[42] It governs the health, safety, and environmental management norms and practices applying in that industry. It focuses on improving performance, communication, and accountability. Its overall goal is to improve the reputation of the industry. The initiative started in 1985 in Canada and is currently active in 52 countries around the world, whose combined chemical industries account for nearly 90% of global chemicals production. It is managed by the International Council of Chemical Associations (ICCA) at the global level. It disposes of a common set of Fundamental Features that all associations must adhere to, ensuring the initiative remains true to its core ethic. Its structure is federated with a central organization and adopts flexible implementation with different emphases

---

40 Baldwin and Cave, supra note 1, 39 et seq., with further references.

41 A. Marti, Selbstregulierung anstelle staatlicher Gesetzgebung? (2000) 566, with further references; Priest, supra note 3, 245 et seq., with further references.

42 http://www.responsiblecare.org/ (last visited 21 November 2009).

in each territory. Responsible Care helps the industry to operate safely, profitably, and with care for future generations. It commits chemical companies through their national chemical associations to make the entire chemical life cycle safer. It is characterized by the high interdependence among industry members. The programme works through the sharing of information and a rigorous system of checklists, performance indicators, and verification procedures. It also requires companies to be open and transparent with their stakeholders. Opinions about the contribution of Responsible Care are divided. According to some, it can be considered to be one of the most sophisticated, established, and successful systems based on private voluntary codes or industry self-regulation. It has been commended for being a significant contribution by the chemical industry to sustainable development by the United Nations Environmental Programme (UNEP). According to others, it presents the weaknesses of self-regulatory regimes. In particular, it favours the interests of large industry players.[43]

The standards defined by private associations are self-regulatory. Normally, membership in an association with a defined code of conduct is made dependent on the readiness and commitment to respect the rules laid down in the code of conduct. The acceptance of the code can be declared compulsory for all members. It is contractually binding. On their side, states bodies and courts are free to recognize or also declare codes of conduct binding. In case such standards or codes of conduct would be officially recognized as binding, that is, universally valid within a sector, it would be expected that similarly defined rules or rules based on a similar structure or model enacted in other sectors would then also be binding. On the other side, it should be taken into account that the recognition of standards applicable in a particular firm or industry by a court can entail the risk that such standards could become binding for an entire sector, although such standards regularly pursue the goal of protecting their industry only and do not apply in the public interest. As far as the actual practice of courts is concerned, there is no unified approach and the assertion of an obligation to respect a code cannot be used as a defence before a court.[44]

At the global level, the use of codes of conduct is very common. Various non-governmental actors define standards, among others the International Swaps Dealers Association, Transparency International, or the Internet Engineering Taskforce. However, one should bear in mind that, here again, governmental authorities are not obliged to consider any of the so-defined standards.[45]

---

[43] B. M. Hutter, The Role of Non-State Actors in Regulation (2006) 4, with further references; Priest, supra note 3, 248–249.

[44] Priest, supra note 3, 247–251, with further references, in particular from practical cases. See also the decision of the Swiss Federal High Court, Case 125 IV 139 of April 1999; Chapter 5, point 3 A Process of Transformation into State Regulation.

[45] P. S. Berman, From International Law to Law and Globalization (2005) 546–549; J. Black, The Decentred Regulatory State? (2007) 267, with further references.

1.3.3 Characteristics

Codes of conduct lay down principles. The value of these codes of conduct or codes of governance first concerns their substance rather than their form. Normally, the incentives for compliance are: the openness of the self-regulatory measure, its adequacy with regard to the field or question to be regulated, and a degree of accountability. As self-regulatory measures, they are not subject to any external control. Basically, they should contribute to the good reputation of a sector and preserve its public standing. Although the interest group or organization is itself responsible for rules implementation, a form of external pressure to be disciplined is possible.[46]

For instance, the CDB defines what constitutes good industry practice, as stated. It neither affects banking secrecy nor does it alter the relationship between the bank and its client. It is a self-regulatory measure declared by the Federal High Court to represent an 'instrument of ethical self-regulation'. It remains the most prominent example of a self-regulatory solution in Switzerland's financial market regime and is often used as a model for other self-regulatory measures. Thus, it is also significant in relation to money laundering. Moreover, it has been endorsed by the supervisory authority, the FINMA. The latter has declared that all banks must observe the CDB, including non-SBA members. The authority also monitors the compliance of banks with the Code insofar as the responsible auditing companies are obliged to control its effective enforcement.[47] Thus, in practice, the Code now constitutes an integral part of banking regulation in Switzerland.

The Code has its own investigatory regime. A private Supervisory Board, de facto an arbitral court, is in charge of investigating and penalizing violations. It is appointed by the SBA together with one or more investigators. The investigator will make recommendations to the Supervisory Board to open proceedings and impose sanctions based on its investigations or to close proceedings. In case the Supervisory Board identifies a code violation, it will impose an equitable sanction upon the culpable bank (article 12 CDB). In case a bank refuses to participate in an investigation, the Supervisory Board may impose a fine. In case a bank refuses to pay a fine, an arbitration tribunal will hand down a ruling, upon a complaint brought by the SBA against the bank (article 13 CDB). The decisions or judgments issued by the Supervisory Board or an arbitral tribunal have a purely private character.

The nature and importance of the CDB remains under discussion. One important issue concerns the attitude of courts. To date, the Federal High Court stipulated in a ruling that the rules of the Code are private and self-regulatory. It denied any recognition. It held that they do not represent any generally binding norms. The Court compared these norms with usances and declared that they could only deploy

[46] Priest, supra note 3, 245 et seq., with further references.

[47] Case 125 IV 139 of April 1999, 144; P. Nobel, Gesetz oder private Selbstregulierung? (1987) 456 seq.; Nobel (1987), supra note 38, 156 seq.; see also the Annex to the Circular of the FINMA: Self-regulation recognized as a minimum standard by the Swiss Financial Market Supervisory Authority of 20 November 2008, FINMA-Circ. 08/10 Self-regulation as a minimum standard.

private effects. Thus, they are not binding for state courts. They could be used solely for the purpose of interpretation, in relation to the penal appreciation of a case. However, observance of the CDB as a set of self-regulatory rules has been declared mandatory for all banks by the supervisory authority following the Court's ruling. It would be interesting to see whether this recognition would lead to a change of attitude of the Federal High Court or not.[48]

2 Firm Own Regulation

The second case concentrates on the own internal regulatory regime of firms or the regulation defined by the firms themselves. The term 'firm' should be understood in a broad sense. It does not only mean commercial businesses. It may also include other firms or organizations, such as universities, and so forth.[49] As a regulatory regime, firm own regulation is regularly discussed under the label of 'enforced self-regulation', a well-known model of regulation first defined by Ayres and Braithwaite.[50] It appears in relation to individual firms, groups, conglomerates, or multinational corporations. It covers intra-firm regulation, which concerns the design and operation of regulation within a single organization, and further includes the relations of a firm with a SRO or an association in charge of representing its interests. The key role within this typology of regulation is played by private firms themselves and their own regulation. However, it should not be ignored that the basic order is first determined by the state, and occurs through the incorporation of a firm under a legal category. It involves a blend of state and corporate regulatory efforts. The government lays down broad standards and rules, which registered companies or firms are expected to meet following their incorporation.[51] This section however focuses on the firm's own regulatory initiative regarding its internal processes, that is, the internal law of the firm.

The following types of firm own regulation are discussed hereinafter: individual firms as well as multinational firms together with their representative associations.

[48] Case 125 IV 139 of April 1999; G. Friedli, Übersicht über die Praxis der Aufsichtskommission zur Sorgfaltspflicht der Banken 1998–2001 (2002) 165–167; see also: Abegg, supra note 38, 266–290.

[49] J. Black, Decentring Regulation: Understanding the Role of Regulation and Self-Regulation in a 'Post-Regulatory' World (2001) Volume 54, 120.

[50] Ayres and Braithwaite, supra note 3, 102–109; J. Braithwaite, Enforced self-regulation: A new strategy for corporate crime control (June 1982) 1466–1507.

[51] Hutter, supra note 43, 5; J.-P. Robé, Multinational Enterprises: The Constitution of a Pluralistic Legal Order (2006) 52–53; E. Rock and M. Wachter, Islands of Conscious Power: Law, Norms and the Self-governing Corporation (2001) 1 et seqq.

2.1 *Individual Firms*

2.1.1 Historical Aspects

The historical approach of the development of the firm can be retraced together with the history of company law. Company law is first territorially limited. Thus, the well-known origin of the firm is the incorporation of the first public limited liability company in the modern sense, the Dutch East India Company (Vereenigde Oostindische Compagnie or VOC in old-spelling Dutch, literally 'United East Indian Company') in 1602. It marks the starting point of company law. It served as a model for the development of that body of law in other territories or countries in Europe, apart from England. The main difference concerned the treatment of shareholders: whereas they all had a say in England, oligarchic ownership structures dominated and continue to dominate matters in the Netherlands.[52]

In Italy, for example, this model of company was used for particular business techniques, such as the 'commenda', to invest capital in a commercial venture, or the practice of the 'compera delle imposte' or purchase of tax receivables. One case in point is the Genoese Maone, a joint-stock company and similar in substance to limited liability companies. In the sixteenth and seventeenth centuries, both the Dutch and English models were adopted in Italy. In the second half of the seventeenth and in the eighteenth century, other kinds of limited companies were formed, whose articles of incorporation were increasingly uniform. Then, in the course of company law codification during the nineteenth and twentieth centuries, the French Code de commerce exercised a determining influence. The Civil Code of 1942 rules on limited liability companies and joint-stock companies. However, it suffered some limitations in particular with regard to the rules governing internal governance structure. In the course of the twentieth century, Italian company law underwent reform not least following the implementation of European Union directives for securities markets, corporate takeover rules, and so forth.[53]

However, notwithstanding all these developments and reforms, it should not be overlooked – as the example of Italian company law shows – that following the incorporation of the VOC in 1602, many of the issues arising at that time are still discussed nowadays in modern company law. Topics such as the principal versus agent relationship, the role and powers of shareholders, principles of good corporate governance or management compensation continue to be fiercely debated and the issues they raise remain controversial.[54]

---

[52] Preface by the Editors, E. Gepken-Jager, G. van Solinge, L. Timmerman (eds.), VOC 1602-2002 400 Years of Company Law, Law of Business and Finance (2005) IX–XII.

[53] G. A. Ferrarini, Origins of Limited Liability Companies and Company Law Modernisation in Italy: A Historical Outline (2005) n 52, 189–215.

[54] For a basic introduction, see: A. A. Berle and G. C. Means, The Modern Corporation and Private Property (1991).

2.1.2 Institutional Arrangements

In the case of firm own regulation, the private firm constitutes the core of the regulatory regime. Other actors involved are the shareholders, the investors, the employees and general public which may exercise a determining influence on the firm's operations, for example when its environmental responsibilities are concerned.[55] The following constellations can be distinguished:

- First, the firm takes over regulatory responsibilities, the initiative to lay down internal rules tailored to its needs, enforce these, and impose sanctions
- Second, it can be prompted by the state or through statute to conduct self-rule, that is, define regulation autonomously
- Third, firm internal rules may be introduced by a firm, but these may not be expressly required by statute although it is allowed to do so
- Fourth, a traditional regime of regulation can be available as an alternative.[56]

Within the regulatory framework applying to firms, company law concerns the broad legal basis only within which firms operate. The statute grants the companies the freedom to organize themselves as far as they respect the legal standards laid down. Private companies are not subject to a state supervisory regime, similar to that applying to financial institutions like banks or securities dealers. They do not have to be granted authorization to operate. Rather, registration suffices and the commercial register exercises a limited control when registering them. The registrar's duty only consists in guaranteeing a single practice and application of commercial law. The submitted articles of incorporation and their subsequent changes are checked, using standard guidelines and directives which provide interpretations of the law for their introduction into the commercial register.

Originally, a firm commits itself to respect the statute with its incorporation. The chosen legal form implies the adoption of a determined organizational behavior. The firm must be willing to take all adequate measures to respect existing basic legal requirements. Then, a private firm will organize itself autonomously. It can (self-)regulate itself. It will lay down its own internal rules. It should organize itself in such a way as to respect the statute, for instance in relation to the organization of general meetings, but it is free to develop individualized, internal rules applicable to its operations and activities. These individual rules will be adapted to its own activities and size. It defines its internal regulation, and subsequently manages and enforces it. It will be tailored to the specific needs and particularities of the firm. A firm may also enact proper rules not required by statute, for instance regarding specific internal requirements in relation to the attainment of determined

[55] Here, the state, with which a relationship exists since it defines company law rules, is considered to be in the background. C. Parker, The Open Corporation, Effective Self-Regulation and Democracy (2002) 277.

[56] Priest, supra note 3, 256.

quality grades for their products or regarding employees' conduct. In doing so, firms can make use of useful SRO support and services.[57]

Ayres and Braithwaite describe firm own regulation as a model of enforced self-regulation. It is a hybrid form of self-regulation which encompasses negotiations between the state and an individual firm. A firm is required to propose its own particular regulatory standards. Otherwise, standards defined by the state will be imposed. As a result, firm self-regulation is 'enforced' in two senses:

- The firm is required by the state to perform self-regulation
- The privately written rules can be publicly enforced.[58]

Ayres and Braithwaite argue that as a matter of fact, the goal of state regulation should be to enhance initiative within the private market and support it. To reach this goal, governmental functions should be more often delegated, not only to firms, but also to other private actors or individuals. To explain how the model works, they suggest transposing Ronald Coase's work on 'The Nature of the Firm' to the legal field when discussing their model of enforced self-regulation. Coase argues that firms should be organized to produce goods and services in case internal production is cheaper than external market transactions. Thus, they would internally produce goods that they could produce cheaper than buy them on the open market. A similar situation can apply to public goods produced by the government, although these goods have other characteristics than private ones or those produced by private firms. As Ayres and Braithwaite state, the same Coasian insights apply to regulatory issues at a basic level. Governments should produce 'public goods' – like regulation – internally only when it is cheaper than producing same through external contracting. Conceptually, they should be thought of as subcontractors of regulatory functions to private actors. In the same sense, as just stated, private firms should be in a position to produce goods and services as long as the internal production is cheaper than external market transactions. This can be applied to firm internal regulation, as produced or defined within firms. The costs taken into account are the internal costs arising from the definition of internal regulation as well as the external costs resulting from the conclusion of agreements or, with regard to regulation, contracts entered into with the state.[59]

As already stated, in the case of firm own regulation, the state only determines the basic structure of company law and firm regulation. Based on a model of enforced self-regulation, it is subsequently presumed more efficacious for firms to

[57] Ibid. 256–257; see also: C. Coglianese, D. Lazer, Management-Based Regulation: Prescribing Private Management to Achieve Public Goals (2007) 423–462.

[58] Ayres and Braithwaite, supra note 3, 101; see also Baldwin and Cave, supra note 1, 133–136; Hutter, supra note 43, 5; see also: B. M. Hutter, Is Enforced Self-regulation a Form of Risk Taking?: The Case of Railway Health and Safety (2001) 29, 379–400.

[59] R. H. Coase, The Nature of the Firm (1937) 386–405; Ayres and Braithwaite, supra note 3, 3 et seq., 102–103; Priest, supra note 3, 257; Rock and Wachter, supra note 51, 16–27, 28–33; see also M. Ruffner, Die ökonomischen Grundlagen eines Rechts der Publikumsgesellschaft (2000) 69 et seqq.

exercise regulatory functions themselves. The focus is placed on these detailed internal rules of firms. Self-regulatory measures are dominant and not the statute. Self-regulation corresponds to a firm-internal regulatory process originally induced by the state. It offers the specific advantage that firms can adopt clear-cut rules on their own initiative and corresponding to their needs. Firms also are free to adapt rules. However, the enactment of their own rules can cost firms a lot of precious resources and may be expensive in particular for small and medium-size companies. Thus, these firms could rely on model rules defined by their SRO. SROs representing firms may contribute significantly to diminish regulation costs through providing standard regulatory models and guidelines and placing these at the disposal of their member firms, assisting them, defining and administering their internal rules. SROs can also play an important role when representing the interests of firms towards a broader public. However, small and medium-size firms may still have difficulties in respecting the requirements of independency and justify rules within the firm. These companies, in particular non-SRO members, may not cope well with systems of enforced self-regulation. They are less influential and often do not have the capacity to entertain a regulatory role, contrary to large and multinationals firms. On their side, larger, more sophisticated firms are most likely to find this managed self-regulation or firm-defined regulation most attractive. They will also largely influence the regulatory functions of their SRO.[60] Finally, such a regulatory structure also bears the risk that the interests of third parties and the public may not be sufficiently taken into account.

A major attribute of the model lies in the original cooperation between the state and the firm. First, the statutes are defined subsequent to extensive consultations between the state, the firms, and the private actors. They are the result of negotiations conducted by the state. Based on this overall framework, firm self-regulation can be embedded in schemes of escalating state interventions. Besides statutes, enforcement decisions rendered by supervisory authorities and courts or other official bodies refine and shape firm regulation. For example, a court decision may require the introduction of specific compliance systems. Jurisprudence will influence all firms with the same legal structure or active in the same field and confronted with similar regulatory questions. They will adapt their behaviour to case-law. However, the model is first of all a scheme which is dominated by the firm's private governance. Its own internal rules determine its daily operations and characterize the multitude of internal transactions. These are based on an own governance mechanism and are almost entirely not legally enforceable.[61]

In relation to firm own regulation, SROs or associations representing firms can fulfil a key function with regard to specific issues and for reasons of efficiency where solutions, which should apply to a whole type, industry or group of firms, are

[60] Hutter, op., cit., n 43, 5. For a detailed discussion of the advantages and disadvantages, see Ayres and Braithwaite, supra note 3, 110–116 and 120–128; see also Priest, supra note 3, 258; Coglianese and Lazer, supra note 57, 423–462; Braithwaite, supra note 50, 1469–1474.

[61] Rock and Wachter, supra note 51, 16–17.

sought.[62] An illustrative example of the role of SROs is the development of codes of corporate governance. It is a core issue regarding the good conduct of firms. After the first OECD Corporate Governance Principles of 1999 had been successfully applied in a number of countries, a revised version was enacted in 2004 to better reflect company law developments. These principles are applied intensively by governments, regulators, investors, companies and shareholders. They are also observed by OECD non-member states. The SROs regularly adapt them to the characteristics of the national markets they cover and where they are used as standards. For instance, in Switzerland, economiesuisse, the leading private enterprise SRO, has developed the Swiss Code of Best Practice for Corporate Governance (Swiss Code).[63] The SIX Swiss Exchange, moreover, has enacted the so-called Directive on Information relating to Corporate Governance.[64] Both entered into force in July 2002. They are the result of the efforts undertaken by private business to enact proper principles of corporate governance. Finally, a Directive on Disclosure of Management Transactions was passed by the SIX Swiss Exchange and entered into force in 2005.[65] The texts are adjusted to each other and constitute a package of self-regulatory measures which cannot be considered separately. Their goal is to encompass 'the full range of principles directed towards shareholders' interest seeking a good balance between direction and control and transparency at the top company level while maintaining decision-making capacity and efficiency.' The Swiss Code consists of recommendations for economiesuisse member firms and the directives of the Swiss Exchange apply specifically to listed companies. Both are mandatory in relation to the information regarding executive salaries and credits granted to organs. As far as the other rules are concerned, the principle of 'comply or explain' applies.[66]

However, it should not be ignored that besides these efforts based on private initiative and where a consensus was rapidly reached, a debate took place regarding possible state intervention. Various parliamentary initiatives have been submitted to introduce a statute on corporate governance. According to Böckli, a race took place at the time between the possible introduction of a state regulation or a private regulatory solution. Thus, private business claimed a narrow victory in the first round with the introduction of the Swiss Code in 2002. The leading opinion finally considered flexible self-regulatory texts appropriate to regulate the issue. In other

---

62 Ayres and Braithwaite, supra note 3, 103–104.

63 Of July 2002, updated 2007, http://www.economiesuisse.ch/web/de/themen/wettbewerb/cp/Seiten/default.aspx (last visited 23 November 2009).

64 Directive Corporate Governance, DCG, version 29 October 2008, http://www.six-exchange-regulation.com/regulation/directives/being_public_en.html (last visited 28 November 2009).

65 Directive Management Transactions, DMT, version 29 October 2008, http://www.six-exchange-regulation.com/admission_manual/06_16-DMT_en.pdf (last visited 28 November 2009).

66 Swiss Code of Best Practice for Corporate Governance, economiesuisse, Annex 1, 6; Directive on Information Relating to Corporate Governance (Corporate Governance Directive, DCG) of July 2002, as of 1 January 2007, Annex, SIX Swiss Exchange, 5; Peter Böckli, Harte Stellen im Soft Law, Zum Swiss Code of Best Practice for Corporate Governance (2002) 982.

words, besides the substantive rationales, one motivation to introduce these rules was to avoid a state regulatory measure.[67] However, the political debate continues and the effectiveness of the private measures is questioned. In the meantime, shareholding company law has already been changed and extensive rules on the disclosure of board's and management's compensation have been introduced in 2007. The main argument used to justify the introduction of statutory rules was to strengthen investor and public confidence in the commercial activities of listed companies and strengthen abuse prevention. Further proposals to change that law are still pending.[68]

2.1.3 Characteristics

All firms and industries self-regulate to some degree or another. Firm own regulation implies that the power of the state is brought to bear on the firm or industry organization to require the delimitation and enforcement of regulatory requirements on a private basis. Statutes may contain basic prescriptions in the fields of company law, securities law, or environmental law. Besides satisfying these requirements, which may have an ethical component, firm own regulation is particular to each firm. It can include rules of conduct or codices, rules regarding internal controlling, compliance and accounting, the organization of the firm as well as general working prescriptions, and in particular specific rules regarding the realization of objectives. Firm own regulation also includes firm external regulation, that is, regarding its relations with third parties or business partners, the organization of general meetings, press contacts, or relationships with the general public. Within a firm, one key objective is to institutionalize behavioral standards and adequate decision-making processes. The methods applied to define and enforce these rules may differ from firm to firm. Each firm has its own internal compliance and control instances responsible for the development of internal rules and their implementation.[69] Some might have fairly sophisticated internal systems.

When defining the form of enforced self-regulation in individual cases, it is useful for policymakers to be aware of the range of self-regulating options available. They should also have a sense of when voluntary self-regulation is to be encouraged. Considered in relation to the other regulatory regimes discussed here, firm own regulation or enforced self-regulation can be situated between the

---

67 Böckli, supra note 66, 981–992.

68 Article 663b^{bis} and article 663c paragraph 3 of the Code of Obligations; Botschaft zur Änderung des Obligationenrechts (Transparenz betreffend Vergütungen an Mitglieder des Verwaltungsrates und der Geschäftsleitung) vom 23. Juni 2004, BBl Nr. 30, 4471 et seq.; Botschaft zur Änderung des Obligationenrechts (Aktienrecht und Rechnungslegungsrecht sowie Anpassungen im Recht der Kollektiv- und der Kommanditgesellschaft, im GmbH-Recht, Genossenschafts-, Handelsregister- sowie Firmenrecht) vom 21. Dezember 2007, BBl Nr. 11, 18 March 2008, 1589–1750, 1606 et seqq.

69 Priest, supra note 3, 266, with further references.

typologies of pure self-regulation and coercive self-regulation. There is an enrolment by the state which concerns the definition of the broad regulatory framework. The regulatory outcome corresponds to a hybrid form of regulation and an intermediate regulatory strategy between state and private regulation. It is distinct from co-regulation, which usually means industry-association self-regulation with some state oversight or ratification. Firm own regulation or enforced self-regulation can be considered to represent an extension and individualization of co-regulation.[70]

Within the range of self-regulatory options applying to firm own regulation, a sub-form of organizational structure of regulation can be distinguished: sector-based regulation. Sector-based regulation represents a regulatory regime applying to a sector and where a regulatory agency is in charge of enforcing rules. The agency enters into enforceable agreements with the supervised firms, but the firms can develop their own strategies, which they may submit to the agency for approval. The proponents of this system opine that it fosters technological innovation, reduces compliance costs, and produces better results.[71] The financial services sector is representative of this type of regulation where it has been applied since the origins of modern financial services regulation. The firms concerned are banks, securities dealers, investments funds, insurances, and other financial businesses. Contrary to business firms, they must be granted authorization and are supervised by an agency on a continuous basis. Like business firms, they can still develop their own regulation, but must comply with exacting and highly specific rules regulating their business activities. They have to submit their rules for approval to the supervisory agency, which can intervene at any time.

Yet another type of regulatory regime applying to firms is 'yardstick competition'. Under this regime, there is a competitive situation between a privately-owned producer and a government-owned one or the regulator places similar firms in competition with one another. No regulation as such applies to the privately-owned, self-regulated firm. However, to be competitive on the market, it must meet the standards set by the government-owned firm. The result is a kind of indirect disciplinary effect which could be compared to state regulation. This form of enforced self-regulation presents a range of weaknesses. In particular, government or regulated firms do not have to provide their services under identical circumstances. Thus, as a form of regulation, it is neither very important anymore nowadays nor much utilized in its pure form. The contrary is rather the case, because the private sector defines which regulatory standards apply in a number of cases.[72]

---

[70] Ayres and Braithwaite, supra note 3, 102.

[71] J. L. Harrison, T. D. Morgan, P. R. Verkuil, Regulation and Deregulation (2004) 495.

[72] Baldwin and Cave, supra note 1, 243–244; A. Shleifer, A theory of yardstick competition (Autumn 1985) 319–327; Harrison, Morgan, Verkuil, supra note 71, 495–496; for a case study, see: P. Parker, K. Namwoon, National Brands Versus Private Labels: An Empirical Study of Competition, Advertising and Collusion (1997) 220–235.

Finally, in relation to firm own regulation, some authors claim that another use of self-regulation refers to the interactions of individuals and firms in devising legal contracts. Self-regulation is determined by contracting. The parties to a contract can decide for themselves whether or not they will comply with the defined rules. However, it should be taken into account that contrary to the multilaterality or collective character of self-regulation, contracting consists in a bilateral relationship. Legally, it corresponds to an enforceable arrangement.[73]

2.2 *Multinational firms*

2.2.1 Historical Aspects

The history of multinational firms (or multinational companies, MNCs) is linked to the history of individual firms. However, the perception of firms as multinationals is a modern phenomenon. It mainly crystallized as an issue in the context of the debate on the globalization and liberalization of business in particular. It has led to an increase of cross-border transactions and a perception of activities dispread by multinational corporations in a broad array of countries.

The above example of the Dutch East India Company, the first large trading company, shows that MNC structures already existed in the seventeenth century. As a limited company incorporated in the Netherlands, it exhibited the typical features of modern multinational companies or companies operating in various countries, whereas diverse forms of organizing activities can be identified. In particular, three phases of the development of multinational companies can be distinguished. First, the nineteenth-century 'international model', meaning that such firms were based in their home country, but sold goods through overseas sales offices. Second, in the twentieth century, the classic multinational firm emerged, that is, the mother company created smaller versions of itself across the world. The third model is the 'globally integrated enterprise' as defined by Samuel Palmisano. This is the current type of multinational company. It shapes its strategy, management, and operations as a single global entity. The right cost, the right skills, and the right business environment are crucial. Operations are integrated horizontally as well as globally.[74]

In connexion with the case of individual firms, the evolution of MNCs reveals remarkable similarities as far as the development of the core issues are concerned: the current corporate governance debate, the related issues of executive and shareholder power as well as conflicting interests in relation to companies and directors acting on their behalf. A more acute topic applying especially to MNCs concerns

---

[73] Black, op cit., n 49, 120–121, with reference to H. Collins.

[74] S. J. Palmisano, The Globally Integrated Enterprise (May/June 2006) 127–136; Hungry tiger, dancing elephant, How India is changing IBM's world, in: The Economist (April 7th 2007) 65–67.

their handling of environmental matters. Their attitude towards social responsibility, too, is fiercely debated and the object of global initiatives, as will be discussed hereafter.[75] Due to their size and financial power, such firms can influence their outcome and the general public expects them to assume responsibility.

2.2.2 Institutional Arrangements

Basically, MNCs work according to the same model of enforced self-regulation applying to individual firms. As stated by Robé, it should first be acknowledged that MNCs do not exist as such in positive law. They are not a legal concept, although their existence under economic and political aspects is generally recognized and not questioned. MNCs are discussed separately here, because they epitomize a special position under institutional aspects and present some specific characteristics. Like individual firms, MNCs are private firms. However, they often constitute whole conglomerates which can be active in different fields at the global level. Together with the associations of firms or SROs representing their interests, they defend specific interests, in particular when trading policy and economic interests are at stake. With their SRO, and contrary to small national firms, they are in a strong position to exercise their influence on economic instances. They can organize themselves and dispose of sufficient means and funds to lobby their interests. They can play a determining role in the formulation of regulations. Moreover, they present the greatest challenge to state sovereignty, whereas the other actors involved, including states, governmental or non-governmental international organizations and transnational networks and the general public, may exercise some pressure, too.[76]

SROs play an important role. They are often dominated by, and largely dependent both economically and financially on, MNCs. They are organized professionally and can exercise their influence effectively. They may represent the interests of their member firms in general or they can be in charge of dealing with specific topics or issues. Both national and international self-regulatory or non-governmental organizations (NGOs) are very active. They have developed their own codes of practice. Since NGOs have been formally recognized by the United Nations, they are expected to participate to the work of those organizations in charge of setting standards, in particular economic law, such as Unctad, Ecosoc, Uncitral, ILO,

[75] E. Gepken-Jager, Verenigde Oost-Indische Compagnie (VOC), The Dutch East India Company (2005) 41–81.

A case study on the mode of action of VOC is presented by: J. G. Nagel, The Company and the Port City: Trading centres of the Malay Archipelago and their role in commercial networks during the seventeenth and eighteenth centuries (2004) 249–273.

[76] Robé, supra note 51, 52–53; see also C. Parker, The Open Corporation, Effective Self-Regulation and Democracy (2002) 277; G. Teubner, Codes of Conduct multinationaler Unternehmen, Unternehmensverfassung jenseits von Corporate Governance und gesetzlicher Mitbestimmung (2007) 2; L. Engwall, Global enterprises in fields of governance (2006) 161–179.

or WIPO. Within these organizations, their role is significant not only with regard to the subsequent specification of member rules. They are also capable of exercising considerable influence on the rule-making function of these organizations.[77]

Besides the participation or representation of MNCs in international organizations through NGOs, MNCs are themselves the subject of a number of initiatives launched at the international level and managed by international organizations. First, the ILO Tripartite Declaration of Principles concerning Multinational Enterprises and Social Policy; secondly, the UN Global Compact; thirdly, the OECD Guidelines for Multinational Enterprises; and fourthly, the United Nations Norms on the Responsibilities of Transnational Corporations and other Business Enterprises with regard to Human Rights can be cited.

The ILO Tripartite Declaration, first adopted in 1977 and subsequently amended, is intended to encourage the positive contribution which multinational enterprises or MNCs can make to economic and social progress and to minimize and resolve difficulties arising from their various operations. It is the result of a debate in the 1960s and 1970s regarding their activities and conduct in host countries, mostly in the developing world. Efforts were subsequently made to resolve labour-related and social policy concerns. The Declaration provides principles regarding the social aspects of the operations of MNCs for the use of domestic and host country governments, employers' and workers' organizations, and MNCs themselves.[78] Its application is still timely and necessary today as MNCs are prominent in the process of social and economic globalization.

The UN Global Compact launched by the United Nations in 2000 is an international initiative, whose objective is to motivate private companies – for instance MNCs and companies active in the Third World – to work together with United Nations bodies, labour and civil society organizations, and other parties on a voluntary basis to foster partnerships and build 'a more sustainable and inclusive global economy'. Companies should cooperate in the fields of human rights, labour, the environment, and anti-corruption as well as support universal environmental and social principles. Global Compact seeks to promote responsible corporate citizenship and master the challenges of globalization. Ten principles have already been adopted in the areas of human rights, labour, the environment, and anti-corruption. These are derived from the Universal Declaration of Human Rights, the ILO's Declaration on Fundamental Principles and Rights at Work, the Rio Declaration on Environment and Development, and the UN Convention Against Corruption. Participating companies should make efforts to observe these

---

[77] See Chapter 2, point 3 Institutional Structure, 3.2 Collectivity: From Associability to Association; J. Delbrück, The Role of the United Nations in Dealing with Global Problems (Spring 1997) 291; W. Cragg, Multinational Corporations, Globalisation, and the Challenge of Self-Regulation (2004) 213 et seqq.

[78] Tripartite Declaration of Principles concerning Multinational Enterprises and Social Policy, International Labour Office, Geneva, 3rd ed., 2001, 2; http://www.ilo.org/wcmsp5/groups/public/—dgreports/—dcomm/documents/normativeinstrument/kd00121.pdf (last visited 28 November 2009).

principles. The objectives are to mainstream the ten principles in business activities around the world and catalyze actions in support of UN goals.[79] Global Compact does not consider itself to be a regulatory authority. It does not supervise the activities of the participating companies and does not inflict sanctions. Its operations rely on public accountability, transparency, and the enlightened self-interest of companies themselves as well as labour and civil society in enforcing the principles on a voluntary basis. Global Compact constitutes a network of different groups: businesses, enterprises, international organizations – first of all UN-sub-organizations and representatives of the governments –, unions and non-governmental organizations. It is a learning forum on what constitutes good practices, based on dialogue among all participants. It should propagate minimal standards through self-regulatory measures, which on their side should promote the good conduct of enterprises. Thousands of companies from all regions of the world as well as international labour and civil society organizations are currently engaged in Global Compact.[80]

The OECD Guidelines for Multinational Enterprises, which were revised in the year 2000, constitute a set of voluntary recommendations to multinational enterprises or MNCs. The Guidelines are part of the OECD Declaration on International Investment and Multinational Enterprises. They are designed to cover commercial activities across a broad range of business transactions. The recommendations cover all the major areas of business ethics, including employment and industrial relations, human rights, environment, information disclosure, combating bribery, consumer interests, science and technology, competition and taxation. They define principles and standards for responsible business conduct and are complemented by explanatory notices. Governments can adhere to these Guidelines, which means that they commit themselves to promote them among MNCs active in their country. However, these recommendations are not legally enforceable. They resemble a form of soft law. They should serve to strengthen the basis of mutual confidence between MNCs and their host societies, help improve the foreign investment climate, and enhance the contribution to sustainable development made by the multinational enterprises or MNCs.

The United Nations Norms on the Responsibilities of Transnational Corporations and other Business Enterprises of 2003 aim at integrating transnational corporations as organs of society and rendering them responsible or even accountable for promoting human rights. They comprise nineteen operative regulations with an explanatory commentary and four closing provisions providing definitions of the key terms used in the document. In particular, the Preamble acknowledges the universality, indivisibility, interdependence, and interrelatedness of human rights, including the right to development. The Norms take the form of recommendations.

---

[79] http://www.unglobalcompact.org/AboutTheGC/TheTenPrinciples/index.html; http://www.unglobalcompact.org/AboutTheGC/index.html (last visited 28 November 2009).

[80] http://www.unglobalcompact.org/AboutTheGC/index.html (last visited 28 November 2009); A.-M. Slaughter, Sovereignty and Power in a Networked World Order (2004) 307–311.

They are not legally binding. However, due to their normative contents, they are considered to constitute an authoritative guide to corporate social responsibility. They should assist companies in conducting business in a socially and politically responsible and sustainable manner. These norms represent the most comprehensive document dealing with corporate human rights obligations and responsibilities. However, in comparison to other norms and codes, they do not introduce new duties for companies. They reaffirm and reinforce existing norms.[81]

Finally, private initiatives and networks should be mentioned. The International Corporate Governance Network (ICGN) stems from the convergence of corporate initiatives in North America and Europe. It is an incorporated, not-for-profit association. Its purpose is to provide an investor-led network for the exchange of views and information about corporate governance issues internationally as well as the development of corporate governance guidelines. The network shall facilitate the exchange of information on corporate governance practices. It also aims at encouraging adherence to corporate governance standards and guidelines and generally promoting good corporate governance practices. A similar role is taken over by the ECGI.[82]

2.2.3 Characteristics

Like national companies or firms, MNCs determine the internal legal order of the firm. They operate on the basis of their own internal behavioural rules. Within the firm, they are perceived as being mandatory. In fact, as far as these rules are concerned, nothing refers specifically to MNCs. The internal constitution of the firm depends on neither size nor location. The order is unitary, closed, unique, and autonomous. It is decided and defined by the firm itself. It will enforce it effectively.[83] What characterizes MNCs, such as IBM, Elf Aquitaine or Nestlé, is their transnational activities and economic power, although this power is also elusive.[84] MNCs are registered in one particular country, in which they may operate at the national level, and the main part of their operations is global. Hence, they face other issues than national companies as regards globalization and on account of their

[81] http://www.unhchr.ch (last visited 28 November 2009); UN Document E/CN.4/Sub.2/2003/12/Rev.2; K. Nowrot, Die UN-Norms on the Responsibility of Transnational Corporations and Other Business Enterprises with Regard to Human Rights, Gelungener Beitrag zur transnationalen Rechtsverwirklichung oder das Ende des Global Compact? (September 2003); C. Hillemanns, UN Norms on the Responsibilities of Transnational Corporations and Other Business Enterprises with regard to Human Rights (October 2003) 1065–1080; M. E. Cloghesy, A Corporate Perspective on Globalisation, Sustainable Development, and Soft Law (2004) 323–328.

[82] http://www.icgn.org/ (last visited 30 November 2009); http://www.ecgi.org/organisation/overview.htm (last visited 30 November 2009); see also P. Nobel, Transnationales und Europäisches Aktienrecht (2006) 703–782, regarding international standards applying to company law.

[83] Robé, supra note 51, 52–53.

[84] W. C. Jenks, Multinational Entities in the Law of Nations (1972) 80.

transnational activities. Such activities may lead to the formulation of specific rules, which will transpose ethical codes defined by international organizations based on international initiatives as just described. Normally, two main aspects will be covered by these rules: the business relationships of the MNCs will be addressed and their social responsibility will be appealed to. In other words, rules may concern issues not limited to commercial interests, environmental or societal issues, or issues of general importance.

According to Sajó, MNCs constitute very powerful transnational networks. These networks emerge from production and distribution processes in the corporate world. Nokia can serve as an example. As an MNC, it is a private business network in which different networks can be distinguished. For instance, there is the shareholder network, which, depending on specific disclosure rules, is either an identifiable or also unidentifiable international network of company owners. It is not excluded that in case of broadly dispersed ownership, no shareholder may reach the disclosure threshold. The channels of product distribution or of suppliers represent other networks. MNC managements, moreover, are international and may be physically hard to locate. For an MNC or global business network, this situation means that it can only operate based on the working of the networks constituting it at the global level. Decisions limited to national territories alone will not be significant. Issues of management, trade, capital, taxes are all global and will often be hard to retrace for outsiders. Similarly to a private company, the MNC will apply its own rules within its networks. Nokia operates according to its own corporate ethics, internal professional standards and codes, which all serve to hold the network together. Furthermore, networks pertaining to an MNC will often represent core economic interests for an indusrtry or also within a country. Thus, they may not only exercise a function of governance or control over their member organizations and partners in competition with the state, but they may also be in a position to decisively influence definite sectors of the state.[85]

Besides corporate governance as a major vehicle for self-regulatory initiatives, the increasing abundance of ethical codes regarding MNC activities over the past few years has largely been influenced by globalization. The perception of MNCs has become unambiguous. Their activities are significant for citizens around the world. The rise of activities generated by MNCs changes the approach applied to commercial, societal, environmental, and other issues. Moreover, states alone cannot satisfactorily adopt and enforce regulatory measures at the global level. They do not have the capacity to regulate the conduct and activities of MNCs apart from the activities developed in their own country. They will be able to identify the shareholders or owners of a MNC based on the enforcement of national regulation or their own particular transparency rules. However, they will not record their capital for tax matters based on their domestic rules. States are in a difficult position to participate as full actors in regulating MNC activities. As a result, there is a perception of a regulatory vacuum regarding such activities. This situation entails

[85] A. Sajó, Transnational Networks and Constitutionalism (2006) 213.

the proliferation of ethical codes of conduct. When compared, these codes cover similar topics or even repeat the contents of other codes. The rationales for their establishment are political. Only broad principles and standards in the form of recommendations are formulated. As a form of soft-law, these are neither legally binding nor do enforcement mechanisms apply, similarly to other instruments of international law. However, public pressure to comply with such codes cannot be ignored. The observation of industry-wide codes may result in MNCs adopting voluntary or self-regulatory measures.[86]

Finally, the influence and role of MNCs and large businesses also prevails in the model of enforced self-regulation as far as the operations of (trade) associations or SROs are concerned.[87] In particular, together with SROs or motivating them, MNCs play a particular role, not least due to their global activities and experience gained. In a way, they are quasi precursors of legal trends. For instance, international NGOs like the ICC largely influence the harmonization of global economic law. They set their own standards and contribute to the development of law through their formal participation in the activities of international and regional state institutions. Their approach is practical, based on the experiences made with the firms participating in their operations. They are also active through lobbying.[88] In the global market, MNCs as private entities, their NGOs, and other international organizations all exercise strategic governance functions.

3 Co-regulation

Self-regulation is determined by the initiative of individuals or groups of interest. In the case of co-regulation, cooperation between private actors, individuals, interest groups, businesses or organizations, and the state is crucial. Co-regulation refers to situations where non-state actors and the state collaborate to introduce or enforce regulatory solutions. The regulatory role is shared between the private actors and the state, as arising from their negotiations and regulatory interactions and on the basis of mutual agreement. The arrangements worked out represent hybrid regulatory solutions. Industry-wide standards are defined and usually effectuated through legislative reference or endorsement of a code of practice. The industry or self-regulatory organization will be committed to attain the regulatory objectives as convened with the state. Co-regulation can be considered to correspond to a kind of industry-association self-regulation with some state supervision or ratification. It represents an intermediate strategy between a model of pure self-regulation and

[86] Cragg, supra note 77, 213 et seqq.; B. Hunt, The Timid Corporation, Why Business is Terrified of Taking Risk (2003) 51–54, 61–67.

[87] Hutter, supra note 43, 5.

[88] K. Nowrot, Legal Consequences of Globalization: The Status of Non-Governmental Organizations under International law (Spring 1999) 589 et seq.

a model of rigid state command and control regulation. As a type of regulation, it can be encountered in different sectors.[89]

Two illustrative cases are discussed hereinafter: securities markets and official codes of conduct.

3.1 Securities Markets

3.1.1 Historical Aspects

The securities industry is a typical case of a self-regulatory regime featuring state involvement or a form of co-regulation. In that sector, self-regulation plays a role in a range of countries. In the United States, for instance, self-regulation is a key component of the securities industry regulation. It is determining in relation to both the organizational structure of the securities markets and the rules applying to financial institutions and operations. It is based on cooperation between private industry and government, and corresponds to a co-regulatory solution. The determination to rely on self-regulation as a cornerstone of securities markets and broker-dealer regulation is reflected in the Securities Exchange Act of 1934, the Maloney Act of 1938 as well as the Exchange Act Amendments of 1975. Self-regulation has a long tradition in these markets in which the securities industry was first subject loosely to state laws.

In 1792, the historic Buttonwood Agreement was negotiated by the New York broker community to form the first organized stock market, the NYSE.[90] In the course of developing exchanges, trading conventions became formalized; they assumed the form of exchange rules. In 1817, the NYSE's Constitution was adopted. Then, the NYSE enacted a range of rules governing its members and listed companies. In 1820, a detailed set of NYSE By-Laws was passed. Federal rules were only introduced over time. A pivotal year is 1934, where rules were enacted following the 1929 stock market crash. In the Exchange Act of 1934, the self-regulatory role of the exchanges was expressly recognized, but they were required to register with the Securities and Exchange Commission (SEC) to operate as self-regulatory organizations.[91]

---

[89] Baldwin and Cave, supra note 1, 133; Ayres and Braithwaite, op. cit. n 3, 102.

[90] See the study by the US Securities and Exchange Commission, Concept Release Concerning Self-Regulation, 17 CFR Part 240, Release No. 34-50700; File No S7-40-04; RIN 3235-AJ36 of November 18, 2004, point II. Foundations of Self-Regulation; Priest, supra note 3, 260–261, point II; R. Sobel, The Big Board, A History of the New York Stock Market (1965) 14–27, as cited in the Concept Release Concerning Self-Regulation.

[91] Sobel, supra note 90, 30–31 and 38–40, as cited in Concept Release Concerning Self-Regulation, supra note 90, point II; J. Seligman, The Transformation of Wall Street: A History of the Securities and Exchange Commission and Modern Corporate Finance (2003) 1–38.

Although some changes have occurred over time, the US self-regulatory regime has not been radically revised or dismantled since its establishment. It is generally admitted that it functions effectively. Its functioning and the analysis of its results have been periodically reviewed. For example, in 1975, US Congress determined that it was 'distinctly preferable' to rely on a co-regulatory system, because it had worked well and a regime based on state intervention may have been ineffective. The existing regime results in a mutually beneficial balance between the government and the securities industry interests. The organizations in charge of the industry are composed of professional experts. They are familiar with its nuances and their regulation appears to be less invasive and less rigid to their members. Moreover, if necessary, they could also set proscriptive standards for their members.[92]

As far as the NYSE is concerned, until 2002, it has often been perceived as a US securities market self-regulator which 'sets the pace for global transparency capitalism by acting as the gatekeeper of foreign securities listings'.[93] However, in the meantime, it has dramatically lost its competitive advantage not least due to regulatory burden. Then, in 2007, the NYSE Group merged with Euronext. The historic combination creates a truly global marketplace group. The same year, a new organizational structure of self-regulatory bodies was approved by the SEC. The Financial Industry Regulatory Authority (FINRA) is a consolidated self-regulatory organization resulting from the merger of the enforcement and arbitration arms of the NYSE and the National Association of Securities Dealers, Inc. (NASD). It operates under the oversight of the SEC. It is responsible for regulating all securities firms doing business with the public and, by contract, for a range of markets. It is now the largest non-governmental regulator for all securities firms doing business in the United States. It is dedicated to investor protection and market integrity through effective and efficient regulation and complementary compliance and technology-based services.[94]

Comparable developments took place in other countries. Hence, historically, securities exchanges have always been private entities in one form or another, organizing themselves in conjunction with the expectations of their members, issuers, and investors. Over time, they have established themselves pragmatically as SROs. State intervention and state involvement followed later,[95] in the wake of

[92] Concept Release Concerning Self-Regulation, supra note 90, point II, with further references.

[93] Braithwaite and Drahos, supra note 5, 492.

[94] http://www.nyse.com/about/history/1089312755484.html (last visited 25 November 2009); http://www.finra.org/index.htm (last visited 25 November 2009); SEC Gives Regulatory Approval for NASD and NYSE Consolidation, 2007-151, July 26, 2008, http://www.sec.gov/news/press/2007/2007-151.htm (last visited 25 November 2009).

[95] The Swiss regime of exchange regulation is briefly discussed hereafter as a case of delegated self-regulation; in particular, it offers less discretionary powers to the exchanges. It corresponds to a form of coercive self-regulation. However, some regulatory aspects remain co-regulatory and can lead to ambiguous solutions, as the example of enforcement measures adopted by the SIX Swiss Exchange discussed in Chapter 4, point 2 Standardization, 2.3 Gradual Transformation, 2.3.2 Impact, will show.

scandals and crises. The leading idea remains that state regulation should be moderate, not least because it represents a high burden to trading activities, incurs costs, and professional expertise is required. However, it cannot be ignored that these markets are also known for their recurrent scandals and a tendency to create direct personal advantages. Consequently, the need for more severe forms of regulation based on state intervention is advocated. In the long term, however, self-regulation shows an impressive success in this sector. It is mainly attributed to the particular interests of its actors.

3.1.2 Institutional Arrangements

Under a co-regulatory regime, the regulatory role is shared between the private sector and the state. It is the result of interactions and negotiations taking place between private interest groups or an industry and the state. According to Ayres and Braithwaite, a co-regulatory solution is based on a tripartite structure insofar as it also involves the participation of interest groups.[96] This is certainly correct, not least because the state has to represent public interest. In practice, it can occur in a more or less formal manner, either directly through state intervention or through the participation of interests groups in negotiations. While rule-making and enforcement functions will be in the hands of either the state, the industry, or the SRO, third parties or interest groups may influence the choice of a co-regulatory arrangement. They can take position in consultations or be represented in working groups.

Various arrangements can represent co-regulatory solutions. According to Priest – who conceives this kind of co-regulatory arrangement as a model of 'Regulatory Self-Management' –[97] the participation of an industry or its SRO has a determining effect with regard to both defining and attaining or enforcing regulatory objectives. The industry or SRO is responsible for submitting regulatory programmes and delimiting the possible extent of co-regulation as a solution. The state will pass the statutes resulting from negotiations. Under a co-regulatory regime, the state may be responsible for approving the self-regulatory measures and rules applying to an industry and which are then implemented by the SRO. They will be mandatory for all industry participants and the state will be responsible for exercising some ongoing oversight. It may also assume some enforcement functions. Industry or its SRO will subsequently have to cooperate with the responsible regulatory agency when verifying that the process of controls guarantees the attainment of the expected results. Cooperation may also be based on an agreement between the state and an industry or its SRO. Under such regimes, the range of SRO responsibilities and

[96] Ayres and Braithwaite, supra note 3, 102; Chapter 2, point 3 Institutional Structure, 3.2 Collectivity: From Associability to Association; P. Grabosky and J. Braithwaite, Of Manners Gentle: Enforcement Strategies of Australian Business Regulatory Agencies (1986) 83.

[97] Priest, supra note 3, 262 et seqq.

powers may differ from those of a SRO operating under a regime of coercive or supervised self-regulation.[98]

Co-regulatory regimes can also consist in arrangements regarding either the rule-making or enforcement functions. Often, there is a convention between the state or its regulatory agency and the industry or SRO concerned. These arrangements will guarantee voluntary industry-level compliance. According to Michael – discussing the regime of ‘Cooperative Implementation’, wherein a federal government leaves many compliance decisions up to the regulated entities themselves – self-regulation is stressed in such a regime. This corresponds to a co-regulatory regime based on the state relying on the regulated entities. These interpret and enforce the rules. However, to work properly, the following conditions must be fulfilled:

- Regulatory standards are written to allow for discretion with regard to methods of compliance and such discretion lies within the competence of the regulated entities
- There are economic incentives to offset the additional costs to these entities
- The entities self-report their own compliance, the (state) agency closely monitors the programme, and the agency maintains a residual programme of traditional surveillance and direct enforcement.[99]

In the securities markets, a concerted industry effort to address regulatory, infrastructural, or other issues can be recognized. This attitude is largely promoted by the state. It will interfere only if necessary and in a restrictive manner. The rule-making and enforcement functions are primarily in the hands of the industry or professional SROs, such as the securities exchanges. In that case, for instance, the state is involved and will have the power to approve or rewrite the rules of the exchanges. It can also require the adoption of determined rules or measures. In this respect, it should be taken into account that the motivation for action is based on gaining and keeping investors’ confidence in the markets. It constitutes the most important incentive. Thus, there is a reciprocal interest of both the state and the exchanges in ensuring the proper, fair, and good working of the securities market. This also concerns the ethical standards of regulation. The authorities are oriented towards the public interest or in relation to securities markets towards the interests of the investors in fulfilling their tasks, but the co-regulatory arrangement in this sector is determined by the prevailing role of self-regulation. State governance is somewhat limited, but there is a continuous dialogue between the state and the exchanges. The state remains responsible for the enforcement of the criminal justice rules. Exchanges or SROs do not have any power to impose penal sanctions.[100]

---

98 As discussed hereinafter; Priest, supra note 3, 262 et seqq.

99 D. C. Michael, Cooperative Implementation of Federal Regulations (1996) 535, 543–553.

100 Concept Release Concerning Self-Regulation, supra note 90, point IV.; Priest, supra note 3, 260–261.

Another form of co-regulatory institutional arrangement may concern cooperation between the state and a private or independent organization to attain a specific goal or realize an objective, for example to ensure rules enforcement. This applies to the British Panel on Takeovers and Mergers. The Panel was established in 1968 as a private organization. Following the implementation of the European Takeovers Directive, whilst the Panel remains an independent body, it now has a statutory basis. Its main functions are to issue and administer the City Code on Takeovers and Mergers. It has been designated as the supervisory and regulatory takeovers authority.[101] Thus, compliance with the Code is no longer solely regarded as a voluntary matter. In addition, although the Panel has limited enforcement action against companies failing to comply with the Code, it may now apply to the court directly in order to seek enforcement of its requirements.[102]

3.1.3 Characteristics

As already stated, an important characteristic of co-regulation is its representation as an order based on negotiations among the state, an industry, and possibly interest groups. The interplay between these actors and their cooperation can assume various forms. The solutions are based on a collective agreement among the actors concerned. When negotiations take place, possible co-regulatory solutions may be introduced based on private market initiative. They represent market-based solutions, which have to be approved by the state. They should then be best adapted to the sector they apply to. Diverse conventions and arrangements can be distinguished with regard to the economic sectors and actors involved, depending on the regulatory rule-making, enforcement, or judicative functions and the interests at stake.

A co-regulatory regime does not necessarily mean that regulatory functions are delegated by the state to a SRO. The state may set the framework and private industry or its SRO plays a determining role in that regime. The government may have some limited rule-making or policy-making function but the existing arrangement may be revised and improved on a regular basis. Where industry processes are complex and highly variable from firm to firm, industry will be largely responsible for rule-making, since a high degree of industry expertise in setting standards is required. However, at the same time, the government must retain its own expertise

[101] Directive 2004/25/EC of the European Parliament and of the Council of 21 April 2004 on takeover bids, OJ L 142, 30/04/2004, 12–23; Chapter 1 of Part 28 of the Companies Act 2006; http://www.thetakeoverpanel.org.uk/structure/about-the-panel and http://www.thetakeoverpanel.org.uk/structure/legislative-basis (last visited 8 January 2010).

[102] Section 955 of the Companies Act 2006 and section 11 of the Introduction to the Takeover Code; http://www.thetakeoverpanel.org.uk/wp-content/uploads/2008/11/code.pdf; http://www.thetakeoverpanel.org.uk/the-code/compliance (last visited 8 January 2010).

and responsive capacity in order to judge the adequacy of the industry standards defined and deal residually with enforcement.[103]

The degree of independence of the responsible SRO should be defined jointly with the authorities. It should also be accountable for its activities and its liability should be regulated. In this respect, transparency may contribute to realize these points. Moreover, the SRO should not only rely on voluntary compliance by its members but have enforcement expertise to guarantee the effective implementation of the regulatory arrangement. A level of enforcement quality should be attained – possibly in conjunction with the state –, and maintained on a continuous basis. As discussed by Michael, it should not be ignored that co-regulatory arrangements work successfully when industry has the right incentives to ensure compliance with existing rules. Regulation costs are one such incentive. Under a co-regulatory regime, they will be reduced, since an industry has to work efficiently. Hence, an industry's willingness to cooperate with the state should increase to develop solutions entailing cost reduction. To summarize, the focus point of co-regulatory solutions is to guarantee industry-level compliance, not least because co-regulatory schemes are established based on industry-wide voluntary standards.[104]

3.2 *Official Rules of Conduct*

3.2.1 Historical Aspects

Rules of conduct can be both public or official and private. Official codes may be enacted by a state or international organization or they may be enacted by a private industry based on statutes. For instance, article 11 of the Swiss Federal Act on Securities Exchanges of 1995[105] – the first federal act on securities exchanges – defines the rules of conduct applying to securities dealers. It states that they have a duty of information, a duty of diligence, and a duty of loyalty towards their clients. With a view to its practical application, this statute had to be concretized. Based on negotiations with the state and the supervisory authority, the SBA as the SRO representing the banking industry took the initiative to formulate a Code of Conduct for Securities Dealers, which subsequently had to be approved by the supervisory authority. In accordance with the statute, the Code lays down detailed rules regarding the responsibilities and duties of securities dealers together with

[103] Priest, supra note 3, 299–300; see also: IOSCO Report of the SRO Consultative Committee of the International Organization of Securities Commissions, Model for Effective Regulation (May 2000).

[104] Michael, supra note 99, 545–546; Priest, supra note 3, 265–267.

[105] Federal Act on Securities Exchanges and Securities Trading (Securities Exchange Act, SESTA) of March 24, 1995, SR 954.1, unofficial translation; P. Nobel, Schweizerisches Finanzmarktrecht, Einführung und Überblick (2004) 23–24, 758–765; E. Stupp, D. Dubs, Verhaltensregeln (2007) 150–166.

explicative comments. Its aim is to guarantee professional, fair, and transparent services to the clients of securities dealers. Although it is based on a statute, the substantiation undertaken by the SBA is considered part and parcel of self-regulation. In fact, it is the product of a co-regulatory compromise reached between the state and private industry. The Code has been in force since 1st August 1997. It applies to all licensed securities dealers, including non-members of SBA.

Another example, the above described practices among credit rating agencies mentioned that IOSCO published a Code of conduct for CRAs. IOSCO took the initiative to formulate this Code although the agencies are neither regulated entities nor involved in the activities of the organization. The code sets minimal standards, which established agencies already respected de facto before its enactment. Thus, some formalization has occurred in the meantime. However, the code would be without value if agencies failed to observe it. The CRAs thus committed themselves to respect the standards defined.

3.2.2 Institutional Arrangements

These codes of conduct can be issued based on various institutional arrangements. Some codes are solely the result of state initiatives and may be enacted either by the state itself or based on a delegation according to the prescriptions of the state. The example of the code of conduct for securities dealers corresponds to a form of weak enrolment by the state. In the statute, only broad principles have been laid down. The responsible SRO had large capacities to interpret these. In other cases, such as difficult or complex technical or other industry-specific questions, the state may renounce defining specific codes of conduct itself. It can limit itself to declaring existing private codes applicable standards or binding, and consequently protect valid standards of self-regulation in a sector.[106]

In the case of state involvement, controlling the implementation of codes can be transferred to auditing companies. There may be an agreement between the state and the entities concerned whereas these entities agree to be audited by a third-party. For example, the SBA rules of conduct applying to securities dealers, which have been approved by the supervisory authority, must be audited by an auditing company based on the dualistic system of supervision that applies in the financial sector.[107]

Nowadays, codes of conduct often have an international or global character. The increasing number of codes defined by international organizations is not least a consequence of the globalization of economic and societal processes. The structure of relations beyond the state is changing. There is a need to develop standards

[106] Marti, supra note 41, 566–567, with further references; Priest, supra note 3, 250 et seq.

[107] Nobel, supra note 105, 484 et seq.; Circular of the FINMA: Self-regulation recognized as a minimum standard by the Swiss Financial Market Supervisory Authority of 20 November 2008, FINMA-Circ. 08/10 Self-regulation as a minimum standard.

applying at the global level. Thus, initiatives are taken in various fields, including the environment, financial sector, human rights, and so forth. To give these initiatives more weight, international organizations will take measures. They may not have sufficient powers to enact binding rules or prospects that binding rules will be observed may be very slim. In particular, there exists no universally applicable and enforceable legal order at the global level. Hence, these organizations may publish declarations or also issue recommendations. Yet another possibility is to edict codes of conduct. For instance, this is the case of the rating agencies as stated where IOSCO published a code, although these entities are not regulated. In other cases, an organization may define codes of conduct or standards and rely on the states to enforce these. States are aware of these developments. Significantly, the Finmasa features an article declaring that the supervisory authority will take international minimum standards into account when exercising its powers (article 7 paragraph 2 letter d.). In such cases, the states play a determining role. They decide on the adoption of the standards and can exercise enforcement powers.

3.2.3 Characteristics

Rules of conduct can represent a form of soft law. They are not legally binding. In case of non-enforcement, they are not backed by sanctions. However, they are observed and may exercise a determined influence on legal life. They represent co-regulatory solutions, because although they may be defined by states or international organizations, they require private sector implementation. In various cases, the private sector will also actively participate in their elaboration.

The main difference between private or voluntary and public or official rules of conduct concerns their enrolment. There will be no state enrolment in the case of private codes of conduct. The industry or SRO will play a determining role when defining a code of conduct on a voluntary basis. On the contrary, in the case of public or official rules of conduct, the state always plays a leading role. This may concern the role of the state when dictating and formulating the standards to be transposed in a code or it may refer to state involvement with regard to the enforcement of a code. It can be interpreted as resulting in a hybrid form of control.

It should also be noted that some schemes of code of conduct defined by international organizations or bodies, notably the OECD Guidelines for MNCs and the ILO Tripartite Declaration of Principles concerning Multinational Enterprises and Social Policy as discussed above, could be compared to soft law measures adopted by states. In practice, these norms address firms directly, recommending determined behavioural measures, largely bypassing states.[108]

---

[108] K. W. Abbott, D. Snidal, The International Standards Process: Setting and Applying Global Business Norms (2005) 112.

4 Coercive Self-regulation

Coercive self-regulation designates a hybrid form of regulation locatable between command and control regulation and co-regulation. Similarly to co-regulation, it is a mixed form of regulation based on an interaction between the state and private business. There is both a part of direct state regulation and voluntary self-regulation.[109] While the model of co-regulation is constructed on the basis of a cooperative arrangement between private individuals, groups of interest or self-regulatory organizations and the state, the state dictates the extent and form of the self-regulatory solution in the case of coercive self-regulation. It can subsist within the limits set by the state following negotiations. The requirements to be observed are defined and delimited by statute. As a form of self-regulation, this corresponds to a kind of statutory self-regulation. It is the result of a delegation of regulatory powers by the state. Private actors like SROs will assume the responsibility to define private rules based on state steering. SROs will implement rules and may also fulfil other regulatory functions, for example in relation to compliance with the rules. Coercive self-regulation is a very important form of regulation, illustrating a possible relationship between the state and the private sector. It appears in various forms.

The following two main cases are distinguished hereinafter: delegated and supervised self-regulation.

4.1 Delegated Self-regulation

4.1.1 Historical Aspects

The delegation of duties by the state has a long tradition. It can assume various forms. Initially, it regularly concerned the implementation of rules. However, it is rather a new phenomenon as far as the rule-making function is concerned. The delegation of rule-making powers is based on an active participation of the private sector. Nowadays, a form of delegation commonly used consists in passing so-called framework statutes. Such statutes contain a provision delegating rule-making functions to agencies and private market actors or SROs. The statute only lays down principles. Thus, private industry or the responsible SROs play an important role together with the responsible agency. Besides taking charge of formulating and implementing detailed rules, SROs represent their industry and are best informed to defend the interests of their members and respond adequately to the requirements set by the statute. Depending on the sector concerned, there may be either a universal industry self-regulator or hybrid models or several self-regulatory

[109] Priest, supra note 3, 266; Marti, supra note 41, 570–577.

organizations or multiple SROs may exist, for instance for the sectoral or functional representation of firms, each fulfilling a different role.[110]

Another form of delegation of regulatory duties which has appeared recently has been principle-based regulation. It has been applied in the financial services industry, for example by the FSA, where principles have been in place since 2001. The basis of principle-based regulation is the reliance on broadly stated principles and not on detailed, prescriptive rules and supervisory actions regarding how firms should operate their business. It is outcome-focused and preference is given to broad-based standards or high-level rules. Principles-based regulation also implies a different approach towards the relations between the responsible supervisory authority and the regulated entities. It is based on trust and an ongoing dialogue between the authority and industry takes place. The aim is to define what type of rule or standards are appropriate to concrete cases or situations. However, following the 2007–2009 financial crisis, the future of this kind of delegation is insecure.[111]

4.1.2 Institutional Arrangements

In the case of delegated self-regulation, strategic focus is first placed on institutional aspects. Delegated self-regulation can appear in different forms and grades, and the range of institutions involved can vary depending on the delegation by the state, the statute, and a possible self-regulatory structure already existing at the point of delegation. In the literature, various categories of a state commitment to delegation are delimited. Marti, for instance, distinguishes the following possible constellations:

- State delegation and order to self-regulate
- Delegation of primary supervision to a self-regulatory organization
- Private, self-regulatory norms declared binding by the state
- Sufficient self-regulation as a condition of authorization[112]

These constellations represent basic structures of delegated self-regulation. They are briefly discussed hereinafter.

The statute constitutes the first form of state delegation and order to self-regulate. It lays down framework rules. Powers to formulate detailed rules are delegated to the private sector by statutory order. Delegation is understood as an authoritative decision that transfers policy- making authority away from established, representative organs to a non-majoritarian institution, whether public or private. Hence, the definition implies that it is largely used as a policy method.[113]

[110] Concept Release Concerning Self-Regulation, supra note 90, point IV.

[111] Principles-based regulation, Focusing on the outcomes that matter. FSA, April 2007, 4–6.

[112] Marti, supra note 41, 570–577. See also the description of C. Errass, Kooperative Rechtssetzung (2010), 81–90.

[113] M. Thatcher and A. Stone Sweet, Theory and Practice of Delegation to Non-Majoritarian Institutions (January 2002) 1, 3; M. Thatcher, Delegation to Independent Regulatory Agencies: Pressures, Functions and Contextual Mediation (January 2002) 125, 125–131; M. Shapiro, Judicial

It results in a fragmentation of rules. The regulatory functions are not concentrated anymore. On the contrary, they are distributed among different actors. Such an arrangement corresponds to undoing a centralized system. However, the degree of fragmentation or dispersion can vary depending on the matter considered and grade of delegation. In fact, it is a consequence of the level of control or power kept by the state. The self-regulatory organization elaborates the detailed rules concretizing the statute and implements these. Insofar as the model of coercive self-regulation delegates powers to the SROs, these can then adapt their exercise of powers to the particularities of the represented industry. This type of self-regulatory arrangement is essentially corporatist. The state endows the SROs with governmental power and the SROs implement the state strategy.[114] In practice, this kind of self-regulation will develop its own dynamic when defining detailed norms.

The second form deals with the delegation of supervisory competences. It is discussed separately hereafter as a case of supervised self-regulation.

The third form of private self-regulatory norms declared binding by the state is generally encountered when the historical development of a sector is considered. Rules often take the form of self-regulation in the first stage of their emergence. They may exist for centuries, such as in the case of the professions. However, in the long term, self-regulation may no longer be left entirely to the discretion of the professional organizations concerned or other bodies. The need for state intervention in the form of either regulation or state controls emerges in the course of time, for instance when there is a sense of a market failure which may be attributed to an unsatisfactory or insufficient self-regulatory solution. At such junctures, governmental intervention is expected. It should represent a corrective. However, a state may not just choose to introduce its own rules. It can follow various strategies and may decide to declare existing self-regulatory norms universally binding. When acting thus, it takes into account public interest. In recognizing a self-regulatory solution publicly and declaring it binding, it 'elevates' it to the status of a binding standard. From the point of view of the state, it is a form of exercising control over norms. Self-regulation acquires legal underpinning and self-regulatory rules become generally applicable.

In the fourth form of sufficient self-regulation as a condition of authorization, private firms or entities must fulfil the conditions set in the statute to be granted a license and be operative in a given business sector. However, prior to authorization, other stages of intervention can be considered. Priest differentiates three grades of state intervention under the category of delegation, whereby each represents a different degree of coerciveness.[115] The first, most lenient grade concerns the registration procedure. Such procedure applies in the case of an activity not regulated by the state. A registration can be used for practical matters, such as

Delegation Doctrines: The US, Britain, and France, (January 2002) 173, 173–175; also Senn, supra note 9, 444; Marti, supra note 41, 572–574.

[114] J. Black, Rules and Regulators (1997) 79.

[115] Priest, supra note 3, 252 et seq.

being introduced in a database in order to be approached for services. Another case is supervision-related registration. A well-known case is the case of rating agencies. Until 2006, these had to register with the SEC before their information could be used by the authority to determine the capital requirements of firms. However, following the introduction of the Credit Rating Agency Reform Act of 2006, the SEC now has more power.[116] In these cases, registration corresponds to a form of control. The second grade concerns the certification procedure. This procedure is a form of recognition of individuals or professionals. For example, it is often applied by professional organizations or also by the state. Rules for professional examinations are subject to state approval and enacted once they conform with professional training statutes. Based on this system, only individuals may bear a title who have passed the corresponding exam and thus been certified. A typical example is the case of auditors or also lawyers. Responsible private organizations, SROs, or the state are entitled to confer the title. In case a SRO grants the title, it acts as a guarantor towards the state and certifies that persons bearing the title hold the necessary qualifications to exercise a particular activity. For the general public, a title provides evidence for a defined professional background and knowledge.[117] Certification procedures are more severe than registration procedures, but less restrictive than authorization procedures. Such procedures do not limit the number of practitioners on the market and there is no issue of competition. On the contrary, they enhance competitiveness. Depending on the professional service offered, there will be more offers at lower prices. The third grade is the procedure of authorization, which is the most coercive measure. The main rationale justifying an obligation to be granted authorization is public interest. Requiring authorization represents state interference designed to limit the activities of private businesses. There are strict statutory requirements as far as the conditions of authorization to be fulfilled are concerned. There must be a sufficient self-regulatory solution. Moreover, authorization is accompanied by state supervision. It is the most imperative form of coercive self-regulation. However, the authorization requirement is not as severe as a measure where the state would regulate all the details itself.[118]

For example, the securities market in Switzerland has always been characterized by a long tradition of self-determination and self-regulation. Securities exchanges were not regulated by the state until the mid 1990s. Exchanges possessed corporative structures and opposed any state regulation. However, the cantons introduced specific rules. The Canton of Zurich, for instance, had its own law since 1883, stipulating that the securities exchange of the City of Zurich is a corporation by constraint, governed by public law. Its trading activities were subject to cantonal supervision. Other cantons, such as Geneva and Basel, also had their own rules.

---

116 See above, point 1 Self-Regulation, 1.2 Credit Rating Agencies; Credit Rating Agency Reform Act of 2006, September 29, 2006, Pub. L. No. 109-291 (2006); 17 CFR Parts 240 and 249b Oversight of Credit Rating Agencies Registered as Nationally Recognized Statistical Rating Organizations; Final Rule, June 18, 2007.

117 Marti, supra note 41, 567 et seq.; Priest, supra note 3, 252–256.

118 Marti, supra note 41, 574.

However, the exchanges themselves did not need authorization.[119] In the course of the 1980s and 1990s, these exchanges began to work together and finally merged to form one exchange, now the SIX Swiss Exchange. Centralization within one exchange was mainly due to international competitive pressure. At the same time, it was recognized that a federal statute laying down authorization requirements, would be necessary to be recognized and in a position to compete at the international level. Since the introduction of the SESTA in 1995, a framework law offering room for self-regulation, exchanges are regulated at the federal level. They must be authorized as self-regulatory organizations and the Act specifies that exchanges are self-regulated entities. Article 4 SESTA reads as follows:

Self-regulation

1. The stock exchange must undertake to ensure that it has an organizational structure in respect of its operations, administration and supervision that is appropriate to its activities.
2. A stock exchange must submit its regulations and any amendments thereof to the Supervisory Authority for approval.

Consequently, exchanges will be granted a license when their self-regulatory measures are sufficient to guarantee the respect of the statute. They have to define their own rules and submit these to the responsible supervisory authority for approval. The main rules concern the organization of a transparent trading, listing rules, rules regarding the admission of members to the exchange, and reporting duties. Supervision by the responsible authority is subsequently exercised on a continuous basis.[120]

4.1.3 Characteristics

From a policy point of view, the model of coercive self-regulation represents a way to strengthen private initiative not only with regard to businesses, but also regulatory matters. It is unambiguously the case, because self-regulation is ordered by the state. However, the delegation of rule-making competences raises a question with regard to the constitutionality of the measure as far as it implies a privatization of regulation. In fact, delegation does not correspond to a full delegation of a rule-making function. The state dictates the extent and expected contents of private, detailed regulation. For example, the Swiss Federal Constitution does not contain any general rule declaring that the delegation of regulatory functions to private market actors would be legal. Its article 178 paragraph 3 states expressly that administrative duties can be delegated to private market participants. Other

---

[119] Gesetz betreffend die Gewerbe der Effektensensale und Börsenagenten of 2nd December 1883; R. T. Meier, T. Sigrist, Der helvetische Big Bang, Die Geschichte der SIX Swiss Exchange (2006) 21–61.

[120] Articles 3 and 4 SESTA; Nobel, supra note 105, 773 et seqq.; P. Böckli, Zum Börsengesetz von 1995: neue Rechtsinstitute und neue Probleme (1998) 228–233.

categories are not mentioned expressly in the Constitution. However, as far as private business is concerned, economic order is based on private-public collaboration. According to article 164 of the Constitution, the enactment of detailed rules can be delegated to private organizations by statute. Thus, delegation to enact basic rules or statutes would not be possible. The detailed rules must also be submitted to a state agency or a supervisory authority and granted formal approval. Such approval is limited to checking the conformity of rules with the statute, which is particularly important when rules also apply to third parties. Hence, approval corresponds to a form of preventive rules control.[121] On the other side, it should be taken into account that in the case of delegating regulatory functions, SROs should be motivated to self-regulate effectively and assume supervisory and enforcement responsibilities as far as their members are concerned. In addition, individuals using SRO services de facto exercise significant pressure on the conduct of their activities and in particular on effective rule enforcement. What results is a self-disciplinary effect, not least because the SRO's reputation is very important.[122] Consequently, it will be motivated to ensure the good functioning of the regime. It will take adequate measures regarding the services offered or also other functions. These may take the form of internal rules applying to working methods, compliance rules, and so forth.

A regime of coercive, delegated self-regulation can enhance the role of private individuals and industries or their SROs. They can adopt a self-reflective approach and the state remains in the background as a higher authority. It can intervene whenever a failure within the self-regulatory system is recognized or the defined parameters need to be revised due to public pressure or other rationales. Hence, delegated self-regulation consists in a dual regime. The state remains responsible and plays a decisive role as far as the definition of the regulatory framework is concerned. It also acts as a kind of guardian whereas it pursues the goal of delegating regulatory functions.[123] As far as day-to-day operations are concerned, it will not be involved. It will be reluctant to intervene once a regime has been defined. However, such a regulatory regime does not necessarily mean that a government delegates the responsibility to ensure rules enforcement. Rather, it means that a strategic approach is applied as far as such enforcement is concerned. As Ayres and Braithwaite observe, the delegation of regulatory or legislative functions does not need to (and cannot) imply a delegation of executive and adjudicative ones. These functions are exercised by the courts and belong to the public sector, while the rules enacted and functions exercised by the SROs are private. A SRO may have the capacity to govern and enforce rules, but not inflict sanctions, in particular penal ones.[124]

[121] Chapter 1, point 4 Institutions; Marti, supra note 41, 570–572, with further references.

[122] Priest, supra note 3, 266.

[123] Ibid. 266.

[124] Ayres and Braithwaite, supra note 3, 103; Priest, supra note 3, 266.

The main advantage offered by a regime of delegated self-regulation is its flexible approach. It can be tailored to concrete cases and adjusted to individual situations. Due to a basic level of cooperation with the state or responsible agency, the introduction of a control is possible. It can take the form of periodical reports, or involve access to these reports or other data. Such a self-regulatory regime also has disadvantages, such as the threat of possibly limiting competition since authorization procedures may represent barriers to a market entry. The requirement of being granted authorization may also induce higher prices or a transfer of income. Yet another disadvantage is a possible mistaken or inefficient use of resources. It may also have a negative impact on incentives for new developments. In the financial sector, the 2007–2009 financial crisis will lead to a re-thinking and re-framing of the relationships between the state and self-regulated entities. It is almost certain that the model of delegated self-regulation will lose its significance.

4.2 *Supervised Self-regulation*

4.2.1 Historical Aspects

The case of supervised or audited self-regulation is based on third-party delegation or inspection. The model relies on decentralized market-based incentive mechanisms. It can be used to promote industrial safety as advocated by Kunreuther et al. This will be the case in particular with regard to environmental matters. Firms may be required to invest in Risk Management Plans (RMP), whose enforcement is subject to third-party inspections, along with insurances, as is the case in the United States. This can occur in the case of chemical firms or other matters, such as hygiene quality in restaurants or annual boiler controls, which were already introduced in the United States in the nineteenth century. Within such a supervisory regime, the main incentive for firms to comply lies in the probability of being subject to inspection.[125]

One interesting example in structural and institutional terms is the Swiss supervisory regime of banks and saving banks. These institutes are audited by external, private auditing companies. This regime is closely linked to the introduction of the first ever federal banking regulation regime in the 1930s, following the recognition that exercising supervision was considered necessary. However, at that time, the state was reluctant to introduce control. It was generally thought that official control would weaken the sense of responsibility of the administrative organs of banks. It was also considered problematic with regard to the liability of the state. Moreover, the use of the terms ‘federal control’ or ‘federal auditors’ could have been misinterpreted. In particular, bank clients, who as is well-known attach great

[125] H. C. Kunreuther, P. J. McNulty, and Y. Kang, Third-Party Inspection as an Alternative to Command and Control Regulation (2002) 309–318.

importance to banking secrecy and should be able to trust it, would most certainly not appreciate this kind of control and perhaps lose confidence in their bank. One possible consequence would probably be the flight of capital deposited in Swiss banks. Obviously, the country had to be preserved from such damage. The Federal Message of 1934 on the Introduction of a Banking Law reads as follows:

> 'The activity of the banks is so complex and polymorphic, that it is not possible to think about a control through the state.'[126]

Hence, at that time, it was decided to transfer the control of banks and savings banks to third, private institutions. Specific rules regarding audits were created. Independent, external auditing companies and auditing institutes were deemed particularly apt to fulfil these serious duties. Under this regime, they have to report to the supervisory authority. They should also indicate deficiencies encountered during their routine audits to both the bank's management and the supervisory authority.[127] As of today, the auditing companies still exercise the same key function – acting as gatekeepers of financial markets – although the supervision exercised by the supervisory authority became more important after the 1970s. In a ruling, the Federal High Court wrote that the legal rules laid down in the Federal Banking Act regarding the Supervision and Audit would be the 'pivotal point of the Act' according to which the idea of legal protection had to be realized.[128] However, it is recognized that control will never replace a bank management's circumspection.[129] Nor should one ignore the examples of foreign states in which neither severe state control nor rigorous auditing helped prevent isolated or collective bank collapses.

In Switzerland, the above solution has proved to be very valuable. However, it also presents weaknesses. To exercise its role, the supervisory authority has recourse to the reports of auditing companies. On the one hand, auditing companies receive their mandates from banks. On the other, they are dependent on the supervisory authority, responsible for checking their reports. The potential for conflicts of interest is inherent in such a model of supervision. To ensure that auditing duties are duly performed, the Banking Act and the Banking Ordinance contain comprehensive catalogues of duties.[130] Thus, the question may arise whether auditing companies are effectively instruments of self-regulation or only outsourced, privatized services companies of the supervisory state agency or its extension. In fact, these companies are only recognized by the supervisory authority and not authorized. Moreover, it should be noted that the Federal High Court did not recognize any responsibility of the state or Confederation for the auditing activities

126 Unofficial translation, Botschaft des Bundesrates an die Bundesversammlung betreffend den Entwurf eines Bundesgesetzes über die Banken und Sparkassen of 2nd February 1934, BBl 1934 I 179.

127 Hutter, supra note 43, 6; Kunreuther, McNulty, and Kang, supra note 125, 309–318.

128 Case 99 Ib 104, 110, E. 5., of 4 May 1973.

129 Unofficial translation, BBl 1934 I, supra note 126, 179–182.

130 See in particular article 44 and 45 Banking Ordinance.

of a private auditing firm conducted in a bank. In a ruling not deemed uncontroversial it was argued that auditing companies are not agencies of the state and do not exercise any function or fulfil any duty corresponding to a 'task of public law for the account of the Confederation'. The missing recognition of state responsibility strongly suggests the existence of a mechanism of self-regulation.[131]

4.2.2 Institutional Arrangements

The regime of supervised self-regulation applies to regulated activities. The main idea lies in the delegation of implementation or supervisory duties to private firms or SROs by statutes whereas they will be subject to continuous monitoring. They are supervised by a state agency and accountable to it. Such an arrangement results in a dual system of supervision. The case of supervised or audited self-regulation can be defined as follows:

> '(Supervised or) 'Audited' self-regulation is the exercise of this delegated power, subject to review by a federal agency. The term 'audit' is not used in strict reference to the functions performed by independent public accountants ... The federal agency relies on information produced by the SRO, but verifies that the processes used by the SRO are sound, that those processes are complied with, and occasionally examines the information directly to spot-check its accuracy.'[132]

The responsible private firm or SRO may define detailed rules or guidelines to clarify the procedures it will apply directly when fulfilling its task. These rules may be discussed with the responsible supervisory authority or agency, examined and approved by it. The agency may also take measures itself to enforce rules if necessary. For instance, it can enact directives regarding the interpretation of rules. The firm or SRO remains responsible for compliance and enforcement. The state agency first exercises a governance function. It will supervise compliance and enforcement, and analyse the reports of the firms or SRO. It may also be confronted with appeals, render decisions, and either conduct investigations itself or together with a responsible firm or SRO. It should take all appropriate measures to guarantee effective rules enforcement. Its influence may be less pronounced when a practice is developed and a regime of supervised self-regulation is working properly.[133]

Basically, the SROs assume direct responsibility, but their autonomy may be relatively limited. The firms or SRO remain entirely accountable to the supervisory authority as far as proper rules application is concerned. They are more embedded in the regulatory system than in the case of delegated self-regulation. The functions

---

131 Case 117 II 317 of 20 September 1991; P. Nobel, Freiheit und Ordnung im Kapitalmarktrecht (1998) 121–126. Whether this will still be the case following the introduction of the Federal Act on Auditors' Authorization and Supervision of 16 December 2005, SR 221.302, remains open at this stage.

132 D. C. Michael, Federal Agency use of Audited Self-Regulation as a Regulatory Technique (Spring 1995) 176.

133 Ibid. 175 et seq.; Priest, supra note 3, 260.

of supervision exercised by the firms or SROs may also be shared with the state agency. State supervision duties consist in checking whether the processes applied by the firms or SRO are adequate to implement the statute. The good functioning of the regime is largely based on the responsible authority's appreciation of the information received from the professional bodies. The supervisory authority will act as a superordinate instance and impose sanctions if necessary. It can also choose to focus on determined functions only.[134]

The state can organize supervision such that it introduces various levels of supervision. In that case, it will determine the basic governance structure. Within an enforcement pyramid, some functions, for example regarding primary supervision, can be delegated to a self-regulatory organization. The powers and role of that organization are then defined in the statute. The state determines the level of regulation and the competences to be delegated to that organization. In a concrete case, the power to grant authorizations within a sector may be delegated to a professional body or a SRO as far as determined business activities are concerned. The SRO will be responsible for granting authorizations, and it may also be responsible for other supervisory matters. It will assume supervisory functions or may have some powers to inflict sanctions on its own. It is directly accountable to the state agency and will report to it. The main rationale for this solution is that a lot of activities are only accessible to specialists and can best be administered by these or their representative SROs. They will have developed their expertise through longstanding experience.[135]

For example, the regulation of money laundering in Switzerland follows the above scheme. According to the statute on Money Laundering first enacted in 1997, it is possible to delegate the supervision of rules observance to specialized SROs. To fulfil this task, a professional body or SRO must be recognized by the responsible authority. It has to submit its rules for approval. Such rules must describe the legal duties of diligence for affiliated financial intermediaries, and will apply in particular to combat money laundering. They will also set the detailed conditions to admit or exclude financial intermediaries from the SRO, thus sanctioning them. In addition, monitoring rules observance and sanctions must be regulated, too. The SRO also has to compile lists of affiliated financial intermediaries and of those refused affiliation. It must inform the authority of every change. It reports at least once a year to the authority and files charges when it suspects possible cases of money laundering. A SRO can also develop a long-term strategy. It can provide training and assistance to the firms or individuals subject to its rules or can function as a centre for information and exchange. Finally, the responsible authority has the authority to revoke an authorization granted to an SRO.[136] The affiliated members of specialized SROs are financial intermediaries which have not already been

---

[134] Priest, supra note 3, 260.

[135] Ibid. 254; for examples of enforcement pyramids, see Ayres and Braithwaite, supra note 3, 35–40.

[136] Article 24-28 Federal Act on Money Laundering of 10 October 1997 (FAML) SR 955.0.

granted a license under another statute, for instance as a bank or broker-dealer, and which are not already supervised. Moreover, besides the fact that money laundering rules offer the possibility to financial intermediaries to affiliate themselves to an SRO, these entities can chose to be directly subject to the authority or authorized and supervised by it. A basic feature underlying this self-regulatory model is the role of the state in taking measures itself in case an SRO is no more in a position to satisfy the statutory requirements. It may act subsidiarily. For example, if an SRO's authorization were revoked, its members would become directly subject to the authority in an initial phase. They could subsequently choose to affiliate themselves to another SRO or remain directly authorized and supervised by the authority.[137] There is a similar situation in the UK where the FSA no longer manages most money laundering rules since 2006. It now relies on regulatory provisions, guidance, and instruments produced by the Joint Money Laundering Steering Group (JMLSG), a private industry association. It applies a risk-based approach to implement money laundering rules. For the FSA, the challenge as a regulatory body has three dimensions: supervision, use of enforcement powers, and working in partnership with the JMLSG and the government.[138]

According to Kunreuther et al., the use of third-party delegation is rapidly becoming very common. However, it is also a controversial issue, although it has proved its worth in many circumstances. Auditors are being delegated tasks in a wide range of cases, like financial matters, as just stated. One prominent example of a company specialized in the inspection, verification, certification as well as risk management, technical consultancy, and products testing or activity monitoring based on third-party delegation is the Société Générale de Surveillance (SGS). It works for governments that have privatized enforcement as well as for private businesses. Insurances could also undertake similar roles. Such delegation may either replace a state supervision or complement it.[139]

4.2.3 Characteristics

Besides the above cases of supervised self-regulation, the regime can adopt various other forms. It can be a form of self-reporting, encountered where no SRO performs supervision. In such cases, the regulated entity reports directly to the agency. It has little or no power to interpret the existing regulation, but must apply it as dictated by the agency. Another form is privatization. The regime of supervised self-regulation can be considered to be a part of what is a broader concept. Privatization not only covers sectors or industries which can be governed by private actors, SROs

[137] Article 14 and 28 FAML respectively.

[138] Black, Decentred Regulatory State, supra note 45, 266–267; Financial Services Authority, Newsletter of the FSA, January 2006; FSA, Reviewing our Money Laundering Regime PS06/1.

[139] Kunreuther, McNulty, and Kang, supra note 125, 309–318; Hutter, supra note 43, 6; Coglianese and Lazer, supra note 57, 449–451; on the Société Générale de Surveillance: Braithwaite and Drahos, supra note 5, 287, 492–493, 618–619.

or private associations instead of the state. With privatization, government services are turned over to the private sector. The questions arising and the techniques used under privatization could prima facie be compared to those arising in relation to the introduction and shaping of a self-regulatory solution. However, privatization is more comprehensive. It corresponds to the introduction of an ad hoc regulatory solution, which consists in entrusting a private firm or industry association with a previous public sector matter. With privatization, the focus is placed on a transfer of ownership from the state to a private body in charge of managing a service or production process. Privatization is accompanied by the question whether the private body replacing the government should be regulated or not and the question of its accountability. In particular, it is expected that private actors should commit themselves to what are traditionally public goals.

In practice, governments often delegate functions to private business or SROs. Due to their expert knowledge, specialized firms or SROs can be adequately suited to determine standards for practitioners and work on compliance and enforcement matters. The binding character of the standards will depend on their relationship to the statute. They may also be declared binding by the state or based on court rulings. However, in the case of supervised self-regulation, the objective of the state should be not to intervene directly. The state should exercise a function of governance, defining the structure of a regime. It exercises supervisory functions solely as a higher instance. Within such a regime, it acts as a guarantor towards the supervised private entities. Supervised self-regulation allows for the development of sophisticated supervisory techniques. It implies that both the state and SROs or firms cooperate and are committed to the same regulatory objectives.[140]

The following requirements should be fulfilled to apply this regime: regulatory standards should be clearly defined and the goal of the regulatory solution should be communicated clearly. The firms or SROs must be in a position to apply the rules defined objectively. Together with the delegation of powers to a firm or SRO, the individuals or institutes concerned by third-party control should be broadly informed. Their capability is determined by their professionalism, experience, authority, and their commitment to adopt effective compliance measures.

Supervised self-regulation presents various strengths and weaknesses when assessed against the public interest criteria. This regime offers cost saving opportunities. The delegation of duties to SROs enhances the probability of efficient enforcement. Moreover, sectors where a model of supervised regulation is applied have often been self-administered for long time or no state regulation existed first. Their conduct of operations was probably satisfactory and various other rationales may have led to the introduction of supervisory solutions governed by the state. It was subsequently redelegated to the private parties concerned with the introduction of a statute. In this way, it is possible to preserve an existing functioning privately organized system, while supervising it at the same time. In addition, in comparison to a regime of state enforcement, a regime of private rules enforcement offers the

[140] Priest, supra note 3, 301.

major advantage of being likely to be free of corruption, on the one hand, but the problem of capture is a major one and cannot be ignored, on the other. Accountability mechanisms are also in place and incentives for compliance exist. On top of this, fairness and natural justice play an important role in the regulatory processes of both the SRO and the oversight agency. It is likely to have a relatively high degree of openness and transparency. However, this regime may be less efficient than other self-regulatory regimes since it gives rise or even encourages a duplication of effort by an SRO and the supervisory agency.[141]

To differentiate between both, the regime of delegated self-regulation and the regime of supervised self-regulation, a functional approach has to be applied. The regime of supervised self-regulation cannot be simply assimilated as such to the regime of delegated self-regulation. While the rule-making function is the main focus of delegated self-regulation, the situation is different in relation to supervised self-regulation where supervision is core to the regime. A private firm or SRO is in charge of supervising the implementation of rules or other measures. The main difference to delegated self-regulation lies in the continuous oversight over the implementation by the state or a state agency. However, its role is less incisive in the regime of supervised self-regulation. De facto, it may correspond to indirect state control.[142]

5 Self-contained Regimes

The cases discussed in this chapter all enhance the phenomenon of fragmentation and decentralization of law. They have been selected, since they belong to the variety of autonomous regulatory fields. They represent complexes of rules with different grades of non-state and private autonomous, bespoke institutional arrangements, and spheres of application. In practice, they initially appear to correspond to a response to technical or functional requirements of matters or sectors to be regulated and which may not be addressed satisfactorily or efficiently enough with traditional legal methods or techniques. As illustrating typologies of regulatory regimes, they may perhaps be limited to determined areas, either geographically, sectorally, or functionally. On their side, self-contained regimes also represent a form of fragmentation of law. They belong to this category of bodies of rules although they are and remain a form of state law. When considering these regimes through the lens of general law, they can be classified as regimes based on their own principles and institutions comparable to environmental law, maritime law, or investment law. The main difference consists in their linkage to international law as a point of departure and their development as a regime within that

[141] Michael, supra note 132, 179–184; Braithwaite and Drahos, supra note 5, 287; Harrison, Morgan, Verkuil, supra note 71, 505–516.

[142] Michael, supra note 132, 171–251; Priest, supra note 3, 259–260.

framework of law. Technically, they contribute to the understanding of a possible passage from legal regimes to private or autonomous regimes,[143] which is the rationale for mentioning them here.

To illustrate these regimes, the S.S. Wimbledon and Hostages cases are discussed hereinafter.

5.1 S.S. Wimbledon and Hostages Cases

5.1.1 Historical Aspects

The use of the term 'self-contained regime' first appeared in rulings regarding two concrete cases. It was initially coined by the Permanent Court of International Justice in the S.S. Wimbledon case of 1923. The Court had to decide whether the provisions of the Treaty of Versailles relating generally to German waterways also applied to the Kiel Canal and, consequently, whether the boat could be granted passage:

> The provisions relating to the Kiel Canal in the Treaty of Versailles are therefore self-contained; if they had to be supplemented and interpreted by aid of those referring to the inland navigable waterways of Germany in the previous Sections of Part XII, they would lose their 'raison d'être'... The idea which underlies [the provisions regarding the Kiel Canal] is not to be sought by drawing an analogy from these provisions but rather by arguing a contrario, a method of argument which excludes them.[144]

Later on, in 1980, the International Court of Justice adhered to this concept and identified diplomatic law as a self-contained regime in the Tehran Hostages case. These cases represent two major precedents. In the Wimbledon case, the Court applied the concept of self-containment to resolve a question of treaty interpretation concerning the relationship between two sets of primary international obligations. In the second case, the concept of self-contained regime was transposed to the level of secondary norms. The regime of

> ... diplomatic law itself provides the necessary means of defence against, and sanction for, illicit activities by members of diplomatic or consular missions. ... [t]he rules of diplomatic law, in short, constitute a self-contained régime which, on the one hand, lays down the receiving State's obligations regarding the facilities, privileges and immunities to be accorded to diplomatic missions and, on the other, foresees their possible abuse by

---

[143] M. Koskenniemi, Fragmentation of International Law: Difficulties arising from the Diversification and Expansion of International Law (13, April 2006) 11–14; A. Fischer-Lescano and G. Teubner, Regime-Collisions: The Vain Search for Legal Unity in the Fragmentation of Global Law (Summer 2004) 1001–1002.

[144] Case of the S.S. 'Wimbledon', P.C.I.J. Series A., No. 1 (1923), 23–24.

> members of the mission and specifies the means at the disposal of the receiving State to counter any such abuse. These means are, by their nature, entirely efficacious, ...[145]

The concept of self-contained regime has then been adopted in the Riphagen Reports to the International Law Commission (ILC) regarding State Responsibility in 1982. According to Riphagen's words:

> ... international law as it stands today is not modelled on one system only, but on a variety of international sub-systems, within each of which the so-called 'primary rules' and the so-called 'secondary rules' ' are closely intertwined – indeed, inseparable.[146]

In the Report, however, the concept of self-contained regimes should not be used as a synonym for subsystem. It should be reserved to designate a certain category of subsystems, namely those embracing a full set of specific rules. These subsystems would then continue working on their own. They would be close subsystems consisting of rules of international law. They would regulate relations exclusively and fall entirely outside the system of general international law. As stated by Simma, this is exactly the main question posed by self-contained regimes. The character of their relationship with the general rules of law and, hence, their very existence as such have to be determined. Prima facie, self-contained regimes represent borderline cases and deviations from general rules, although they can be considered to be based on general international law. In such a case, human rights law, like diplomatic law, could also have been regarded as a subsystem or a self-contained regime. However, the arguments furnished to support that point of view were not convincing and the question remained very controversial. Self-contained regimes were considered to represent exceptions or third regimes, and international law was considered to represent true law.[147]

Since that report, the situation regarding self-contained regimes has not changed. The evolution of the law has not brought new elements which could have contributed to an understanding and classification of these regimes. In the recent UN-Report finalised by Koskenniemi in 2006, the result of the analysis leads to the discussion of a 'failure' of the concept of self-contained regimes. In the course of time, taking into account the evolution of the understanding and interpretation of these regimes, the conclusion was reached that the claim that they were completely

---

[145] Case concerning the United States Diplomatic and Consular Staff in Tehran (United States of America v. Iran) I.C.J. Reports 1980, 38, para. 83; United States Diplomatic and Consular Staff in Tehran, I.C.J. Reports 1980, 38 and 40; see also: B. Simma, Self-Contained Regimes (1985) 113.

[146] W. Riphagen, Third Report on State Responsibility (1982) para. 35; Simma, supra note 145, 115; Koskenniemi, supra note 143, 74. Primary and secondary rules are not to be understood in the sense of Hart's distinction between primary and secondary rules; H.L.A. Hart, The Concept of Law (1997) 79 et seqq.; see Chapter 4, point 2 Standardization, 2.3 Gradual Transformation, 2.3.2 Impact.

[147] Simma, supra note 145, 117–119, 135–136.

cocooned outside international law was mistaken. They are now considered to be part of general law.[148]

5.1.2 Institutional Arrangements

Self-contained regimes are understood to be specific regulatory orders with their own rules applying to determined fields or issues. As autonomous regimes, they should work on their own. They develop their techniques of rules interpretation and administration, which deviate from the rules of general law. Two uses of the notion of self-contained regime can be distinguished. One may denote a special set of secondary rules under the law of state responsibility that claims primacy over the general rules regarding the consequences of a violation. The other may refer to interrelated wholes of primary and secondary rules that cover some particular problem or specific sector differently from the way it would be covered under general law. Furthermore, these regimes may designate entire sectors of functional specialization, diplomatic and academic expertise, or also regulation. In the fields typically classified as self-contained regimes, that is, diplomatic law, trade law, humanitarian law, or also space law, these regulatory regimes have their own institutions. They qualify as self-contained or special regimes, because they operate based on their own principles, methods and techniques and not primarily based on the rules of international law. The rules are adapted to the peculiarities of their field.[149]

In the field of trade law, for instance, the WTO dispute settlement regime can be considered to represent a self-contained regime. In particular, article 23 of the Dispute Settlement Understanding (DSU) excludes unilateral determinations of breach or countermeasures outside the 'specific subsystem' of the proper WTO-regime. Trade law disposes of its own institutions, which operate according to their own rules. They should not be interpreted in application of the principles of general international law. The WTO treaties differ fundamentally in their general orientation from the orientation of regular public international law. International law is implemented through national governments and finds its justification in the theory of comparative advantage. On the contrary, like the IMF and the World Bank, the WTO aims at enhancing the process of globalization. It should establish and administer a free trade area. As a consequence, its rules should be interpreted according to different, proper principles. The WTO Dispute Settlement organs have to take trade rationality into account, which may not correspond to the protection of sovereign interests. Hence, the general objectives and principles of

[148] Koskenniemi, supra note 143, 91–100. On self-contained regimes, see also: L.A.N.M. Barnhoorn and Karel Wellens (eds.), Diversity in Secondary Rules and the Unity of International Law (1995).

[149] Koskenniemi, supra note 143, 68; Barnhoorn and Wellens, supra note 148; Fischer-Lescano and Teubner, supra note 143, 999–1046; on the distinction between primary and secondary rules, see: Hart, supra note 146.

trade law will apply.[150] However, it should be noted that academic opinion is divided on the question whether the WTO forms a closed system. One view holds that the WTO is part of international law and operates within the general system of international law rules and principles. The other focuses on the provisions of the DSU that require that the obligations under the covered treaties should be neither added nor diminished. An analogous situation could apply to space or environmental law. Here, too, the question whether these regimes can be designated as special branches of international law leading to the exclusive application of proper interpretative principles instead of the ones generally applied is controversial.[151]

5.1.3 Characteristics

Basically, the term 'self-contained' reads thus:

> Having all that one (it) needs in oneself (itself); independent of external means or relations [...][152]

What characterizes self-contained regimes is their deviation from the rules of general law. They differ from those of national or international law or from the conception of law as the sovereign's coercive order. They can also be characterized as instruments used to interpret rules. The following technical definition can apply to self-contained regimes:

> A regime is a union of rules laying down particular rights, duties and powers and rules having to do with the administration of such rules, including in particular rules for reacting to breaches. When such a regime seeks precedence in regard to the general law, we have a 'self-contained regime,' a special case of lex specialis.[153]

When considering self-contained regimes as a strong form or a special case of lex specialis, the question of the fragmentation of law arises, as stated. The issue raised by self-contained regimes is an issue of their coherence with international law. These regimes have their own distinctive rules and dynamic, and a particular approach is applied. They are auto-constitutional regimes, which means that a development of rules or rule-regimes that have no clear relationship to each other is possible. Self-contained regimes not only create highly specialized primary norms, but they also produce their own procedural norms on law-making, law-recognition, and legal sanctions. These regimes are also neutral institutions in the sense that their emergence occurs independently, in isolation from third legal

[150] Koskenniemi, supra note 143, 71–72, 87; Sassen, supra note 4, 267–268.

[151] Koskenniemi, supra note 143, 70, with further references, 87–90.

[152] The Oxford English Dictionary, Volume XIV (1991) 917.

[153] Fischer-Lescano and Teubner, supra note 143, 1013, with reference to Koskenniemi; Fischer-Lescano and Teubner, Regime-Kollisionen, supra note 3, 50; Koskenniemi, supra note 143, 65–73.

influences.[154] They focus on the regulation of factual matters and mainly represent a technical regulation. In practice, the development of these regimes is also linked to the activities of their pressure groups and the specific norms which have to be created must be adapted to the particularities of the fields they regulate. Thus, a possible issue which arises here concerns the process of juridification. Should these regimes be understood to correspond to rules situated one stage before traditional law, and which should be 'officialized'? Which conditions ought to apply to their establishment? These regimes add to the fragmentation of international law and it should not be overlooked, as the Report finalized by Koskenniemi concludes, that no such regime can be created outside the scope of general international law. Such regimes are considered to belong to the traditional concept of law. Neither do they emerge outside that concept nor do they disaggregate or violate it. Rather, they present their own specificities within it.[155]

6 Global Networks

Global networks are certainly the prime example of autonomous regimes. As a form of regulatory governance, they could already be recognized in relation to other cases discussed above, for instance commercial arbitration or multinational firms. In fact, a large number of modern developments can be classified as global networks. These networks can both be public or private, governmental or non-governmental. Some matters can be delimited only through them, as their order will be solely able to be operative based on their global character. There is now a proliferation of specialized types of mainly private, non-state authority at the global level. In the literature, the phenomenon, nature, power, characteristics, and influence of global networks is vividly debated. Grasping and understanding how they emerge, what they are, and how they can be linked to or included in traditional modes of state regulation still represents a challenge.

The following cases are briefly discussed hereinafter: digital networks, technological standard setting networks, and financial standard setting networks.

---

[154] Fischer-Lescano and Teubner, supra note 143, 1014–1017; on the concept of neutrality, see Sajó, supra note 85, 14–15.

[155] Koskenniemi, supra note 143, 83 et seqq.; Fischer-Lescano and Teubner, supra note 143, 1015; Simma, supra note 145, 111, 245.

6.1 Digital Networks

6.1.1 Historical Aspects

The proliferation of global computer-based networks, the Internet and the accompanying digitization of activities in a broad array of domains has occurred mainly since the 1980s and 1990s. The process of digitization is all-embracing. It encompasses telecommunications, copyright, communication, or also technological issues, to name a few.[156] From the point of view of regulation, the efforts made to regulate the process of digitization and the rules developed are generally summarized under so-called lex digitalis or lex cybertoria. The main characteristic of this body of rules is its non-state character. Both regulation and rules enforcement, and supervision based on the concept of the state would be largely useless and noneffective. In particular, they would fail, because digitization cannot possibly be associated and limited to the concept of territoriality. Digitization is global. Hence, instead of state regulation, non-state and self-regulatory solutions began to permeate and a range of autonomous self-regulatory regimes have appeared.[157] They take the form of epistemic communities, networks or specialized organizations, each dealing with specific, mostly technical questions raised by the use of electronic communication means. Besides traditional, established standard-setting organizations like the International Organization for Standardization (ISO), International Electrotechnical Commission (IEC), and the International Telecommunications Union (ITU), which also develop standards in relation to information technology, a range of specific organizations have emerged since the 1990s. These include: the Internet Architecture Board (IAB), Internet Assigned Numbers Authority (IANA), Internet Corporation for Assigned Names and Numbers (ICANN), Internet Engineering Steering Group (IESG), Internet Engineering Task Force (IETF), Internet Research Steering Group (IRSG), Internet Research Task Force (IRTF), Internet Society (ISOC), RFC-Editor, or the World Wide Web Consortium (W3C). The list is not exhaustive. Further, specialized organizations may be created at any time.[158] This is due not least to the fact that many challenges still need to be mastered when crafting governance frameworks aimed at defining regulations. For example, the regulation of search engines still requires resolution. There is an ongoing endeavor to establish policy principles.[159]

---

156 For a discussion of practical issues, see D. Weinberger, Everything is Miscellaneous, The power of the new digital disorder (2007); D. L. Spar, Lost in (Cyber)space: The Private Rules of Online Commerce (1999) 31–51; D. L. Spar, Ruling the Waves, Cycles of Discovery, Chaos, and Wealth from the Compass to the Internet (2001); D. L. Spar, The Public Face of Cyberspace (1999) 344–362.

157 Sassen, supra note 4, 328–329.

158 Berman, supra note 3, 397–400.

159 U. Gasser, Regulating Search Engines: Taking Stock and Looking Ahead (Spring 2006) 124–157.

Each organization pursues its own objectives and fulfils different functions either in relation to technical matters or to set standards to ensure the stability and good functioning of the Internet worldwide. Among these organizations, ICANN is probably the most well-known. It serves as a case in point here. While it appears as a private organization operating at the global level, it is originally based on a Memorandum of Understanding (MOU) with the US Department of Commerce to transition the management of the Domain Name System (DNS) to the global community. It will be fully independent when it reaches the goals defined in the MOU. Hence, it is formally a private-public partnership. De facto, however, it is run on a private basis. It calls itself an 'internationally organized, non profit corporation'.[160] In comparison to other organizations active in the field of digitization, it is certainly one of those organizations most closely linked to the state. It is dedicated to managing and coordinating the DNS and it is responsible for handling technical DNS elements. Further, it contributes to the development of substantive – and globally enforceable – legal standards in that field. ICANN coordinates its activities with other interested groups and also issues directives. Its goals are to ensure that every Internet address is unique and to guarantee that every user can find valid addresses. It is also responsible for accrediting domain name registrars. Its Uniform Domain Name Dispute Resolution Policy (UDRP) has already been used to resolve more than 9,000 disputes regarding the rights to domain names by early 2005. Moreover, it develops a strategy based on a consensus among participants and encourages competition. Its achievements are based on its global presence. It also tries to represent as many Internet organizations as possible. As such, it is part of a third network. However, ICANN does not make Internet policy. The organization is also criticized. It is alleged that it mainly acts in the interests of the US Government, whose influence stems from its historical role. Its other members are less influential. They usually represent the interests of their respective states, although they have no formal duty to do so.[161]

6.1.2 Institutional Arrangements

The process of digitization creates new institutional challenges. These are based on the transnational character of regulatory issues. States have been overstrained by the process of digitization. They recognized that an individual handling of this matter would neither deliver the expected results nor be responsive. The global dimension of activities and the necessity to work out corresponding regulatory solutions rapidly became obvious. Braithwaite and Drahos argue that this kind of regulation is the result of a worldwide collaboration of various epistemic groups or

[160] Memorandum of Understanding between the U.S. Department of Commerce and Internet Corporation for Assigned Names and Numbers, of 25 November 1998; http://www.icann.org/en/general/icann-mou-25nov98.htm (last visited 25 November 2009).

[161] http://www.icann.org/; http://www.icann.org/en/general/bylaws.htm; http://www.icann.org/en/factsheets/ (last visited 25 November 2009).

groups of experts. Transnational communities of experts or epistemic communities appear to be in a much better position to adopt effective measures. These communities develop on an ad hoc basis and can work out global regulatory solutions. Over time, formalization occurs and transnational networks are constituted. From an institutional point of view, these transnational network structures mostly correspond to communities or networks of private ordering, although networks comprising state representatives or both can also be encountered. They can adopt different forms on an ad hoc basis, depending on the environment and issues at stake. In their field, they will define a regulatory frame autonomously. Their activities correspond to working out self-regulatory solutions, which will take a shape proper to the network concerned.[162]

With regard to ICANN, its operations are based on the collaboration of a collectivity of different actors. Participation in the organization is open to all who have an interest in global Internet policy, however only as far as this relates to ICANN's mission of technical coordination. ICANN works together with private companies, governments, other organizations, and private individuals. Through the full participation of the international community, it enjoys worldwide presence. It holds public meetings. Its working manner is transparent and collaborative. Its bottom-up policy guarantees the acceptance of the measures taken. Its board and staff come from a range of countries and also reflect its global character. Although it does not represent any government, it deploys specific mechanisms to consider governmental inputs. However, the enduring influence of the US Government is a hindrance and ICANN faces significant challenges regarding its authority and legitimacy.[163]

According to some authors, network phenomena 'are rooted in the information-technology revolution' or simply the process of digitization. De facto, private, non-state networks correspond to an empowerment of individuals and groups while dismantling and reducing state authority at the same time.[164] Network participants operate on the basis of their members' adherence to common principles. Their good functioning, moreover, is primarily based on the willingness of precisely these members to cooperate and exchange ideas with others participating in the network or also with other communities or networks. They should agree to cooperate among each other not only with regard to defined common principles and rules, but also as far as communication and decision-taking processes are concerned. The expected benefits of network participation act as a cohesive force, thereby encouraging collaboration. On the other hand, members are also co-dependent to some degree[165] and the self-regulatory standards defined by networks persist without state participation. States or other representatives of groups of interest like environmental

---

[162] Braithwaite and Drahos, supra note 5, 501–506; Hutter, supra note 43, 11; Senn, supra note 9, 461–463; S. L. Schwarcz, Private Ordering (Fall 2002) 319–350.

[163] http://www.icann.org/en/factsheets/ (last visited 25 November 2009).

[164] Sajó, supra note 85, 22–23, with further references.

[165] H. Willke, Systemtheorie III: Steuerungstheorie (1998) 112–121.

representatives may be excluded from these self-regulating processes. However, with regard to future developments, the process of digitization will require massive and detailed coordination between states and transnational regulators in many areas, including customs, taxation, electronic payments systems, and model contracts for electronic commerce.[166]

6.1.3 Characteristics

As noted, the process of digitization is governed by transnational epistemic communities and networks. It results in a polycentric structure or a decentralized network of networks. For a transnational (regulatory) network to function properly, several conditions have to be satisfied: a high level of professionalism, a widely-shared (regulatory) philosophy, and a good deal of mutual trust among network members. These conditions may be difficult to fulfil, but the very existence of an epistemic community or a network should provide an environment conducive to the development of the requisite properties. The pursuance of mutual interests is a central criterion and a motivating factor for a network, although unanimous consensus is not essential throughout. While like-minded group participants, sharing similar interests and pursuing similar goals, will have a positive influence on network quality and worthiness, significant differences of opinion between members may undermine its integrity and credibility.[167]

Epistemic communities and networks are genuine representations of the process of globalization. Their dominant role with regard to digitization raises questions concerning the nature of the measures adopted and the rules enacted. As observed, state institutions cannot cope satisfactorily with the challenges of enacting rules with a claim for validity and global implementation. Apart from particular rules or statutes regulating isolated questions – for instance the introduction in the Swiss Code of Obligations of a rule regarding the use of emails by courts[168] – at the national level, independent national statutes (or representing a state measure) would not make sense. Coordination at the global level is needed anyway. On their side, national court rulings – such as the French Yahoo! ruling[169] – illustrate the

[166] Braithwaite and Drahos, supra note 5, 112.

[167] Sassen, supra note 4, 261, 330; G. Majone, The New European Agencies: Regulation by Information (1997) 262–275; G. Majone, The European Commission: The Limits of Centralization and the Perils of Parliamentarization (2002) 382–388; G. Majone, Delegation of Regulatory Powers in a Mixed Polity (2002) 336; Senn, supra note 9, 462.

[168] Article 14 paragraph 2bis Code of Obligations, CO, SR 202, which entered into force on 1 January 2005 together with the Federal Act on Certification Services in the Domain of the Electronic Signature (Law on the Electronic Signature, SCSE, SR 943.03), which entered into force on the same date.

[169] In that ruling, a French court has addressed the jurisdictional issue and claimed the power to regulate the content of an American website accessible in France. The suit was brought both against Yahoo.fr and Yahoo.com. The court issued a preliminary injunction against Yahoo.com, ordering the site to take all possible measures to dissuade and prevent access in France of Yahoo!

problems raised by unilateral, territorially-based, national approaches to global communication media. Thus, any solution can work efficiently only if it takes into account the global aspects of digitization. Digitization leads to an increase of interconnections and, closely linked to these, interdependencies of national economies and societies. To some extent, this accounts for recharacterizing the rules adopted by global networks or organizations. These rules will be presumed to be applicable and recognized as valid on a global scale. They may qualify as quasi-governmental rules.[170]

Although the activities developed by epistemic communities and transnational networks raise issues of legitimacy[171] and democratic deficit, it is out of the question that they can constitute valuable alternatives to constitutional and democratic decision-making structures to be observed within states. There are important arguments in their favor. They operate based on the voluntariness of their members and the necessity to cooperate transnationally, which is a significant element for their success.[172] Epistemic communities and networks provide alternative forms of regulation, enforcement, and control to be applied at the global level. Such forms are advantageous in relation to issues traditional state structures have not handled efficiently enough so far. Moreover, the credibility of the members of epistemic communities and networks depends on their reputation and good governance principles of the network. In particular, reputation plays an important role and exercises a kind of disciplinary effect. Each member must submit to such discipline to participate in network operations.[173] Members of an epistemic community or network will monitor or hold each other to mutual account. Such internal and inherent self-discipline may ensure both their good conduct and working manner and the effective implementation of the rules enacted by these epistemic communities and networks.[174] However, it should not be overlooked that these developments

auction sites that sell Nazi memorabilia or other items that are sympathetic to Nazism or constitute holocaust denial, because it would violate French law. Yahoo.fr complied with requests that access to these – indeed non-French – sites stored on Yahoo!'s non-French servers should be blocked. Tribunal de Grande Instance de Paris, Ordonnance de référé, 22 mai 2000, UEJF et Licra c/ Yahoo! Inc. et Yahoo France; Tribunal de Grande Instance de Paris, Ordonnance de référé du 11 août 2000, UEJF et al. c/ Yahoo! Inc. et Yahoo France; Tribunal de Grande Instance de Paris, Ordonnance de référé du 20 novembre 2000, UEJF et Licra c/ Yahoo! Inc. et Yahoo France; http://www.juriscom.net/txt/jurisfr/cti/tgiparis20000522.htm (last visited 16 December 2009); Berman, supra note 3, 336.

170 Berman, supra note 3, 397–398.

171 On legitimacy, see Chapter 4, point 2 Standardization, 2.4 Nature of Autonomous Regulatory Regimes, 2.4.2 Legitimacy and Accountability.

172 See also K. Raustiala, The Architecture of International Cooperation: Transgovernmental Networks and the Future of International Law (2002) 6, in relation to international law.

173 Majone (1997) supra note 167, 262–275; Majone (July 2002) supra note 167, 382–383; Majone, (September 2002) supra note 167, 336; Senn, supra note 9, 462; Willke, supra note 165, 112–121; A.-M. Slaughter, supra note 80, 312; Raustiala, supra note 172, 10 et seqq.

174 Majone (1997) supra note 167, 262–275, 262, 272; see also R. O. Keohane, Governance in a Partially Globalized World (March 2001) 1–13, at 9.

are extremely new and states will unavoidably interfere more actively with their own rules in the course of time.

Finally, it should be mentioned that the process of digitization is not the only case where rules should apply at the global level, that is, without territorial limits. Other regulatory regimes do not fit the concept of territoriality either, such as rules governing ethnic or religious communities, which transcend geographical boundaries. Rather, they may apply at any place in relation to these communities.[175]

6.2 Technological Standard Setting Networks

6.2.1 Historical Aspects

Standards are very important. Although they are often invisible or pass unnoticed by the individuals applying them, they will raise the levels of quality, safety, reliability, efficiency, and interchangeability of products. International standardization began in the electrotechnical field. The International Electrotechnical Commission (IEC) was established in 1906. Pioneering standardization work in other fields was carried out by the International Federation of the National Standardizing Associations (ISA), established in 1926. In 1946 a new organization was created, whose objective was 'to facilitate the international coordination and unification of industrial standards'.[176] This new organization, the International Organization for Standardization (ISO), officially began its operations in 1947. It replaced the ISA and the UNSCC (a United Nations Standards Coordinating Committee). Today, ISO is a network of the national standards institutes of some 157 countries operating on the basis of one member per country. They can be part of the governmental structure of their countries, be mandated by their government or have their roots uniquely in the private sector. It is the world's largest standards developing organization in all fields except in the fields of electricity and electronic where the IEC and the International Telecommunication Union (ITU) respectively set the standards. These three organizations cooperate under the banner of the World Standards Cooperation (WSC) to better coordinate their activities and the implementation of the standards set. They complement each other, collaborate, and are the principal standards setters worldwide. Together with IEC and ITU, ISO has built a strategic partnership with the WTO to pursue the common goal of promoting a free and fair global trading system and the enhancement of the global market.[177]

---

175 Berman, supra note 3, 437–440.

176 http://www.iso.org/iso/about/the_iso_story/iso_story_founding.htm (last visited 16 December 2009).

177 http://www.standardsinfo.net/info/livelink/fetch/2000/148478/6301438/inttrade.html (last visited 16 December 2009).

ISO is a global network of organizations, an NGO specialized in the process of standardization. It is run by its members and operates based on consensus reached among them. Since 1947 it has published more than 16,500 International Standards. Its work programme ranges from standards for traditional activities, such as agriculture and construction, over mechanical engineering to medical devices and the latest information technology developments, such as the digital coding of audio-visual signals for multimedia applications. The vast majority of ISO standards are highly specific to a particular product, material, or process. The ISO 9000 and ISO 14000 families have earned a worldwide reputation. ISO 9000 is concerned with 'quality management' and ISO 14000 is primarily concerned with 'environmental management'.[178] ISO standards have important economic repercussions and make a positive difference to society as a whole. They make an enormous contribution to most aspects of living in numerous domains.

Another important international standard setting organization is the International Accounting Standards Board (IASB). Since 2001 it has assumed accounting standard-setting responsibilities from its predecessor body, the International Accounting Standards Committee, which was formed as a not-for-profit corporation in 2001. The IASB is

> 'the independent standard-setting body of the IASC Foundation. Its members (currently 15 full-time members) are responsible for the development and publication of IFRSs, . . . and for approving Interpretations of IFRSs . . . All meetings of the IASB are held in public and webcast. In fulfilling its standard-setting duties the IASB follows a thorough, open and transparent due process of which the publication of consultative documents, such as discussion papers and exposure drafts, for public comment is an important component. The IASB engages closely with stakeholders around the world, including investors, analysts, regulators, business leaders, accounting standard-setters and the accountancy profession.'[179]

6.2.2 Institutional Arrangements

ISO is a private organization and its members do not have to be representatives of their governments, although only one member for each country can participate in ISO. Its members can both be private bodies or also official bodies or institutions part of a state structure. Each ISO member will be the national body most representative of standardization in its country of origin. Nevertheless, the organization occupies a special position between the public and private sectors. It is able to act as a bridging organization in which a consensus can be reached on solutions that meet both the requirements of private business of all types, industrial organizations, and the broader needs of society, such as the needs of citizens, consumer groups, or users of specific products.

---

[178] http://www.iso.org/iso/home.htm (last visited 17 December 2009).

[179] http://www.iasb.org/The+organisation/IASCF+and+IASB.htm (last visited 16 December 2009); Hutter, supra note 43, 9.

From an organizational point of view, ISO members meet for the Annual General Assembly and take all strategic decisions. The Council, which resembles a board of directors, prepares the proposals to be submitted to the Assembly. It is chaired by the President of the organization. Operations are managed by the Secretary-General, who reports to the Council. ISO distinguishes between three membership categories. First, ISO membership is open to the national standards institutes. As full members, known as member bodies, they have one vote each, independently of the size or strength of their domestic economy. Correspondent members constitute the second category of members; these can participate as observers without voting rights. This category is representative of countries which do not yet have a fully-developed national standard activity. The third category are subscriber members. These are institutions originating from countries with very small economies while maintaining contact with international standardization. While individuals or enterprises are not formally eligible for membership, they have a range of opportunities to participate in ISO activities. This is especially due to the fact that expert knowledge is required for the definition of most standards. The ISO approach is strictly professional. Annually, no less than some 50,000 experts are involved in developing standards. These are defined by technical committees comprising experts from various sectors (industrial, technical, business) requesting the definition of standards, and subsequently implementing these. Around 3,000 technical groups exist. They are transnational standard setters. Committee experts are not expected to represent the views of their institution or country, but must represent the views of all parties interested in a standard. They must be in a position to competently evaluate technical aspects. As technical committees, they fulfil specific tasks. They provide strategic guidance regarding standards to be developed based on a market approach. While the elaboration and specification of the content of basic standards is shaped and discussed on an informal basis, that is, within epistemic communities in the first place, new, specific standards are defined only when there is a market requirement. They correspond to a response to a market demand.[180]

6.2.3 Characteristics

Standards are technical agreements. They provide a framework for the assessment of many products for conformity. When the large majority of products or services in a particular business or industry conforms to the standards defined, there exists a state of industry-wide standardization. The definition and adoption of standards by ISO is achieved through consensus agreements between the national delegations representing the economic groups concerned by a standard in their respective country. This is, of course, crucial to their acceptance and to retaining their position

---

180 http://www.iso.org/iso/home.htm (last visited 16 December 2009); for a discussion of a concrete example, The Birth of MP3, see Spar (2001) supra note 156, 337–341.

as the state of the art. In practice, international standards provide a reference framework, or a common and compatible technological language, between suppliers and their customers worldwide, although it should be borne in mind that all ISO standards are voluntary. Thus, the particular situation of ISO standards concerns their widespread recognition and applicability, mostly at the global level. In fact, as an NGO, ISO has no legal authority to impose its standards. It does not have any power to regulate or legislate in any country. However, due to their global recognition, ISO-standards set the pace and largely facilitate the definition, comprehension, and conceptualization of products or affairs. Understandably, states will therefore prefer to refer to defined standards instead of creating their own definitions and introducing their own product criteria for regulatory purposes. Consequently, a certain percentage of ISO standards are included in the regulatory framework of individual countries.

As far as ISO as an organization is concerned, the community of states refrains from creating and entertaining their own standard-setting organization since this would qualify as an international organization under international law.[181] The main rationales for this attitude are that ISO's work is extremely specific and not at all politically motivated. Contrary to state activities, it requires highly specialized expert knowledge to define standards. Such work is first of all dominated by commercial, business, and trade interests. States hence have a range of motives to opt for a policy of non-intervention. This attitude is reinforced by the fact that every state can be represented in the organization. ISO operations, moreover, are conducted in a very professional, serious, and successful manner. Thus, ISO is an example of an associational regime whose scope has grown beyond the confines of the association.[182] Its success may also explain why states do not hesitate to refer to ISO standards in their legislation where such standards serve as the technical basis, although states are free to adopt these standards or not. In addition, these standards have a global character. When referring to them in their legislation, states know that these standards are compatible at the global level, thereby enhancing cooperation and trading opportunities with other states or organizations.[183]

---

[181] For criteria applying to the definition of an international organization in the sense of international law, see: I. Seidl-Hohenveldern and G. Loibl, Das Recht der Internationalen Organisationen einschliesslich der Supranationalen Gemeinschaften (2000) 1–7; see also D. Zaring, International Law by Other Means: The Twilight Existence of International Financial Regulatory Organizations (1998) 304–308, with a focus on organizations in the field of financial markets.

[182] C. Scott, Regulating Private Legislation (2007) 4.

[183] http://www.iso.org/iso/home.htm (last visited 16 December 2009); Black, supra note 45, 266, 270; Braithwaite and Drahos, supra note 5, 503; Seidl-Hohenveldern and Loibl, supra note 181, 3–5; E. E. Meidinger, Look Who's Making the Rules: International Environmental Standard Setting by Non-Governmental Organizations (1997) 52–54; see also V. Haufler, Private sector international regimes (2000) 123–137.

6.3 *Financial Standard Setting Networks*

6.3.1 Historical Aspects

Finance has a very long history. Financial usances first began to develop with the appearance of money used for trading transactions. Later, customary merchant norms served to regulate banking. Modern financial regulation began to develop with nation-states establishing their own financial systems and institutions.[184] The 1930s mark the beginning of the modern era of banking regulation in a range of countries with the enactment of banking acts at the national level.

Financial transactions have always had a high propensity to cross borders. With the end of the Second World War, it was recognized that the international monetary system had to be (re-)organized. The Bretton Woods system was set up, establishing institutions, procedures, and rules for commercial and financial relations among the world's major industrial states. The system collapsed in 1971, but its institutions are still operative: the International Monetary Fund (IMF), and the World Bank, including the International Bank for Reconstruction and Development. The architecture of the financial markets evolved in the course of time. Capital markets and multinational banking expanded. New markets arose, like the derivatives market. The Bank for International Settlements, established in 1930 and initially a much lower-profile organization than the IMF or the World Bank, has since become a core forum for central bankers.[185] It hosts the BCBS, a standard setting network constituted in 1974 by the Group of Ten countries central bank governors. Since the mid-1970s, a range of other standard setting networks and organizations has emerged: IOSCO was founded in 1984 and the International Association of Insurance Supervisors (IAIS) in 1994. The 2007–2009 financial crisis leads unavoidably to question the current financial architecture and re-design it. Structural, institutional and regulatory aspects are now analyzed.[186]

---

[184] For an overview, see for instance: Braithwaite and Drahos, supra note 5, 88, 92–93.

[185] Braithwaite and Drahos, supra note 5, 116; M. Giovanoli, A new architecture for the global financial market: legal aspects of international financial standard setting (2000) 6–10; B. A. Simmons, The Legalization of International Monetary Affairs (Summer 2000) 573–602; B. A. Simmons, International Law and State Behavior: Commitment and Compliance in International Monetary Affairs (December 2000) 819–835; M. Marcussen, The transnational governance network of central bankers (2006) 180–204; for an introduction, see also: A. Kern, R. Dhumale, J. Eatwell, Global governance of financial systems – The International Regulation of Systemic Risk (2006) 79 et seqq.

[186] See for instance the Report of the Financial Stability Forum on Enhancing Market and Institutional Resilience, 7 April 2008, http://www.financialstabilityboard.org/ (last visited 8 January 2010). A number of studies have been published before the crisis: H. Davies and D. Green, Global Financial Regulation, The Essential Guide (2008); Giovanoli, supra note 185, discussing the 'old' architecture; Kern, Dhumale, Eatwell, supra note 185; R. H. Weber and D. W. Arner, Toward a New Design for International Financial Regulation (Winter 2007) 391–453; V. Schreiber, International Standards, Neues Recht für die Weltmärkte? (2005) 15 et seqq.

As a network, the BCBS comprises representatives of thirteen central banks and bank supervisory authorities. It provides a forum for regular cooperation on banking supervision. Its objective is to enhance understanding of key supervisory issues and improve the quality of banking supervision worldwide. BCBS issued the first Basle Concordat in 1975, a set of capital adequacy standards in 1988, and a refined one, known as 'Basel II', in June 2004. It developed a set of Core Principles for Effective Banking Supervision.[187] On its side, IOSCO – which has no charter and was not constituted by a treaty, but incorporated by a private bill of the Quebec National Assembly – participation is much wider. Its members are the national supervisory authorities of the securities markets. The exchanges themselves are represented under the statute of affiliate members. The aim of IOSCO is that its members coordinate their efforts to establish standards of regulation and the effective surveillance of international securities transactions, exchange information on their respective experiences to enhance the development of domestic markets, and provide mutual assistance to ensure the integrity of the markets.[188] The regulatory standards developed and the recommendations produced are based on reports established through the organization's working committees. Its Objectives and Principles of Securities Regulation of September 1998 are its masterpiece.[189] Finally, the IAIS – a non-profit organization incorporated in Illinois – is an organization representing insurance regulators and supervisors. It covers the insurance market almost worldwide and pursues three objectives: first, to contribute to improving the supervision of the insurance industry through domestic and international cooperation in order to maintain efficient, fair, safe, and stable insurance markets; secondly, to promote the development of well-regarded insurance markets; and thirdly, to enhance global financial stability. The IAIS issues global insurance principles, standards, and guidance papers related to insurance supervision. Its masterpiece is the Insurance Core Principles of October 2003.[190]

These three organizations work closely together and belong to a superordinate network of organizations together with other national and international representatives responsible for financial stability, the FSB. The initial mandate has been given to the FSF in 1999 by the Finance Ministers and Central Bank Governors of the Group of Seven industrial countries. Then, its mandate has been broadened by the

---

187 On the Core Principles, see: http://www.bis.org/publ/bcbs129.htm (last visited 7 January 2010); on Basle II, see: International Convergence of Capital Measurement and Capital Standards: A Revised Framework – Comprehensive Version, June 2006 (first published in September 1997), http://www.bis.org/publ/bcbs128.htm and http://www.bis.org/bcbs/index.htm (last visited 7 January 2010); Zaring, supra note 181, 287–291; K. P. Follak, International Harmonization of Regulatory and Supervisory Frameworks (2000) 291–322; T. Porter, States, Markets and Regimes in Global Finance (1993) 58 et seqq.; P. Nobel, Globalization and International Standards with an emphasis on Finance Law (2005) 56–57.

188 http://www.iosco.org/about/ (last visited 7 January 2010); Zaring, supra note 181, 292–297.

189 http://www.iosco.org/library/index.cfm?section=pubdocs&year=1998 (last visited 7 January 2010); Porter, supra note 187, 111 et seqq.

190 http://www.iaisweb.org/ (last visited 7 January 2010); Zaring, supra note 181, 297–301.

Heads of State and Government of the Group of Twenty in 2009 and re-established as the Financial Stability Board with a stronger institutional basis and enhanced capacity.[191] Its goal is to promote financial stability through addressing vulnerabilities and developing and implementing strong regulatory, supervisory and other policies. It comprises senior representatives of national financial authorities, international financial institutions, standard setting bodies, and committees of central bank experts.[192] Thus, the creation of these organizations was mainly a reaction to financial crises and must also be attributed to the recognition that financial regulation cannot remain national only. The global financial system and transactions have no national borders. Consequently, an important task of these organizations is to promote convergence among national regulatory frameworks. They define common principles and make recommendations regarding prudential supervision; these should be observed by all and operate as channels among supervisors.[193] As of today, a wide range of codes and standards can be met. The FSB conducts a comprehensive Compendium of Standards in economics and finance that are internationally accepted as important for sound, stable, and well-functioning financial systems. It highlights 12 key standards designated as deserving priority implementation.[194] Following the 2007–2009 financial crisis the working of these financial institutions is now scrutinized. Improvement proposals and adaptations are evaluated.

6.3.2 Institutional Arrangements

The field of finance is constantly evolving. Correspondingly, the institutional structure is submitted to changes, too, and adjusts to the prevailing circumstances. New communities, networks or organizations may emerge or exercise a prominent role while the overall objectives, such as creditor protection and financial stability, remain unchanged over time. Currently, the dominating and most influential transnational networks or organizations are the FSB and its affiliated organizations while the IMF and the World Bank group play an important role in relation to emerging countries. These two groups constitute proper institutional zones.

---

[191] G20, London Summit, 2 April 2009, "Declaration on Strengthening the Financial System"; http://www.financialstabilityboard.org/index.htm (last visited 8 January 2010). Regarding the efforts undertaken by the European Union to introduce a new institutional order, see: E. Wymeersch, The reforms of the European Financial Supervisory System – An Overview, (July 2010) 240–265.

[192] http://www.financialstabilityboard.org/about/overview.htm (last visited 8 January 2010). Zaring, supra note 181, 287–304; Giovanoli, supra note 185, 11–14.

[193] A.-M. Slaughter, Global Government Networks, Global Information Agencies, and Disaggregated Democracy (2003) 1045, 1046–1048; Braithwaite and Drahos, supra note 5, 97, 101–105; Berman, supra note 45, 500–502; D. W. Arner, Financial Stability, Economic Growth, and the Role of Law (2007) 74 et seqq.

[194] http://www.financialstabilityboard.org/index.htm (last visited 8 January 2010); Giovanoli, supra note 185, 12–13.

The FSB and its participating organizations were first instituted based on the initiative of state representatives, as stated. However, there is neither any direct state representation nor participation in the Board. Rather, it brings together national authorities responsible for financial stability in significant international financial centres, international financial institutions, sector-specific international groups of regulators and supervisors, and committees of central bank experts.[195] Like the BCBS, IOCSO and IAIS, the FSB has a unique structure. All these organizations primarily constitute transnational networks. They do not constitute recognized legal bodies. They do not qualify as international organizations in the sense of international law. Nor do they meet the legal definition applying to international organizations. In particular, they are neither organizations composed of states only nor constituted by a formal treaty. Further, they have not been subject to any process of ratification. Their creation has occurred only through transnational administrative agreements or the promulgation of by-laws, which might not even have been made public. Hence these organizations do not represent legal subjects benefiting from the rights and duties of international organizations. They do not have any legal rights granted by international law such as international personhood, the capacity to conclude treaties, and the protection of legal immunities.[196]

These organizations have various commonalities. Although official state organizations participate in their activities and working procedures, they are constituted by state representatives operating in relative isolation from the state on account of the high level of specialization and expert knowledge required in the respective field. They all have own, flexible internal organization and decentralized administrative units. Their administrative procedures are discretionary. They may consider broad consultations with regard to the enactment of important recommendations or regulatory measures. In addition, their work is oriented not only towards national issues but also global issues and external relations, such as transborder cooperation and coordination. Not only do they represent the general public's interest in sound and fair markets, but also the private interests of creditors and investors. Business globalization and its accompanying aspects hence gives rise to the formation of a new, institutionalized intermediary space.[197]

To complete the picture, the role of the OECD should also be mentioned. It is an important analyst and chronicler of financial regulatory trends. It also works extensively on the analysis of regulation and regulatory techniques and, as such, on issues related to financial markets and institutions, encouraging the convergence of policies, laws, and regulation.[198]

---

195 http://www.financialstabilityboard.org/index.htm (last visited 8 January 2010).

196 Zaring, supra note 181, 285, 304–308; Seidl-Hohenveldern und Loibl, supra note 181, 1–7.

197 Sassen, supra note 4, 261; Zaring, supra note 181, 304–308; Giovanoli, supra note 185, 21 et seqq.; Benjamin, supra note 32, 510–517.

198 Braithwaite and Drahos, supra note 5, 119; Chapter 1, point 2 The Impact of (Public) Policy Issues; 2.8 Contribution of the OECD; http://www.oecd.org/topic/0,3373,en_2649_37421_1_1_1_1_37421,00.html (last visited 16 December 2010).

6.3.3 Characteristics

Financial markets are now the standard example of genuinely global markets. Their globalization has been supported by digitization.[199] Epistemic communities and global regulatory networks characterize finance today. While a state-centred system of international law presumes that the views of the states will be reflected in the work and measures adopted by international organizations, these transnational financial communities and networks reflect their participants' own voices. The operations of the FSB and the other networks linked to it are based on a functional approach. These transnational financial regulatory organizations are best understood as task-specific entities pursuing the objective of creating cooperation on a global technical level that is likely to spread. They represent an increasingly important means of global relation unfettered by national oversight. In particular, their standards and measures are implemented by states in their own financial markets. It is expected that they will become even more influential and fragmented, particularly given the wide array of transnational challenges which have emerged following the 2007–2009 financial crisis.[200]

Basically, the standards defined by these networks set out good principles, practices, or guidelines which should apply to a given area. They may be classified according to their scope, orientation (sectoral or functional), or category when taking into account the implementation perspective. As regulatory measures, they are not compulsory. They cannot be classified as measures of international law. They will be implemented by the industry when representing widely accepted good practices. While international law offers the opportunity to conclude binding treaties and to seek redress in case of their breach, this is not possible with the measures adopted by these networks. They may be considered to assume the character of customary international law in case they gain acceptance over a period of time. That said, they could, provided an opinion juris would recognize their binding character, become binding. However, such a process of juridification will take a number of years prior to realization.[201] For example, the BCBS plays a preeminent role regarding the globalization of banking regulation. De facto, it is 'just a club of gentlemen who get together',[202] but they have a tremendous impact in practice. The Committee does not possess any formal supranational or global supervisory authority, and its conclusions do not, and were never intended to,

---

[199] Braithwaite and Drahos, supra note 5, 8; Sassen, 2006, supra note 4, 328; S. Sassen, Global financial centers (1999) 75–87, 1999; see also: R. K. McGill and T. A. Sheppey, The New Global Regulatory Landscape, Impacts on Finance and Investment (2005) 3 et seqq.; Nobel, supra note 186, 46 et seqq.

[200] Zaring, supra note 181, 312, 327; Global Trends 2025: A Transformed World, National Intelligence Council, NIC 2008-003, November 2008, x–xi, 10.

[201] http://www.financialstabilityboard.org/cos/index.htm, Compendium of Standards (last visited 8 January 2010). See also Giovanoli, supra note 185, 33–36; Cragg, supra note 77, 213–227; Zaring, supra note 181, 329.

[202] Braithwaite and Drahos, supra note 5, 117, citing an 1991 OECD interview.

have legal force. Rather, it formulates broad supervisory standards and guidelines, and recommends statements of best practice in the expectation that individual authorities will take steps to implement these through detailed arrangements best suited to their own national systems. It encourages convergence towards common approaches and common standards without attempting any detailed harmonization of member countries' supervisory techniques. Its working manner is characterized by differentiation and specialization. Experts sitting on the sub-committees are at the core of the whole process. The representatives are senior officials responsible for banking supervision or financial stability issues in central banks and authorities with formal responsibility for the prudential supervision of banking business where this is not the central bank. There is no official nomination procedure to designate these experts. Rather, the selection of network or sub-committee members follows its own, often non-transparent course. The national professional authority does not have formal powers to control these independent experts. The professional and policy-implementing work first takes place within these committees. They act in their own capacity and their activities follow their own principles and logic. In practice, these networks are very powerful and influential nowadays. They determine the leading standards applicable to the whole industry. As such, they exercise a kind of public authority on the financial markets.[203]

7 Conclusion

This chapter has discussed concrete cases which can be classified as either private, non-state autonomous regulatory regimes and alternative forms of regulation or present some of their features. It has concentrated on cases situated on the periphery or outside the state regulatory framework, co-opted by it or possibly linked to it in some way. The following six typologies have been distinguished: self-regulation, firm own regulation, co-regulation, coercive self-regulation, self-contained regimes, and global networks. The description of these concrete cases will serve to illustrate the analysis of theoretical aspects of autonomous regulatory regimes in the next chapter, thereby contributing to their evaluation.

[203] Sajó, supra note 85, 209 et seqq., 8–10, with further references; Zaring, supra note 181, 287–304; Giovanoli, supra note 185, 30–32, 45 et seqq.; Benjamin, supra note 32, 510–517; A.-M. Slaughter, Governing the Global Economy through Government Networks (2000) 181 et seqq.

Chapter 4
Analysis

Abstract The fourth chapter is the analysis. It attempts to cast some light on the concept of alternative forms of regulation and non-state, autonomous regulatory regimes. It also tries to show that non-state regimes are the result of a fragmentation of regulation and at the same time of a need for standardization. The components leading to fragmentation – polycentrism, transnational aspects, institutional transformation – and standardization – in particular cooperation and auto-constitutionalism – are examined in detail. The interplay of the state and civil society approach is explored. The process of transformation, which characterizes the development of these forms of regulation, is discussed at length, including aspects of cooperation, auto-constitutionalism, and effectiveness or impact of the regimes. Finally, the nature of these regulatory regimes is debated.

The first and second chapters of this study have established a framework for a possible conceptualization of private autonomous regimes or alternative forms of regulation. Departing from the concept of the state regulatory regime and its broadening in Chap. 1, Chap. 2 elaborated an approach to the constitution of (private) autonomous regimes. Chapter 3 discussed illustrative cases taken from practice that operate at the boundaries of state and international law. These included autonomous regimes and regimes co-opted by the state. This chapter aims to cast some light on the features, modes of operation, and nature of these regimes and forms or regulation. No theory of private ordering, self-regulation non-state regimes, or alternative forms of regulation exists to date. Although it is recognized that non-state actors possess their own regulatory capacities and are increasingly influential,[1] the very existence of these – often hybrid and global – regimes and forms of regulation is subject to heated debate. To grasp some of their characteristics, discussion focuses on their identification and emergence. This is not an easy task, since these regimes are not at all uniform, but correspond to ad hoc solutions on a case by case basis. They grow incrementally and adapt to the issues at stake. In addition, their existence, basic mechanisms, and impact are largely accentuated by the process of globalization, shaped predominantly by the activities of transnational networks.

---

[1] B. M. Hutter, The Role of Non-State Actors in Regulation (May 2006) 1.

M. Senn, *Non-State Regulatory Regimes*,
DOI 10.1007/978-3-642-14974-0_5, © Springer-Verlag Berlin Heidelberg 2011

The attempt to conceive these regimes is a multi-faceted issue. In fact, non-state, private autonomous regulatory regimes and alternative forms of regulation may give rise to the need to redefine the regulatory framework. Thus, the approach is both analytical and heuristic. Two main features, ensuing from the previous chapters, are highlighted: fragmentation and the mechanisms of standardization. Both represent a paradox as far as the fragmentation or dispersion of regulation initiate a process of standardization. The structural components of the phenomenon of fragmentation are discussed, including polycentrism, the transnational dimension, and institutional transformation. Then, mechanisms leading to standardization are explored: cooperation and trading, auto-constitutionalism, gradual transformation, and the nature of the regimes. Throughout, analysis focuses on the institutional and structural framework rather than substantive issues.

1 Fragmentation

When trying to identify the very existence of private autonomous regimes, the path of the contest of fragmentation and dispersion of regulation prevails. These regimes typically contribute to the fragmentation or dispersion of the regulatory order. As autonomous orders, they are situated at the periphery or outside the state order. They are either private or non-state orders or fragment that order.

In fact, the approach based on fragmentation is regularly used to show the scattering of orders. To begin with, it is worth considering the meaning of fragmentation:

1.1 Fragmentation or Dispersion?

In relation to regulation, fragmentation is currently much discussed in academic circles in connection with the proliferation of non-state, private, chiefly global, autonomous regimes.[2] *Fragmentation* can be defined thus:

> A breaking or separation into fragments; in biology: separation into parts which form new individuals.

a *fragment*:

> A part broken off or otherwise detached from a whole; a broken piece, a small detached portion of anything.

---

[2] For a representative study, see M. Koskenniemi, Fragmentation of International Law: Difficulties arising from the Diversification and Expansion of International Law (13 April 2006) 11–12, with a range of further references.

and *to fragment*:

> To break or separate into fragments.[3]

In the legal field, Wilfred C. Jenks already discussed the term in the 1950s. He drew attention to two particularities. Since no general legislative body in the international world existed, he observed:

> ... law-making treaties are tending to develop in a number of historical, functional and regional groups which are separate from each other and whose mutual relationships are in some respects analogous to those of separate systems of municipal law.[4]

Second, Jenks suggested that fragmentation was a result of the law itself. That situation has remained unchanged up to this day. However, the number of regulatory regimes has increased significantly since.[5]

Fragmentation comprises various aspects and lends itself to different interpretations. It can occur within a state regulatory regime through conflicting interpretations of general law, through the emergence of special law as an exception to the general rule of law, or as a differentiation between types of special law.[6] It may also occur outside a state regulatory regime and symbolize the division of international law as well as the appearance of a diversity of specialized, often technical regimes.

According to the above definition, the term implies that the point of departure for other, third, non-state, or civil society regulatory regimes is the state regulatory regime, or with regard to globalization also international law. It departs from a centre, the concept of the state, which is then divided or becomes fragmented. As a matter of fact, there is often the unspoken, unconscious, or non-articulated assumption that these regimes implicitly belong to a regime of state law or at least have the same origin, from which they subsequently taper off in different directions. Fragmentation thus corresponds to a decentring and disembedding from state regulation. Indeed, besides considering fragmentation in etymological terms, the functional aspects of its application cannot be ignored. Conceptually, fragmentation pertains to the decentralization of regulation. It implies a fragmentation of knowledge, power, and control.[7] The regulatory functions are not concentrated anymore, but distributed among different actors. The undoing of a regime or the existence of a decentralized regime of regulatory governance results in fragmentation as an intrinsic component. However, the degree of fragmentation can vary, depending on the level of central or centralized control. Thus, autonomous regimes are considered to be inherently linked to a state regulatory regime in one way or another from the outset. This implies that state law can be understood as an umbrella concept. With regard to

---

[3] The Oxford English Dictionary, Volume VI (1991) 137–138.

[4] W. C. Jenks, The Conflict of Law-Making Treaties (1953) 403, as cited by Koskenniemi, supra note 2, 10.

[5] Koskenniemi, supra note 2, 10.

[6] Ibid. 30–34.

[7] Chapter 1, point 5 Decentred Analysis of Regulation.

whether these regimes are part of state law or whether they are completely detached from it, however, the term *dispersion* becomes relevant. Dispersion means:

> The action of dispersing or scattering abroad; the condition or state of being dispersed; scattering, distribution, circulation.
> The action of diffusing or spreading; diffusion. ...
> Dispersion medium, a substance that may contain another substance 'dispersed' in it.

and *to disperse* means:

> To cause to separate in different directions; to throw or drive about in all directions, to scatter, to rout. ...
> To separate into parts; to part, divide, dispart.
> To distribute from a main source or centre.[8]

Pursuant to this definition, while fragmentation implies that the origins of autonomous regulatory regimes or orders remain centred, that is, within the state, or in its context, this is not necessarily the case with dispersion. Unlike fragmentation, dispersion is a more open and broader notion, implying a scattering of orders with no definite source, or diverse possible sources, which are not necessarily linked to a state regulatory regime or state-oriented system. Instead, these are non-state sources, or a so-called acephalous system of regimes. Hence, the use of the term dispersion instead of fragmentation may be more appropriate to focus on discovering the origins of these regimes. The term dispersion should be used at least as long as a regime can be attributed neither to state or non-state sources. Better than fragmentation, dispersion clearly underlines that the sources of a regime are not to be found prima facie within a state regulatory regime. It is not excluded or may even be the case that a regime has developed independently, outside the existing state regulatory order or other established orders. In the following, both terms will be used, depending on whether attention is placed on the notion of a source within the state or one linked to the state regulatory regime, or whether the source is presumed to lie outside the state regulatory regime.

On the other hand, it should be taken into account that fragmentation is not a concept linked and limited to a state regulatory regime. It is typically used in international law and also applies to circumstances within society. In these terms, as discussed by Luhmann, the state regulatory regime belongs to society as a whole. It is part of society. It is a differentiated functional system within society.[9] As a consequence, autonomous regimes may be situated at the contact points or at the periphery of a state regulatory regime, but they are within society. Both state and non-state regulatory regimes are part of different spheres. In this respect, so-called 'globalization' is very important. A vibrant globalization debate is taking place. It is a driving force in relation to the fragmentation and dispersion of regimes. Globalization is both an elusive and pervasive concept. Three broad schools of thought can be distinguished: the hyperglobalizers, the sceptics, and the transformationalists.

---

[8] The Oxford English Dictionary, Volume IV (1991) 812–813.

[9] N. Luhmann, Law as a Social System (1989) 136–150, 138.

The hyperglobalizers argue that the sovereignty and autonomy of nation-states is eroding. There is a denationalization of economies and nation-states have become unnatural. The sceptics apply an empirical approach, draw on statistical evidence, and negate the existence of globalization. They reject the 'myth' that the power of nation-states is being undermined. Finally, the transformationalists are convinced that globalization is a central driving force behind societal changes. It transforms and reconstitutes the power and authority of nation-states. However, a theory of globalization is still missing and there is no generally recognized definition either. It is understood as a process of degree in itself. As defined by David Held et al., globalization can be considered to be

> 'a process (or set of processes) which embodies a transformation in the spatial organization of social relations and transactions – assessed in terms of their extensity, intensity, velocity and impact – generating transcontinental or interregional flows and networks of activity, interactions, and the exercise of power.'[10]

It implies changes within the legal, economic, political, technological, military, cultural, and environmental spheres. Within these spheres or sectors, states, firms, markets, and regulation are all directly affected by the process of globalization. It comprehends society as a whole and – according to Anthony Giddens – results in

> 'the intensification of worldwide relations which link distant localities in such a way that local happenings are shaped by events occurring many miles away and vice versa.'[11]

Globalization entails a systemic change in the organization of society, economics, or the regulatory space. It leads to a qualitative transformation. Territorial boundaries are overcome. Significant components of globalization are cooperation schemes building on trading opportunities, technology, or digitization. The emerging regimes are functionally oriented and often technical. They regularly apply to specialized fields and follow their own logic based on their own mechanisms and

[10] D. Held and A. Mc Grew, D. Goldblatt and J. Perraton, Global Transformations, Politics, Economics and Culture (2008) 2–10, 16; D. Held, Democracy and the Global Order: From the Modern State to Cosmopolitan Governance (1995) 62; J. Braithwaite and P. Drahos, Global Business Regulation (2000) 8. There is still no general consensus on the nature of the concept of globalization; see also: D. Held and A. McGrew, Globalization Theory, Approaches and Controversies (2007), and for other useful analyses: D. Thürer, Globalisierung der Wirtschaft: Herausforderung zur 'Konstitutionalisierung' von Macht und Globalisierung von Verantwortlichkeit – Oder: Unterwegs zur 'Citizen Corporation' (2000) 107–122; E. Loquin and C. Kessedjian, La mondialisation du droit (2000); M. Chemillier-Gendreau and Y. Moulier Boutang, Le droit dans la mondialisation, Une perspective critique (2001); J.-B. Aubry, La globalisation, le droit et l'Etat (2003); U. Beck, Was ist Globalisierung? (2007) 29–32, 150–152; B. Stern, How to Regulate Globalization? (2000) 247–250; R. O. Keohane and J. S. Nye Jr., Governance in a globalizing world (2002) 193–202. For a critical view, see J. E. Stiglitz, Globalization and Its Discontents (2003); A. Peters, The Globalization of State Constitutions (2007) 251–308.

[11] A. Giddens, The Consequences of Modernity (1990) 64. Giddens distinguishes the following four dimensions of globalization: nation-state system, world capitalist economy, world military order, and international division of labour or the global spread of industrial development, 70–71; B. Z. Tamanaha, A General Jurisprudence of Law and Society (2001) 121–122.

possess distinctive dynamics.[12] Thus, these regimes add to fragmentation or may just characterize it. They may also be dispersed regimes, unlinked to the concept of the state.

1.2 Polycentrism

Regulation has been regarded as inextricably related to state attempts to control economic activities during the nineteenth and twentieth centuries. However, its development in the course of time has been uneven. Periods of regulation were followed by periods of deregulation. Periods of re-regulation were followed by claims of overregulation. Then, regulatory reforms should have brought about more flexibility in regulation and diminish its costs. Presently, there is a growing understanding that regulation is not exclusively centred towards the state, but effectively polycentric. It occurs in multiple sites. Autonomous, mostly transnational regimes are identified. As stated, these regimes characterize the phenomenon of fragmentation. Based on functional differentiation, they are oriented towards problem-solving in relation to factual questions, develop solutions adapted to their applicable sector and may assume the form of rules or rules complexes. Their boundaries are determined by the issues they are presumed to solve and they have some continuity over time.[13] Koskenniemi subsumes fields of law such as trade law, investment law, the law of the sea or environmental law under this category. These regimes emerge without taking into account existing rules or regulatory complexes like international law. Nor are they related among each other. Koskenniemi's analysis pleads for the unity of law, similarly to Dupuy. His approach focuses on 'seeking relationships' to link the different regimes. It is centred towards the state or international law.[14] It applies to regimes which origins deviate from the state legal system. Regimes emerging autonomously, that is, without state participation, or outside the state, as discussed in Chap. 3, are not covered. They are both non-state and private autonomous regimes, dispersed, and can appear under a range of variations. Such regimes are quasi flourishing nowadays, shaped by practical issues and spatial events. Merely their legal character is controversial.[15] Thus, instead of a centred system of rules, there are many possible centres, constituting a polycentrist system.

---

[12] A. Fischer-Lescano and G. Teubner, Regime-Kollisionen, Zur Fragmentierung des globalen Rechts (2006) 25–33; Chapter 2, point 3 Institutional Structure, 3.3 Private Regulation: From Association to Self-Regulation.

[13] Hutter, supra note 1, 1; J. Black, Constructing and contesting legitimacy and accountability in polycentric regulatory regimes (June 2008) 139–141; L. Hancher and M. Moran, Organizing Regulatory Space (1989) 271–299; J. L. Harrison, T. D. Morgan, P. R. Verkuil, Regulation and Deregulation, Cases and Materials (2004); on the Regulatory cycle, see Chapter 1, figure 1.

[14] P. Marie Dupuy, L'unité de l'ordre juridique international (2002) 9–489; Koskenniemi, supra note 2, 20–25, 245.

[15] Chapter 3, point 1 Self-Regulation, point 2 Firm Own Regulation, and point 6 Global Networks. Koskenniemi, Fragmentation, supra note 2, 9 et seqq.; B. de Sousa Santos, Toward a

Polycentrism, or a polycentrist approach to regulation implicates that different state and non-state regimes might coexist. The regulatory functions might be exercised by diverse organizations and not be concentrated within the same one. Various state or civil society actors might participate to regulatory processes at diverse levels such as national, international, supranational, or also transnational, and they might be interrelated in a myriad of different ways.[16] Under an organizational point of view, polycentrism indicates that the approach does no more concentrate on the state only. The focus can be placed on a multitude of centres, like regimes, actors, levels, or also issues in which regulation might occur.

In seeking to provide a background for explaining autonomous regimes, the first two chapters departed from the state approach and examined the impact of public policy issues, public theories of regulation, and institutions (Chap. 1) as well as the public policy debate and possible state regulatory strategies (Chap. 2). With regard to the patterns and nature of these autonomous regimes, one must ask whether or not they are linked to the state or international law approach, and if so how. Which interactions or interconnections exist between them, and which possible rationales might there be for these relationships. Why does the state or international law approach apply or fail to apply in relation to these regimes, substantiating polycentrism?

1.2.1 State Level

Public Policy Issues: Confirmation and Denial

The examination of public policy issues has shown that they may apply to any field or matter where the state may intervene or be expected to intervene by the general public. The state is motivated by public interest, or the governance of conduct in the public sphere.[17] The rationales for the introduction of state regulatory measures lie in the assumption that it is the responsibility of the state to adopt (possibly corrective) measures. In case of a crisis, there is then the idea of a state 'remedy' as a response.[18] On the contrary, autonomous regimes develop spontaneously. They are not the result of crises, but are instead driven by the pursuance of privately motivated economic interests. The criterion of a public sphere or public interest justifying the introduction of (state) measures does not apply as such. In principle, the general public – that is, potentially everyone or large groups of citizens who can express a common concern about regulatory questions[19] – is not directly concerned

New Common Sense. Law, Science and Politics in the Age of the Paradigmatic Transition (1995) 114 et seq. See also the discussion by B. Kingsbury, The Concept of 'Law' in Global Administrative Law (2009) 23–57, focusing on the case of global administrative law.

[16] For a somewhat different approach to polycentrism, discussing polycentric and decentred regulation interchangeably, as synonyms, see Black, supra note 13, 139–141.

[17] Chapter 1, point 2 The Impact of (Public) Policy Issues.

[18] It corresponds to stages 2 and 3 of the regulatory cycle, see Chapter 1.

[19] Braithwaite and Drahos, supra note 10, 24.

and not targeted by the activities of these regimes, but rather by communities or groups of interest attempting to regulate their relationships and exchanges. In practice, the general public may not even be aware of the existence of such regimes.

Seen in relation to the phases of a regulatory cycle,[20] these regimes could be interpreted as corresponding to the first phase of a free market. They do not present any relation to state regulation and result from regulatory efforts occurring spontaneously only within the private economy or civil society. In such a case, a state intervention in the form of the introduction of regulatory measures will only take place when such a regime fails to work, the responsible private actors are unable to master the challenges regarding their effective implementation, or there is the recognition that the introduction of a state regulation serves public interest. Another possible explanation for the emergence of these regimes is to link them to the last phases of a regulatory cycle – the fifth stage, Regulatory reform, or the sixth stage, Deregulation. In such cases, it merely presents the opposite case. The constitution of these regimes is the outcome of a process of regulatory reform. It is the product of a deregulation, resulting in the privatization of rules. For instance, the deregulation occurring in the law of international direct investment led to the freedom of contract, which in turn gave rise to the development of substantive standards. The determining impulse came from private industry associations, SROs, and international standard organizations. However, in such cases, the emerging regimes will be narrowly linked to the state regulatory regime. Their emergence depends on state's attitude and it can be assumed, moreover, that the general principles of law will most probably apply or influence the shaping of these regimes, as also discussed in Koskenniemi's Report.[21]

Public Theories of Regulation: Testing Their Application

Public theories of regulation or currents of thoughts contribute to explaining and motivating the choice of regulatory measures. These theories may be used to justify regulatory solutions, which in turn should reflect them.[22] They evolve in the course of time and in case any theory or current would dominate at a point in time, it may not be the only means of explaining or justifying a regulatory regime. Moreover, in relation to these theories, it should be taken into account that regulation is understood as a subset of governance not limited to the state only. Now, it may be interesting to test whether these theories apply to non-state autonomous regulatory regimes. Among the few basic theories discussed, the first, so-called proceduralist theory, concentrates on the role of the state as a regulator. It focuses on governmental procedures, in particular on the role of regulatory agencies. It is also

[20] Chapter 1, point 2.1 Regulatory Cycle.

[21] C. Baudenbacher, Globalisierung und Regionalisierung des Wirtschaftsrechts (2004) 30; Koskenniemi, supra note 2.

[22] Chapter 1, point 3 Public Theories of Regulation.

oriented towards the general public, which will not be the case of autonomous – and thus specialized – regimes primarily searching to govern the relationships of determined groups. However, should the state delegate regulatory powers to such a regime or decide against intervention or regulation in a determined field, proceduralist theory may apply insofar as the recourse to a private autonomous regime can be considered from the perspective of representing an alternative to a state regulatory solution. In that case, the state provides the necessary framework for the emergence of a non-state regulatory regime.

Second, the core of an approach based on the welfarist theory of regulation consists in trying to ensure the welfare of individuals as the ultimate goal of regulation. It is linked to utilitarianist philosophy, which seeks to realize the greatest happiness for individuals. Efficiency plays a central role within this theory, which also holds true for autonomous regulatory regimes. Utilitarianist theory may be more adequate to explain the emergence and functioning of autonomous regimes, although it is again linked to the state or a state activity. Moreover, some autonomous regimes may be part of a state regulatory strategy or present hybrid characteristics. They may also subsist not least because heavy administrative state solutions may prove to be unsatisfactory or inefficient enough. Political issues and processes may hinder or block their constitution or effective implementation. Thus, epistemic communities and networks of experts may be in a better position to develop adequate solutions, which in fact corresponds to the goals pursued by welfarist theory of regulation.[23]

Third, in relation to the neoclassical theory of regulation, the efficiency of the measures adopted plays a central role again. The emergence of non-state autonomous regimes is best explained with this theory. Efficiency is linked to the idea of the privatization and marketization of regulation. It legitimates regulatory measures adopted by the private sector. Efficiency is the central aim of setting regulation and, as such, tends to replace the adoption of regulatory measures pursuing the goal of covering public interest.[24] Besides efficiency, neoclassical theory focuses on individual welfare and not on the welfare of society. Autonomous regimes are not aimed at ensuring the general welfare of society either. Instead, these regimes focus on their own group and tend to ensure the best solution for their members. They pursue singular goals in order to satisfy their own needs.

Fourth, the current described as regulatory capitalism takes into account the developments occurring with non-state regulation. It seizes regulation in a broad sense and includes private autonomous regimes in its approach. Regulation is no longer only a state activity. The concept has been broadened to include a mode of governance within society. It is argued that it best captures the complex interdependence of

---

23 Ibid.

24 Ibid.; S. Sassen, Territory, Authority, Rights, From Medieval to Global Assemblages (2006) 196–199.

state, society, and the economy in the establishment of a political-economic order.[25] Whether this is the right concept and designation, and whether all non-state or private autonomous regimes are to be understood as the product of 'capitalist' phenomena, still has to stand the test of time and accuracy.[26] Finally, Boyer and Saillard make an interesting case for a mode of regulation which takes into account different institutional frameworks and the influence of macroeconomic regimes and structural changes. Indeed, the trend toward institutional transformation and greater diffusion of networks is likely to accelerate.[27] Their study also covers questions regarding the process of globalization.[28] Non-state autonomous regulatory regimes primarily appear in relation to the phenomenon of globalization.

Public Policy Debate: Marginal Similarities

Within the public policy debate on whether to regulate or not, who should be regulated, and how, three aspects are distinguished: public interest, public administration, and public choice.[29] In relation to regulation, the public interest means that a (state) regulatory measure in the traditional sense should be general and applicable to everybody. Non-state autonomous regimes, however, do not primarily pursue the goal of representing general interests, as stated. They are specialized regimes, which tend to respond to the specific expectations and needs of groups of interest, experts, epistemic communities, or also individuals. The measures adopted may be of general or public interest in that they apply to or affect everybody, such as the lex digitalis. However, this is not their primary objective. Contrary to the state, they do not consider public interest as such when enacting their rules, nor are they accountable to the general public. This attitude may not only apply to fully private epistemic communities, but also to communities involving governmental experts. A typical example is the BCBS, which is composed of governmental experts acting independently and which sets standards applying to the financial industry. Thus, state involvement exists, but de facto it operates indirectly. The shaping of highly specific regulatory measures is influenced by the interests of industry or (business) groups aiming to have some specific issues regulated in their own interest. Consultations take place and as a result, the interests of these specialized groups will be

---

[25] J. Braithwaite, Regulatory Capitalism, How it works, ideas for making it work better (2008); J. Black, The Decentred Regulatory State? (2007) 253; D. Levi-Faur, The Global Diffusion of Regulatory Capitalism (2005) Volume 598, 12–32.

[26] Chapter 1, point 3 Public Theories of Regulation.

[27] National Intelligence Council, Global Trends 2025: A Transformed World, NIC 2008-003, November 2008, x, 81. On the phenomenon of globalization, see above point 1.1 Fragmentation or Dispersion?

[28] R. Boyer and Y. Saillard, Théorie de la régulation, l'état des savoirs (2002).

[29] Chapter 2, point 1 Embedding Autonomous Regulatory Regimes, 1.1 Traditional State Approach, 1.1.1 Public Policy Debate.

largely taken into account, although in the case of finance, the ultimate goal of investors' protection remains.[30]

The second aspect is public administration. It concentrates on the simplification, adequacy, and efficiency of the measures adopted by the state. As stated, ensuring efficiency is also a core characteristic of non-state autonomous solutions. These regimes emerge spontaneously. They are not subject to the cumbersome administrative burden of the state. They represent practical approaches, defining a basis to enable cooperation and exchange and the setting of relationships between their members. Their operations and the measures they adopt will be scrawny. Decisions can be taken by a few representatives and transposed at low costs, contrary to state measures. However, it should not be ignored that in the course of time and with the increasing sophistication of a regime, weaknesses similar to state regulatory solutions cannot be excluded.

Finally, seen in relation to the public choice perspective, the emergence and persistence of autonomous regulatory regimes may well be considered to merely represent an opposite reaction or a response to public choice. This approach analyses the collective decision-making processes. In theory, it suggests that states can best represent the interests of individuals and the markets. In practice, states regularly act as self-interested entities, which are under the pressure of influential bodies. The regulatory measures adopted do not always match the specific interests of groups or individuals they should represent, and they often lead to inefficient results. On the contrary, regulatory regimes adopted and implemented on a non-state or private basis by either epistemic communities, groups of experts, or networks will be adapted to the needs of the industry or sector represented and they are likely to be efficient. They are able to move around obstacles to achieve their objectives.[31]

State (Regulatory) Strategies: Pointing to the Public–Private Divide

As far as state strategies are concerned, interplay between the state and private economy will often take place, facilitating the adoption of a range of forms. With regard to the state (regulatory) strategies discussed in Chap. 2, autonomous regulatory regimes may be considered to represent a strategy themselves. While some strategies are solely limited to state intervention, such as the imperative forms of regulation, the incentives systems determined by the state, the strategy of disclosure based on state statutes, or also direct state intervention, the strategy of self-regulation will apply to autonomous regulatory regimes.[32] In relation to the state, these regimes

---

[30] On lex digitalis and BCBS see: Chapter 3, point 6 Global Networks; J. Benjamin, Financial Law (2007) 510–517.

[31] Chapter 2, point 1 Embedding Autonomous Regulatory Regimes, 1.1 Traditional State Approach, 1.1.2 State (regulatory) Strategies.

[32] Chapter 2, point 1 Embedding Autonomous Regulatory Regimes, 1.1 Traditional State Approach, 1.1.2 State (Regulatory) Strategies.

may result from cooperation and coordination of the exercise of regulatory activities between the state and the private economy. Cases include co-regulatory solutions or coercive self-regulatory solutions, according to the examples discussed in Chap. 3. They represent hybrid forms of self-regulation, based on either cooperative or authoritative schemes. However, the strategy of self-regulation will not apply to pure self-regulatory solutions, which are assumed to be originally entirely detached from the state and emerge within civil society.[33] State strategies – at the national and international (such as the UN) or supranational (such as the EU) levels – may also define or provide a framework for autonomous or quasi-autonomous regulatory regimes to develop and subsist. The examples of trade law or investment law or also 'self-contained' regimes, as designed by courts are all cases of regimes akin to state law, but consistent with their own logic and dynamics.[34] In these cases, regulation appears to be more functional and sector-oriented than motivated by other rationales, although it remains basically a form of state regulation. Yet another point with regard to state (regulatory) strategies is the fact that policy-making towards the state or influence on the state by actions of private markets actors either individually or through their representative SROs may also largely determine the shaping and definition of state rules. In case the introduction of state rules is based on an existing self-regulatory solution, the state regulation will first reflect this regulation, giving it another character vis-à-vis the general public. It will bear a state stamp. A further possibility consists in a possible – albeit criticized – opting out of a state regime, which means that interested parties can choose the regime they want to submit to. An illustrative example is arbitration. It represents a private autonomous regime, which is often used as an alternative to a state judiciary system. It is typical in the case of foreign investment. Private investors seek the protection of international standards and reject the national legal standards and institutions which are preferred by their home state.[35]

Polycentrism: Confirmed

The discussion of the state approach shows that there is no general answer to the question of the influence and role of the state in relation to non-state or private autonomous regimes. Rather, it confirms polycentrism: Regimes may emerge within the state regulatory framework or outside of that framework, within civil

---

[33] Respectively: Chapter 3, point 1 Self-regulation, point 3 Co-regulation and point 4 Coercive Self-regulation.

[34] For an example, see Chapter 3, point 5 Self-contained Regimes.

[35] C. Chinkin, Monism and Dualism: The Impact of Private Authority on the Dichotomy Between National and International Law (2007) 154–158, in particular discussing the case of Société Générale de Surveillance S.A. (SGS) v Islamic Republic of Pakistan, Case No ARB/01/13, Decision on Objections to Jurisdiction of 6 August 2003, and Société Générale de Surveillance S.A. (SGS) v Republic of the Philippines, Decision of the Tribunal on Objections to Jurisdiction, Case No ARB/02/6.

society. Case by case appraisal is necessary. In fact, the basic orientation of autonomous regimes is opposite to the state's. From the point of view of the state, autonomous regulatory regimes correspond to a change from a public interest motivated regulation (or officially declared as such) to a private interest motivated regulation or a regulation focused on the satisfaction of the specific interests and needs of the communities it represents and thus belonging to civil society. It is defined by experts and will finally lead to a new institutional status, as discussed below. Diverse rationales may explain this phenomenon, which results in a change of sphere. Besides the functional orientation of a sector and within it the factual and professional precision, criteria can include operations of a sector, efficiency, acceptance, efficacy, confidence, the costs aspect, the subsidiarity of a state intervention, the process of globalization, and the development of new technologies.[36] It may also be due in part to the difficulties of states to respond and react adequately and in a reasonable time period to the expectations and needs of the private economy at the national level and international. State bureaucracies tend to dither and they are submerged by the specificity and complexity of global regulatory networks. Still another rationale in relation to states is the institutional deficit of an international scene formed of aging post-World War II institutions not in a position to fill gaps generated by political and technological developments.[37] There is an abandonment of the state sphere, that is, a transition to another sphere. At the same time, there is often a shift from the national to the global level. The aspect of territoriality loses its significance and regimes become transnational. The rationales are influenced by the search for global solutions. Transnational coordination takes place and the regulatory regimes emerge at the global level – where multinational corporations (MNCs), epistemic communities, and networks of experts have an advantage. Their know-how and their efficient way of operating and cooperating when concluding business transactions contribute to improving their position as powerful actors in comparison to states operating through a range of international organizations, in the absence of an official global legislative body. MNCs and other businesses or networks have a good knowledge of both the rules and the situation in the markets they cover. They can communicate with their entities easily and develop standards themselves or through their SROs, which will then apply to their industry. They constitute quick-witted, market-driven networks performing at low costs and not subject to the burden of regulatory competition among states. In addition, uncertainty and informational problems linked to the state regulatory process may prove expensive as firms attempt to make plans and investment decisions. Hence, they will prefer to avoid that burden and develop their own,

---

[36] P. Nobel, Zur Regulierungsarchitektur im Finanzmarktbereich (2004) 124–126, with further references; see also: D. Held and A. McGrew, Political Globalization: Trends and Choices (2003) 185–199.

[37] A. Fischer-Lescano and G. Teubner, Regime-collisions: The vain search for legal unity in the fragmentation of global law (Summer 2004) 999–1000; Braithwaite and Drahos, supra note 10, 495; National Intelligence Council, Global Trends 2025, supra note 27, x, 81; see also Chapter 1, point 2 The Impact of (Public) Policy Issues.

ad hoc solutions.[38] Further, taking into account that no actor possesses all the information regarding a determined market or area, the weight of well-organized businesses will be considerable. They will be in a position to decisively influence the standards and rules which will finally be defined by states or international organizations of states where they may also be directly represented, such as the ILO. As a result, non-state regimes cannot just be subsumed under a public policy or state approach. Considered from the point of view of the state, they are much more a reaction to, an escape from, or a consequence of a state approach, thus, an emanation of polycentrism.

1.2.2 Non-state Level

To cross over from the state to the non-state level, the role of international organizations as official representatives of states, as well as further, parent organizations, is briefly mentioned. Similarly to states, international organizations work based on a consensus among their members. With regard to the passing and implementing of regulation, these organizations suffer weaknesses similar to those affecting states. They may also be undermined by political tensions and the process of defining (regulatory) solutions and reaching a consensus may be very time-consuming. Their enforcement powers may be limited. In particular, they largely depend on the willingness of their members to translate into practice the measures in their respective state. However, besides the official international organizations, other organizations or networks play a somewhat different role at the international or global level. They can comprise both state and non-state representatives. Currently, a proliferation of such organizations, communities, or networks can be observed, such as in the field of international finance. On the one side, like the IAIS, BCBS, or IOSCO, they may solely be able to define recommendations or adopt non-binding measures. On the other side, and paradoxically, it should not be ignored that de facto they exercise a very large influence on their industry and define standards to be applied worldwide. These organizations constitute transgovernmental networks of experts or technocrats. They are new types of structured cooperation, reflecting the practical necessities of international economic and political interdependence. Thus, they add to the decentralization and fragmentation of regulation.[39]

---

[38] R. Baldwin and M. Cave, Understanding Regulation, Theory, Strategy, and Practice (1999) 184.

[39] As discussed in Chapter 3, point 6 Global Networks, 6.3 Financial Standard Setting Networks; A.-M. Slaughter and D. Zaring, Networking Goes International: An Update (2006) 215; D. Zaring, International Law by Other Means: The Twilight Existence of International Financial Regulatory Organizations (1998) 281–330; A.-M. Slaughter, Governing the Global Economy through Government Networks (2000) 181–185, 194–198; see also K. Pistor, The Standardization of Law and Its Effect on Developing Economies (Winter 2002) 97–130; below, 1.4 Institutional Transformation.

To go a step further, besides these organizations and governmental or hybrid networks, there are global self-regulatory solutions which are effectively developed by autonomous, civil society networks. As a form of self-regulation, they differ from the traditional form of self-regulation understood as an atavistic notion of private regulation, mostly bearing medieval sources. They are a new, global form of self-regulation constituted by private, non-state regulatory regimes emerging spontaneously. They are the result of the operations of epistemic communities and global networks or – formally – associations that have a genuine propensity to self-regulate and are highly conducive to self-regulation based on their own dynamics. They accompany the developments occurring at the global level. The rationales for their emergence are economic and they are guided by efficiency and the Pareto optimum. In fact, they are the catalyst of a global civil society. They define appropriate concepts, norms, and principles for their field of operations. These (global) regulatory regimes can be considered to resemble a form of private government and private justice. Among others, this is the case of digital networks or also MNCs. For instance Nokia, as discussed in Chap. 3, (self-)regulates itself, applies its own rules and manages the relationships to its own networks: the network of branches, the employees network, the shareholders network or the network of its international owners, the marketing network, the communication network, the networks of suppliers, or the product distribution network. It also develops its own corporate ethics, internal professional standards and codes. In addition, the proliferation of industry codes of conduct by SROs representing MNCs and other businesses or other bodies exemplifies their role. The norms, rules, and standards emerging are self-imposed among the private members of an epistemic community or network to govern their behaviour and transactions.[40] Global, spontaneous civil society regimes based on transnational networks are constituted. They are characterized by the fact that they represent non-hierarchical regimes or systems of regimes, which result in a horizontal cooperation occurring between the private actors or organizations concerned. These actors pursue similar interests and are dependent on each other to some degree. They will cooperate on a voluntary basis. While they rely on a non-complicated organizational framework, they are complex communities or networks insofar as they deal with highly specific matters necessitating expert knowledge. As a consequence, there is a risk that their way of operating may not be transparent and undemocratic. However, the approach is adapted to the realities of the area or sector covered, which is likely to be due to the inherent flexibility of autonomous regimes.

To return the fragmentation of regulation and polycentric regulation in an attempt to locate the sources of these regimes, they seem to result from a decentralization and dislocation of power and authority. Decentralization has already been

[40] On Nokia: Chapter 3, point 2 Firm Own Regulation, 2.2 Multinational Firms, point 1 Self-regulation, and point 6 Global Networks; G. P. Fletcher, Basic Concepts of Legal Thought (1996) 155–171; G. Teubner, Global private regimes: Neo-spontaneous law and dual constitution of autonomous sectors in world society? (2004) 71–87; A.-M. Slaughter, Sovereignty and Power in a Networked World Order (2004) 311–313.

discussed in the first two chapters. Scholarship and practice have delimited and explored various criteria to define the concept of decentred regulation. The shape decentralization takes differs according to the area considered, and depends on the regulatory objectives and parameters of that area. The concept of decentralization implies that regulatory responsibilities are shared between central, regional, and local governments. Decentralization of a state administration can also occur insofar as the responsibility to deliver services can be devolved upon different bodies within a state. Beside state decentralization, the abiding external aspects have to be considered, too. Non-governmental and private actors take the responsibility of assuming regulatory, administrative, or other duties. Various perspectives can be adopted. Here, however, decentralization does not suffice to understand these private regimes.[41] They do not necessarily apply existing state concepts of regulation. Fischer-Lescano and Teubner use the approach of the centre towards the periphery to seize them. Hence, these regimes would be situated at the periphery of a centred state regime. Centrifugal tendencies become more important, instead of the centripetal dynamics typical to the development of nation-states.[42] They emerge autonomously, from dispersed sources. In fact, the developments of these regimes indicate that they may be completely dissociated from the state in extreme cases. They may emerge at any place. There is no (state-)centred approach anymore or a decentralization of a state regulatory regime, but, on the contrary, a polycentrist system of regimes. The shaping of these regimes is largely influenced and determined by the phenomenon of globalization, which as a matter of fact has fundamentally altered the capacity and willingness of nation-states to regulate generally and commercial activity in particular.[43] The resulting fragmentation or dispersion is more pronounced at the global level, where there is no unity at all among the regulatory regimes. The emerging regimes may deviate from general rules of law. They may be entirely original. However, the deviations should not be understood as a refusal to apply general rules of law. Rather, they are an expression of legal pluralism. They develop their own conceptual framework, reflecting the features of their sector. They correspond to technical, functionally oriented regimes and are typically transnational. Instead of a centre, there is a polycentric status. Regimes are scattered, which is underlined by the fact that there is no overall legal perspective,

---

[41] Chapter 1, point 5 Decentred Analysis of Regulation; Chapter 2, point 1 Embedding Autonomous Regulatory Regimes, 1.2 From State to Civil Society Approach: A Decentred Perspective; J. Black, Decentring Regulation: Understanding the Role of Regulation and Self-Regulation in a 'Post-regulatory' World (November 2001) 103–146. See also Hancher and Moran, supra note 13; C. Scott, Analysing Regulatory Space: Fragmented Resources and Institutional Design (2001) 329; G. Teubner, Dilemmas of Law in the Welfare State (1986); C. Scott, Regulating Constitutions (2004) 226–245; M. Senn, Decentralisation of Economic Law – An Oxymoron? (October 2005) 442.

[42] Sassen, supra note 24, 398; Fischer-Lescano and Teubner, supra note 12, 48–52; Black, supra note 13, 139–141.

[43] Braithwaite and Drahos, supra note 10, 13; W. Cragg, Multinational Corporations, Globalisation, and the Challenge of Self-Regulation (2004) 221; S. Sassen, The Places and Spaces of the Global: An Expanded Analytic Terrain (2007) 79–105.

but a dispersion of regimes represented by a structural heterarchy. The regimes are neither hierarchically nor otherwise linked. They are all regimes with their own properties; these collocate and are self-monitored and self-determined. As a result, there is a state of governance without government. A main function of the sovereign state, the organization of the regulatory space needs to be reinterpreted. Regimes are dispersed and lead to a polycentric system of regimes, which includes both state and civil society regimes. Typical examples at the moment are transnational copyright, the lex constructionis, global financial regulation, or issues related to the operations of digital networks like transnational cybercrime. In fact, some, such as the National Intelligence Council advance the view that

> 'The trend toward greater diffusion of authority and power occurring for a couple decades is likely to accelerate because of the emergence of new global players, increasingly ineffective institutions, growth in regional blocks, advanced communications technologies, and enhanced strength of nonstate actors and networks.
>
> By 2025, nation-states will no longer be the only – and often not the most important – actors on the world stage and the 'international system' will have morphed to accommodate the new reality. But the transformation will be incomplete and uneven. Although states will not disappear from the international scene, the *relative power* of various non-state actors – including businesses, tribes, religious organizations, and even criminal networks – will grow as these groups influence decisions on a widening range of social, economic, and political issues.'

While this view may represent an alternative, it ignores the current efforts of states to design or re-design the institutional framework governing financial markets as a case in point. In that regard, Zaring, for instance, argues that the crisis has revealed the weakness of networks rather than their possible contribution. The outcome may well be a reinforcement of the role of the states and international organizations.[44]

1.3 The Transnational Dimension

An important feature ensuing from the discussion of the dispersion and fragmentation of regulatory regimes and adding to polycentrism is their transnational character. The prefix *trans-* denotes:

> across, to or on the farther side of, beyond, over.

and *transnational*:

> Extending or having interests extending beyond national bounds or frontiers; multinational.[45]

---

44 Respectively: National Intelligence Council, Global Trends 2025, supra note 27, 81; D. Zaring, International Institutional Performance in Crisis (Winter 2010) 475–504, 485.

45 The Oxford English Dictionary, Volume XVIII (1991) 385 and 417 respectively.

Philip C. Jessup, Judge at the International Court of Justice, first used the term of '*transnational law*':

> 'to include all law which regulates actions or events that transcend national frontiers. Both public and private international law are included, as are other rules which do not wholly fit into such standard categories. ... Transnational situations, then, may involve individuals, corporations, states, organizations of states, or other groups.'[46]

The sources of the concept of transnationalism are rooted in the Cold War. Transnationalism designated the persistence of interstate cooperation despite political controversies. Relationships between non-state actors were studied. Since then, it has taken many forms.[47] It is now used to indicate that it is essentially opposed to the regime of international law. The prefix *inter-* designates:

> between, among, amid, in between, in the midst.

and international signifies:

> Existing, constituted, or carried on between different nations; pertaining to the relations between nations.[48]

The traditional concept of regulation or rather state regulation is linked to the notion of the nation-state. This rests essentially upon territoriality. The territory of the state limits the extent of the application of regulation and recognition of rules. Accordingly, 'inter-national' law applies between states. It emanates from a state regulatory regime. States shape such a regime through their participation in international organizations and decide on its implementation and enforcement within the confines of their territory. Still in the traditional sense, national law regulates the actions of individuals and legal persons within states. By contrast, the fragmentation and dispersion of regulation allows for perceiving non-state, autonomous regimes. These are particularly relevant to promoting global regulatory solutions. Regulation appears beyond state institutions. It is dissociated from the national territory. It is sector- or also process-oriented[49] and applies to domains where a global, transnational cooperation is necessary. Transnationalism can adopt diverse

---

[46] P. C. Jessup, Transnational Law (1956) 2–3.

[47] Slaughter and Zaring, supra note 39, 213; H. J. Steiner, D. F. Vagts, H. Hongiu Koh, Transnational Legal Problems (1994); C. Kaufmann, Globalisation and Labour Rights, The Conflict between Core Labour Rights and International Economic Law (2007) 263; A.-M. Slaughter, Global Government Networks, Global Information Agencies, and Disaggregated Democracy (2001) 4–9; A. Sajó, Transnational Networks and Constitutionalism (2006) 209–225.

[48] The Oxford English Dictionary, Volume VII (1991) 1081 and 1123 respectively.

[49] N. Luhmann, Das Recht der Gesellschaft (1993) 571 et seqq.; N. Luhmann, The World Society as a Social System (1982) 131–138; Koskenniemi, supra note 2, 71; Chinkin, supra note 35, 136; Fischer-Lescano and Teubner, supra note 37, 999–1000, 1007–1009, 1021; see also the analysis by G. Teubner, Self-Constitutionalizing TNCs? On the Linkage of "Private" and "Public" Corporate Codes of Conduct (2010) 1–20, focusing on Corporate codes of conduct; M.-L. Djelic and K. Sahlin-Andersson, Introduction: A world of governance: The rise of transnational regulation (2006) 3–8. On process-based regulation, see Chapter 1, point 8 Alternatives to Regulation, 8.4 Process-based Regulation.

forms and be approached from diverse perspectives. The non-territoriality of autonomous regimes is an important attribute. It first indicates that the traditional distinction made between national or domestic and international law is breached. The typical hierarchical order governing the organization of state and international law, which upholds a traditional view of the role of the state, has disappeared. The emerging rules belong neither to the traditional sources of state law nor the principles of international law. Instead, there is a shift from the vertical concept of state and international regulation to a horizontal concept of state and, mostly, non-state or private regulation issuing from ad hoc cooperative schemes. Prima facie, transnational law is not linked to the national or international state regulatory regime, but resides beyond it or at its periphery. It follows its own principles and processes, and these may differ from those of the state. In particular, with transnational law, the dichotomy between public and private is abandoned.[50] Instead, distinct, original rules or regimes of rules are developed. These are moulded to fit a sector and directly applicable, rendering obsolete or useless national or state law. They lead to a breakdown of the classical order of rules established by states and international organizations in favour of a structural bias in the relevant functional expertise.[51] Transnational relations get the overhead, spontaneously constituting autonomous regimes. They lead to a polycentric global society.

Despite the power of the centralized state, transnational non-state and private authorities flourish and evolve. They are not necessarily oppositional to the state and can be involved in common enterprises with it. Transnational regimes can be both private rule-making regimes or regimes of rules defined by both state and private experts. The rules they define will first apply to the private domain, but may also apply to the public one. Although states may participate in hybrid forms of regimes either through the experts they delegate or exercise their influence in another way, they will manage their own transgovernmental networks and mainly act within the limits of their traditional role in implementing state and international law. They may also transpose transnational rules into their legal order.[52] On their

---

50 Fischer-Lescano and Teubner, supra note 37, 1007–1009; A. Fischer-Lescano and G. Teubner, Fragmentierung des Weltrechts: Vernetzung globaler Regimes statt etatistischer Rechtseinheit (2007) 45–48, with further references; C. Chinkin, A Critique of the Public/Private Dimension (1999) 387–395; C. Brölmann, Deterritorialization in International Law: Moving Away from the Divide Between National and International Law (2007) 84–109; Sassen, supra note 43, 88–90, 94–98.

51 M. Koskenniemi, The Fate of Public International Law: Between Technique and Politics (January 2007) 4; M. Koskenniemi, From Apology to Utopia: The Structure of International Legal Argument, Reissue with a New Epilogue (2005) 600–615; J. Black and D. Rouch, The development of the global markets as rule-makers: engagement and legitimacy (May 2008) 224 et seqq.; Brölmann, supra note 50, 96.

52 Chapter 2, point 3 Institutional Structure, 3.6 Transnational Networks: From Legal Pluralism to Autonomous Regulatory Regimes; Chapter 3, point 6 Global Networks, 6.3 Financial standard setting networks; Chinkin, 2007, supra note 35, 135; A.-M. Slaughter, A New World Order (2004) 131–165; Slaughter, supra note 40, 312 et seqq.; A.-M. Slaughter, The Power and Legitimacy of Government Networks (2004a); Slaughter, supra note 47; Sajó, supra note 47.

side, private regimes, SROs or NGOs pursue different strategies with respect to the use of national and international law and courts.[53]

Thus, a dual approach could be applied to assess these regimes. On the one hand, when departing from the point of view of the state, the understanding of a regulatory regime in the strict sense of state regulation is broadened. It is a sector-oriented regime of rules applying at the global level. On the other, when departing from the private economy, the dominant view is that the institutional structure changes and evolves. There follows a process-based logic, unfolding from autonomous, non-state sources. The regimes are presumed to produce a global law. In such cases, however, the problem of physical location will often arise when the existence of such a regime is actually recognized, but not concretized through a determined organization. Moreover, there is also a potential for a regulatory vacuum with respect to private authorities or networks undertaking public tasks under international law. What distinguishes these approaches is that while the state approach is primarily based on politics, the non-state approach is motivated by efficiency and economic considerations.[54] Politics is linked to state activities only. It is not a feature of the transnational dimension.

Whether transnational law can be considered to represent a distinct category of state law, or a legal regime emerging from autonomous or self-governing networks, is still debated. At this stage, it can be stated that it is basically a form of autonomous governance, resulting from civil society and non-state interactions. Its emergence and persistence are largely motivated by private and economic interests. Transnationalism has two advantages: It breaks and evades the hierarchy of state and international law. In particular, it is possible to work out and finalize ad hoc, flexible solutions. Subjects for further research and theorization will have to focus on the degree of specificity of the spaces where regimes interact and overlap as well as on their level of interactions and complexity.[55]

1.4 Institutional Transformation

Fragmentation or dispersion of regulation is a multifaceted phenomenon. Besides the institutional issue, the substantive issue and the issue of territoriality are two other important facets. This study primarily assumes that institutions play a key role and exercise a determining function with regard to the fragmentation and dispersion of regulation. As an institutional issue, the aspects of the process of formation of

---

[53] Chinkin, supra note 35, 146, 154; see also Chapter 5.

[54] P. S. Berman, From International Law to Law and Globalization (2005) 530–533; C. A. Cutler, V. Haufler, and T. Porter, Private Authority and International Affairs (1999) 9–15; C. A. Cutler, V. Haufler, and T. Porter, The Contours and Significance of Private Authority in International Affairs (1999) 336–344; Stern, supra note 10, 252–255, 261–265; critical: T. Risse-Kappen, Bringing transnational relations back in: introduction (1995) 7–13.

[55] Sassen, supra note 24, 390.

institutions, their competencies, and their relations inter se are relevant. Seen thus, autonomous regulatory regimes assume an intermediary role in this context. Rather, an actor-based approach addresses the emergence and transformation of institutions leading to the formation of regulatory regimes. Chapter 1 explored the concept of regulation as representing an institutional issue. As such, it included a range of state and non-state actors fulfilling diverse roles and at the global level, epistemic communities, transnational networks, and SROs. Another aspect briefly mentioned in Chap. 1 was the alternative possibility of the application of non-state regulation in the public sector by private institutions or private actors regulating the regulator. Regulation then appears to lie beyond state institutions as the product of private institutions. It may have a strong normative dimension leading to behaviour modification.[56] Hence, two key questions arise: what institutions are these and what is their role in a global, fragmented society?

Chapter 2 delineated a hypothetical trajectory to understand regulatory developments from an institutional point of view. It showed the process leading to just the formation of epistemic communities and, in a next step, networks, as the institutional basis leading to the constitution of autonomous regulatory regimes and the enactment of non-state regulation. However, the cases discussed in Chap. 3 show that not all regulatory solutions can be solely attributed to one category. They cannot always be classified as either state regulation or pure forms of self-regulation or non-state regulation. There are hybrid forms of regulation, or that bear a state stamp. In practice, there are many interconnections of private and public elements. With the practical cases, it was possible to see how the affiliation of rules to a category can be split up. In what follows, the argument regarding institutions is developed along the same lines as in Chap. 2 under Institutional structure (point 3), and is linked to the cases described in Chap. 3. From individual interests (Theory of interest in Chap. 2), it moves to the association of interests (Collectivity in Chap. 2; the case of Self-regulation in Chap. 3), the organization of business (Private regulation in Chap. 2; Firm own regulation in Chap. 3), state intervention and international organizations (State intervention in Chap. 2; and the cases of Co-regulation and Coercive self-regulation in Chap. 3), non-state orders (Non-state orders in Chap. 2; the case of Self-contained regimes in Chap. 3), the constitution of epistemic communities (Transnational networks in Chap. 2; the case of Global networks in Chap. 3), and finally, the appreciation of transnational networks as regulatory institutions (Networks as regulatory institutions in Chap. 2). In accordance with the structure of Chap. 2, the actors are regrouped into three categories: private actors, public actors, and epistemic communities and transnational networks.

---

[56] Chapter 1, point 4 Institutions; C. Scott, Private Regulation of the Public Sector: A Neglected Facet of Contemporary Governance (March 2002) 56–76; see also the example of Credit rating agencies, Chapter 3, point 1 Self-regulation; Hutter, supra note 1, 13, with further references.

1.4.1 Private Actors

The notion of private actors encompasses individuals, experts, firms and private businesses, epistemic communities, private networks, and organizations, NGOs or SROs. Individuals constitute the basis of processes of institutionalization and origin of all forms of regulation. Within civil society, they are the primary source to enrol states or businesses in regulatory matters when representing their interests. Although their institutional power as isolated individuals is limited and not comparable to the dominant position of families in feudal or early modern times, for instance, they are influential,[57] not least through taking position when making use of their voting rights. Individual action is also important to understand the unfolding of global regimes. However, it is not the same quality of individual action. Epistemic communities and networks are composed of individual experts. Their non-hierarchical character is an incentive for a more active participation of these experts and their interactions with others are determining. They are crucial for the emergence of autonomous regimes when becoming organized to represent their interests, that is, the interests of their industry or sector. In particular, the knowledge of private actors reaches beyond authority. These actors dictate the choice and form of regulatory solutions in their field.

For instance, as far as firms and private businesses are concerned, both individual national and multinational firms operate as self-regulated bodies with regard to their practices. They have their own codes of conduct and usances, and act in conjunction with other firms on their markets. In Chap. 3, a distinction has been made between individual firms and MNCs. They are all private firms, but their weight is different with regard to regulation. MNCs are global leaders and play an influential economic role. To a large part they dictate the role and operations of their professional representative bodies or SROs. While national firms will focus on influencing the state of their incorporation and operations, multinational firms will exercise their influence at the national and global level. This is the case of MNCs and companies active in the Third World and participating in the UN Global Compact, an initiative seeking to prompt them to foster partnerships and enhance cooperation to build a more sustainable global economy, for instance. Further, national and transnational SROs represent either businesses or other groups of interest, thereby constituting a proper private autonomous institutional zone. They exercise a growing influence nowadays and are important for lobbying matters. On the one hand, in pushing for a specific cause, both SROs and NGOs act as catalysts of further specialization and fragmentation. These organizations are specialized in their field and will be able to take (regulatory) measures only based on the expectations and requirements of their own members or the epistemic communities constituting their basis. On the other hand it should not be ignored,

---

[57] B. M. Hutter and C. J. Jones, From government to governance: External influences on business risk management (2007) 27–45; Braithwaite and Drahos, supra note 10, 494–495.

as Braithwaite and Drahos underline, that the impact of ordinary citizens or the general public is not mediated through NGOs or SROs.[58]

1.4.2 Public Actors

The notion of public actors encompasses the states and all national and international bodies and organizations of states. As far as the nation-state is concerned, there is the idea of the 'regulatory state'. This is regularly linked to the creation of specialized state regulatory agencies, which mainly occurred in the course of the 1980s and 1990s, although the 'regulatory state' already existed long before.[59] Then, the often discussed 'rise of the regulatory state' concerns the debate on the increasing centralization of regulatory powers and state control. The concept of state regulation is based on a strategy of command and control, which also applies to state regulatory agencies as far as they have to enforce statutes. Thus, the authority is centralized towards the state. It is a hierarchical order wherein the state acts as the ultimate sovereign. This hierarchy also applies to international law and autonomous fields of state law such as trade law, investment law, financial law, or also self-contained regimes. The state regulatory order is marked by fragmentation 'internal' to the state insofar as many state agencies, bodies, and courts are created, each covering specialized fields. This form of fragmentation is only partly autonomous. It is based on state delegation. The state determines the extent of the delegated powers. Formally, it also has the ultimate authority to change or rescind its delegation. A division occurs within the state. It is largely motivated by specialization requirements and is likely to increase in the future. In fact, it symbolizes an area of domination by experts and technocrats. They are in a position to influence economic developments with their advice. However, their relation to the state is semi-permeable. Although they act in the name of the state, as its representatives, they may be independent and not directly submitted to political processes.[60]

The notion of 'external' fragmentation covers various regulatory arrangements between public and private or non-state actors. The state and private economy may cooperate on a range of issues. In the case of a delegation by the state, the degree of statutory underpinning may range from compulsory schemes to voluntary

[58] Braithwaite and Drahos, supra note 10, 497–501; R. Geiss, Non-State Actors: Their Role and Impact on the Fragmentation of International Law (2006) 318–320; Cutler, Haufler, and Porter, supra note 54, 5–19; S. Roberts, After Government? On Representing Law Without the State (January 2005) 23. On the UN Global Compact, see Chapter 3, point 2 Firm Own Regulation, 2.2 Multinational Firms; Chapter 2, point 3 Institutional Structure, 3.2. Collectivity: From Associability to Association.

[59] Black, supra note 25, 251–253, with further references; G. Majone, The Rise of the Regulatory State in Europe (July 1994) 77–101; G. Majone, The New European Agencies: Regulation by Information (1997) 262–275; Braithwaite, supra note 25, viii-ix, 9–10.

[60] Koskenniemi, supra note 2, 8 et seqq., 11.

approaches. For example, a state may adopt and apply international standards based on its own initiative, implicitly recognizing the standard-setting bodies concerned or it may delegate rule-making or enforcement powers to third, private bodies. In fact, due to the increasing complexity and technicality of matters to be regulated, a question of regulatory instrument choice arises. It is typically framed as a choice between management-based, technology based, or performance-based regulation. Regulators can craft rules that either:

- Require firms or organizations to engage in their own planning and internal rule making efforts that are supposed to aim toward the achievement of specific public goals (management-based regulation)
- Mandate specific technologies or behaviors (technology-based regulation) or
- Require that certain outcomes will be achieved or avoided (performance-based regulation)

In other words, regulation may intervene at one of three stages of any organization's activities: the planning, acting, or output stages. Other regulatory techniques, like market-based, principle-based, or risk-based regulation are then linked to either of these approaches. Deciding how to classify these regulatory techniques – under management-, technology-, or performance-based regulation – will depend on their intended purpose, not least because they provide distinctive incentives.

The application of these regulatory techniques adds to fragmentation and the polycentrism of regulation. The state may make use of framework statutes, risk-based, or principle-based regulation, which means that it will only define the basic rules and principles to be applied. In practice, it means moving away from dictating through detailed, prescriptive rules and supervisory actions. The detailed rules are laid down by either state agencies, and possibly non-state or private bodies with rule-making and possibly enforcement capacities.[61] They take over public functions and are accountable for their fulfillment. Then, firms are responsible to decide how best to align their operations and objectives with the regulatory outcomes specified. Diverse rationales may lead states to enact such statutes and chose such instruments, due regularly to the level of specialization of the matter to be regulated. The use of these forms of regulation is becoming more frequent. In fact, multiple levels of state involvement are possible. Hence, the mapping of arrangements with state participation and other public actors may vary widely. Solutions may correspond to cases falling under the categories of co-regulation, coercive or also supervised self-regulation, as discussed in Chap. 3.[62]

As far as international state organizations are concerned, they are characterized by great diversity. They have expanded their influence to the globalization of

---

[61] C. Coglianese and D. Lazer, Management-Based Regulation: Prescribing Private Management to Achieve Public Goals (2007) 423–462 or 1–4; S. Breyer, Regulation and Its Reform (1982); Principles-based regulation, Focusing on the outcomes that matter, FSA (April 2007) 3–5.

[62] Concrete examples are co-regulatory solutions, or also delegated and supervised self-regulation, Chapter 3, point 3 Co-regulation and point 4 Coercive Self-regulation.

regulation through their sheer growth in numbers. While there were about 50 such organizations in 1914, there were over 600 in 1980 and the number of these organizations is increasing. Their nature, power, and influence will vary largely from one organization to another. While the influence of some organizations has risen in the course of time, the influence of others has declined, such as the ILO currently. Considering these organizations collectively, as an institutional group, their role has certainly increased in the course of time. Although they cannot cope efficiently with all the issues emerging from the process of globalization, they are very important, not least due to the diversity of interests they represent, their possibilities to take measures, and the support they enjoy from their member states. Although not all qualify as organizations in the sense of international law, they may constitute powerful transnational networks, such as the FSB and its sub-organizations in the field of finance for instance.[63]

Often, these state organizations will lack the power and competences to define and in particular effectively implement rules. Their main difficulties to assert themselves effectively and efficiently as global players are due to the clumsiness of their internal decision-making processes. Such organizations, moreover, are also largely dependent on the goodwill of their member states to implement the rules adopted. Often they will just issue recommendations or codes of conduct. It is also possible, that neither the member states nor their organizations may have the necessary expertise. As a consequence, private market actors with expert knowledge may prefer to organize themselves within networks and apply their own practices and standards in some cases. Notwithstanding these reservations, the influence of international organizations is significant and perceptible in a range of fields – for example, shipping laws which are written at the IMO, air safety laws at the ICAO, food standards at the FAO, telecommunication laws at the ITU, nuclear safety standards at the IAEA, or motor vehicle standards at the ECE.[64] With regard to the court system too, there has been an almost explosive expansion of independent and globally active, yet sectorally limited, courts, quasi-courts, and other forms of conflict-resolving bodies. No less than 125 international institutions where independent authorities reach final legal decisions have been identified – 43 permanent, independent international tribunals delivering binding decisions and 82 quasi-judicial implementation control and dispute settlement bodies. These include the International Court of Justice (ICJ), the International Tribunal for the Law of the Sea, various tribunals for reparations, international criminal courts and tribunals, hybrid international-national tribunal instances, trade and investment judicial bodies, regional human rights tribunals and convention-derived institutions, as well as other regional courts and bodies, such as the European Court of

---

63 Braithwaite and Drahos, supra note 10, 485–488; on the FSB, see Chapter 3, point 6 Global Networks, 6.3 Financial Standard Setting Networks.

64 Braithwaite and Drahos, supra note 10, 485–488.

Justice, the EFTA Court, and the Benelux Court or also the WTO Appellate Body, or the ICTY.[65]

Finally, globalization presents new, sector-oriented challenges for the public actors. Contrary to the concept of the state applying its power within its territory, there are no territorial limits at the global level. Interstate regulation may not be adequate or will not be required anymore, unless there is global coordination. National borders do not confine markets. The regulatory power of states loses its significance in some fields, in particular where global coordination is necessary, like with the lex digitalis. At the same time, states may find themselves involved in regulatory competition with other, third bodies. The public sphere is shaped by global networks.

1.4.3 Epistemic Communities and Transnational Networks

Epistemic communities and in particular their more sophisticated forms, transnational networks,[66] are a hallmark of fragmentation and dispersion. State, non-state, or mixed epistemic communities and networks can be encountered. Indeed, as Berman states:

> 'Such non-state jurisdictional assertions include a wide range of entities, from official transnational and international regulatory and adjudicative bodies, to non-governmental quasi-legal tribunals, to private standard-setting or regulatory organizations.'[67]

In an attempt to grasp private autonomous regimes and alternative or non-state forms of regulation, the following discussion focuses on mixed and non-states communities. These are primarily groups of interest emerging spontaneously. From an instrumental point of view, these regimes can be formally embedded in different forms of agreements, conventions, norms, rules of conduct, or other standardizations, often situated at the intersection between traditional legal and alternative, non-state regimes. As discussed in Chap. 2, their emergence is based on a fundamental epistemic agreement among their members, who share common attitudes and cooperate to defend their interests. The characteristics of these epistemic communities are: (1) a shared set of normative and principled beliefs, (2) shared causal beliefs, (3) shared notions of validity and (4) a common policy

---

[65] H. Hestermeyer, Where Unity Is at Risk: When International Tribunals Proliferate (2008) 125–126; Fischer-Lescano and Teubner, supra note 37, 1000–1001; Fischer-Lescano and Teubner, 2006, supra note 12, 57 et seqq., with further references; W. W. Burke-White, International Legal Pluralism (2004) 963–979.

[66] As discussed in Chapter 2, point 3 Institutional structure, 3.3 Private Regulation: From Association to Self-Regulation, and 3.6 Transnational Networks: From Legal Pluralism to Autonomous Regulatory Regimes.

[67] P. S. Berman, The Globalization of Jurisdiction (December 2002) 324.

enterprise.[68] They have no pre-determined organizational structure or arrangement, the organizational grade may vary from informal to more sophisticated regimes, and finally, they may take the form of associations or SROs. Transnational networks are characterized by non-hierarchical structures. They can be endowed with different powers, depending on their objectives, and can encompass a strikingly wide array of possible cooperative schemes. Their nature is not political, although they may have important strategic and political repercussions.

According to Sajó, from an institutional point of view, two types of epistemic communities or transnational network structures can be distinguished. The first type is a network of private ordering confirming the process of the dismantling of the state, which, however, does not exclude a possible participation of administrative bodies. The second type originates from supranational organizations that operate beyond the nation-state.[69] They constitute a proper institutional zone characterizing globalization and add to polycentrism. The bedrock of these communities or networks is the expert knowledge of the members. Sajó describes indepth what he calls a typical process in the making of a transgovernmental network issuing from a traditional international organization with the consent of the participating states and where an international secretariat works out substantive decisions based on the participation in the preparatory work by the national bureaucracies represented in the organization. It marks the beginnings of transgovernmental networking. These networks, which de facto emerge from policy decisions of the states, are sector-orientated.[70] Science and technological developments play a key role in their development and operations. Information gathering – including data organization, exploration, and analysis within their geographic, societal, institutional, and cultural context –, the forming of opinions, and standard setting are their core activities. The OECD is a case in point. It is an important builder of business regulatory epistemic communities in a range of fields. It brings government officials and experts together for the purpose of addressing specific common issues and making recommendations or promulgating codes of conduct for its solutions. As mentioned

68 Chapter 2, point 3 Institutional Structure, 3.6 Transnational Networks: From Legal Pluralism to Autonomous Regulatory Regimes, providing a definition of epistemic communities; P. M. Haas, Introduction: Epistemic communities and international policy coordination (1992) 1–35; Slaughter and Zaring, supra note 39, 214; for an example of lack of value agreement and thus little networking in the context of European privacy regulators, F. E. Bignami, Transgovernmental Networks vs. Democracy: The Case of the European Information Privacy Network (2005) 807–868.

69 However, networks emerging from the states themselves should be mentioned too. Sajó, supra note 47, 209–225, 212–213.

70 Sajó, supra note 47, 213–215. It is also described as the ‚club model' of international institutions. The model became particularly important after the Second World War. Trade Ministers dominated GATT; finance ministers the IMF. R. O. Keohane and J. S. Nye Jr., The club model of multilateral cooperation and problems of democratic legitimacy (2002) 219 et seqq.; A.-M. Slaughter, Governing the Global Economy through Government Networks (2000) 177–205; Kaufmann, supra note 47, 266–267. On Thatcher's view regarding institutional transformation, see point 3 Evaluation, A process of institutionalization.

in Chap. 3, the OECD published its own OECD Principles of Corporate Governance. Considering that good corporate governance is key to the integrity of corporations, financial institutions and markets, and central to the health of our economies and their stability, it disposes of a Steering Group on Corporate Governance. This Group co-ordinates and guides the Organisation's work on corporate governance and related corporate affairs issues, including state-owned assets, market integrity, company law, insolvency and privatisation. As of 2008, it was chaired by a financial markets regulator. It provides a key forum for dialogue with the Regional Corporate Governance Roundtables.[71]

In the first place, the networks articulate the norms and guidelines which shall apply to their members. Decisions are taken on a consensual basis; their activities as well as the standards and rules they define are not limited to national borders, but are global. They can also take the form of activities resulting from the networks of international organizations or transgovernmental networks, which rely on the principle of unilateralism. For example, the proceedings of the G7-states against Offshore Financial Centres can be cited. In these cases, the observations and perception of the situation in a country by the G7-states are subjective and politically motivated. Based on these observations, they will adopt measures like the Watchlisting or Blacklisting of these non-member countries, without prior consultation. These countries will find themselves subject to these measures through peer pressure. They cannot be submitted for examination to any court by non-members. In April 2000 for instance, Switzerland, Luxembourg, Ireland, Singapore, and Hong Kong were listed as offshore financial centres in a report published by the former FSF. Switzerland declared refusing to accept that qualification in a letter addressed to all FSF members and in a press release, but could not change it. The situation could be compared to the extraterritorial application of law by states.[72] In practice, other forms of activities or cooperation can also be considered to emanate from transgovernmental networks. They can be constituted by international agreements, which, for instance, may delimit mechanisms to solve disputes. However, in these cases, rules may often be non-binding and ineffective.

[71] Hutter, supra note 1, 2–3; H. Willke, Systemtheorie III: Steuerungstheorie (1998) 125; www.oecd.org/daf/corporate-affairs (last visited 26 November 2009).

[72] Report of the Working Group on Offshore Centres, Financial Stability Forum (5 April 2000) 14; http://www.financialstabilityboard.org/list/fsb_publications/from_01011999/index.htm (last visited 8 January 2010); Schweiz weist Qualifikation als 'Offshore'-Finanzzentrum zurück, 30 May 2000, http://www.efd.admin.ch/dokumentation/medieninformationen/archiv/00392/index.html?lang=de (last visited 23 November 2009); Chapter 2, point 3 Institutional Structure, 3.3 Private Regulation: From Association to Self-regulation; P. Nobel, Schweizerisches Finanzmarktrecht, Einführung und Überblick (2004) 164–166; Baudenbacher, supra note 21, 30. Another case is the Financial Action Task Force blacklisting in relation to money laundering. However, these measures are different from freezes imposed pursuant to sanctions, as discussed by W. Blair, Interference of Public Law in the Performance of International Monetary Obligations (2000) 395–412, in particular 410–411. On the FSB, see Chapter 3, point 6 Global Networks, 6.3 Financial Standard Setting Networks.

In the literature, the nature, power, and mechanisms of functioning of epistemic communities and networks are vividly debated. It is generally assumed that they evade state influence and diminish the extent of the sovereignty of the state. Transgovernmental networks raise concerns in terms of democratic control. They represent state interests, but they also reflect their limitations or perhaps powerlessness to tackle definite issues on their own, or compete with other regimes. Moreover, how can states make sure that their delegates are advancing their interests? In particular, national government delegates who participate in them as experts have a dual loyalty – both to their national constituents as well as to their commitments in respect of solving border-transcending problems. In practice, it is a genuine feature of epistemic communities and networks to first constitute themselves based on experts' and scientists' individual, initiative. Initially, such endeavour consists in the exchange of information. Later on, relationships become more organized. For instance, the spreading and use made of the Internet induced a range of regulatory issues. For various reasons, governments were somewhat overstrained and not immediately in a position to define generally applicable rules in a relatively short period of time.[73] The process of digitization as discussed in Chap. 3 was an uncontrollable phenomenon at both the national and global level, and many challenges still need to be mastered. In a first phase, states did not have the necessary expertise and skills to rule on a new technology. They also recognized that an isolated handling of this matter would not lead to the expected results. Large-scale coordination was necessary at the global level. Another case is the financial services industry. It is probably the most blatant case, illustrating how states have delegated (or even abandoned) some of their rule-making functions to governmental and non-governmental entities or networks of experts who – without being formally any official body or (international) organization – are extremely influential. The organizations pertaining to the FSB, in particular the standards defined by the BCBS, IOSCO, or IAIS, as discussed in Chap. 3, can be mentioned. De facto, these organizations emerged spontaneously. They exercise a leading (regulatory) function worldwide. Not only do they determine the standards applying to their members, but also those of the entire industry. Even non-member states feel compelled to implement them in order to operate on the world financial markets and be recognized as players applying good-standing measures. However, it is also argued that besides a market-based perspective, which asserts that market forces enhance cross-national convergence on these international standards, national regulatory authorities remain a key actor in voluntary convergence on international standards. They play a crucial role, not least because they have the power to decide to adopt

[73] A. Hamann, H. Ruiz Fabri, Transnational networks and constitutionalism (2008) 489–491; Slaughter, supra note 40, 311–313; Sajó, supra note 47, 210–211; Braithwaite and Drahos, supra note 10, 29; Chapter 3, point 6 Global Networks, 6.1 Digital Networks; Sassen, supra note 43, 85–90; see also S. Deakin, The Return of The Guild? Network Relations in Historical Perspective (2009) 53–73; M. Amstutz, The Constitution of Contractual Networks (2009) 309–346; National Intelligence Council, Global Trends 2025, supra note 27, x–xi, 80 and seqq.

these standards and declare them binding in their jurisdiction.[74] Nevertheless, as international players, they are not entirely free. Public pressure and possible reputational damages as well as national interests will exercise a disciplinary effect and actually be comparable to sanctions, although these standards are not legally enforceable. Hence, these regimes have a strong normative force, although they are undemocratic as far as the citizens do not take position and their proceedings are largely non-transparent for uninvolved. A similar situation applies to supranational administrative and adjudicative bodies, for instance the WTO dispute resolution panels. 'WTO panels face the objection that they are not accountable to any electorate. . . . Thus, we see a 'democratic deficit' because lawmakers lack electoral responsibility to the 'people' whose 'sovereignty' they exercise.'[75]

Epistemic communities and transnational networks or SROs and NGOs constitute the institutional basis for autonomous regulatory regimes as bodies defining their own global rules. SROs or in particular NGOs also exercise an ever-growing influence on the creation of law through regional and international organizations, and states.[76] They are in a position to operate successfully where states cannot meet normative expectations, which should be compatible with universal normative values in various sectors. This results in the constitution of self-regulatory regimes of rules. However, autonomous regulatory regimes also pertain to the state and can well develop within a state regulatory regime. The case of the self-contained (special) regimes or genuine self-contained regimes, as defined by the International Court of Justice (ICJ) in its Tehran Hostage-case Decision, illustrates this situation. According to the ICJ, these regimes can be subsumed neither under national legal regimes nor international law. Rather, they develop their own norms. Not only are they defined as extremely specialized substantive norms applying to particular fields (these are positive primary norms), but they also constitute autonomous secondary bodies of norms in Hart's sense, other than international law secondary norms. They produce their own procedural norms on rule-making, rule-recognition, and legal sanctions. Hence, they form autonomous or alternative regulatory regimes. While they are based on reflexive processes of norm-setting, they are not considered to be constitutional or auto-constitutional regimes or bodies of rules. They are intersystemic linking institutions over secondary legal norms, which relate law to fundamental principles of rationality. Moreover, it should be noted that they

---

[74] H.-K. Chey, Do markets enhance convergence on international standards? The case of financial regulation (2007) 295–311; Chapter 3, point 6 Global Networks, 6.3 Financial Standard Setting Networks; Sajó, supra note 47, 217. A similar view is now shared by Zaring, supra note 44, 479, who admits to first have been impressed – similarly to other scholars – at how widespread and adequate networks appeared to be as a tool of international governance. However, following the 2007–2009 financial crisis, he recognized that they failed to furnish appropriate responses.

In addition, it should be mentioned that some authors hold the view that standards may represent instruments to avoid or appease crises. For a discussion see: H. Zimmermann, Risiko und Repräsentation: Über Krisen des Finanzsystems (2008) 31–36.

[75] Berman, supra note 67, 390–395.

[76] On the treatment of NGOs within the UN, see Chapter 2, point 3 Institutional Structure, 3.2 Collectivity: From Associability to Association.

are applied by states. In his Report on Fragmentation, Koskenniemi qualifies these regimes as a subcategory, namely a strong form of lex specialis. He concludes that these regimes cannot be created outside the scope of general international law. His view is most certainly correct, not least because these bodies of rules emerge within state law or concepts of international law. Their sources are not dispersed. They are the result of fragmentation. They are autonomous, but belong to the state legal regime. The rules are state rules.[77]

Besides the case of autonomous, self-contained regimes as state regimes, there is also a body of rules called 'law without a state'. It is the product of specialized types of private, non-state authority that proliferate through the expansion and development of epistemic communities and networks, in particular accompanying the emergence of new issues. Their primary source lies in civil society. The groups of interest or various epistemic communities meet on a regular basis at some central geographical location. They share their knowledge and understanding in a determined field or market and exchange experiences. Through their interactions, the position of functional experts is reinforced. Their contacts result in the formation and crystallization of just these groups with a convergence of interests and may lead to the creation of associations or self-regulatory organizations at the global level. The cohesiveness of private relationships may be more efficient than the official, politically embossed way of international relations, which is laborious and cumbersome and whose solutions may finally not be appropriate.[78] They are outside an approach based on a concept centred towards the state. They do not know territorial boundaries and are transnational. Their emergence is dispersed and not necessarily the result of fragmentation. Markets, transnational alliances, and spontaneous, self-governing networks are taking over. Whether they create a genuine 'law without the state' is presumed,[79] but also widely doubted and criticized.[80] Autonomous regimes producing a 'law without a state' are regimes developed by civil society and solely belong to that order. There is a shift of responsibilities onto civil society. Besides the issue of qualifying them as regimes in relation to the state legal regime, there is the issue of their qualification when departing from a dispersed statute, that is, from civil society sources. The rationales leading to the constitution of these regimes are economic, and emanate from developments on private markets and the necessity to

---

[77] Koskenniemi, supra note 2, 65–67 and 99–101; B. Simma, Self-Contained Regimes (1985) 111 et seqq.; Chapter 3, point 5 Self-contained Regimes.

On Hart's distinction between primary and secondary norms, see below, point 2 Standardization, 2.3 Gradual Transformation, 2.3.1 From Standards to Rules.

[78] S. Bernstein and B. Cashore, Can non-state global governance be legitimate? An analytical framework (2007) 354–363.

[79] Fischer-Lescano and Teubner, supra note 50, 48–49; Bernstein and Cashore, supra note 78, 352–354.

[80] Koskenniemi, supra note 51, 1 et seqq.; F. Schauer, Playing by the Rules: A Philosophical Examination of Rule-Based Decision-Making in Law and in Life (1991) 31–34, 47–52.

transact and resolve cooperation problems. The private actors act opportunistically. The regimes shape themselves and their market through defining cooperative schemes and rules. They assume a role of governance in their sector and steer themselves toward collective goals. Through their formalization, they operate through their associations or SROs.[81]

1.4.4 Result: Multiplicity of Actors, Regimes, Institutions

The institutional issue is a core feature of the phenomenon of fragmentation and dispersion of regulation. The entire regulatory system is a constructed system based on the working of institutions or, according to North, 'Perceptions are derived from the mental constructs of the players'. Its configuration is neither stable nor definite, and transformation occurs in both the public and private regulatory orders at any time. These institutional changes are based on the continuous interactions between institutions and organizations in a competitive setting. The system evolves and depends on the present forces as well as the issues and interests at stake. When trying to understand regulatory regimes, the mechanisms are first those used to recognize and categorize actors. The approach is actor-based. Indeed, a variety of actors can be involved. As discussed, state and non-state actors, including individuals, businesses and multinational corporations, NGOs or SROs and the general public, states, international organizations of states, epistemic communities, and transnational networks can be distinguished. Indeed, there is a plethora of actors. They may act either unilaterally or in cooperation with others to defend their interests and realize their objectives. State and non-state actors or combinations of them can be organized in different ways depending on the circumstances and target objectives goals.[82]

The proliferation of epistemic communities and networks characterizing current regulatory developments best underlines the occurring institutional transformation. It is largely due to non-state initiatives. These indicate that there is not only a decentralization and fragmentation of regimes, but much rather a dispersion of regimes, characterized by their plurality and diversity. It is accompanied by a

[81] For a detailed discussion of the emergence of these institutions, see Chapter 2, point 3 Institutional Structure

[82] D. C. North, Understanding the Process of Economic Change (2005) 59; D. C. North, Institutions, Institutional Change and Economic Performance (1990) 3–10; see also Braithwaite and Drahos, supra note 10, 15–17; B. Kingsbury, N. Kirsch, & R. B. Stewart, The Emergence of Global Administrative Law, in: Law and Contemporary Problems (Summer/Autumn 2005) 15–61, 23–27, focusing on global administrative law. In relation to the interpretation of regulation: R. Zäch, Tendenzen der juristischen Auslegungslehre (1977) 313 et seqq.; Black and Rouch, supra note 51, 219 et seqq.; Djelic and Sahlin-Andersson, supra note 49, 8–15; S. Cassese, The Globalization of Law (2005) 986–990; National Intelligence Council, Global Trends 2025, supra note 27, x–xi, 80 and seqq.

growing multiplicity and diversity in both types and kinds of actors. Networks and SROs are in the process of becoming more significant. Some authors regard SROs or also NGOs as key to future regulatory developments. There is the perception that the increase of the number of non-state regulators and regimes is related to transformation at both the state and transnational level.[83] These regimes present original forms of cooperation and their progressive development and persistence leads to the recognition that the institutional structure is changing. It now entails autonomous, non-state regimes. They are best suited to accompany the ongoing expansion of private ordering. In particular, global non-state autonomous regimes producing global rules represent a new order. Instead of traditional state regulation, ad hoc solutions are worked out by these regimes which are outside or different from the scope of traditional state-centred law, although they may be transposed into state law. This results in a multiplicity of regimes mainly pursuing economic interests.[84] The development of these regimes, and linked to these of substantive rules, is the result of technical and functional requirements quintessential to transnational regimes and motivated by policy decisions of multiple actors. However, it should not be overlooked, that their emergence is primarily determined by policy choices of the states to intervene or just not to intervene as well as the absence of concerted efforts by international institutions or states.[85]

2 Standardization

The very existence of alternative, autonomous regulatory regimes is perceived through their regulatory impact. Essentially, they correspond to a process of standardizing relationships between interested members. In the course of a progressive development, a range of stages can subsequently be distinguished, leading from the crystallization of usances or informal rules to a process of self-normativity and codification, to finally constitute a regulatory regime.[86] The issues arising in this connection concern the mechanisms leading to their constitution and subsistence, the rules they produce, the actual effectiveness of the regimes and their nature, not least in relation to state regulation. To explore these issues, the argument proceeds dialectically, but is discursively constructed. The following aspects are discussed below: cooperation and trading, auto-constitutionalism and self-regulation, the process of transformation, and the nature of these regimes.

[83] Hutter, supra note 1, 7; Braithwaite and Drahos, supra note 10; for a numeric example regarding the rise of SROs see Chapter 2, point 3 Institutional Structure, 3.2 Collectivity: From Associability to Association; National Intelligence Council, Global Trends 2025, supra note 27, 80–87.

[84] Sassen, supra note 24, 242–247.

[85] Koskenniemi, supra note 2, 13–14; Chapter 3, point 6 Global Networks, 6.1 Digital Networks; National Intelligence Council, Global Trends 2025, supra note 27, x-xi.

[86] Koskenniemi, supra note 2, 22–23.

2.1 Cooperation and Trading

Historical evidence suggests that cooperation and trading are the source and driver of all kinds of interaction. Both appear in numerous disciplines like economics, mathematics, anthropology, or also biology. Their operations are based on individual or group activities aimed at increasing benefits, while running the risk of suffering a loss or obtaining little return on investment. As a result, their attitude is motivated by opportunistic considerations. They have to make choices between small, secure and immediate profits or substantial but future ones. These choices represent recurring dilemmas. Thus, cooperation theory regularly focuses on 'lower-level' building blocks such as short-term payoffs from behavioural encounters. Individuals or groups recognize that they are interdependent and develop mechanisms to ensure the greatest satisfaction of their needs and expectations. There would be no necessity for cooperation in case no transactions were concluded; nor would trading exist without cooperation between the parties to a transaction.

Cooperation and trading should be understood in a broad sense. Trading is not limited to the physical exchange or trading of goods only. It encompasses all forms of exchange, including intellectual exchanges or relationships in a court, between the judge and the accused. It epitomizes the relationships between individuals or groups. These are multilateral rather than bilateral. Cooperation is a non-linear concept, based on consensus. Nor is it stable. It applies to intrinsically unstable or evolving relationships. In particular, a range of informal avenues of cooperation exist. De facto, a great diversity of forms of cooperation can be identified. Functional and systemic challenges revolve around the issue of cooperation. Different forms of cooperation require different kinds of theoretical models, but most can be subsumed under the following basic categories of individuals' interactions:

- The first category is the dyadic interactions or interactions taking place in the context of a large number of individuals that can potentially interact. They constitute a 'market'. However, the actual interactions are intrinsically dyadic. For instance, an individual customer will buy goods in a single shop.
- The second category covers the polyadic interactions. Multiple individuals have to act together in order to obtain an outcome that will be beneficial to some or all of them. This form of collective behavior is oriented toward long-term interests and in such cases, individuals renounce to reap short-term personal profit. Examples are the management of public goods or the production of benefits through collective action for instance within the framework of self-regulatory organizations representing an industry.
- The third category regards cooperation between entities consisting of multiple individuals. Recently, it has been shown that the evolution of specific forms of cooperation between individuals can be attributed to a form of 'cultural' group selection. This process can probably be linked to the evolution of language, which acts as a tool for synchronisation and also policing. By the same token, trading between firms or companies can be seen as cooperation between groups

rather than individuals. Decisions adopted at the company level are usually the result of the dynamic interaction between individuals involved in the decision-making process.

– While the above categories imply face-to-face interactions with the possibility of communication between actors, the last category is characterized by anonymous trading and can entail completely anonymous interactions. This can be the case of trading taking place on securities markets or at certain forms of auctions for instance.[87]

Cooperation is a central focus of inquiry in a range of disciplines. Linked to trading, it corresponds to a necessity to develop a strategy among various possible opportunities to attain a goal. A weighting of interests – first between self-interest and cooperation – takes place to resolve the dilemmas of choice. Mechanisms to solve the issues have to be developed. In some situations, cooperation will lead to effective trading markets, while in others it may break down or never develop. The evolution of cooperation is accompanied by trade. Both concepts have essential elements in common. They involve the presence of a number of actors, exchange opportunities, and transactions. In practice, a multitude of contracts or agreements are concluded. Hence, cooperation and trading methods will need to be unified. Cooperation methods management and the intensification of relationships will lead to the search for standardizing and simplifying processes leading to trading and the conclusion of transactions. Cooperation and exchanging views, ideas, and practices will facilitate developing a common approach to trading. It will mark the beginning of a process of transformation towards formalization, and standardization. The normative orders that will finally emerge are negotiated orders, that is, resulting from cooperation-specific negotiations. They constitute the basis that will ultimately lead to the formation of regimes.[88]

Empirical research and social science literature assert that there are instances in which institutions led states to behave in a more cooperative manner than they otherwise might have. For instance, while states develop from and around a center, the widespread global administrative institutions of states develop through mutual

---

87 Unpublished paper on The Evolution of Cooperation and Trading, Tect – Eurocores, 2005, 3–4, on file with author; P. J. Richerson and R. Boyd, Not by Genes Alone, How Culture Transformed Human Evolution (2005). While these categories are logically constructed and based on the idea of an existing order, they ignore fortuitous, unexpected, or accidental interactions.

88 K. A. Oye, Cooperation under Anarchy (1986); P. Drahos, The regulation of public goods (2004) 325; Cutler, Haufler, Porter, supra note 54, 9–15; Cutler, Haufler, and Porter, supra note 54, 334–336; Roberts, supra note 58, 23; K. Raustiala, The Architecture of International Cooperation: Transgovernmental Networks and the Future of International Law (2002) 64–70; E. A. Posner, Law and Social Norms (2000) 4–5, 11 et seqq.; G.-P. Calliess, J. Freiling, and M. Renner, Law, the State, and Private Ordering: Evolutionary Explanations of Institutional Change (2008) 400–406. On the theoretical problem of cooperation, see: North (1990) supra note 82, 11–16.

For a discussion from an historical point of view, see: M. Schulte Beerbühl, J. Vögele, Spinning the Commercial Web, International Trade, Merchants, and Commercial Cities, c. 1640–1939 (2004).

connections from peripheral points, in federative or associate forms.[89] Indeed, cooperative behavior is shaped by the societal environment, institutions, cultural information, and the webs of circuits used by information and commercial networks. In addition, the development of regulation based on such a cooperative scheme largely depends on the determination of individuals and groups to develop their relationships. Cooperation is the basic mechanism of functioning transnational (regulatory, self-organizing) networks. The pursuance of mutual interests is central, although it is not essential to have only one opinion about all questions. However, like-minded group participants or members will have a positive influence on the quality and worthiness of their community or network.[90] The advantages members expect to gain from participating in a network act as a cohesive force, motivating participants to cooperate and exchange their views. As a result, they may be interwoven in a subtle mixture of dependences and independences.[91] Cooperation-based communities or networks are also expected to enhance creativity and innovation. They are good vehicles to react in a flexible way to crises and organizational changes within society. Moreover, with regard to the impact of cooperative schemes or networks, reputation plays an important role and exercises a kind of disciplinary effect among network members through its pressure.[92]

Cooperative schemes comprising both state and private actors could be considered to represent a corporatist or neo-corporatist solution and a need could be located to introduce a new repartition of tasks between the state and these actors. However, contrary to the autonomous regulatory schemes emerging spontaneously, corporatist schemes are largely based on the dominating role of the state. It defines the structure of the cooperative framework. This may not be the case of the cooperative schemes discussed here. The cooperative model can be based on an

---

[89] S. Cassese, Administrative Law without the State? The Challenge of Global Regulation (2005) 674; B. A. Simmons and L. L. Martin, International Organizations and Institutions (2002) 199; most recently A. Greif, Institutions and the Path to the Modern Economy, Lessons from Medieval Trade (2006); L. L. Martin, The Political Economy of International Cooperation (1999) 51–64; Oye, supra note 88.

[90] Majone (1997) supra note 59, 262–275; G. Majone, The European Commission: The Limits of Centralization and the Perils of Parliamentarization (2002) 382–383; G. Majone, Delegation of Regulatory Powers in a Mixed Polity (2002a) 336; Senn, supra note 41, 461–463; see also point 1 Fragmentation, 1.4 Institutional Transformation; Chapter 2, point 3 Institutional Structure, 3.6 Transnational Networks: From Legal Pluralism to Autonomous Regulatory Regimes; Haas, supra note 68.

[91] Posner, supra note 88, 5, 11 et seqq.; Willke, supra note 71, 112–121; Slaughter, supra note 40, 312; Majone, supra note 59, 262, 265; Senn, supra note 41, 461–463; Raustiala, supra note 88, 10 et seqq.; see also: E. Fehr and U. Fischbacher, Social norms and human cooperation (April 2004) 185–190; Chapter 2, point 3 Institutional Structure, 3.6 Transnational Networks: From Legal Pluralism to Autonomous Regulatory Regimes.

[92] Majone (1997) supra note 59, 262–275; Majone (2002) supra note 90, 382–383; Majone (2002a) supra note 90, 336; see also S. Barrett, Creating Incentives for Cooperation: Strategic Choices (2003) 308–328.

intensive collaboration between the state, the economy and other market actors, but it is not determined by the state only.[93]

In their study 'Global Business Regulation', Braithwaite and Drahos question how the regulation of business is generated and how it shifts from national to global institutions, that is, the process of globalization and the role played by organizations such as the WTO, OECD or the World Bank, NGOs, SROs, professional bodies, and some individuals. These institutions constitute epistemic communities that meet at the national and international level. Their interactions and exchanges are all based on cooperative schemes. They develop a common and shared understanding of the required standards and regulation. The standards they set shall prevail within an industry (be privately implemented) or be adopted by the states (be publicly implemented), at the national level, when laying down rules. Their cooperation results in regulating other businesses and states.[94] Constituting networks, they are very efficient vehicles to develop standards in part, since they present non-hierarchical structures offering the possibility to elaborate ad hoc, practical ways to solve issues. However, the issues of effective implementation of the measures, their regulatory impact, and performance remain open. In case of private implementation, no sanctioning instrument and mechanism may be available to enforce the rules. In case of implementation by states, their role cannot be ignored. States remain largely determining. As stated by Oye:

> 'At times, the absence of centralized international authority precludes attainment of common goals. Because as states, they cannot cede ultimate control over their conduct to a supranational sovereign, they cannot guarantee that they will adhere to their promises. The possibility of a breach of promise can impede cooperation even when cooperation would leave all better off.'[95]

The financial markets are a case in point, for instance, where rule-making and enforcement functions are co-opted by the states and professional SROs. In this sector, most transactions are typically global. There are multiple financial nodes and the financial landscape is multipolar. There is a general systemic risk, and therefore a necessity to cooperate and develop common standards applying to financial markets worldwide. Consequently, businesses, financial institutes, banks, or securities exchanges first work together to define the modality of their – often transnational – transactions themselves. Such definition usually occurs in an informal way first, in the form of ad hoc agreements or contracts concluded between private parties before further development to subsequently constitute standards either finalized or approved by their representative networks or regulators. Their cooperation is originally based on loosely-structured, peer-to-peer relationships developed through frequent interactions rather than formal negotiations.

---

[93] Chapter 2, point 3 Institutional Structure, 3.2 Collectivity: From Associability to Association.

[94] Indeed coercive orders such as the EU-order should also be taken into account. Braithwaite and Drahos, supra note 10; see also: R. Axelrod and R. O. Keohane, Achieving Cooperation under Anarchy: Strategies and Institutions (1986) 226–254, discussing cooperation in world politics.

[95] Oye, supra note 88, 1.

In practice, this form of regulation is predestined to be more efficient than rules defined by international organizations, other intergovernmental cooperations, or agreements, at least in the initial stage. One important incentive is that it consists in the representation of vital interests of an industry. In practice, examples could be classified under the forms of transnational committee standards-setting, transactional standards-setting, market standards-setting, and individual standards-setting, as suggested by Black and Rouch.[96] Under the transnational committee standards-setting form, regulators produce standards to be enforced by their members. Authority is based on associational schemes. Typical examples are IOSCO, or the IAIS, both belonging to the FSB. However, the standards they define have to be adopted by the states. In practice, the work of these committees is practical and comprehensive. For instance, following the 2007–2009 financial crisis, the former FSF established a Report comprising more than 60 recommendations. It expects the members to implement them and give account of their progress.[97] In the transactional standards-setting form, expertise is determining. National and transnational groups of market participants draw up standardised documentation to facilitate transactions in particular types of securities. It can include the documentation produced by ISDA, the Loan Market Association (LMA), or the Global Master Securities Lending Agreement (ISLA), for instance. In the market standards-setting form, national or transnational groups of market participants develop standards, guidance or codes of practice for industry participants. They are the industry representative associations or SROs. For instance, similarly to the FSF, the Institute of International Finance (IIF) – a private initiative and global association of financial institutions (major international banks) created in 1983 in response to the international debt crisis – also published a Report[98] drawing the consequences of the 2007–2009 financial crisis, containing a range of (self-disciplinary) proposals to be applied by banks to strengthen the financial industry and financial markets. At the national level, the Swiss Bankers Association publishes codes and guidelines, which are binding on its members, like the Code of Conduct for Securities Dealers of 1997. In these cases, a state participation is not excluded. Depending on the issue at stake and the statute, the state can invite, delegate, or agree that industry representatives produce or develop codes or standards, or establish reports before getting active itself. Such codes or rules may be subject to approval. This is the case with the said Code for Securities Dealers, which has to be approved based on article

---

[96] Although this classification may be questionable as far as it mixes approaches based on the subjects with approaches based on business transactions or the institutional framework, it is useful as far as it allows seizing the outcome of diverse forms of cooperation. Black and Rouch, supra note 51, 226; see also National Intelligence Council, Global Trends 2025, supra note 27, 10–14.

[97] Report of the Financial Stability Forum on Enhancing Market and Institutional Resilience, Financial Stability Forum (7 April 2008); see also Chapter 3, point 6 Global Networks, 6.3 Financial Standard Setting Networks.

[98] Final Report of the IIF Committee on Market Best Practices: Principles of Conduct and Best Practice Recommendations, Financial Services Industry Response to the Market Turmoil of 2007–2008, Institute of International Finance (July 2008).

11 SESTA. Moreover, the former Federal Banking Commission (now Financial Market Supervisory Authority), considering the dual system of supervision, declared that the compliance with the self-regulatory measures had to be revised by the responsible audits companies, thus 'elevating' them to a status of rules recognized by the state.[99] It is also common practice for states to sponsor or commission experts. Industry associations can do the same.[100] In addition, market standards may also be standards issuing from coordinated networks of market participants. In the individual standards-setting form, standards or other norms are developed at the micro-level, by individuals, and then adopted by others. It can be the result of day-to-day legal and regulatory decision-making by the staff of financial institutions regarding regulatory and legal issues. It can then represent the logical continuation of former experiences and practices, or models adopted from practices developed in the course of relationships with other individuals or firms or according to counselors' opinions, precedents produced by law firms, or correspond to the implementation of judgments. Standards set by third parties or parties not directly participating in the market, like credit rating agencies, may also be used by others, or as discussed in Chap. 3, by regulators. Finally, they may be the result of the creativity of individuals themselves. Cooperation and trading and the conclusion of transactions will enhance the emergence of standards. Although not primarily developed for use by others, practices may nevertheless become standardized throughout sectors of the market, in relation to specific kinds of transactions. In the end of the process of standard-setting, they may indeed be adopted by regulators themselves.[101]

From an organizational point of view, epistemic communities, networks, and SROs can adopt a number of cooperative forms, as just discussed. They can comprise different types of members who pursue similar substantive goals. Basically, there is no monitoring by a mother organization. However, these entities can be considered to represent systems, with the ability to function not only as closed and immovable systems, but also as open and dynamic ones. Hence, they can cooperate with third, external entities, either as a whole or through their sub-groups composed of definite categories of actors and they can be oriented towards state governance or also private market economy.[102] As such they may also constitute

---

[99] Chapter 3, point 3 Co-regulation, 3.2 Official Rules of Conduct; Circular of the FINMA: Self-Regulation Recognized as a Minimum Standard by the Swiss Financial Market Supervisory Authority of 20 November 2008, FINMA-Circ. 08/10 Self-regulation as a minimum standard.

[100] Black and Rouch, supra note 51, 226; see for example the expertise by P. Nobel and I. Stirnimann, Zur Behandlung von Entschädigungen im Vertrieb von Anlagefonds- und strukturierten Produkten durch Banken Eine Untersuchung im Lichte des Bundesgerichtsentscheids BGE 132 III 460 (2007) 343–356, ordered by the Swiss Bankers Association.

[101] Black and Rouch, supra note 51, 226; Chapter 2, point 3 Institutional Structure, 3.1 Theory of Interest: From Interest to Associability, and 3.2 Collectivity: From Associability to Association; Chapter 3, point 1 Self-regulation, 1.2 Credit Rating Agencies; B. Jacobsson and K. Sahlin-Andersson, Dynamics of soft regulations (2006) 253–262.

[102] Willke, supra note 71, 112, 125; Senn, supra note 41, 461–463; Haas, supra note 68, 15–20.

third, transnational networks, insofar as they may cooperate voluntarily with other or similar entities, or other organizations working in the same field. For instance, in the case of financial markets they can be encountered among responsible national authorities or among private groups. Practically, this means that they can also be members of international organizations or be represented in working groups of these organizations as well as ad hoc groups, task forces, or committees. They may also take the initiative to constitute distinct, third communities or networks with similar entities.

2.2 *Auto-Constitutionalism and Self-regulation*

The mechanisms on which autonomous regimes are based and operate are characterized by their particular, unique, and unconstrained development. They are self-constituted, follow their own logic, adapted to the field they regulate, and develop spontaneously. In fact, some of these characteristics may also apply to regimes belonging to state regulation like trade law or investment law,[103] as stated, insofar as auto-constitutionalism designates the process of self-constitution of regimes. Here, however, discussion focuses on non-state and hybrid regulatory regimes. In practice, these regimes may apply to sectors such as the economy, science, technology, education, and the environment. They may be global or local, and create and administer their own, (self-regulatory) rules. They are auto-constitutional regimes.

When discussing auto-constitutional regimes, Fischer-Lescano and Teubner state that the following pre-conditions must be fulfilled to find them outside a state regime:

1. The development of an explicit constitutional discourse and constitutional self-consciousness
2. A claim to foundational legal authority, or sovereignty, whereas sovereignty is not viewed as absolute
3. The delineation of a sphere of competences
4. The existence of an organ internal to the polity with interpretative autonomy as regards the meaning and scope of competencies
5. The existence of an institutional structure to govern the polity
6. Rights and obligations of citizenship, understood in a broad sense
7. Specification of the terms of representation of the citizens in the polity

Fischer-Lescano and Teubner also suggest that there is a world constitution for the economy, a world constitution for education, etc. Indeed, their concept of auto-constitutionalism implies that the regimes cover societal sectors comparable to the political constitutions of states. As a result, they form auto-constitutional private,

[103] Chapter 3, point 5 Self-contained Regimes.

non-state regimes, parallel to political constitutions. They are civil constitutions which should apply broadly to civil society as well as merit its respect.[104] Notably, Koskenniemi – although he otherwise disagrees with Fischer-Lescano and Teubner – applies a similar approach. He refers to the rise of the nation-state in the late nineteenth century, suggesting that this resembled the emergence of autonomous regulatory regimes. He also applies this view to the international legal system, where the fragmentation into technical regimes when examined from the point of view of the law of treaties is not too different from the traditional fragmentation into more or less autonomous territorial regimes called national legal systems.[105] The concept of auto-constitutional regimes applies to global regimes, but it may also comprehend local or regional regimes or regimes operating at the national level. A participatory scheme or partnership involving the private and public sectors is not excluded. On their side, self-contained regimes consolidate themselves and become auto-constitutional regimes or present auto-constitutional elements. Nor can it be safely asserted that the claim for standing of these regimes is global and universal. These regimes will often be global, but it is not their objective. Neither do they aspire to covering or satisfying the needs of entire civil society. Their main incentive is functional and sector-orientation. They primarily tend to satisfy the needs of the members of their community, operating in accordance with expectations or instructions. In case of a global character, it will be a consequence of their orientation.

As auto-constitutional regimes, autonomous non-state regimes are first centred towards the knowledge or self-knowledge of their members communicating and cooperating among each other. As such the concept belongs to the field of cybernetics. Cybernetics is defined as:

> The theory or study of communication and control in living organisms or machines.[106]

Cybernetics[107] explores and describes the workings of all kinds of systems. It is a multidisciplinary scientific approach which discusses these processes in an abstract way. Its goal – by formulating abstract concepts common to all systems – is to understand their behaviour. Cybernetics tries to discover how large systems can be governed with little energy. Such self-monitoring processes are well-known in nature, ecological systems, and human society. One case in point is the well-known notion of the self-regulated market, which relies on Adam Smith's concept of an 'invisible hand' governing supply and demand for products and services as well as the price building process. The market self-regulates the exchange of goods

---

104 Fischer-Lescano and Teubner, supra note 37, 1014–1016; Fischer-Lescano and Teubner, supra note 12, 53.

105 Koskenniemi, supra note 51, 1, 24–25; Koskenniemi, supra note 2, 15.

106 The Oxford English Dictionary, Volume IV (1991) 188.

107 N. Wiener, Cybernetics, or control and communication in the animal and the machine (1948). For cybernetic-approaches in the field or regulation, see C. Hood, Administrative Analysis (1986); C. Hood, H. Rothstein and R. Baldwin, The Government of Risk (2000) 23–24.

and price formation.[108] Self-regulation is a process of self-monitoring or self-governing, without any external influence. When examining autonomous regulatory regimes as self-regulated processes through the lens of cybernetics, it becomes clear that they can be based on various institutional arrangements. Their nature remains not easily amenable. As far as their specific form of regulation qualifies as self-regulation, it constitutes a system outside or at the periphery of the state legal system. But which conditions must such a regime fulfil? Page argues that there must first be an organized interest group, a collectivity. This group will be formalized within an association or SRO. Second, as self-regulation emerges from the activities of a group of interest, motivation is an important feature. The group or SRO must be willing to reach a determined goal through regulating member behaviour. This goal will be made public as well as the rules adopted by the association or SRO. However, self-regulating through an association or SRO again shows that both the phenomenon and process of self-regulation are complex. Member interactions may vary continuously, on the one hand; on the other, the reasons for adopting certain measures as well as the environmental factors may change. In other words, self-regulation is governed by many interrelated factors with changing constellation. The third condition for self-regulation to work is that the association or SRO must maintain sufficient control over its members. It has to be credible towards the market and individuals, in particular as regards counteracting a possible introduction of state regulation.[109] While these conditions are most certainly feasible, it should also be taken into account that the very existence of a group of interest or association implies knowledge, which is even more important than motivation. Indeed, the rationale for self-regulating as well as the genuine reason for the very existence of self-regulatory solutions resides in the fact that a system offers the advantage of expertise and profound domain knowledge, which the state lacks or must acquire. Self-regulation is based on knowledge.[110]

This leads to the theory of autopoiesis or the theory of reflexive law developed by Teubner at the beginning of the 90s. Originating in biology, autopoiesis is also inspired by cybernetics. Specifically, it refers to the self-regulation, self-production, and self-organization of systems or regimes. Its basic assumption is that (state) governance is based on the self-organization and self-governance of differentiated functional regimes into which society is divided, like economy, law, politics, etc. These regimes or systems are self-defined and self-referential. They have the capacity to regulate themselves. They follow their own rationality, but interact continuously with the outside world. They are closed regimes or systems as far as their organization is concerned, but they are open to situations in the outside world

[108] A. Smith, An Inquiry into the Nature and Causes of the Wealth of Nations (1976); A. Marti, Selbstregulierung anstelle staatlicher Gesetzgebung? (2000) 563, 568, with further references; see also Thürer, supra note 10, 107–122.

[109] A. C. Page, Self-Regulation: The Constitutional Dimension (March 1986) 148–151; see also Slaughter, supra note 52, 169; Chapter 2, point 3 Institutional Structure, 3.3 Private Regulation: From Association to Self-regulation.

[110] Slaughter (2004) supra note 52, 169.

or other regimes where present, so as to self-generate and reproduce.[111] In relation to self-regulatory measures adopted by autonomous regimes and considered within a societal or a legal regime, the latter must be taken into account. Self-regulation can regulate itself, but it must be harnessed for 'government at a distance' to be effective.[112]

As auto-constitutional regimes, non-state, private autonomous regimes are based on reflexive norm-building. Such regimes operate based on self-regulatory and self-defined rules. Thus, they auto-constitute themselves. The term 'auto-' is defined as:

> self, one's own, by oneself, independent-ly, combining form of self. . . . In free composition as a prefix element, its chief meanings are: of oneself, one's own; self-; self-produced or -induced (pathologically) within the body or organism; spontaneous, self-acting, automatic.[113]

Auto-constitutionalism is closely related to self-regulation. Both notions are effectively co-dependent. While auto-constitutionalism is a basic feature of an autonomous regime, self-regulation (and standards)[114] represents the mechanism and instrument concretizing and realizing it. However, self-regulation is a difficult construct. It is a broad concept and a complex phenomenon.[115] While the content of self-regulation is a clear given, self-regulation escapes easy definition and the conceptual issue still needs to be explored. Elucidating its meaning is a challenge. The term 'self-regulation' is constituted by two distinct parts. The particle 'self' is defined as:

> In concord with a sb. or pron., to indicate emphatically that the reference is to the person or thing mentioned and not, or not merely, to some other.

or:

> In agreement with a possessive genitive . . ., the word may be rendered 'own'. Hence the use of the uninflected self in 16-17th century for: Own, peculiar.[116]

Black suggests that 'self' denotes both an individual person as well as a collective. It refers to individuals disciplining their conduct or a collectivity 'self-'regulating its members. As such, self-regulation should be distinguished

---

[111] G. Teubner, Recht als autopoietisches System (1989); H. Willke, Entzauberung des Staates, Überlegungen zu einer sozietalen Steuerungstheorie (1983); see also G. Teubner, Law as an Autopoietic System (1993); J. Black, Critical Reflections on Regulation (2002) 5; G. Teubner, R. Nobles, D. Schiff, The Autonomy of Law: An Introduction to Legal Autopoiesis (2003); Baldwin and Cave, supra note 38, 31.

[112] Black, supra note 111, 5.

[113] The Oxford English Dictionary, Volume I (1991) 799; in French: auto- means Elément, du gr. Autos 'soi-même, lui-même', autoanalyse, autodérision. Contr. Hétér(o)-; allo-. 183. Hétér(o)- Elément, du gr. Heteros 'autre', contr. Homo-, is(o)-; auto-. Le Nouveau Petit Robert, Dictionnaire de la Langue Française (2003) 1262.

[114] On the distinction between self-regulation and standards, see below, 2.3. Gradual transformation.

[115] Hutter, supra note 1, 4; A. I. Ogus, Regulation: Legal Form and Economic Theory, (2004).

[116] The Oxford English Dictionary, Volume XIV (1991) 905.

from what may be termed 'individualised' regulation.[117] Thus, there is a zone of autonomy and self-reliance within a domain and in relation to a collective, such as an organization, association, or self-regulatory organization, as far as this includes what the collective can do for itself, its members, and towards the outside world. However, it should not be understood as a kind of individual 'laissez-faire'.[118]

Self-regulated thus means:

> Regulated from within or automatically.

and *self-regulation* signifies:

> Regulation, control, or direction by or of oneself (itself).[119]

The OECD defines self-regulation as:

> The process by which an organized group regulates the behaviour of its members.[120]

The basic idea of self-regulation is a process occurring or governing itself from within. As a consequence, self-regulation has been considered to be an oxymoron during a long period of time. It was the result of the traditional understanding of regulation as representing an activity only belonging to the state. Regulation signified that regulatory measures were imposed from outside, thus contrary to self-regulation. Regulation was solely a form of state governance regarding citizen behaviour or the private economy. In the meantime, this understanding of self-regulation has been superseded and has lost its oxymoronic character. This shift is in part due to the fact that independent state agencies have become more influential and effective while attempting to counter the allegations of over-regulation confronting them. They tend to enhance network-based, (state-controlled) self-regulatory solutions. At the same time, due to diverse rationales, there is a general tendency to increasingly provide space to alternative regulatory resources, or alternative forms of regulation formulated and finalized by groups of experts.[121]

Self-regulation represents the rules enacted by a SRO or association, for example a commercial association controlling and governing itself, and imposing its rules on its members. It may also exercise control over a broader group of persons than solely its members.[122] The notion of self-regulation concerns – as far as specifying its content is concerned – a process governed from inside, within itself, autonomously, and which can persist thus. It results from the activity of a collective or a group of interest with incentives to take measures. It is motivated by the need to

---

[117] J. Black, Constitutionalising Self-Regulation (1996) 26–27.

[118] Nobel, supra note 36, 126.

[119] The Oxford English Dictionary, Volume XIV (1991) 929.

[120] OECD, Meeting on Alternatives to Traditional Regulation, OECD (1994) 7.

[121] Harrison, Morgan, Verkuil, supra note 13, 494 et seqq.; National Intelligence Council, Global Trends 2025, supra note 27, x-xiii, 81–87.

[122] Baldwin and Cave, supra note 38, 39, with further references.

satisfy and protect its individual members.[123] Self-regulation does not mean the constitution of self-regulatory models of organization, but rather the constitution of domain-specific rules by experts. Its nature is voluntary. Rules enforcement or good working practices largely depend on actors involved in a self-regulatory regime recognizing that they constitute a network, and on the assumption that they are interdependent, willing to interact and cooperate in a fair and constructive way. In addition, no territorial limits abide. Autonomous, self-regulatory solutions may thus extend well beyond national borders.

Considered in relation to state regulation, self-regulation can be examined with regard to the state monopoly to regulate as its most exclusive task. Due to its powers, it can act through unilateral, binding command or based on heteronomy. The relation between state regulation and self-regulation relies on the following key variables, as identified by Ogus whose view is centred towards a predominant role of the state and state regulation: first, there is no clear dichotomy between self-regulation and public or state regulation or in other words between private regulation through private interest groups, networks or associations at one extreme and state rules at the other. Second, the rules issued by these associations may have varying degrees of legal force. There may be formally binding codes of practice or purely voluntary measures. Third, regimes may differ according to their degree of monopolistic power. Historically speaking, self-regulation may represent a preliminary stage to a statute. It is predestined to become part of the state monopoly to regulate. Lastly, when discussing the configuration of a traditional state regulatory regime and self-regulation, two important characteristics appear to play a determining role: delegation and subsidiarity.[124]

From the point of view of the state, cooperation may take place with the private economy when it empowers civil society with competencies to regulate or enforce regulation. In relation to cooperation and trading mechanisms, the delegation of regulatory powers by the state to an association, SRO or other private market actors depends on the attitude of the state and the self-regulatory capabilities of a market or sector. Delegation often occurs as a result of cost-benefit considerations. At the basis, there is a model of participatory governance and a state regulatory system favouring the transfer of rule-making or enforcement functions to third entities, whether public or private. The delegation of regulatory powers is closely related to the accountability of the institutions, private bodies or associations concerned. The state delimits the extent of the delegation and expects specific results. It will introduce control mechanisms. It will require the association or SRO to inform or report on a regular basis and determine liability conditions.

---

[123] Black, supra note 117, 26–27; Page, supra note 109, 144–145; A. I. Ogus, Rethinking Self-Regulation (Spring 1995) 99 et seqq.; G. De Minico, A Hard Look at Self-Regulation in the UK (2006) 183–211; J. Braithwaite, Enforced self-regulation: A new strategy for corporate crime control (June 1982) 1466–1470; Chapter 2, point 3 Institutional Structure, 3.3 Private Regulation: From Association to Self-regulation.

[124] Ogus, supra note 115; Ogus, supra note 123, 97; De Minico, supra note 123, 183–211.

In such cases, moreover, there is the possibility for a judicial review of the measures taken by these associations or SROs.[125]

As stated in Chap. 2, the second issue of subsidiarity concerns the policy of task allocation. This is linked to the state monopoly to regulate. Accordingly, the state has the ultimate regulatory authority. Any matter can be regulated by other authorities or private associations as long as the state does not intervene. Based on the subsidiarity of state regulation, the presence as well as the enactment of self-regulatory rules in economic or other systems can be justified and subsumed under state regulation, as long as no state regulation is enacted. Regulatory alternatives can subsist as far as they are tolerated by the state and linked to the state system of rules. From a liberal point of view, subsidiarity can be interpreted as a duty of the state to first provide space for other solutions to develop and intervene only when there is no other possible solution, and then restrictively.[126]

2.3 Gradual Transformation

Autonomous regulatory regimes are best perceived through the rules they define and the observance of these rules in practice or, in other words, their impact. To analyze these rules, the basic regulatory roles distinguished are: information gathering, standard setting or rule-making and behaviour modification, that is, enforcement or impact.[127] While the role of information gathering can be implicitly comprehended and included in the cooperation and trading scheme as well as constituting the basis of regimes, insofar as the epistemic communities and networks meet and congregate just based on their knowledge and to exchange information, the focus is now placed on the two other roles. Similarly to the emergence of institutions accompanied by a transformation of modes of interactions, there is the idea of a gradual standardization and codification of elements of knowledge which first exist as societal practice, towards the elaboration of rules. Based on standards, rules crystallize in the course of a codification process. To discuss that process, the passage draws on the development of practices and standards and their transformation into either state or non-state rules. The argument proceeds in two main stages. First, that standard setting or rule-making covers a wide range of activities, mirroring them. It departs from designing relationships discursively, based on interactions, draws on and reproduces particular structures, finally

[125] To the concept of delegation, see Chapter 1, point 5 Decentred Analysis of Regulation, with the references given at n 59; Chapter 2, point 1 Embedding Autonomous Regulatory Regimes, n 5; Chapter 3, point 4 Coercive Self-regulation, n 113 and the example of Co-regulation, Chapter 3, point 3

[126] Chapter 2, point 3 Institutional Structure, 3.4 State Intervention: From Self-regulation to State Regulation; Harrison, Morgan, Verkuil, supra note 13, 494–496; Hutter, supra note 1, 7; Braithwaite and Drahos, supra note 10.

[127] Hutter, supra note 1, 2–3.

appearing to take the form of rules. That process comprises both constitutive and transformative elements. Second, that the possible impact of a regime of rules can be both formal and informal. It can correspond to a form of voluntary compliance or be appreciated by the enforcement of sanctions dictated by a court. The impact is an indicator of the effectiveness or success of a regime, although, as will be discussed, it remains incommensurable as such.

2.3.1 From Standards to Rules

Brief Overview of the Cases

Non-state regulation or self-regulation is regularly perceived as an innovative kind of regulation, not least because it regularly appears in conjunction with the regulation of new fields or issues not regulated by the state before. Initially, the debate over regulatory design is framed in epistemic communities. The individuals and groups concerned form collectivities that need it to transact their business. They have to rely on a generally accepted normative structure. It will take the form of practices or usances first, which are then concretized to form standards applying to their field. To cooperate, they recognize that they would be better off if they could follow specific standards or rules delimited in common and applying to all. At the same time, their attitude also emphasizes their self-responsibility within their field. The standards or rules they define may be advisory or also voluntary. Nowadays, standards abound.[128]

Braithwaite and Drahos argue that regulation is the result of a worldwide collaboration of various epistemic groups or groups of experts forming transnational networks. This process is not limited to economic activities. It is extremely conducive to self-regulation. Self-regulation as a system working on its own largely relies on the specialized knowledge of the private interest groups, associations or SROs represented. The essence of self-regulation is a process of collective government. The specific expertise of the collective – groups of expert, epistemic communities, or networks – in a determined field is a key characteristic distinguishing it from the individuals or other regimes. The process leading to self-regulatory solutions corresponds to an informal way of communicating expertise and where the actors involved in the community pursue similar substantive goals and interests.[129] They can take efficient action in response to the pressures they are subject to in order to produce solutions operating as safeguards.

At the global level, a range of issues needs to be addressed. In the absence of national or international standards and rules, alternative forms of regulation appear

---

[128] Ibid. 13; see also V. Haufler, Self-Regulation and Business Norms: Political Risk, Political Activism (1999) 199–203; N. Brunsson and B. Jacobsson, A World of Standards (2000).

[129] Braithwaite and Drahos, supra note 10, 501–504; Black, supra note 117, 27; Slaughter (2004) supra note 52, 14, 41–45; Drahos, supra note 88, 324–326; Chapter 2, point 3 Institutional Structure, 3.2 Collectivity: From Associability to Association.

more adequate. The epistemic community or network sets the frame wherein self-regulation can emerge, take shape, and define rules proper to an issue. Specific arrangements must be adapted to the environment and concrete circumstances, as the cases discussed in Chap. 3 show.[130] Nowadays, the global dimensions of these non-state regulatory activities are prominent. They are driven by the genuine business interests of their members, profit maximization instead of the normative validity based on value legitimacy. At the global level, the rules applied by networks can be regarded as a form not only of self-regulation, but global non-state regulation and self-regulation. This is in part due to the fact that self-regulation is not a concept which is stable or static and strictly defined. The rules represent a set of values and principles governing common activities rather than formal regulation. As such, they are genuine representations of the process of globalization.[131] At the same time, networks also challenge the state as an institution. Globalizing networks are increasingly capable of shaping what remains in the public sphere and determine what is private. The regulation of public goods takes place by means of global standards. For example, financial stability is guaranteed by the application of standards and guidelines defined by the FSB and its sub-committees, which apply to the world's financial system. By this way, it has become a global public good. As a result, in the context of business regulation, states can be both regulators and regulatees.[132] Specifically, these networks are able to replace state law with their own regimes of norms. They reconfigure regulation and become the norm generators. They are well-placed to impose their norms on those entering into contact with their regime and they may be responsible for their implementation.[133] They can make use of the fragmentation of knowledge and the information asymmetry existing between their members or their group and the state. It is also often assumed by some authors that networks diminish the sovereignty of the state. This trend is going to accelerate with the enhanced strength of non-state actors and networks.[134]

In the course of the process of reshaping the public-private divide, hybrid organizational forms can be created, too. State functions and tasks can be delegated to state agencies or directly to SROs endued with professional expertise or to networks of experts. The state will share its power to decide on the public-private

---

[130] Chapter 3, point 1 Self-regulation, point 2 Firm Own Regulation, point 3 Co-regulation, point 4 Coercive Self-regulation, point 6 Global Networks.

[131] Sajó, supra note 47, 210–211, 213–217, 223–224; Baldwin and Cave, supra note 38, 76–82; Sassen, supra note 24, 197.

[132] Drahos, supra note 88, 323; Braithwaite and Drahos, supra note 10, 421–422, 27.

[133] Bernstein and Cashore, supra note 78, 349–351; Baldwin and Cave, supra note 38, 63–64; Black and Rouch, supra note 51, 218–223. On the establishment and operations of these standards-setters, see: J. Sloan and G. Fitzpatrick, The Structure of International Markets Regulation (2007) 455–500.

[134] A vehement representative of this view is Slaughter who ascertains the phenomenon of a 'disaggregated democracy' due to the increasing influence by transgovernmental networks. Slaughter, supra note 47; National Intelligence Council, Global Trends 2025, supra note 27, x–xi, 81.

divide. It may underwrite what was developed privately and private codes may become standards for all. In the case of delegated self-regulation, both private and public actors are concerned by the regulatory measures, whereby public actors lead the way as they define the basic framework. However, private businesses and organized entities represented by their own SROs will be in a position to influence the measures adopted by the state. The basis of the model remains cooperative. The state maintains control of the process and can take measures in case of non- or insufficient enforcement.

The configuration of autonomous, civil society regimes occurs in the pursuit of determined objectives. The basic motivation is formed by the representation of the interests of individuals or collectivities which crystallize with the constitution of groups of interest, networks or associations.[135] In case of a state involvement, the statutes or a basic agreement can also coordinate and organize member behaviour and relationships both among members and towards third parties. By establishing regimes, the substantive content of the rules and standards to be defined may cover an extremely wide range of issues, as the cases discussed in Chap. 3 have illustrated:

Among the self-regulated regimes discussed first, the credit rating agencies are an example for a regime whose regulatory statute has been fiercely debated and is now in a transformation process. To exercise their activity, they have to be independent. Thus, their self-regulatory statute ensured that they could operate without regulatory constraint, and self-control occurred through the pressure and need to preserve their reputation on the financial markets and deliver high-quality, reliable ratings. The observance and appreciation of the ratings by the market participants set the standards to be applied by the agencies. Following the publication of wrong ratings, they lost the confidence of the public and a debate has been launched by supervisory authorities to work out a regulatory solution, that is, introduce a state regulation and supervision. However, although they made errors and are heavily criticized, these agencies have been keen to preserve their autonomy. They are now expected to comply with the standards set by international bodies such as IOSCO and the rules passed.[136]

Another case has concerned firm own regulation.[137] This is a case of hybrid or enforced self-regulation, with a large influence of the state or international organizations, as far as they determine broad standards. For instance, the OECD Code of Corporate Governance has been taken over in a number of states, calling for compliance by firms. The Code is particularly important for listed firms and regulatory efforts to enforce it are still going on. Moreover, the self-regulatory status of firms as private sector organizations is also significant. They have the possibility to develop their own strategies and initiatives on private markets, applying an economic approach and aiming to maximize their profits. They are

[135] Chapter 2, point 3 Institutional Structure, 3.1 Theory of Interest: From Interest to Associability.

[136] Chapter 3, point 1 Self-regulation, 1.2 Credit Rating Agencies.

[137] Chapter 3, point 2 Firm Own Regulation.

responsible for developing their own risk management systems and rules to monitor compliance and supervise operations. At the same time, they are in competition with other firms, which provides an incentive to remain competitive, not least by meeting the prevailing standards. Furthermore, industry input largely contributes to reinforce the compliance culture.[138] To sum up, the state sets the 'external' standards and the firms develop their own business or 'internal' standards. They are in a position to adapt them at any time.

Then, co-regulation has been discussed. In that case, global, state, as well as privately defined standards apply, as the example of securities regulations showed. The operations of securities markets are genuinely global. Standards are first laid down at the global, transgovernmental level and then adopted by the states. States will concretize and implement them by issuing national statutes or rules or declaring these standards binding for the industry. Their regulatory capacity is affected by these standards. They can be both objects and subjects of regulation or they can autonomously define national standards and rules applying to their own market, as 2007–2009 financial crisis follow-up measures strikingly shows. The private industry also elaborates its own standards. For instance, at the global level, the IIF listed a range of measures in its Report as a response to the 2007–2009 financial crisis. They were addressed to its members and should be respected. Codes of conduct too may set standards and may be encountered either at the global, national, or private level.[139]

Yet another case considered is supervised self-regulation, in particular introducing third party controls or having recourse to external auditors to require operations scrutiny, drawing up reports, and especially reporting shortcomings uncovered during corporate finance audits to company management and supervisory authorities. It largely relies on the respect of standards. One important rationale leading to third party control as a viable option is the efficiency gain. Also, the delegation to auditors or private market participants is an incentive itself. It allows for harnessing their specialized knowledge and marketability, and saving cumbersome and expensive state resources.[140] Moreover, although there is potential conflict of interests, such private actors are generally well-accepted by market participants. They can easily adapt to the circumstances. To recapitulate, the standards are set or defined by the state. The arrangement is based on a form of cooperation or negotiation.

Finally, the case of global networks examined the digital, technological and financial standard setting networks.[141] Organizations setting standards like the ISO pursue the goal of producing highly technical data. Every standard defined is based on the specialized knowledge of experts. Standards are developed on a continuous

---

[138] Hutter, supra note 1, 5; Chapter 3, point 2 Firm Own Regulation; see also Teubner, supra note 49, 1–20.

[139] Chapter 3, point 3 Co-regulation; Drahos, supra note 88, 321–324; IIF-Report, supra note 98.

[140] Chapter 3, point 4 Coercive Self-regulation, 4.2 Supervised Self-regulation; Hutter, supra note 1, 5–6; H. C. Kunreuther, P. J. McNulty, and Y. Kang, Third-Party Inspection as an Alternative to Command and Control Regulation (2002) 309–318.

[141] Chapter 3, point 6 Global Networks.

basis. They are also part of a transformation process when they are adopted by the states in the form of statutes. The same applies to standard setting networks in the field of finance. The proposals and decisions made by specialized networks or committees at the global level, on the basis of scientific criteria and negotiations among the members represented – for instance the Basel II framework –, and perhaps concluded by agreement have to be adopted and implemented by the states.[142]

Transformation

The configuration of autonomous regulatory regimes and their role as standard-setters or rule-making organizations is the result of the need to organize them in order to set standards for business behaviour. It is based on cooperation and negotiations. It consists in giving a definite form or shape to issues and relationships, affording them formal standing or endorsement (or possibly rendering them legitimate or official) through observing proper, transparent procedures. Within a transformational process of gradual norm-setting, standardization, and formalization there is first the question of the definition and nature of standards that can be encountered. *Standards* can be:

> A rule, principle, or means of judgement or estimation; a criterion, measure. ...
> Having the prescribed or normal size, amount, power, degree of quality, etc. . . .
> Of a law: That has the chief authority with reference to a particular subject.

standardization:

> The action of standardizing.

and *to standardize*:

> To bring to a standard or uniform size, strength, form of construction, proportion of ingredients, or the like.
>
> To test by a standard.[143]

while *rules* are defined as:

> A principle, regulation, or maxim governing individual conduct. . . .
> A principle regulating practice or procedure; a fixed and dominating custom or habit. . . .
> An order made by a judge or court, the application of which is limited to the case in connexion with which it is granted. . . .[144]

The nature of standards is largely undefined. They are not mandatory directives or rules. There is no idea of coercion as such. The approach to the constitution of standards and the process of their formulation is informal. They emerge out of

142 Cassese, supra note 89, 669.

143 The Oxford English Dictionary, Volume XVI (1991) 505–508; also: Brunsson and Jacobsson, supra note 128, 10–16.

144 The Oxford English Dictionary, Volume XIV (1991) 228.

diffuse processes and are not based on systematic consultation or preparatory works (apart from professional standards as set by ISO). They are diverse phenomena. Often, they represent ad hoc solutions. They reflect a general consent on a matter or can be established by authority or custom. Standards are linked to or associated with an idea of appropriateness or appropriate response to a given situation. They enable a higher degree of global order in the modern world than would exist without them. They also facilitate coordination and cooperation even among people and organizations that are far apart. The formation and definition of standards is often the source of a process of codification and formalization towards determined and definite rules. In the case of states, when formulating rules, they may in fact transpose standards. In a way, they act then as regulatees, although they may have participated in the formulation of just these standards.[145] In Switzerland, for instance, this applies to the case of article 8 paragraph 3 SESTA on the 'Admission of securities', which declares in relation to accounting rules for listing companies that international standards have to be taken into account when formulating or elaborating the national rules. The Finmasa too states in its article 7 paragraph 2 letter d. on the 'Principles of regulation' that the supervisory authority shall take international minimal standards into account when regulating. It reads as:

> It exercises its regulatory powers only to the extent required by its supervisory objectives. In doing so, it takes account in particular of:
>
> . . .
>
> d. the international minimum standards.'

It is not stated whether these should be official standards or not, but in practice the standards set by international organizations or other transgovernmental and possibly non-state networks or bodies are meant. Diverse rationales have led to the introduction of these rules. They demonstrate officially the commitment of the country to respect and implement international or global standards. They contribute to reinforce its good reputation, standing and competitiveness, all goals of the supervision of financial markets as stated in article 5 Finmasa. Moreover, it should not be overlooked that Switzerland is itself member of a number of leading international and global organizations and transgovernmental networks. As a consequence, it already participates actively in the elaboration and adoption of international or global standards. Still another rationale may be to counter possible pressure, which may result from unilateral measures of other countries or bodies, as discussed. However, it should be noted that the transposition of these standards into national statute does not occur based on the doctrines or techniques of international law, that is, incorporation and transformation of rules. According to these approaches of international law theories or techniques to integrate international

[145] V. Schreiber, International Standards, Neues Recht für die Weltmärkte? (2005) 137–145, and to article 8 paragraph 3 SESTA, 171–174; Brunsson and Jacobsson, supra note 128, 2 et seqq.; F. Schauer, The Tyranny of Choice and the Rulification of Standards (2005) 803–814.

rules into the national legal regime, every state may adopt its own approach. The technique adopted by a state is laid down in its constitution. It will refer to how international law will be treated in that particular state. The doctrine of incorporation holds that a rule of international law will automatically become part of national law. There is no express adoption process. The rule will apply immediately unless there is some statutory provision or precedent that indicates otherwise. As a result, a treaty signed and ratified by a state will be binding on the citizens without any further procedure or without laying down further legislation. The constitution of the state will provide that rules of international law should automatically become part of the national statute. On its side, the doctrine of transformation requires a positive act of the state or an express act of adoption of the rules of international law. These rules are transformed into domestic law and will then become part of national law. Thus, a treaty ratified by a state would only be given effect when corresponding domestic legislation has been enacted to integrate it into national law. The two doctrines are linked to the doctrines of monism and dualism. The monist doctrine holds that international law and state law are part of a single system. As a consequence, the incorporation doctrine applies. On the contrary, the dualist doctrine holds that they are two distinct systems of law. Thus, a rule of international law will not operate within state law as long as it is not transformed into that regime.[146] In application of these doctrines, standards can be considered to belong to the national regime of rules without any procedure or they can be the source of national rules as far as they have to be transposed into national rules. As far as Switzerland is concerned, it applies the theory of incorporation. Thus, international law or rules will become state rules. There is an enrolment by the state. However, it should not be overlooked, that basically, to incorporate or transform standards or rules into state regulation, the following conditions have to be fulfilled: The regulation must be in the public interest and it should have a majority appeal or be capable of winning a majority. Specialized rules, as is the case of the Basel II framework, do not represent any international law standards. Rather they are global standards set by a transgovernmental network and apply to specialized institutes only. They are transposed into state law as far as detailed rules adapted to the national particularities of the state concerned are defined and enforced.

Besides such rules, standardization is also determined by the organization operating in their background. The type of organization concerned can vary from loose contacts to organizations of states or associations with fixed structures. In the last case, there will be formal memberships based on a contractual agreement with the association or SRO, as discussed in Chap. 2. In reality, a range of organizational structures can determine the standard setting procedure or instrumental process. At the global level in particular, it cannot be covered by national

[146] J. O'Brien, International Law (2001) 113–114.

institutions. However, the multitude of individuals or actors participating in a network needs a common basis to ensure communication and cooperation. Their interactions and communication methods need to be formalized in the course of a process ultimately resulting in the constitution of precisely these global regimes. As a result, besides international organizations, like the UN or World Bank which have fostered an expansion and homogenization of normative standards, principles, and rules together with national legislatures and multinational companies, nationally registered but globally operating SROs or NGOs as specialized institutions play a key role in a range of sectors at the global level, concentrating on specific issues and filling vacuums left by states and international organizations. Each applies its own strategy. The emerging regimes are negotiated regulatory orders which have developed gradually.

Hereinafter, 'standard' is used as a superimposed concept, a general term to design regulatory rules or measures. Indeed, a range of instruments can be classified as standards. Various regimes of rules too can be subsumed under standards: norms, technical standards, and principles, standardized contracts, agreements of professional associations, legal or non-legal rules, codes of conduct, guidelines, conventions among groups of interest like the media, routines of formal organizations, technical and scientific standardization, behaviour normalization, and informal consensus between NGOs or SROs. Indeed, there is a plethora of instruments. Essentially, they correspond to a process of standardizing relationships between interested members. In the course of a progressive development, various stages can be distinguished subsequently, leading from the crystallization of informal practices or usances to a process of self-normativity, codification, and juridification, to finally constitute a regulatory regime of rules.

In the literature, the distinction between these instruments or concepts is fluid. While some authors consider that an existing rule may become a directive, a norm, and a standard in the course of time, others depart from the opposite, the norm, which is then concretized through just norms, principles, standards, or guidelines, and in a next step legal or non-legal rules. Indeed, these instruments cannot be classified within a static hierarchical scheme similar to the one applying to state rules. The distinction between standards, principles, rules or other regulatory instrument is a matter of degree. They can be combined, assembled, and conceptualized in different ways to build theories of regulation. At this place, it is not entered into all possible forms of regulatory instruments. In the following, the main distinction is made between standards and rules, albeit it is submitted that 'norms' designate the all encompassing concept. As a basis for all kind of measures possibly leading to a regulation, norms can also be used to represent non-tangible public goods, such as order or good governance. They are considered to be at the background while the approach departs from standards, which will be concretized and finally adopt the form of rules. Although both the notions of standard and rule are somewhat indeterminate and let room for interpretation by their very nature, their grade of abstractedness allows for seizing them as sub-forms of norms. In comparison to rules, standards are a broader concept and also less specific than rules. Rules are the ultimate or highest degree of specialization, formalization or also concretization.[147] Indeed, the focus is placed on the degree of abstractness and bindingness in relation to the issue at stake. Instead of standard, 'principle' could be used. However, here again, it is a matter of degree. As stated by Hart,

> 'principles are, relatively to rules, broad, general, or unspecific, in the sense that often what would be regarded as a number of distinct rules can be exhibited as the exemplifications or instantiations of a single principle.'

Both instruments – standards and principles – are considered to be at a similar level or, in a way, linked together. However, it is assumed that principles are a more comprehensive concept, which does not only embrace regulatory matters or matters with a potential to be regulated, or as stated by Hart, 'principles ... refer more or less explicitly to some purpose, goal, entitlement, or value ...".[148]

The transformation of norms to standards or rules is often the result of a diffuse, evolving process. Stages of development can be distinguished from their emergence to their effective implementation. Within each stage a range of conditions must be fulfilled for a norm to develop to standards and then rules. When discussing the norm – to which he subsumes legal rules – Morgenthau defines it as a

> 'prescription of the will: it designates between various possible actions the one to be chosen.'[149]

According to Morgenthau, there are four fundamental challenges to grasp and understand what a norm is. The approach includes first, the logical structure of the norm, second the reality of the norm, third its content, and fourth its realization. Indeed,

> 'The norm is one due to its fundament, its general character and its object ...; but it is complex and diverse with regard to the intensity of the social reaction which results from its violation.'[150]

Thus, Morgenthau sees two constitutive elements in a norm, which also apply to a standard or rule as discussed in this study: the normative character and the validity, as has already been suggested by Thomas Hobbes and Thomas d'Aquin. Similarly, Hart sees in the rules or social rules what he calls

> 'the practice theory' of rules 'comprising both patterns of conduct regularly followed by most members of the group and a distinctive normative attitude to such patterns of conduct ... called 'acceptance'. It consists in the standing disposition of individuals to take such

---

[147] Generally: H. Morgenthau, La réalité des normes, En particulier des normes du droit international, Fondements d'une théorie des normes (1934); H. L. A. Hart, The Concept of Law (1997) 6–13, 254–263; see also: Braithwaite and Drahos, supra note 10, 18–20; Brunsson and Jacobsson, supra note 128, 10–15, 14; Schauer, supra note 145, 803–814.

[148] Hart, supra note 147, 260; see also Braithwaite and Drahos, supra note 10, 18–20.

[149] Translation by the author, original: 'prescription de la volonté: elle désigne, entre diverses actions possibles, celle qui doit être choisie.' Morgenthau, supra note 147, 22.

[150] Translation by the author, original: 'La norme est une par son fondement, par son caractère général et par son objet' ...; 'mais elle est complexe et diverse par l'intensité de la réaction sociale que produit sa violation.' Morgenthau, supra note 147, 24–25.

patterns of conduct both as guides to their own future conduct and as standards of criticism which may legitimate demands and various forms of pressure for conformity.'[151]

As a result, it can be stated, that the perception and implementation of norms, standards, or rules is characterized by two main features: their validity and their observance or, in other words, their effectiveness or also efficacy. Both their substantive and normative validity, as well as their psychological and normative effectiveness can be distinguished. Standards and rules are valid when they mirror the will of the actors concerned and subjectively effective when they determine it effectively.[152]

Then, in relation to the distinction between standards and rules, the same applies to the nature of their relationships or some of their particularities. They can be complementary or referential, functional or have a normative value, correspond to a logical subordination or be the result of a delegation or competition.

Standards can be both, public or private. They can be defined by the state or emerge from civil society, as stated. As far as states are concerned, they can define and apply regulatory standards on the one hand or also follow leading standards on which policies to pursue, or how to handle matters on the other hand. Within civil society, the relationship between standards as a form of non-state regulation to self-regulation needs to be clarified. Both concepts are narrowly linked. Self-regulation means that those subject to the regulation have some say in the initiation or operation of the regime. They regulate themselves. On the contrary, standards are a broader concept. Similarly to self-regulation, they can be voluntary. They may involve industry participation and their provenance may be either with industry or other non-state actors. As such, they can represent the outcome of a self-regulatory solution. However, they cannot be systematically subsumed to the concept of self-regulation, because they may be neither solely, nor directly defined by the members of a collectivity, industry, or group to regulate themselves. They may be defined by the state or other organizations. The following categories can be distinguished: standards defined by private groups, an industry, committees, networks, or organizations.[153] A typical example of private standards is the standards defined by ISO. These standards may be adopted both by states or the private economy, but they are not strictly self-regulatory. They are defined by a specialized organization and apply to third parties. However, self-regulation and standards remain largely interconnected. First, they represent arrangements involving the setting of rules. There are no mechanisms for monitoring and enforcing them. Their observance mainly relies on compliance. Secondly, they are not generally binding rules on anyone, unless they are linked to a membership agreement within an association.

---

[151] Morgenthau, supra note 147, 2, 24–35, with further references; Hart, supra note 147, 254–263, 255.

[152] Morgenthau, supra note 147, 32–49, 157 et seqq.; Hart, supra note 147, 259–263; see also: Schreiber, supra note 145, 164–169; D. W. Arner, Financial Stability, Economic Growth, and the Role of Law (2007) 121–125, to the Rule of Law.

[153] D. Kerwer, Rules that Many Use: Standards and Global Regulation (2005) 626; Brunsson and Jacobsson, supra note 128.

Finally, they are observed as far as they reflect expertise, which is an incentive to recognize their validity and comply with them. The incentives to adhere to these rules are mostly economic ones.[154] At the same time, it is not excluded that standards are self-regulatory. They may then reflect the prevailing practices and governance rules of their own group. Hereinafter both terms are used, depending on the focal point.

Initially, the codification process leading to the formulation of standards occurs spontaneously. Such standards are the result of cooperative mechanisms initiated by the collective action of individuals on a voluntary, private basis, finally leading to the definition of substantive rules. They will give rise to the emergence of voluntary, self-regulatory solutions in a first stage, and which are situated at the border of a state legal regime, indifferent to it. The standards they propagate or apply are dislocated from national legal regimes. They have their own relational links to their societal environment. Similarly to self-contained regimes, they define own values and principles, developed on an ad hoc basis. Multiple agents will ensure and execute their normative order. They will constitute regimes which prove to be important governance mechanisms. The standards set are based on economic and societal criteria. They add to pluralism and are legitimated as far as they are accepted by their members.[155] In fact, the use of standards is very old. 'Standards have existed as a source of an industry' self-discipline almost since the beginning of modern market economies.' In political science, both private and public standards are viewed as alternatives to public regulation. However, the emergence of standards from private regulatory regimes is also characterized by a tendency of juridification and dependence on state rules resulting from the displacement of societal norms.[156]

On its part, the process of globalization evolves through the development of practices which solidify in the course of time in the form of principles and then follow a process of codification into standards, guidelines, conventions, rules, or other kinds of global norms. Indeed, globalization offers many possible points of entry. Sequences can be distinguished. For instance, compliance habits may develop in a first stage. These are subsequently institutionalized as bureaucratic routines in the long run and the formation of principles. Basically, the transformation can occur both towards the state and within or towards civil society. Non-legal rules can crossover or be rendered legal and legal rules may be rendered legal from an international to a state level. In particular, these rules are free from ties of fealty. According to Braithwaite and Drahos' unidirectional view, the globalization of regulation can be understood by means of the modeling of self-regulatory principles

---

[154] C. Scott, Self-Regulation and the Meta-Regulatory State (2006) 133; Brunsson and Jacobsson, supra note 128, 57.

[155] Sassen, supra note 24, 242–243, 265–268; Fischer-Lescano and Teubner, supra note 50, 45–48; G. Teubner, Globale Bukowina: Zur Emergenz eines transnationalen Rechtspluralismus (1996) 255 et seqq.; on the issue of legitimacy, see below in discussion.

[156] T. Padoa-Schioppa, Regulating Finance: Balancing Freedom and Risk (2004) 41–43; Brunsson and Jacobsson, supra note 128, 1 et seqq.; C. Scott, Privatization and Regulatory Regimes (2006) 654; along similar lines: Tamanaha, supra note 11, 77 et seqq.

and rules of private justice. States do not run things but rather regulate them or monitor self-regulation. It is also possible to consider this process to be the result of interactions among an array of regulatory webs: webs of influence, webs of dialogue, and webs of reward and coercion. Coercion can be conceived as corresponding to a transformative sequence that will ultimately lead to the formation of (binding) rules. This accounts for providing another character to the rules adopted by global networks or organizations. The rules will be presumed to be applicable and recognized as valid at a global scale. Thus, they could qualify as quasi-governmental rules.[157] In sum, the globalization of business occurs as a two-tiered process. The first tier occurs at the level of standards and the second at the level of rules, comparable to Hart's distinction between primary and secondary rules. Hart argues convincingly that law is defined by the existence of a constitutional difference between primary and secondary rules: rules of the first type impose duties, concern actions involving physical movement or changes, and control conduct. Rules of the second type confer powers, public or private, and provide for operations leading not merely to physical movement or change, but to the creation or variation of duties or obligations in order to produce law.[158]

The situation can be illustrated with the following schematic structure (Fig. 4.1)

2.3.2 Impact

Throughout the study regimes of diverse regulatory structures have been discussed. The focus has been placed on non-state autonomous regimes and such linked to the state, or in other words voluntary and compelling orders. Depending on the case discussed, the regulatory role considered has been information gathering, standard-setting or rule-making, behavior modification or enforcement. Although it is recognized that there is a need for such regimes and fragmentation of orders will increase in the future – not least given the apparently waning ability of international

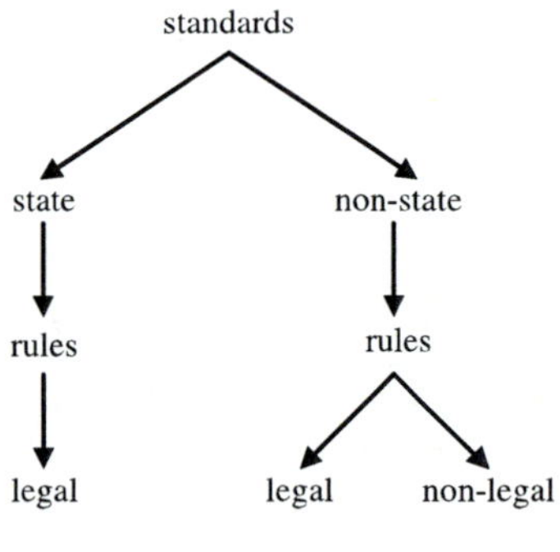

Fig. 4.1 Transformation from standards to rules

[157] Braithwaite and Drahos, supra note 10, 15–16, 28, 550–563; Berman, supra note 67, 397–398.

[158] Hart, supra note 147, 79–81.

institutions do address new transnational challenges as convincingly argued in the study on Global Trends 2025 – there has been no direct discussion of the actual success of these regimes in initiating a behaviour modification, which is linked to their validity. Their real value depends on just that point and can be appreciated through their impact, efficacy or also effectiveness. In this study, efficiency has been mentioned as the main rationale, especially motivating the introduction of alternative, non-state regulatory measures. Effectiveness has not been discussed as such. Yet, as a preliminary remark, it should be noted that the view encountered in the literature that effectiveness applies to state rules while efficiency applies to privately defined rules is rejected as too exclusive at this place. Most regimes are based on efficiency rationales. However, they can only be fully perceived and appreciated when they lead to effective behavior modification in the sense that the addressees adopt the expected behavior, as suggested by the rules. In terms of effectiveness, this means that they have to be adhered to, observed, and implemented in practice. Accordingly, the impact or effective implementation or in Morgenthau's terms realization of regulatory regimes is an indicator of their functional operativeness.

At first, the choice of the term 'impact' instead of effectiveness is briefly explained. The study has distinguished both state and non-state as well as elaborated and less-elaborated standards and rules. Contrary to state rules, non-state orders are not compelling, unless there is a member's contractual agreement. When discussing classical, that is, state rules, a distinction is made between rule-making and enforcement. This does not apply in the same sense to non-state rules or rules defined by networks or non-state organizations. As far as the enforcement is concerned, non-state orders cannot be enforced similarly to state rules. In particular, non-state organizations do not offer the necessary infrastructure to implement the rules, enforce them and control their enforcement. They cannot impose penal sanctions. Enforcement is possible based on a broad consensus about the legitimacy of rules. It is part of the implementation of state rules. Moreover, the institutional enforcement infrastructure itself is a product of the representation of what constitutes proper behavior within a state. Non-state autonomous regulatory regimes regularly are constituted by not nearly defined norms, standards, or rules, which cannot be enforced as such or primarily they would have to be adopted by the states. Hence, it would not be satisfactory to limit the discussion of the effectiveness of these regimes to the enforcement of rules only. To cover the whole panoply of standards and rules examined, a broader concept has to be applied. The term of impact is used hereinafter. Similarly to the terms of standards or norms, it should be understood as an overall term at this place, a general term which can stand for designating effective behavior modification, implementation, or effectiveness of regimes or rules considered or their mechanisms. One could ask why the impact aspect is not dealt with in the next chapter, Evaluation. Any appreciation of the impact of regulatory regimes is actually part of their assessment. However, it also belongs to the characteristics of the regimes as such and contribute to determining their nature. It is an indicator of their role consisting in behavior modification. For that reason, it is discussed here.

To evaluate the impact of these regimes, the point is to devise how effective they are in practice. The argument proceeds in two main stages. First, theoretical aspects are considered. The approach embraces the following elements: validity and efficacy and mechanisms of implementation. Second, the impact is assessed based on the examination of practical cases. Methodologically, we concentrate on institutional and structural aspects of regulation, not on the substantive ones, as in the whole study. This contextual exclusion does not undermine the utility of the approach.

Validity and Efficacy

To seize the concept of impact, that is, appreciate the efficacy of the rules, Morgenthau's distinction between efficacy and validity of rules is helpful. Morgenthau applies it to the 'norms'.[159] At this place, instead of norms, the terms of standard and rule are used, while the 'norms' are understood as the overall concept, as stated. Efficacy serves as an indicator of the impact of the regimes of rules or standards. It is an indicator for the power of these rules or standards to influence or determine others, their behaviour, to act in the way they prescribe. Morgenthau distinguishes two elements characterizing efficacy: a psychological one and the other pertaining to the domain of rules. The first corresponds to the ideal to be attained or the ideal representation of the objective of the norm. The second corresponds to the realization or, in other words, the compliance with the norm, rule of standard. Between the content of the rule or standard and its realization, there is a causal link. According to Morgenthau, the realization and its objective efficacy are synonyms and in case a distinction is made between the objective and subjective efficacy, the subjective efficacy then corresponds to the psychological aspects, while the objective efficacy regards its realization.

Similarly to Morgenthau, Hart discusses the efficacy of rules. According to him

> 'by 'efficacy' is meant that the fact that a rule of law which requires certain behaviour is obeyed more often than not.'

Validity on its side means that the addressees recognize the rules and accept them. Discussing validity, Hart too asserts that

> 'the statement that a particular rule is valid means that it satisfies all the criteria provided by the rule of recognition.'

Indeed, the concept of validity is linked to the concept of legitimacy. In particular in case of non-state rules, the acceptance of the rule is determining. It can be interpreted as corresponding to a form of informal legitimation of the rules or standards by the addressees.[160] Both notions apply as well to state or legal as to non-state or non-legal standards or rules. Hereinafter, they will be discussed in the

---

[159] Morgenthau, supra note 147, 2. For a complementary discussion, see Fehr and Fischbacher, supra note 91, 185–190.

[160] Morgenthau, supra note 147, 29–35; Hart, supra note 147, 103–104; to the concept of legitimacy, see below, point 2.4; see also: A. Chayes, A. Handler Chayes, The New Sovereignty, Compliance with International Regulatory Agreements (1995) 17–22.

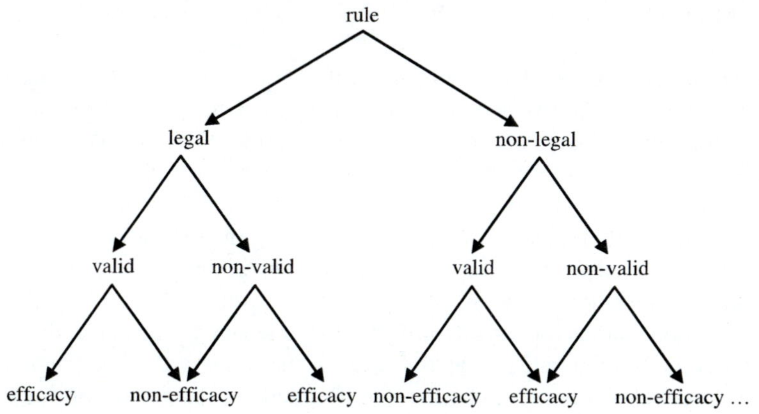

Fig. 4.2 Validity and efficacy

sense as just stated. Schematically, the situation can be illustrated by the following Fig. 4.2:

Regulatory regimes are successful and effective when they contribute to reach the goal pursued by their members. Their standards and rules specify what constitutes appropriate behavior. They regularly induce a modification of behavior, in the sense that it should result in adopting the prescriptions they define.[161] Once set, the next step consists in their respect and observance by the addressees and perhaps third persons or also the general public. Indeed, the configuration and perception of autonomous regimes within civil society is linked to their impact. They represent arrangements involving the setting and implementation of standards and rules. However, there are basically no mechanisms for monitoring and enforcing them. They are not generally binding standards and rules on anyone, unless they are linked to a contractual membership agreement within an association or are standards defined by international organizations or transgovernmental networks, which are then transposed into state statutes and must be observed. Thus, how far will the addressees adapt or modify their behaviour, or how far will they behave accordingly, in other words, which is their impact? To answer this question, the following stages of implementation are distinguished hereinafter: responsibilisation, guidance, compliance, enforcement, legal sanctions and arbitrage. In fact, the approach corresponds to a gradual process of juridification of rules: The steps are: the emergence of informal, societal norms, private, prima facie non-binding or valid standards or rules, legitimate standards or rules, legitimate and binding state rules enforceable by sanctions.

[161] Brunsson and Jacobsson, supra note 128, 14–15.

Stages of Impact

A first, possible measure of their impact is the appreciation of their respect and observation by the addressees or also third parties or the general public. It first occurs informally, through a sense of responsibilisation. For example, it applies to public goods. Actors concerned might conform voluntarily with standards or rules to avoid side-effects for themselves and others. This attitude may be reinforced by a kind of informal policing, such as possibly tarnishing the reputation of free-riders, or a degrading qualification, or the threat of an announcement of sanctions. Responsibilisation is narrowly linked to guidance. Guidance can be both exercised by state and non-state actors or SROs. Within an industry for instance, the interactions between a large number of actors leads to the necessity to specify standards and rules to develop a basis of cooperation. Regulators, regulated firms or regulatees and third market participants develop practices and await generally applicable interpretations to proceed. It regularly occurs in the form of guidance or non-binding instructions provided by either the regulators or also SROs. The FINMA for instance maintains a collection of circulars for practitioners, which comment on the statutory provisions. Besides this form of guidance, another method used by the FINMA is to 'certify' industry guidance by officially declaring that it recognizes it. This confirmation is the object of a specific circular.[162] Whether this confirmation provides self-regulation the formal status of a safe harbor is still open. FINMA circulars do not have any binding character. They are interpretations of the statute published by the supervisory authority to serve as guidance to market participants and indicate how the authority expects the statute to be interpreted and applied in practice. Market participants observing them will not have to expect any enforcement action against them. However, it does not mean that non-conformity with them will be illegal or inevitably lead to enforcement measures or even court judgments. Yet, it should be noted, that the Swiss Supreme Court is not bound to the FINMA circulars, neither to self-regulation, as discussed. Still another category of guidance cases can include third parties. They can act as intermediary for private market actors. For instance, lawyers may assist firms applying for the granting of licenses by a supervisory authority. They can be appointed advisors as is the case of the SIX Swiss Exchange as far as the admission of firms to listing is concerned. These advisors' role is then to guide the firms, assist them and if necessary monitor issues regarding the application of the rules.

In-between guidance and the next step, compliance, there is the case of the credit rating agencies. Initially, they have represented a purely private, self-regulatory solution. There has been a form of compliance as such with their rules or the ratings they published, as far as the market participants and regulators have observed these

[162] Circular of the FINMA: Self-regulation recognized as a minimum standard by the Swiss Financial Market Supervisory Authority of 20 November 2008, FINMA-Circ. 08/10 Self-regulation as a minimum standard; to the collection, see: FINMA Circulars: http://www.finma.ch/d/regulierung/seiten/rundschreiben.aspx (last visited 23 November 2009); Case 125 IV 139 of April 1999; Chapter 3, point 1 Self-Regulation, 1.3 Voluntary Codes of Conduct.

ratings and behaved accordingly. Ratings have been understood as a generally accepted form of market guidance. In a way, it can be stated that there was an efficacious infrastructure for compliance insofar as the market participants meant to be able to verify the ratings based on their judgment, information analysis, and the reputation of the agencies. Their impact has been considerable, although it could only be judged by their observance by market participants. However, following the publication of wrong ratings, the compliance solution does not appear to be satisfactory anymore. In particular, there is a reproach of a lack of transparency and traceability of the ratings. State oversight is now considered necessary. State rules should provide for adequate remedies or enforcement and offer some guarantee for the standing of the ratings.

Then, another case discussed in Chap. 3, arbitration, is typical for the compliance approach. Private, arbitral tribunals act based on their own judgments only. They are free from the constraints under which authorities operate. They represent purely cooperative solutions where the parties involved reach an agreement acceptable to all, often based on compromises, and will then comply with it. As a result, these rules or judgments are recognized by the parties involved as valid, although there is no instrument or infrastructure to enforce them. In addition to being effective insofar as they are observed by the addressees, there can be a competitive situation in relation to state rules. Thus, arbitrational standards and rules characterize a network with no determined authority at an initial stage, and whose operating role is based on agreements among the parties involved in a case. The rationales leading to compliance are non-selfish, they may be reputational, reciprocal, or economic, or result from other form of pressure.

The good functioning of these regimes of private regulation is based on their role as providers of guidance or private justice to their members or also third parties. They are based on the sense of self-responsibilisation of the addressees and their willingness either to observe their information or comply with the measures dictated by the regime. There are no enforcement measures or mechanisms and no (penal) sanctions. Indeed, compliance without enforcement applies to private regulatory regimes as well as in relation to state behavior, in particular in the case of regulatory treaties, as discussed by Chayes and Chayes. In practice, a whole infrastructure of compliance can be discerned. First, there is the scheme of transparency accompanied by reporting rules, which allows verifying the rightness of the information or relevant data. Information processing and analysis can be part of a compliance scheme within a bureaucratic system or a also system of dispute settlement. Second, policy planning and regulation are part of compliance. They may not foresee sanctions as such, but exert subjective pressure, for instance through reputation and shaming.

On their side, voluntary codes of conduct are also based on a compliance approach. They are voluntary in case they are defined by private associations themselves, on their own initiative. Thus, it is up to the addressees to respect them. However, they are regularly binding to the members of an association when membership is based on a contractual agreement compelling the members to observe the codes and standards defined by the association. As associations do not have an infrastructure to enforce rules, it largely relies on the willingness of the members to respect the rules they have defined to defend their interests, which is an incentive. De facto however, associations have the power to impose sanctions as far as they can decide to exclude members as the ultimate or most severe sanction. Exclusion will have force of a sanction.

In addition to the cases mentioned above, the compliance approach also applies to SROs, NGOs, international organizations, or global networks. The 'law without the state' and the globalization of jurisdiction represent a challenge regarding the impact of these bodies of rules or regimes. Linked to the issue of effectiveness of implementation or possible enforcement measures, there is the issue of their legitimation. In particular, global networks do not have coercive power or jurisdiction to prescribe, adjudicate, and enforce rules similarly to states. Enforcement measures are too costly and difficult to be mobilized as a tool. There is no infrastructure to enforce the rules, which is not least also due to the often indeterminate nature of the networks or regimes themselves. An enforcement of rules as such does not exist or cannot be compared to the enforcement of rules by states. Nevertheless there is regularly a reasonably reliable performance of the networks, regimes or treaty obligations of states in practice or it is expected. The actors concerned rely on compliance, but the core issue is: based on which criteria are these regimes operating satisfactorily? Why do members or third parties comply with them? Incentives may be the global reputation of a network or regime, economic interests, rationales like anti-corruption or political rationales.[163] Indeed, two features appear to be important: reliability and predictability. They will play a crucial role in cases of standards defined by standard setting bodies, the implementation of rules of conduct, or arbitration, for instance. In practice, adequate conception and implementation of standards or rules based on a compliance approach will occur on a case by case basis, albeit various levels of compliance can be distinguished. Cases of partial or incomplete compliance or non-compliance are not excluded. In particular, as far as networks are concerned, they have no authority as such and largely operate based on their members' goodwill to cooperate and their sense of responsibilisation. They cannot impose sanctions and have no infrastructure to that effect. Compliance is determined by other incentives, as stated. Members or other, third parties, will honor their commitments at least as long as it is convenient to them.

A compliance approach can also correspond to a situation of bargaining in the shadow of the law. It can be illustrated with the FSAP evaluations, a joint IMF and World Bank initiative that aims to increase the effectiveness of efforts to promote the soundness of financial systems in member countries. Experts seek to identify the strengths and vulnerabilities of a country's financial system and help prioritize

---

[163] A. Chayes and A. Handler Chayes, Compliance Without Enforcement: State Behavior Under Regulatory Treaties (January 1991) 311–330; Chayes, Handler Chayes, supra note 160, 1–28, 109 et seqq.; Berman, supra note 67, 478 et seqq.; see also: K. W. Abbott, D. Snidal, The International Standards Process: Setting and Applying Global Business Norms (2005) 128–129, to the schools of thought on the proper response to non-compliance; for a discussion of an approach to enforcement in relation to public international law, see: A. van Aaken, Effectuating Public International Law Through Market Mechanisms? (2008).

policy responses. Detailed assessments of observance of relevant financial sector standards and codes are established and published. They represent a measure of pressure on states as far as their reputation is at stake. Consequently, they can lead to voluntary compliance with international standards and codes.[164]

Yet another set of cases are hybrid regimes. Securities markets are a case in point, typically entailing both private, self-regulatory, and state regulatory solutions. The reason for putting the emphasis on securities markets is also that it is most adequate and representative to illustrate changes currently occurring to the governance and enforcement structure. In this area, the coordination of regulation and the development of a consistent policy are crucial. Thus, both compliance and enforcement strategies can apply. When there is a transformation towards state rules, these rules should incorporate those provisions, which have proved their worth in a private regulatory scheme. They should pursue the two-fold aim of efficiently protecting the investors and guaranteeing the good functioning of the securities markets, whereby transparency is to play a central role. It is expected that once in place they will have a positive effect on the whole economic activity. Due to the complexity of relationships between private regulators and the state ones, the attribution of responsibilities among actors – supervised institutes, responsible associations or SROs, and supervisory authorities – regularly needs to be clarified, first of all with the means to create incentives to ensure the consistent enforcement of the regulatory provisions. Mixed solutions are not excluded and cooperation among authorities will often be necessary regarding matters of supervision and enforcement. The coordination of these rules should pave the way towards an equivalent intensity of enforcement.

In the case of securities exchanges, regulatory solutions have long been typically self-regulatory. Basically, there is a tendency to preserve that order, because exchanges are private institutions and the values of self-regulatory solutions are recognized. States tend to intervene reluctantly, following crises, when it appears to be urgent, or for strategic rationales. With the introduction of the first federal act on securities exchanges in Switzerland in 1995 (SESTA), exchanges have been officially given a status as self-regulatory organizations. According to that statute not less than six private and public bodies are now in charge of the enforcement and adjudication of legal matters. Beside the official responsible supervisory authority, the FINMA, the SIX Swiss Exchange – which has been granted an authorization as self-regulatory body according to articles 3 and 4 SESTA – acts itself as an enforcement body. It shall maintain its own rules – which must be approved by the FINMA – as specified in the statute, as well as the corresponding specialized authorities as required. They are: the Regulatory Board (former Listing Authority), the Sanction Commission, the independent Appeal Board, and the Arbitral Tribunal. Not least due to that situation, the outcome of regulatory arrangements can be somewhat bemusing or puzzling in some cases, in terms of effectiveness.

---

[164] http://www.imf.org/external/NP/fsap/fsap.asp (last visited 23 November 2009).

The results may be equivocal as the following example regarding the application of the Listing rules and the role of the Sanction Commission unambiguously shows.

The exchange disposes of a specific regulation for the Sanction Commission, a commission composed of seven members whose actions are governed by the Rules of Procedure of the exchange. It may govern its own organization and proceedings to the extent that they are not already regulated. The disciplinary measures it can take are: reprimand, suspension, expulsion, suspension and revocation of permission for order systems, and fines against participants and reprimand, suspension and revocation of registration against traders. Appeals to the Arbitral Tribunal are possible against decisions rendered by that Commission. However, in case of decisions rendered by the Commission on the suspension or exclusion of participants or traders or the suspension of trading or delisting, a recourse may be lodged with the independent Appeal Board first and only in a second place with the Arbitral Tribunal. Against other decisions, a member can appeal directly to the Arbitral Tribunal.[165]

The Appeal Board (article 9 SESTA) is composed of the same experts as the Sanction Commission, but there is an own regulation for each body. The rules applying to the Appeal Board are also different from the rules applying to the Regulatory Board, a separate, proper body. Complaints can be filed to the Appeal Board as stated in articles 83–83a of the Listing Rules. The Appeal Board will also appraise sanctions imposed by the Sanction Commission, as stated. A judgment rendered by the Appeal Board signifies the end of the exchange own, internal appeal procedure. Then, a complaint shall be lodge with the civil judge (article 9 paragraph 3 SESTA) and, according to the order of the SIX Swiss Exchange, it may also be lodged with its Arbitral Tribunal in such cases. However, there is no specific regulation applying to that Arbitral Tribunal. Thus, a first issue is to determine whether this way of doing satisfies the requirement to submit recourses to a civil judge or whether it can be estimated to be equivalent. It can be considered justified as far as under a technical point of view the Arbitral Tribunal is recognized as valid when the parties submit themselves to its jurisdiction. The parties have to accept that order, which most certainly applies to exchange members. However, in case a non-member is involved, it will not be bound based on a unilateral declaration only. De facto, the Arbitral Tribunal operates as a civil court, but the character of an appeal is not easy to determine. In case of disciplinary measures, the situation can be compared to the appreciation of conventional sanctions. The listing conditions can be considered to represent listing prerequisites. The submission of a listing request to make use of the facilities of the exchange can serve as proof that the claimant recognizes and accepts these conditions.

Sanctions of the Exchange are considered to be sanctions of an association towards its members. They first have a private character. They apply to the members of the exchange, that is, authorized securities dealers trading on the

---

165 Nobel, supra note 72, 738 et seqq., 781–786; on securities markets, see also Chapter 3, point 3 Co-regulation.

exchange. They will not apply to issuers who are not members of the exchange. In particular, it is not given prima facie whether they are bound to the exchange judgments or whether other civil courts are capacitated. However, certain authors opine that this argument should also apply to securities dealers, because the sanctions have a character of administrative measures. According to them, in case of authorized securities dealers, the FINMA, as responsible supervisory authority in charge of granting licences to securities dealers and supervising them, can and has to intervene in application of the principle of guarantee for the proper conduct of business. De facto, it can pre-empt the competences of these market participants and initiate an investigation although it will first consult in such cases and the principle of proportionality will have to be respected.[166] Moreover, in such cases, it should also be taken into account that judgments rendered and behavioural measures dictated by private courts may also seep into the decisions of state courts.

Litigation affects firms' behavior, their innovation aptitude, market efficiency, and competition. In case of an admission to listing, it is most probable that competitive aspects play a determining role. Thus, due to the fact, that the market should be open, a civil law recourse will be a competition law recourse (article 12 of the Federal Act on Cartels and Other Restraints of Competition) at the same time. However, in practice, the Arbitral Tribunal may judge such matters, while, the Regulatory Board has to take the public interest into account. It can decline a listing when 'it is required by the public interest.' (article 5 Listing Rules), which may lead to a recourse. In addition, it should also be taken into account, that, on its side, the FINMA will examine possible competition issues when it approves the Listing Rules. It has to ensure the good functioning of the securities markets (article 1 SESTA) and it will check competitive aspects. If necessary, it can consult with the Competition Commission (article 13 SESTO). This does not influence the value of the judgments of the Arbitral Tribunal as such, but the FINMA could require some regulatory adjustments if necessary.

As this example has shown, the ways through instances are complex, not always logical and sometimes difficult to understand. It also indicates that de facto enforcement can be close to the intersection of a state regulatory regime with private litigation or judicial and non-judicial legality. The introduction of the SESTA has led to a role change among instances and their nature. It has led to a transformation from private to state regulation. Negotiations have taken place, which have been framed in terms of re-defining the meaning and applicability of both private and legal rules. Although institutions are generally keen to keep their powers, a partly new distribution of roles among the diverse of actors has been introduced. However, at the institutional level, it does not mean that it corresponds

[166] Nobel, supra note 72, 784–786; S. Kilgus, Effektivität von Regulierung im Finanzmarktrecht (2007) 104–105.

to a radical new repartition of powers. As far as the exchange is concerned, its self-regulatory order has been largely preserved, while at the same time, some powers have been attributed to the state. It enacts basic principles and legislative powers are attributed to the supervisory authority. It is in charge of approving the rules and enforcing them.[167] However, the example shows that the distribution of powers can lead to somewhat ambiguous results, may be unclear and require further changes. Ad hoc approaches often apply. The distinction between public and private competences is not always satisfactory. No official instance to admit recourses and judge ultimately is available within the organization of the exchange. Moreover, state courts are not obliged to respect private decisions. Thus, regimes collisions are inherent to the whole organization. Solutions are not clear-cut and there is room for interpretation. In addition, the (overall) goal of the protection of the investors should not be ignored, but it is not excluded that it may be impinged in such cases. However, alternative modes of redress for aggrieved investors should be basically promoted within a regulatory system.

In practice, rule enforcement should be effective, efficient, fair and predictable. Rapid and sure enforcement against wrongdoing, sufficient means to assure fair and accurate enforcement, and clarity of enforcement norms is necessary. Developing such capabilities is a priority. Practices of enforcement bodies should be well integrated within the overall regulatory approach. Regimes collisions should represent an opportunity to put in place truly efficient and effective means of enforcement that avoid some of the complexities discussed here. The risk that these enforcement decisions disrupt rather than enhance the development of regulatory practices and the achievement of public policy objectives by creating sudden changes in expectations and new, insecure avenues, which may finally damage the market and investors, cannot be ignored.[168]

Enforcement is a challenge. It remains a territorially based concept. It designates state enforcement. The sovereignty of the state is determining. It legitimates its role as enforcer of the legal order. Originally or historically, the concept of the state, as an actor in charge of implementing the rules is based on an agreement and negotiations. In the setting of an enforcement model, dialogue plays a central role. Various approaches are explored. Ayres and Braithwaite distinguish the following escalating stages forming an enforcement pyramid applying to their concept of enforced self-regulation for firms: persuasion, warning letter, civil penalty, criminal penalty, license suspension, and ultimately license revocation. On its side, Chayes and Chayes' approach distinguishes the following formal enforcement measures: incentives, punitive measures which encompass a second-level enforcement comprising retaliation, withdrawal, expulsion and withdrawal of membership privileges, and formal sanctions in the form of coercive penalties.

[167] N. Moloney, New frontiers in EC capital markets law: from market construction to market regulation (2003) 813–817.

[168] Institute of International Finance, Proposal for a Strategic Dialogue on Effective Regulation, December 2006, 14–15.

In principle, it should only be undertaken in concert with considered regulatory strategy and existing rules.[169]

In the case of state or governmental solutions, the principle of primacy of state law applies. State jurisdiction is prescriptive. States have the jurisdiction to enforce and adjudicate. They dispose of the necessary infrastructure and state courts have effective enforcement powers to pronounce both civil and penal sanctions. State authorities are able to take direct action against private actors to ensure compliance with the rules. However, enforcement remains a challenge for states too. Currently, the enforcement issue is largely discussed in academic cycles. In a remarkable study, Coffee explores the practical implementation of measures, the reality of enforcement, its impact in financial markets. He acknowledges that there is a relative need for enforcement. Its approach is comparative, based on the recognition that common law countries are more inclined to enforce rules. In particular, when comparing enforcement styles and practices, the issue raised is why would common law countries need to invest more in regulation and enforcement? Although it is difficult to measure the enforcement intensity, various attitudes and practices of enforcement can be distinguished between countries. They are determined by the regulatory structure, enforcement inputs, and enforcement outputs. Indeed, various bodies worldwide are active in the securities markets, belonging to self-regulatory or state models of regulation. Both state regulatory and supervisory authorities as well as self-regulatory organizations behave differently. Some tend to advice, request, and even admonish, but are slow to punish. Other tend to punish, in particular impose punitive fines. In that regard, the United States are a special case. The number of annual enforcement cases the SEC had to deal with between 2002 and 2006 was much higher than those of the British FSA for instance. Also, on an adjusted basis, it appears that the SEC imposed financial penalties that exceeded those of the FSA by a nearly ten-to-one margin in 2004 and 2005. Although public enforcement in the United States is becoming increasingly punitive, it is interesting to note that, as discussed by Coffee, a comparison of public and private enforcement shows that the average payments from 2000 to 2002 imposed greater financial penalties in the case of private than public enforcement. In fact, the dispersion of self-regulatory and state authorities and their diverse practices produce a political demand for enforcement. Which enforcement policy should be applied, based on which criteria? As a possible approach, Coffee mentions an enforcement policy of enterprise liability versus one of agent or managerial liability.[170]

[169] I. Ayres and J. Braithwaite, Responsive Regulation, Transcending the Deregulation Debate (1992) 35–38; Chayes and Handler Chayes, supra note 163, 314–320; see also: Berman, supra note 67, 468–498.

[170] J. C. Coffee, Law and the Market: The Impact of Enforcement (December 2007) 229–311; H. E. Jackson, Variation in the Intensity of Financial Regulation: Preliminary Evidence and Potential Implications (August 2005).

Global Aspects

As far as global networks are concerned, they most certainly represent one of the greatest challenge with regard to a possible appreciation of their impact. They formulate standards or also more specialized or clearly defined rules. They often are based on informal or sparsely structured arrangements. They do not have any possibility to enforce these standards. However, they add to the perception that enforcement is no longer a purely domestic event, although they are informal, not legitimated bodies. The assessment of their impact is much more linked to their power. Their operations are largely based on the acceptance and adoption of their standards by states participating in their activities in the case of transgovernmental networks. In practice, they may lead to uncertainty with regard to the center of gravity of an alleged offence. In case of a non-state regime, it requires membership in good standing in the organization and regimes. Global networks and regimes do not have the prescriptive jurisdiction, the coercive power of states. Their standards and rules may be adhered to or also adopted by states to form state rules. However in other cases, like the Yahoo! case in France, the enforcement power of state courts is limited to their territory and may prove to be ineffective if not internationally observed or taken over by other jurisdictions or directly by the firms concerned. Nevertheless, some global networks already operate very efficiently, as is the case with the Uniform Domain Name Dispute Resolution Policy (UDRP) applied by ICANN. Globalization of jurisdiction is a challenge in that regard as rules or also enforcement measures would have to be implemented by third, other jurisdictions. Basically, standards set by global networks would have to be transformed into state or international law rules. Greater attention will have to be given to the understanding on whether, where, and how enforcement actions involving global issues and the competent jurisdiction of courts should be brought.[171]

Global public policy networks will also be limited with regard to the contingent adoption of enforcement measures. Their policies will merely apply to the global or international level, apart from political sanctions imposed by international organizations to states or international war tribunals for example. The nature of their enforcement measures remains largely indeterminate. In addition, NGOs are increasingly involved in the activities of global public policy networks. Their involvement constitutes a self-enforcing process. However, it is uneven both in the standard-building process and in the implementation of standards. Their influence can be put at the same level as the one of the states. They can participate indirectly in judicial proceedings and submit amicus curiae briefs. In international adjudication, NGOs have also found an increasing role in providing information to

[171] Berman, supra note 67, 336, 502–511; Chapter 3, point 6 Global Networks, 6.1 Digital Networks; Tribunal de Grande Instance de Paris, Ordonnance de référé, 22 mai 2000, UEJF et Licra c/ Yahoo! Inc. et Yahoo France; Tribunal de Grande Instance de Paris, Ordonnance de référé du 11 août 2000, UEJF et al. c/ Yahoo! Inc. et Yahoo France; Tribunal de Grande Instance de Paris, Ordonnance de référé du 20 novembre 2000, UEJF et al. c/ Yahoo! Inc. et Yahoo France; http://www.juriscom.net/txt/jurisfr/cti/tgiparis20000522.htm (last visited 26 November 2009).

the decision makers. They underline the fact that dialogue plays a central role also with regard to enforcement. They can affect outcomes, mobilize the general public, and constrain states, although they lack the political legitimacy of states.[172]

Incommensurability of Impact

The examination of aspects of the impact of regulatory regimes following an approach based simultaneously on the gradual strength of the measures one the one hand and the grade of bindingness and legitimacy of the rules on the other hand allows appreciating their perception by directly concerned actors and society. To measure and estimate their actual impact and performance, there is first the question of the criteria to be considered. In some cases, this relates to the standards or the activities of groups without any further measures. In other cases, the adequacy and success of a regime will have to be measured considering the enforcement of penal sanctions by a state. Possible measures can be first based on formal regulatory inputs – for instance staffing or budgets – and outputs – for instance enforcement actions or monetary sanctions – of the responsible bodies or authorities. However, these criteria are limited and not regarded as sufficient. Criticisms include the reproach of incompleteness, misdirection, and inadequate granularity. On its side, cost benefit analysis is most certainly a useful tool to assess the impact of regulatory regimes. However, the considerable attention given to cost benefit analysis mainly in academic circles and by regulators and the number of studies published show that it is very difficult if not impossible to find a satisfactory basis to quantify enforcement measures. Moreover, narrow efforts at quantification alone are too limited to assess the impact. Still other aspects which could be taken into account are the financial performance and the behavior of market participants. That approach still has to be developed to rely on a staunchly basis and serve as a common denominator. Furthermore, as far as the enforcement of state rules itself is concerned, the measurement of its impact still remains a big challenge. As a result, it is hold from the beginning that there is no generally recognized and reliable way to measure the impact or effectiveness of regulatory regimes or rules as such. It is incommensurable and any appreciation or statement remains largely subjective.[173] A basis of comparison is lacking in respect to quality status. The concrete cases just discussed to describe and appreciate the situation have been valuable to show how various regulatory regimes are implemented and work in practice. At the same time, they point to the difficulties or specificities of their own implementation as well as a possible measurement of their efficacy. Moreover, with the move beyond the state as the sole responsible enforcement authority, the point is where to draw the line of

---

172 Chayes and Handler Chayes, supra note 163, 311–330; Geiss, supra note 58, 313–320; R. Wedgwood, Legal Personality and the Role of Non-Governmental Organizations and Non-State Political Entities in the United Nations System (1999) 26–28.

173 Posner, supra note 88, 184–202.

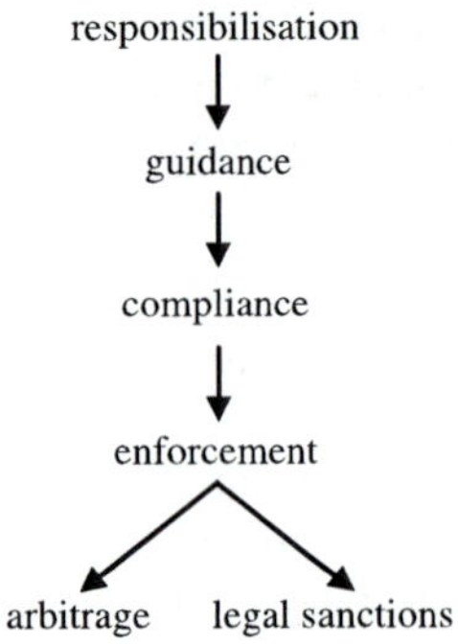

Fig. 4.3 Stages of impact

acceptable and recognizable enforcement measures between private or non-state bodies such as networks or self-regulatory organizations, as discussed above, and the state itself or international organizations as well as between forms or stages of impact. The main distinction regarded compliance versus sanctions. While legal sanctions promise to assert the effectiveness of rules, they still have to be imposed by courts and effectively enforced. On the other hand, in the case of compliance, there are no measures to enforce the standards or rules, but, they may be even more effective in practice. Their acceptance and observance are determining (Fig. 4.3).

2.4 Nature of Autonomous Regulatory Regimes

2.4.1 General Considerations

Throughout this study, a distinction has been made between autonomous and self-regulatory or non-state regimes of rules related to the state regulatory regime and regimes of rules emerging and situated outside, or at the periphery of that regime, that is, (entirely) distinctive, non-state rules. Indeed, autonomous regulatory regimes may create rules with or without state involvement. In the latter case, the classic hierarchy of state and international rules collapses.[174] The rise of rule-making epistemic communities and networks generates a regulatory pluralism which is further supported by the decentring of state regulation. On its side, state activity can be devolved upon private interests in a number of forms. Then, the structure of the regulatory solutions is hybrid and reflects a public-private partnership. Hybrid forms of regulation based on framework statutes delegating regulatory functions to agencies or private organizations are becoming even more common.

[174] See Fischer-Lescano and Teubner, supra note 50, 48–49.

It is expected that the detailed rules which will be enacted will be better adapted to practical circumstances.[175] They constitute decentred regimes which derive from the state and remain linked to it. The question of the nature of these regimes has already been largely studied, for instance in the Report on Fragmentation finalized by Koskenniemi, which concludes that these regimes cannot be approached and understood apart from the scope of state law or international law, as stated.[176] On their part, autonomous regulatory regimes with origins outside a state regulatory regime, that is, existing in a polycentric environment, result from rules dispersion. They will not fit into analytical frameworks applying to bodies of state rules. Conceptually, they lead to a different understanding of the nature of state to civil society, intra-state and intra-society relationships as well as of the nature of the regulatory issue. The norms are civil society norms first, following their own analytical frameworks and approaches. Discussion below intents to focus primarily on the nature of these rules and standards, while bearing in mind hybrid regimes or state-linked regimes.

Non-state, autonomous regimes are integrated complexes emerging from formal or informal institutions, epistemic communities, or networks, as discussed. They are a source of governance, constituting neither an alternative to regulation[177] nor non-regulatory measures, but alternative forms of regulation. The word 'autonomous' implicitly means that there is a notion of self-discipline with regard to regulation adapted to an organization or firm.[178] The term 'alternative forms of regulation' is ambiguous. It can cover a range of interactions and apply to diverse kinds of regulation. Alternative forms of regulation are significant in relation to the development of values, principles, rules, and a notion of order. It is a pervasive concept of regulation. Such alternative forms can belong to diverse institutional frameworks. They can differ due to the content of the rules, their grade of (legal) bindingness or the members involved as well as a possible degree of state involvement, influence, or governance role.[179]

Non-state regulatory regimes have their own proper mechanisms to create standards and rules without using conventional sources of law. Arising from interactions designed to define self-applicable regulation, these regimes will have a strong normative dimension both inherent in networks and necessary to their very existence. In principle, the network effect will be an indicator for the value of a membership. Networks claim validity for their members, whereas the binding force of their claim represents an important difference in relation to state regulatory regimes. The normative power may vary among networks, but may basically extend

---

175 P. N. Grabosky, Using Non-Governmental Resources to Foster Regulatory Compliance (October 1995) 529.

176 Koskenniemi, supra note 2, 83 et seqq.; B. Simma, Self-Contained Regimes (1985) 111, 245.

177 As discussed in Chapter 1, point 8 Alternatives to Regulation.

178 Black, supra note 117, 26, with further references.

179 Ogus, supra note 123, 100–102; J. Freeman, The Private Role in Public Governance (June 2000) 543–675.

well beyond their members.[180] For example, financial, digital or technological standard setting networks, as discussed in Chap. 3, have set their own standards and rules. They are adapted to their sector and the existing structural technicalities. This is the case with standards defined by the FSB or the BCBS, which in fact represent autonomous regimes composed of independent experts linked to their respective governments. As stated, their standards are observed by non-members on a almost worldwide scale. Another case in point are digital networks, whose rules – for instance, the explicit rules of the UDRP – apply to all internet users and are not the preserve of the members.[181]

Each of these regulatory regimes also has its own operative rationality and develops its own dynamics. Their sources are based on distinct technical and highly specialized processes. Such regimes may operate in different environments, but they are usually modelled on patterns of regulation motivated by their members' interests.[182] In the economic sector, they regularly centre on industry morality and institutionalizing responsibility. Although the networks leading to the constitution of these regimes may operate opportunistically, without clearly defined goals, there will be a unity and coherence within a regime as far as their standards are largely respected, which underlines their functional operativeness.[183] However, contrary to state legal orders, there is no coherence among these regimes. For instance, rules applying to securities exchanges, multinational companies, rating agencies, or codes of conduct all constitute different regimes. As a form of global law, they are sector-oriented and can be encountered in any area of society. Depending on the grade of development of an alternative regulatory regime, a measure can primarily consist in an implied behavioural pattern. The basic approach first consists in identifying 'good' and 'bad' forms of behaviour. The different economic sectors will deduce rules or instructions from the behaviour of 'their best practitioners' taken as a point of reference and to be followed or imitated. They serve as directives or rules of conduct. It will often be implicitly assumed that they should apply to the whole sector. In fact, they are developed by powerful practitioners and experts. The motto is: 'What the best do is valid for all', whereas the measures taken rely on the principles applying to economic law: equality of treatment, transparency, fairness.[184] Regimes can also be more elaborated formally, take the form of principles, standards and finally rules enacted by a SRO to govern its members or industry.

---

[180] Hutter, supra note 1, 13; N. Luhmann, Soziale Systeme (1985) 512 et seqq.; H. Ulrich, Das Unternehmen als soziales produktives System (1970).

[181] See above, point 1 Fragmentation, 1.2 Polycentrism; Chapter 3, point 6 Global Networks.

[182] Chapter 2, point 1 Embedding Autonomous Regulatory Regimes, 1.1 Traditional State Approach, 1.1.1 Public Policy Debate, Public Interest and point 3 Institutional Structure, 3.1 Theory of Interest: From Interest to Associability.

[183] Hutter, supra note 1, 13; Fischer-Lescano and Teubner, supra note 37, 1005–1009; Koskenniemi., supra note 2, 35–36, 246; A. Aviram, A Network Effects Analysis of Private Ordering (2003).

[184] P. Böckli, Neun Regeln der ‚Best Practice' für den Rückkauf nichtkotierter eigener Aktien (2001) 576.

The appreciation and value of the rules by the market will depend on the motives of the SRO when defining them, the explosiveness of an issue, and the quality of these rules.[185] Under these aspects, the formation of these regimes corresponds to the initial phase of a process of juridification first occurring within civil society. It could be portrayed as an integral part of the broader systematization of regulation.[186]

Whether these regimes are solely regimes of private ordering or have a genuine legal character is extremely controversial. The question of their dogmatic classification remains unsolved to date. This is rendered even more difficult, because there is no one single mark of identification of non-state and private authority and the concept is contingent, fluid and cultural.[187] Although they may not be subsumed under legal, state regimes, they may apply somewhat similar principles or observe the same ethical values. To classify these alternative regimes from the point of view of the traditional scheme of legal state regimes, criteria establishing the relationship should be identified. Methods of international private law cannot be applied, because these are first directed at solving inter-state cases and coordinating the application of national rules. They are linked to the territory of states. Alternative regulatory regimes, however, are neither limited territorially nor do they constitute state regulatory regimes. They operate on their own and are not accountable to states, although states may support them or provide a framework favouring their development and operations. In relation to the state, a classification will become possible when these forms of regulation are portrayed as the product of a delegation by the traditional regime of state regulation and analysed in relation to that legal regime.

Fischer-Lescano and Teubner discuss this issue.[188] They argue that self-regulatory regimes are essentially corporatist arrangements rather than legal regimes. The point is to determine criteria allowing for their distinction or affording them a legal character. Fischer-Lescano and Teubner suggest further that the application of the binary code 'legal / illegal' is not sufficient, but that the institutionalization of secondary normative processes will afford them a legal character. The secondary process is to be understood in Hart's[189] sense, but instead of being structurally oriented, it is oriented towards processes and operations. Then, there is a 'global law without the state' or an autonomous regulatory regime. Their approach can certainly be endorsed. Emerging transnational law concerns a different category of regulatory regimes, belonging to neither national nor international law. Rather, it emerges from global civil society, follows its own process, and is self-rational and

---

185 Marti, supra note 108, 564, with further references.

186 Tamanaha, supra note 11, 206 et seqq.; Roberts, supra note 58, 17 et seqq.; Zäch, supra note 82, 330 et seqq.; E. Meidinger, Competitive Supragovernmental Regulation: How Could It Be Democratic? (Winter 2008) 513–534.

187 Chinkin, supra note 35, 141; Richerson and Boyd, supra note 87.

188 Arguments for their legal character can be found in: Teubner, supra note 155, 255 et seqq.; for a very good discussion, see Roberts, supra note 58.

189 See above: 2.3 Gradual Transformation; Hart, supra note 147.

self-normative. It may also contain a latent constitutional norming.[190] These regimes are structurally coupled with the independent logic of the sectors they apply to.

There is an enormous demand for regulation, which eludes both national and international institutions in a range of fields, like the globalized economy, science, technology, the mass media, medicine, education, and transportation. The emerging regimes are multi-dimensional, constituted by different environmental influences characterizing the sector represented. Such regimes will also be intersystemic. As a consequence, they will reproduce, albeit in a different form, the structural conflicts already existing between the various functional systems within the law. There will be collisions of regimes, which can occur everywhere. These are not only policy-conflicts between diverse regulatory regimes involving the use of power and negotiation. These collisions of regimes reflect multifaceted conflicts among societal regimes rationalities.[191] In addition, there is also an inherent duality within every regulatory measure taken. It has the potential to increase economic development and there is a need to intervene and protect private market participants at the same time. Finance and labour rights are a case in point: these collide with each other, and dilemmas arise when measures are adopted, as is the case of the Bretton Woods Institutions. The question is whether their policies should include labour standards or not. In case the matter is discussed, the debate is first driven by economic considerations. The issue of labour rights should be pursued only if these contribute to reaching objectives defined in economic terms. The economic approach to labour rights presents shortcomings, and periods of economic growth may not be backed by sustainable social protection policies. To solve this collision, as far as the Bretton Woods Institutions are concerned, there would be the need to adopt a comprehensive legal framework for addressing labour rights.[192]

Another path followed by some authors when trying to classify autonomous regimes and alternative forms of regulation is the 'governance path'. These regimes present a clear resonance with notions of governance. Like the concept of globalization, it is currently subject to heated debate. 'Governance' encompasses a range of meanings and there is still no generally recognized definition of the concept.[193] One definition reads thus:

> The action or manner or governing; . . .
> Controlling, directing, or regulating influence; control, sway, mastery. . . .

---

[190] Fischer-Lescano and Teubner, supra note 37, 1007–1014; see also J. Griffiths, What is Legal Pluralism? (1986) 1 et seqq.; Sassen, supra note 24, 378–386.

[191] Fischer-Lescano and Teubner, supra note 37, 1000 et seqq.; Teubner, supra note 155, 255 et seqq.

[192] As argued by Kaufmann, supra note 47, 127–134.

[193] J. N. Rosenau and E.-O. Czempiel, Governance without Government: Order and Change in World Politics (2000); R.A.W. Rhodes, Understanding Governance, Policy Networks, Governance, Reflexivity and Accountability (2001) who concentrates on the situation in Great Britain in his study of governance and public administration. D. Held, Reframing Global Governance: Apocalypse Soon or Reform! (2007) 240–260.

> The office, function, or power of governing; authority or permission to govern; the command ...[194]

Rosenau has provided the following comprehensive definition:

> ... a more encompassing phenomenon than government. It embraces governmental institutions, but it also subsumes informal, non-governmental mechanisms whereby those persons and organizations within its purview move ahead, satisfy their needs, and fulfill their wants ... Governance is thus a system of rule that is as dependent on intersubjective meanings as on formally sanctioned constitutions ... or regulatory mechanisms in a sphere of activity which function effectively even though they are not endowed with formal authority.[195, 196]

Two main directions can be distinguished. The first is closely related to the notion of government. As argued by Foucault, the object and activity of government are not instinctive and natural. The practices of government have been invented and learned.[197] Governance applies to the development of governing styles. It is used to explain globalization where governance is becoming more prominent to the detriment of government. Emphasis is now placed on the process of governing. That process implies that the distinctions between national and international law as well as between law and politics are becoming blurred.[198] It is also linked to the concept of New Public Management, applied to develop best practices to render more efficient management by public administrations.[199] Government agencies and private actors may exercise public authority. Along with other similar institutions, they have emerged as important governance mechanisms whose authority is not entered into by the state. There are multiple agents that ensure and execute a new, multilayered, normative order. They steer and guide towards goals. Thus, governance is used to redefine and give another meaning to government.[200] This approach may be helpful to understand the relationship between autonomous private regimes and with the state.

---

194 The Oxford English Dictionary, Volume VI (1991) 710.

195 J. N. Rosenau, Governance, Order, and Change in World Politics (2000) 4–5.

196 The OECD has not provided an official definition. It applies an outcome oriented approach. The Commission on Global Governance produced a definition of governance in: Our Global Neighborhood: The Report of the Commission on Global Governance (1995) http://web.archive.org/web/20020119151837/http://www.cgg.ch/. However, it has been largely criticized, attacked, and rejected.

197 M. Foucault, Naissance de la biopolitique (2004) 3–28, 323 et seqq.

198 Black, supra note 25, 252–254, with further references; Rosenau, supra note 195, 1–29; M. Koskenniemi, Carl Schmitt, Hans Morgenthau, and the Image of Law in International Relations (2000) 25–34; Roberts, supra note 58, 17; Sajó, supra note 47, 214–216; K. J. Holsti, Governance without Government: Polyarchy in Nineteenth-Century European International Politics (2000) 30–57; Keohane and Nye, supra note 10, 202–213.

199 Chapter 2, point 1 Embedding Autonomous Regulatory Regimes, 1.1 Traditional State Approach, 1.1.1 Public Policy Debate, Public Administration; Rhodes, supra note 193, who concentrates on the situation in Great Britain in his study of governance and public administration.

200 Sassen, supra note 24, 242–246; Chapter 3, point 1 Self-regulation; J. N. Rosenau, Governing the ungovernable: The challenge of a global disaggregation of authority (2007) 88–97.

According to the second direction, the concept of governance is conceived as a form of regulatory governance. It is less broad. This approach focuses on the governance of behaviour or also 'smart' regulatory techniques, in contrast to 'command and control' regulation. Within it, regulation is considered to be a part of governance, focusing on behavioural aspects of others. This emphasizes the interdependence of public and private actors and the significance of networks of these actors at the national or transnational level. Regulation is a dimension of governing in any case. Such an approach is certainly useful to understand and grasp the role and patterns of private, non-state autonomous regimes or alternative forms of regulation. It also confirms that fragmentation of society has attained legal significance. It is accompanied by the emergence of specialized and autonomous rules or rule-complexes, legal institutions and spheres of legal practice. However, it departs from a very broad perspective and tries to reduce it to 'regulation', which in fact should merely comprise one of the governance elements.[201]

2.4.2 Legitimacy and Accountability

The operations of private autonomous regimes and their rules enforcement raise an issue of representation or, in other words, regarding their legitimacy and accountability. Who is entitled to determine the right order and to whom shall it be accountable? Legitimacy and accountability are relational concepts which are institutionally and discursively constituted. Accordingly, the contemporary debate over the concepts of legitimacy and accountability covers national or state and international bodies, SROs, NGOs as well as the operations and governance of networks, as stated. In fact, the perception of regulatory regimes evolves in accordance with the societal and political context. In addition, the impact of globalization and transnationalism raise new issues, not least because there is now a multileveled system of governance.[202]

In the following, these two main features are briefly discussed together with the characteristics of due process or fairness, expertise, efficiency, and aspects of enforcement issues. Baldwin and Cave most soundly suggest that these criteria represent the rationales employed in regulatory debate to appreciate regulatory measures. According to them, the assessment of regulation or regulatory measures

---

[201] Black, supra note 25, 252–253; Koskenniemi, supra note 2, 11; L.A.N. M. Barnhoorn and K. Wellens, Diversity in Secondary Rules and the Unity of International Law (1995); K. W. Abbott, Toward a Richer Institutionalism for International Law and Policy (2005) 16–18; see also: Arner, supra note 152, 121–125; C. Knill, D. Lehmkuhl, Private Actors and the State: Internationalization and Changing Patterns of Governance (January 2002) 41–52.

[202] J. Delbrück, Exercising Public Authority Beyond the State: Transnational Democracy and/or Alternative Legitimation Strategies? (2003) 29; Bernstein and Cashore, supra note 78, 347–371; T. Risse, Transnational Governance and Legitimacy (2006) 179–199.

should first be based on the assessment of its legitimacy.[203] However, as will be discussed, efficiency has dislodged legitimacy in the case of private autonomous regimes.

With regard to legitimacy, the legitimacy of the state and international organizations on the one hand, and the legitimacy of private bodies on the other, needs to be distinguished. Within the state approach, a legislative measure is presumed to be legitimate. In a liberal democracy, the government has appropriate powers to introduce regulatory measures, not least because originally they have been voted on and decided by the electorate. The setting and enforcement of rules implies the idea of state domination. Rules are centralized towards the state and administered by the state's court system. In addition, states can actively attempt to manage and sustain their legitimacy – both procedural and substantive –, for instance when responding to demands made on them by others, and taking appropriate measures.[204] The sovereignty of the state is a constitutive element of legitimacy. It is generally recognized that its legitimacy as a body is formally provided by the constitution. Constitutions are understood to 'take stock of the values that comprise the preferred forms of life of a given community'. This does not mean, however, that values with universal aspirations are also shared by all citizens. Rules based on these values are followed to varying degrees. According to Weber, however, the legitimacy of governments rests on an empirically verifiable acceptance.[205]

In relation to non-state or private networks and organizations, the issues of legitimacy and accountability are currently broadly discussed. Bernstein and Cashore try to answer the question whether their rules can actually be legitimate? They develop an analytical framework and a set of causal propositions to determine whether legitimacy might be achieved. They identify a three-phase process through which non-state regimes might gain legitimacy in the course of their emergence and institutionalization: initiation, building support, and political legitimacy. Black too discusses how to render polycentric regulatory regimes legitimate and accountable. Her focus is placed on the significance of the institutional environment, the dynamics of accountability and legitimacy relationships, and how they respond to multiple legitimacy and accountability claims in regulatory regimes. She also examines how they themselves seek to build legitimacy in complex and dynamic situations.[206] Besides these approaches, in relation to non-state or private networks and organizations, instead of normative validity based on value legitimacy, a trend exists

---

203 Baldwin and Cave, supra note 38, 76–85; R. Baldwin, Rules and Government (1995) 47; see also Schreiber, supra note 145, who focuses on legitimacy, 150 et seqq. For a detailed analysis of the concepts of legitimacy and accountability in the modern context, see: Black, supra note 13, 137–164, and Black and Rouch, supra note 51, 218–233, with a focus on financial markets.

204 Roberts, supra note 58, 17; Delbrück, supra note 202, 31–32; T. M. Franck, Fairness in International Law and Institutions (1995) 25–46; M. Thatcher, Regulation after Delegation: Independent Regulatory Agencies in Europe (2002) 954–972; C. Scott, Regulating Private Legislation (2007) 4–7.

205 M. Weber, Grundriss der Sozialökonomik (1947); Delbrück, supra note 202, 33.

206 Bernstein and Cashore, supra note 78, 347–371; Black, supra note 13, 137–164.

towards efficiency and interest maximization as a source of legitimacy. Efficiency and legitimacy are deeply intertwined. Contrary to state rules, the members of networks are more directly involved in the regulatory process and networks are specialized entities or bodies focusing solely on the representation of their very specific interests. In comparison, constitutional solutions under traditional rule of law cannot compete with what the professional networks promise to achieve, although the criteria of efficiency, transparency, and accountability also appear within the concept of state legitimacy.[207] In particular, state regulation applies to all citizens, including citizens or groups not supporting the rules or voting against their introduction. Gaining their support will be a key task, since failing to do so will undermine the legitimacy of the rules enacted. In addition, the legitimacy of state regulation may also be equivocal due to the fact that it should represent a normative definition of an issue, which may be difficult to justify in practice. These problems will not arise under that form in relation to self-regulatory or non-state regulatory measures.

Decentred regulatory regimes – including self-regulatory, non-state regulatory measures at either the national or transnational level – may well overcome some problems or difficulties of legitimacy of state regulation. Legitimacy is largely rooted in the acceptance of a regime or rules by civil society. Interest groups, networks or SROs 'by providing for a close institutionalized interface between public authorities and specific groups in civil society' may be in a position to adopt better adapted and accepted rules. Moreover, it should not be overlooked that in practice the success of networks or SROs at delivering adequate outcomes will lead to greater acceptance by the general public. This idea of legitimacy induces voluntary compliance with the rules by the general public. It is an outcome-based legitimacy. Its focus is placed on the policy applied and performance reached. This outcome-based legitimacy will be accompanied by a questioning of transparency and accountability in case the solutions offered and results obtained are not satisfactory.[208] It will thus be easier to enforce self-regulatory measures towards members, because they are the result of negotiations and based on their agreement to respect the rules. On the other hand, when self-regulatory measures affect third parties and require their observance although they are not members of a network, association or SRO, the legitimacy basis and enforcement of measures will remain more questionable.[209]

Basically, when switching from individuality to an associative order and gaining membership, individuals accept to lose some of their independency and autonomy, which they then transfer to the network or organization. At the same time, they can rely on structures they have initially defined themselves when constituting the

---

[207] Sajó, supra note 47, 223–224; Slaughter (2004a) supra note 52, 5 et seqq.; Delbrück, supra note 202, 34; Sassen, supra note 24, 196–199.

[208] W. Streeck and P. C. Schmitter, Community, market, state – and associations? The prospective contribution of interest governance to social order (1985) 22; Slaughter (2004a) supra note 52, 6 et seqq.; see also M. Weber, Wirtschaft und Gesellschaft (2002) 16.

[209] Baldwin and Cave, supra note 38, 125–126.

association and within which the rules and modes of participating and influencing decisions are set out. Possible incentives to comply with the measures adopted by an association are: the openness of the self-regulatory measures, their professionalism, their adequacy with regard to the issue at stake, and their degree of accountability. As a practical example, the IOSCO's Model for Effective Regulation states that the effectiveness of a self-regulatory solution should be assessed against the elements of: industry specialized knowledge or expertise, industry motivation, contractual relationship, transparency and accountability, flexible SRO compliance programs, coordination and information sharing arrangements, and be defined within the context of government oversight.[210] Insofar, and contrary to claims that associations or SROs lack legitimacy, there is no problem of legitimacy from this point of view. Members will take decisions and expect their association to adopt corresponding measures and implement policies opted for. Within an association or SRO, however, it is difficult to implement rules and an association will be reluctant to inflict sanctions on its members. There is a problem of capture.[211] However, the quality of participation and deliberation may be constrained due to the pressure of a possible state intervention, which the association may seek to avoid.

However, self-regulation or also non-state regulation may also overcome problems of enforcement inherent to state regulation, not least due to the fact that it is based on the voluntariness of the members of an SRO. Members are active market participants and perfectly know the needs of their market. It will be easier to recognize the legitimacy of the measures dictated by their SRO. These represent their members' interests, negotiate the regulation to be applied, and are responsible for its enforcement. It will be better tailored to the needs of their members. However, a weakness of self-regulation may lie in the claim that, contrary to the state, there is no separation of powers within a SRO or association. Democratic criteria are compromised.[212] On the other hand, SROs act in a less formalistic way than state bodies and are better placed to take individual needs into account.[213] In practice, self-regulation offers the advantage of a pragmatic approach. This is not least important, because similarly to soft law, self-regulation cannot be sued before courts. It cannot be enforced by civil or criminal courts procedures as such, unless it would have been formally recognized as part of state regulation.[214] Depending on the grade of formalization, that is, an epistemic community, an informal network, or the elaborated form of a (registered) association or SRO, the organization can

---

210 IOSCO Report of the SRO Consultative Committee of the International Organization of Securities Commissions, Model for Effective Regulation, May 2000.

211 See hereinafter in the text.

212 Some authors consider the rule-making function of SROs or associations an abuse of power. Ogus, supra note 123, 98–100; Page, supra note 109, 141, 163. See also T. Risse, Transnational Governance and Legitimacy (2004) 6 et seqq.; S. Peltzman, Toward a More General Theory of Regulation (1976) 19, 211–240.

213 Streeck and Schmitter, supra note 208, 22; Ogus, supra note 123, 100–102.

214 See hereinafter in the text.

negotiate its powers with its members and operate on the basis of a contractual relationship with them. Moreover, it exercises a control through the admission, rejection, or exclusion of members. The issue of legitimacy is then linked to negotiations occurring between members and their entering into a contractual relationship. The bindingness of the rules derives from the contracts themselves and can be enforced as such.[215]

Another feature is the criterion of accountability or control. Private and non-state autonomous regulatory regimes raise concerns about accountability and, linked to it, transparency. The debate regarding accountability occurs in relation to the measures taken to improve representativeness and transparency and also in relation to the exercise of power and the legitimacy of the measures adopted as well as the standards defined.[216] Similarly to legitimacy, there are many understandings of the notion of accountability. It is a multidimensional phenomenon. It represents a communicative relationship entailing responsiveness. Accordingly, in a state, regulators are obliged to justify their actions.[217] They are accountable to democratic institutions and controlled by them, albeit that control can also be delegated to third or external institutions.[218] In a way, accountability can be interpreted as a means to assess legitimacy. The extent of the accountability and its formalization can vary. It depends on the degree of discretion allowed. In particular, tackling issues of accountability is vital to prescribing and designing regulatory networks that address specific governance problems. As discussed in Chap. 3, transgovernmental networks such as the BCBS act informally, aided by strong contacts of their expert members. They can often operate more quickly and effectively than formal state bodies. However, they are perceived as mysterious to a broader public. Typically, they are 'only accountable to a small set of relatively powerful elites' and serious issues of accountability arise. Private regimes are subject to different pressures. They derive from the relationships to the members and private regulatory processes have the potential to add additional layers of scrutiny and accountability for the rules they define. Scott defines the situation as a form of 'extended accountability'

[215] Ayres and Braithwaite, supra note 169, 102–106; Scott, supra note 204, 4–7; J. Black, Rules and Regulators (1997) 79–88. For a detailed discussion of various practical cases, see Black, supra note 13, 137–164; see also: S. Macaulay, Non-Contractual Relationships in Business: A Preliminary Study (February 1963) 1–19, stating that in practice few contractual disputes are litigated and most are settled without resorting to government-enforced laws.

[216] Delbrück, supra note 202, 29; Berman, supra note 67, 399–400; Black, supra note 13, 137 et seqq.

[217] R. O. Keohane and J. S. Nye Jr., Between Centralization and Fragmentation: The Club Model of Multilateral Cooperation and Problems of Democratic Legitimacy (February 2001) 12–15; A. C. Page, Regulating the Regulator – A Lawyer's Perspective on Accountability and Control (2001) 127–149, provides an interpretation based on the example of financial services; R. Mulgan, Accountability: An Ever Expanding Concept? (2000) 555 et seqq.; O. R. Young, The Effectiveness of International Institutions: Hard Cases and Critical Variables (2000) 176–178.

[218] Baldwin and Cave, supra note 38, 76–82; Keohane and Nye, supra note 217, 12–14; see also Baldwin, supra note 203, 47; Berman, supra note 54, 500–503; Young, supra note 217, 175 et seqq.

premised on interdependence and/or redundancy. The idea of interdependence is based on the observation that in many settings key actors lack the capacity to act alone, and must cooperate with others to bring actions to fruition. Redundancy means that if a mechanism of rule-setting fails, it will be met by another overlapping mechanism; regimes of rules are in competition with each other.[219] Accountability is closely related to transparency. Transparency entails accountability and constitutes a form of accountability. Explaining the measures adopted by a state or private organizations and proving their expertise and rationality when introducing them are important means of accountability. Public information concerning the goals and nature of a policy is very important and a private organization or association may act as a facilitator or intermediary between different interests. Such practice works in a market-oriented way, and represents a form of autonomous governance. In practice, the requirement for more accountability and transparency is translated, for instance, in the case of firms with the number of codes enacted generally for the conduct of business or according to the sector concerned, either at the national or international level,[220] and whose designated role is to contribute to explain activities.

The basic idea underpinning the criterion of due process or fairness is that regulators act in a fair and consistent way. They treat individuals equally and procedures must be accessible and open to them. Thus, they merit public support. The underlying rationale lies in the assumption that there is a proper democratic influence on regulation.[221] The next criterion – expertise – is due to the fact that specialized knowledge may be required in order to exercise certain regulatory functions. Here, the point is how the public will accept and interpret regulatory measures decided by experts. These experts can be politicians and primarily represent the interests of their political persuasion. The last criterion – efficiency – concerns the adequacy and costs of the regulatory measures taken. Regulators should be able to justify that the measures introduced are cheap and that their implementation requires the least possible level of input. Furthermore, regulation should be efficient insofar as the goal pursued is attained. Efficiency can be estimated by taking into account and comparing alternative solutions.[222]

As stated in Chap. 2, an association or SRO may also apply enforcement powers and take disciplinary measures or inflict sanctions on its members. Similar to Ayres and Braithwaite's model of enforced self-regulation, it can be argued that it is easier to get convictions within an association, because the rules are more precise and less complex than in the case of state regulation. However, the problem of capture

---

219 Scott, supra note 204, 14–15; Keohane and Nye, supra note 217, 16; Slaughter and Zaring, supra note 39, 212; Ogus, supra note 115, 99 et seqq.; G. Borrie, The Regulation of Public and Private Power (1989) 552–567; Freeman, supra note 179, 543–675.

220 For some examples of international codes, see Chapter 3, point 2 Firm Own Regulation, 2.2 Multinational Firms. See also Young, supra note 217, 176 et seqq.

221 Page, supra note 217, 137–142; Franck, supra note 204, 83–139.

222 Baldwin and Cave, supra note 38, 76–82.

cannot be ignored.[223] But the working of these disciplinary measures and sanctions will contribute to forge an association's public credibility.[224] Thus, in a polycentric or transnational context, the issue of jurisdictional integrity, which traditionally applies to state-centred regimes, is rendered more complicated.[225]

Additional difficulties may arise especially in the case of long-established associations or SROs. These organizations will have developed structures in the course of time and they often enjoy a monopolistic market position. This is the case of the professions. Lawyers and doctors have to be members of an association before they can practise on a market. Membership of a powerful professional organization is compulsory and changes made to its rules are unwelcome. Such professional bodies have traditional structures, which have survived many generations.[226] The problem of legitimation may arise as far as any new generation, which has to adapt to existing structures, is concerned. Professional associations define the conditions of entry to the market. Questions arising concern whether existing self-regulation continues to legitimate established practice, and whether the order created by self-regulatory measures represents an ideal past? Newcomers could prefer another order.

2.4.3 Competition and Capture

Competition and capture are two other significant features of the operations of private autonomous regimes. Competition is important in relation to alternative forms of regulation or self-regulation. Beside state regulation, voluntary or self-regulation is an opportunity for competitive advantage. However, competition and self-regulation are paradoxical. On the one hand, within the decentred analysis of regulation, self-regulation can be understood to represent a genuine appearance of decentred regulation. As an autonomous regime, it is in competition with state regulation.[227] It is detached from such regulation and adds diversity as an alternative form of regulation, not least because it can assume different forms. Regulatory arbitrage is possible. On the other hand, the paradox lies in the fact that self-regulation at the same time represents centralization within an industry or a market. It can occupy a dominant position within a market. It is common for self-regulation

---

223 Ayres and Braithwaite, supra note 169, 55–56, 115; Page, supra note 217, 140–144; M. Priest, The Privatization of Regulation: Five Models of Self-Regulation (1997–1998) 257; see also Chapter 2, point 3 Institutional Structure, 3.3 Private Regulation; Chapter 3, point 2 Firm Own Regulation, on the model of enforced self-regulation. On the issue of capture, see below in discussion; R. Baldwin, Why Rules Don't Work (1990) 323–324.

224 Delbrück, supra note 202, 35.

225 C. Skelcher, Jurisdictional Integrity, Polycentrism and the Design of Democratic Governance (2005) 89–110.

226 Regulating the professions, Taking care of their own, in: The Economist (December 18th, 2004) 62, 64.

227 B. Hunt, The Timid Corporation, Why Business is Terrified of Taking Risk (2003) 232.

to be determined by one predominant SRO in a sector. A typical case is industry self-regulation. The organization determines the rules and it regulates the entry to the association. In the course of time, and with the process of gaining power, it will be in a position where it can exercise its monopoly over its members and the market. This situation leads to an inherent danger to exploit this position. It can also be misused to protect itself, introduce higher thresholds for non-members, and impose externalities on third actors instead of reducing them. As a result, industry self-regulation may be highly anticompetitive.[228] Moreover, there is a latent problem of intransparency. The market may miss important information and be largely disadvantaged in comparison to association members.

There are some remedies to avoid the negative consequences of an anticompetitive, monopolistic situation. The simplest logical conclusion is to ensure that there is a competitive situation. This can be achieved in different ways. Ogus defines the following three possibilities: (1) Unconstrained market competition, which means there is a competitive situation between self-regulatory organizations. (2) Agency-assisted competition, which means that in case of negative externalities for the market the imposition of a state regulation may be introduced and as far as information is concerned, an agency may act in a way to correct the situation either by intervening itself or by requiring a determined behaviour from the self-regulatory organization concerned. A pressure arises due to the possible introduction of a state regulation. As a third solution, (3) Ogus suggests ex-ante competition for ex-post monopoly, which means that the creation of an independent, public agency to exercise residual control over self-regulatory organization can be used to demonstrate that allowing for monopoly power does not exclude the possibility of a competitive self-regulatory solution.[229] Yet another situation is constituted by yardstick competition. In this situation, competition is guaranteed, because a business, firm or organization belonging to the state is active in a market or industry and as such sets standards. Thus, a private business, firm or organization, which is not regulated by the state, but only self-regulated, will have to compete with a state-owned business in order to offer its services to the public. Minimal standards will have to be enforced anyway.[230] Finally, it should be mentioned that an agency may also authorize several SROs.

An important drawback of self-regulation is that it can become the ultimate form of capture. A whole range of theories exists to explain this phenomenon. It is considered here as developed by George Stigler in 'The Theory of Economic Regulation'. This theory recognizes that interest groups or also other actors will use or rather misuse their regulatory powers, or in the case of governments that they will use their coercive powers to enact rules and regulation offering them the

[228] Harrison, Morgan, Verkuil, supra note 13, 342–343.

[229] Indeed, this list is certainly not exhaustive. Ogus, supra note 123, 103–107; Scott, supra note 204, 19–20.

[230] Chapter 3, point 2 Firm Own Regulation, 2.1 Individual Firms; Baldwin and Cave, supra note 38, 243–244; A. Shleifer, A theory of yardstick competition (Autumn 1985) 319–327; Harrison, Morgan, Verkuil, supra note 13, 495–496.

possibility to gain advantages for themselves or in favour of their vested interests at the expense of public interest objectives, from which intervention originated.[231] Due to the power of self-regulatory organizations to act, decide, and opt for the measures to be taken, the danger of capture is a current one. It is often the result of the influence exercised by economically powerful groups. In the large sense, capture belongs to public choice theory. According to this theory, capture is derived from the financial force of the interest groups involved. In this regard, regulatory agencies may well act as a corrective and limit the risks of capture. They act in the interest of both the public and the groups of interest or SROs. In a way, their position could be described as neutral towards both. However, to take measures, they rely on information received from same interests groups, whom they may favour notwithstanding public statements to the contrary. Thus, capture can recur, albeit not due to technical factors or the form of regulation. It is a general problem, possibly due to political, institutional or economic factors rather than a specific problem of self-regulation.[232]

Finally, with regard to the autonomous regimes discussed in this study, it is important to consider their temporal evolution. Many of these regimes are new, in the process of constituting themselves, evolve. The role of the actors and institutions involved still has to take shape. These regimes regularly represent competing conceptions of the 'right order', which they construct themselves and seek to attain. Between them, cooperation and collaboration play an important role. A dialogue takes place between the actors and institutions involved. As efficiency dominates, the approach is practical and the advantages offered by exchanges between actors or institutions as well as their motivation and initiative are determining. For example, it is partly because of the perceived expertise that those setting standards in the context of transnational committees are increasingly entering into a dialogue with transactional and market standards-setting bodies.[233]

3 Conclusion

This chapter has drawn on the previous discussion of non-state and private autonomous regulatory regimes and alternative forms of regulation. Its analysis is based on theoretical issues and illustrated with various cases. Is has aimed to explore the characteristics of autonomous, non-state regimes and alternative forms of regulation. First, the structural aspects have been discussed in relation to fragmentation and

[231] G. J. Stigler, The Theory of Economic Regulation (Spring 1971), 3 et seqq.; Chapter 2, point 3 Institutional Structure, 3.1 Theory of Interest: From Interest to Associability.

[232] Baldwin and Cave, supra note 38, 36–37; to the Public choice theory, see Chapter 2, point 1 Embedding Autonomous Regulatory Regimes, 1.1 Traditional State Approach, 1.1.1 Public Policy Debate, Public Choice.

[233] J. Benjamin and D. Rouch, The International Financial Markets as a Source of Global Law: The Privatisation of Rule-making? (March 2008) 78–86; Black and Rouch, supra note 51, 227.

dispersion: polycentrism, the transnational dimension and the institutional transformation. Second, the mechanisms of standardization have been examined. The aspects explored have been cooperation and trading, auto-constitutionalism and self-regulation, transformation and impact of the regulatory measures. Finally, the nature of these regimes has been discussed.

Seizing and understanding these regimes and the standards and rules they define necessitates a comprehensive approach. They appear to be diffuse, pervasive, complex and unspecified first. Their formation is incremental, uneven. They follow a process of transformation and their degree of specificity and determination evolves. Regularly, they apply to global issues and at the same time are specific. They underline the move away from the typical concept of state centralization and toward cross-border convergence of denationalized components. Their embeddedness depends on their acceptance and implementation. To judge of their real and effective impact, compliance and enforcement mechanisms have to be considered.

Chapter 5
Evaluation

Abstract The focus of the chapter is the evaluation. Regulation is evaluated as an institutional issue that should be adapted to the sectors and activities it regulates. The concept can be summarized as an issue of governance and of shifting the balance between the following key institutions: the state and the market actors within civil society, and their representative organizations.

So far, this study has examined autonomous regulatory regimes and alternative forms of regulation as a multifaceted concept. It has suggested that the concept involves a contest of institutions, institutional issues, and an issue regarding the nature and characteristics of rules as well as their impact. These regimes of rules cannot be considered separately from examining the interactions and structural differences existing between the state and the private economy or, in other words, without taking into account the public–private divide. These spheres are inseparable. The practical examples discussed show that manifold interrelations between them exist at both the organizational or substantive level, and based on diverse mechanisms. Another important point is that alternative forms of regulation and regimes constitute a paradox insofar as they lead to the fragmentation or dispersion of regulation while inducing formalization and standards-setting. Accordingly, there are several challenges.

First, as stated, the very existence of these regimes is still contested by some authors and their dogmatic classification debated. This study assumes that these regimes must be understood in terms of their actual regulatory impact. They are perceived both through their recognition and acceptance, their assertion and success. Put differently, what matters is the adherence and observance by interested actors seeking to devise a mode for their interaction and possibly for relations with third actors. Compliance and enforcement capacity play a major role in this respect. These features will determine the degree of bindingness and be an indication regarding the legitimacy of the regimes. Second, dogmatic aspects of alternative forms of regulation, non-state or self-regulation are clarified. Originally, they find their roots within civil society and are part of autonomous regimes. They are driven by private forces. The presence of epistemic communities, networks and private associations or non-governmental, self-regulatory organizations as distinctive regimes of interest representation taken in relation to the state leads to the substantiation and

M. Senn, *Non-State Regulatory Regimes*,
DOI 10.1007/978-3-642-14974-0_6,

formalization of these forms of regulation. In relation to state regulation, they either depend on a delegation of regulatory powers by the state or correspond to self-regulatory solutions (implicitly) recognized by the state as far as they can rely on the principle of subsidiarity. It is possible to have a range of private, public or hybrid regulatory arrangements, and a regulatory marketplace emerges.[1] Third, while new institutions emerge and develop to become powerful actors, the role of the traditional, state institutions is changing. Technical capacities and the knowledge of experts are the dominating force while political influence is tightened. To enshrine its position, the state assumes governance.

With a view to this situation, the following parameters are now assessed: the institutional issue and the public and private turn of regulation. Indeed, the process of institutional transformation occurs at two main levels: the public level or the level of state and international law and the private level or the level of private and self-regulation. It is further assumed that these regimes are not entirely estranged. Their normative foundation is based on the same ethos. Manifold interdependencies exist between them, and hybrid regimes are common. To understand the context of these regimes, the historical dimension is important. It largely contributes to developing an analytics of change based on a new spatio-temporal order.[2] This situation can be compared to the evolution of self-regulatory regimes from medieval times until now. Approaching these regimes and their interrelationships also encompasses the issue of linkage. How can their relations inter se be conceived? Can the rules be compared, and are they compatible? Communicative and interpretative mechanisms have to be defined. It is reckoned as most probable that the transformation and formalization of rules in the course of time will unavoidably induce the convergence of these regimes and consistent interpretation while the role of the institutions involved is subject to continuous change – in particular of the relations of power – and progression. The regimes tend to coalesce in the long run while remaining distinct.

1 A Process of Institutional Transformation

Alternative, transnational forms of regulation and the polycentrism of regulatory regimes are shaped by institutional economics. Changes occurring in the field of regulation are produced by institutions. North comments thus:

> Institutions are the rules of the game in a society or, more formally, are the humanly devised constraints that shape human interaction. In consequence they structure incentives in

---

[1] Chapter 1, point 7 Regulation as a Marketplace.

[2] D. Held and A. Mc Grew, D. Goldblatt and J. Perraton, Global Transformations, Politics, Economics and Culture (2008) 14–17, 430; S. Sassen, Territory, Authority, Rights, From Medieval to Global Assemblages (2006) 11–18, 378 et seqq., 382; Chapter 2, point 2 A Brief Evolutive View.

> human exchange, whether political, social, or economic. Institutional change shapes the way societies evolve through time and hence is the key to understanding historical change.[3]

Institutions are understood as organizations responsible for defining and enhancing the implementation of rules, standards, or norms. They can also just be represented by formal and informal rules together with their idiosyncratic enforcement mechanisms.[4] They epitomize systems of interrelated elements governed by interest representation. Departing from the level of interacting individuals, their constitution is central to economic and societal development, albeit that the temporal aspect plays an influential role. Processes must be instituted and organizations either formal, such as associations, state institutions, firms, or informal, such as epistemic communities or business networks, produce and disseminate rules that aim at influencing and determining behavioural patterns of market actors.[5]

The process of institutionalization is twofold. It is not a process which only applies to non-state law. The definition and setting of state regulation or hybrid forms of regulation also constitutes institutionalization. State regulatory activities have striven to include multiple national and international developments when shaping governance rules constitutive of internationally diversified or possible transnational markets. The current institutional changes occurring with regard to the role of the state are regularly due to the fact that states are not in a position to control the activities of governmental experts who sit (sometimes together with industry representatives) in the sub-sub-committees or organizations where most of the professional and policy-implementing work takes place. States still work and cooperate within an aging institutional order. Its construction has been largely politically motivated and built to surmount and master the consequence of the Second World War. It has not been adapted to the ensuing societal changes. Thus, there is now a structural vacuum. Non-state actors, epistemic communities and networks become active and try to fill the gap.[6]

Quite often the sub-sub-committees of independent experts act in their own capacity. Although the state or state agencies may formally enact and be formally accountable for state regulation, such bodies may have only a limited influence on

---

[3] D. C. North, Institutions, Institutional Change and Economic Performance (1990) 3; A. K. Sen, Global Justice: Beyond International Equity (1999) 116–125; R. W. Scott, Institutions and Organizations (2001) 47–70. For an example, see: R. L. Tõkés, Institution-Building in Hungary, Analytical Issues and Constitutional Models, 1989–1990 (October 2001).

[4] As defined in Chapter 2, point 3 Institutional Structure, 3.7 Networks as Regulatory Institutions: From Autonomous Regulatory Regimes to Meta-regulation; K. W. Abbott, Toward a Richer Institutionalism for International Law and Policy (2005) 26.

[5] Chapter 2, point 3 Institutional Structure; R. D. Lipschutz and C. Fogel, 'Regulation for the rest of us?' Global civil society and the privatization of transnational regulation (2002) 115–125; A. Greif, Institutions and the Path to the Modern Economy, Lessons from Medieval Trade (2006) 13–14, 39–44; G.-P. Calliess, J. Freiling, and M. Renner, Law, the State, and Private Ordering: Evolutionary Explanations of Institutional Change (2008) 397 et seqq.; Scott, supra note 3, 91 et seqq.

[6] National Intelligence Council, Global Trends 2025: A Transformed World, NIC 2008-003 (November 2008) x, 1, 81.

the definition of mostly highly specialized rules. De facto, their authority to determine rules is largely exercised by the governmental experts represented in specialized committees. This view is also held by Thatcher. He examines when, how and why internationalization or globalization affects national economic institutions, through which mechanisms decisions about national institutional reform are affected, and what are institutional outcomes. Technological and economic forms of internationalization are distinguished from policy forms, notably decisions in powerful overseas nations and supranational regulation. Thatcher rejects the hypothesis that technological and economic forms of internationalisation drive institutional change in and of themselves. Instead, policy forms are determining. They become part of domestic decision making and induce the transformation, even of deeply-entrenched national institutions. Therefore, there is scope for the specification of diverse rule-making mechanisms, which engender institutionalization and ultimately the emergence of a plurality of regimes involving state, hybrid, and private autonomous regimes. Here, mixed temporal and sectoral orders serve to formalize rules.[7]

In the private sphere, the rise of non-state orders and alternative forms of regulation, at the national as well as global level, corresponds to a gradual process of institutionalization. Epistemic communities, (sectoral) networks, and private associations are orders which compete with other orders, such as the state legal order or the order of international law. At the same time, there is a trend toward the institutionalization of transnational relations, which affects state practices. Increased interactions and transnational developments are due to increased ease of communication, transportation, financial transactions, or also travel. On their side, institutionalist theories of regulation tend to emphasize the interdependency of state and non-state actors in the pursuit of both public benefit and private gain within regulatory regimes. Thus, networks can be regarded both as the cause and consequence of that process.[8] As institutions, they can be considered to belong to meta-regulation, that is, the regulation of regulation, which deals with the process and responsible institutions of regulation.[9] From a meta-regulatory perspective, a weighting of the possibilities should take place to opt for the most appropriate regulatory solution, whether public or private. In other words, emphasis is placed on

[7] M. Thatcher, Internationalisation and Economic Institutions, Comparing European Experiences (2007). See also: O. R. Young, The Effectiveness of International Institutions: Hard Cases and Critical Variables (2000) 160–194.

[8] B. Morgan and K. Yeung, Introduction to Law and Regulation, Text and Materials (2007) 16–17, 74–76; S. Bernstein and B. Cashore, Can non-state global governance be legitimate? An analytical framework (2007) 347–371; T. Risse-Kappen, Bringing transnational relations back in: introduction (1995) 3–33; National Intelligence Council, Global Trends, supra note 6, x, 81.

[9] For more details, see Chapter 1, point 6 Meta-regulation; Chapter 2, point 3 Institutional Structure, 3.7 Networks as Regulatory Institutions: From Autonomous Regulatory Regimes to Meta-regulation.

controlling the process of regulation itself.[10] From a perspective of regulatory pluralism, different regulatory paths exist. Indeed, the pluralistic conception of law derives from the need to adapt to new facts. A blend of public and private resources is involved.[11] At the same time, there is a regulatory competition among a number of institutions. An issue of institutional competences arises. Not at least with regard to the challenges posed by transnationalism and the enlarged understanding of regulation, individuals or groups dispose of a number of escapes and are not only dependent upon the state. Its judicialization also belongs to the widened regulatory framework, and is not constituted by courts solely in the traditional sense. Rather, it is also characterized by instances of non-judicial legality, which are often encountered in the context of (non-)governmental economic policy-making, like compliance with rules, as stated in Chap. 4.[12] Chapter 3 has discussed various cases of juridification besides the traditional state regulatory regime.[13] Hence, mainly private institutions can emerge and develop. Conversely, the institutional setting and role of states is changing. They adopt a more cooperative attitude towards individuals and interest groups. They are no longer merely commanders, but also act as brokers or intermediaries.[14]

With regard to rules, these first constitute secondary norms as defined by Hart. They follow a process of formalization and possibly institutionalization. Process of codification occurs through the initial definition of broad, general standards. A subsequent range of possible instruments, such as conventions or agreements, can emerge, as discussed in Chap. 4, exemplifying gradual rules formalization monitored by civil society actors. For instance, in the case of the lex digitalis, autonomous bodies of secondary norms remain dominant, with a claim for validity to internet users. They are perceived through a range of instruments depending on their grade of formalization and specification.[15]

Various approaches and explanations exist to conceive this process of institutionalization and provide a framework for the conceptualization of regulation, in particular including non-state autonomous regulatory regimes or alternative forms of regulation. The emergence of various forms of regimes, private and hybrid

---

[10] B. Morgan, The Economization of Politics: Meta-Regulation as a form of Nonjudicial Legality (2003) 489–491.

[11] J.-P. Robé, Multinational Enterprises: The Constitution of a Pluralistic Legal Order (2006) 68–71.

[12] Chapter 4, point 2 Standardization, 2.3 Gradual Transformation; Morgan, supra note 10, 491–496.

[13] Chapter 3, point 1 Self-regulation, point 6 Global Networks.

[14] P. N. Grabosky, Using Non-Governmental Resources to Foster Regulatory Compliance (October 1995) 545; C. Parker, C. Scott, N. Lacey and J. Braithwaite, Regulating Law (2004) 4 et seqq.; National Intelligence Council, Global Trends, supra note 6, x–xiii, 81 et seqq.

[15] H. L. A. Hart, The Concept of Law (1997) 79–81; Chapter 3, point 6 Global Networks; Chapter 4 point 2 Standardization, 2.3 Gradual Transformation; A. Fischer-Lescano and G. Teubner, Fragmentierung des Weltrechts: Vernetzung globaler Regimes statt etatistischer Rechtseinheit (2007) 46–47, with further references; P. S. Berman, The Globalization of Jurisdiction (December 2002) 329 et seqq. and 366 et seqq.

regulatory regimes, as well as state regulation leads to a status of rules beyond homogeneity, unity, and coherence. The traditional hierarchy of state rules is broken. Lex specialis techniques, lex posterior, inter se agreements, or peremptory norms cannot be applied. As a result, no hierarchical meta-system is realistically currently available to surmount such conceptual issues.[16] From a meta-regulatory point of view, the techniques used are heuristic. Indeed, diverse, and not always clearly categorizable regimes, abound and should be distinguished. New regimes evolve on a continuous basis, subject to institutionalizing and fragmentation is likely to increase in the future. Linked to them, there is an issue of coordination. Yet it is argued that the multiplicity of actors accompanying the emergence of regimes will even incapacitate international cooperation, in particular given the wide array of transnational challenges facing the international community. The international order appears to be a misnomer, hybrid and heterogeneous and will be in transformation during years.[17] In concrete cases, it should therefore be possible to ask which institutional constellation is best suited to solve a determined issue. Is it guided by efficiency criteria only?

The crystallization of standards and rules and their affiliation either to state or non-state regulatory regimes just constitutes or is the result of a process of institutional transformation. But the question is: how should institutional transformation be approached? Which are transformation criteria? Transformation is not a theory of international law, because it is not international law. It covers various approaches, legal and non-legal. It marks the passage from a system or regime to another, from standards to rules, from the state to civil society and vice versa. Transformation is part of an evolutionary theory whose favourites are adaptation and differential selection. It is also a sociological approach. In relation to the globalization debate, the transformationalist thesis argues that contemporary globalization is transforming, reconstituting, or 're-engineering' the power, functions and authority of national states and governments. The transformationalist approach rejects both the hyperglobalist thesis of the end of the sovereign state and the sceptics' view that there is no change.[18] In relation to regulation and institutional changes, transformation applies to political and economic thinking. It points to the changing, transformative relationship between knowledge and government as well as technological and societal developments. At the same time, it also suggests that the perception of a state of things by the members of a collectivity is changing. They come to think of themselves as somehow bound to other collectivities or regimes. New relations of power are established. There is an institutional shift from

[16] M. Koskenniemi, Fragmentation of International Law: Difficulties arising from the Diversification and Expansion of International Law (2006) 249.

[17] National Intelligence Council, Global Trends, supra note 6, x, 1.

[18] A. Giddens, The Constitution of Society, Outline of the Theory of Structuration (1984) xxviii–xxix, 228–233; see also: Held and Mc Grew, Goldblatt and Perraton, supra note 2, 7–9.

defined relationships to different or third forms of relationships. Thus, a transformation occurs.[19]

Foucauldian theories of governmentality provide a possible theoretical basis for analysis. The perception of networks and autonomous regulatory regimes mirrors the continuous and multiple relations pertaining to the 'art of government', something that should be defined in its specificity. It is linked to the emergence and perception of an increasing influence of civil society in regulation that correlates a liberal art of government. Civil society does not repel and contest the will of government. It is a concept belonging to governmental technology. However, with regard to that situation, Foucault underlines that the concept of governmentality, or 'l'art de gouverner', needs a new basis or reference. According to him, it must embrace and refer to civil society for three main reasons: Governmentality must preserve its 'global' character within a state – which is not the case of the traditional state concept –, it should not be entirely dependent on economic aspects, and it should not be divided into economic governmentality and legal governmentality. There should be a

> 'unité de l'art de gouverner, sa généralité sur l'ensemble de la sphère de souveraineté.[20]

Tamanaha explores the relationship between law and society along theoretical and sociological lines. He develops a blended approach to law, integrating legal theory and sociological approaches. Law is understood to be a mirror of society that functions to maintain societal order. Tamanaha attempts to mark out a general jurisprudence. He observes that

> ' 'law' can be said to exist whenever it is recognized as such in society.'[21]

However, finding a common denominator for various regulatory regimes proves difficult in a world of proliferating sectoral particularities. For Teubner, the idea of the unity of the regulatory order is significant for the perception of phenomena at supra-, infra-, and trans-state levels. Consequently, he forecasts a new evolutionary stage in which law will become

> 'a system for the co-ordination of action within and between semi-autonomous societal subsystems'.[22]

---

[19] Giddens, supra note 18, 234 et seqq., 256–262; see also: C. Knill, D. Lehmkuhl, Private Actors and the State: Internationalization and Changing Patterns of Governance (January 2002) 52–57, discussing possible trends of regulatory transformation based on the example of 'internet'.

[20] 'a unity of the art of government, its generality over the whole sphere of sovereignty.', translation by the author. M. Foucault, Naissance de la biopolitique (2004), Leçon du 4 avril 1979, 295–320, 299; A. Ferguson, An Essay on the History of Civil Society (1767), http://www.constitution.org/af/civil.htm (last visited 10 November 2009), Part first, Section I; C. Gordon, Governmental rationality: an introduction (1991) 22–24.

[21] B. Z. Tamanaha, A General Jurisprudence of Law and Society (2001) 166, 171 et seq.; B. Z. Tamanaha, On the Rule of Law, History, Politics, Theory (2004); S. Roberts, After Government? On Representing Law Without the State (January 2005) 20–21.

[22] As cited in Roberts, supra note 21, 4, 21–22.

which, in fact, is similar to a meta-regulatory approach. By contrast, Roberts does not offer a solution, but adopts a very sceptical and conservative attitude and claims caution towards representing mainly autonomous regimes – or negotiated orders – at either the regional or global level as legal orders.[23]

Similarly to Keohane, Abbott applies a rationalist/instrumentalist approach. It supports the idea that international law is a regime that serves national interests. Compliance with international law is a winning strategy that nations will follow by rational choice as long as they see the benefits. Abbott pleads for an approach based on a more expansive institutionalist theory. He discusses theoretical approaches or major 'schools' of international relations theory: realism, institutionalism, liberalism, and constructivism. Realist school focuses on states. They pursue security. Differences in state power are determining. States may cooperate and make legal commitments, but the powerful set the terms of cooperation. Institutionalist school comes in many varieties, neoliberal institutionalism is the most well-developed one. It is centred towards the state, but recognizes that states are legal fictions. It also incorporates international institutions and can accommodate other actors as well. States pursue many interests. The school identifies conditions that impede beneficial cooperation and analyzes how institutions can help overcome them, for example by monitoring behaviour or other mechanisms affecting behaviour. Liberalism places individuals, business firms, NGOs and other non-state actors in its center, acting primarily in domestic politics. They determine state activities and policies to be applied at both the national and international level as well as with regard to cooperation with state agencies. Liberal theory also furnishes normative arguments for international cooperation and law. Finally, the constructivist school of thought is based on Grotian heritage. States, institutions, or agencies are constructed as shared subjective understandings. Law is influential. It plays a determining role in forming identities and preferences and 'constructing' an international society. The first three schools share a rationalist methodology. Actors behave purposively.[24] On the background of these theories, Abbott discusses the whole panoply of cooperative arrangements among the actors or institutions – states, international organizations, state agencies, non-state actors and transnational bodies – involved. The complexity of institutions and governance issues increasingly lead to a call for multifaceted governance strategies encompassing all actors types and policies. With view to the governance problems caused by the territorial approach, a 'global public policy' should be developed. There is not only a 'legal gap' due to territoriality, but also a 'participation gap' between non-state actors and international institutions.[25]

---

[23] Roberts, supra note 21, 23–24; in that context, see also: S. Roberts, Against a Systemic Legal History (7 April 2003); M. T. Fögen, Geschichte der Evolution eines sozialen Systems (24 March 2003).

[24] Abbott, supra note 4, 12–13.

[25] Ibid. 17–26; W. H. Reinicke, Global Public Policy: Governing Without Government? (1998) 85–90; I. Kaul, I. Grunberg, M. A. Stern, Global Public Goods, International Cooperation in the 21st Century (1999); I. Kaul, P. Conceicao, K. Goulven Le, R. U. Mendoza eds, Providing Global Public Goods, Managing Globalization (2003).

Thus, Abbott argues that institutionalism seems to provide a natural framework to respond to challenges posed by global issues. However, it should not be associated with interactions among states. The notion should be enlarged and bring to bear liberal insights into the role of the actors, constructivist insights into the role of values and norms, and realist insights into the role of power.[26]

A main focus of the study has been the institutional issue. The emergence and development of regulatory regimes points to a structural gap in relation to the institutions. There is a vacuum left by states and the international state order and at the same time an evolution of the issues to be dealt with. The goal of creating a working after war institutional order is no longer relevant. Instead, economic and technological issues drive changes. New policy forms and approaches should be developed and the understanding of 'governing' should be 'Foucaulded'. At the same time, an enlarged institutionalist approach should apply.

2 A Process of Transformation into Private Regulation

The process of transformation into private regulation can be attributed either to the private or public sector, as discussed. Rendering a sphere 'private' was originally the preserve of the state authority. It had the privilege to decide on the privatization of tasks or businesses. It was a public policy issue.[27] However, it can now be observed that autonomous regimes largely enhance private regulation, both at the national and first of all global level. They are detached from the state. They lead to a fragmentation and dispersion of rules that derives form societal processes and contradictions. In particular, this development is beyond the reach of the public power at the global level. The private market dictates the rules in various sectors and circumstances as a result of the increasing diversification, technicalization, and specialization of societal sectors. The formalization and institutionalization of these regimes occurs in relative ignorance of existing state regulatory regimes. Multiple variations of regulatory types of relationships, arrangements, and regimes can be encountered, applying their own self-regulatory rules, without any statutory underpinning. Policy is determining. In this regard, an important finding is that global regulatory norms follow globalizing self-regulatory practices. Transnational networks play a key role, determining the rule to be applied. At the global level, where there is no official global authority, the public domain is governed by private norms, thereby curtailing the power of the state.[28] However, only states are equipped to provide and account for public goods. Indeed, it is their core role and duty. With the

[26] Abbott, supra note 4, 17–28.

[27] Chapter 1, point 2 The Impact of (Public) Policy Issues.

[28] J. Braithwaite and P. Drahos, Global Business Regulation (2000) 491; A. Sajó, Transnational Networks and Constitutionalism (2006) 223–224; J. Black, Constitutionalising Self-Regulation (1996) 25–26.

development of transnational activities and governance by epistemic communities and networks, both public and private actors are becoming de facto decision-makers, albeit at different levels. Networks or SROs form regimes, set standards and define own (self-regulatory) rules, but they have limited powers to ensure the implementation of measures and impose sanctions in particular on non-members. They rely on voluntary compliance. Not surprisingly, a range of authors conclude that self-regulatory regimes are difficult to maintain without explicit sanctions.[29] Depending on the circumstances, this relativizes their significance, effectiveness, and binding force. Criticism first regards the efficacy of non-state regulators in modifying behaviour. However, the outcome may not be worse in practice than in the case of state regulation. It depends on the issue, interests at stake and relations of power.[30] Power induces actors to behave differently than they would have otherwise. The distribution of power can change to include non-state actors and organizations. Then, compliance is no longer obtained by states by the nature of constitutional legitimacy, but rather because there are common needs of all the actors in question. As a result, authority and power do not disappear. They are relocated either to transnational or subnational groups. In practice, it is part of a creeping process. Indeed, states have gradually delegated or relinquished parts of their functions to private, societal actors in various cases. Sassen attributes changes of activities from the public to the private sector or also vice versa not only to changes in property regime, but to changes in velocity, toward a new spatio-temporal order. Efficiency or what Sassen would call the 'shift from a bureaucratized time-space to a private accelerated global time-space' is determining. According to Sassen, the temporality of the national or state has been constructed historically, through the expansion of bureaucratized systems and the associated standardizations. The national, state project was to neutralize other temporalities and other spatialities. An idea of appropriateness emerges which is associated with unification of rules and standardization.[31]

Furthermore, private and also non-state actors have no obligation to satisfy public needs. They are primarily oriented towards the needs and interests of their members. Contrary to the state, they are not accountable towards the general public. The addressees of the standards set are the standard-setters themselves or entities linked to them. In the financial services sector, for instance, both specialized

---

[29] B. M. Hutter, The Role of Non-State Actors in Regulation (May 2006) 14; N. Gunningham, Environment, Self-Regulation, and the Chemical Industry: Assessing Responsible Care (1995) 57–109; Chapter 4, point 2 Standardization, 2.3 Gradual Transformation, 2.3.2 Impact.

[30] In that regard, see for example the conceptual analysis of the role of self-regulation prior to the creation of the British Financial Services Authority (FSA), in: A. C. Page, Self-Regulation: The Constitutional Dimension (March 1986) 141–167. Then, Page also analyzed the situation with regard to accountability and control in relation to the newly created FSA: A. C. Page, Regulating the Regulator – A Lawyer's Perspective on Accountability and Control (2001) 127–149; J. Black, Rules and Regulators (1997) 77–79.

[31] Sassen, supra note 2, 378–386, 395; N. Brunsson and B. Jacobsson and Associates, A World of Standards (2000) 15; see also: Held and Mc Grew, Goldblatt and Perraton, supra note 2, 77–86.

transnational and transgovernmental networks set standards which will be observed by the whole industry, actors not directly involved in the standard-setting process, or supervised institutes. This is the case of the IIF, where a few private industry representatives dictate standards to be observed by the whole industry or also of the IAIS, BCBS, or IOSCO, where experts linked to the state formulate specialized rules. In practice, these rules are destined to apply to supervised financial institutes. As a result, these networks play a role in organizing the public sphere at the national level, once the rules are transferred onto the states. Thus, they compete with the state authority or may cost states some of their sovereignty at both the global and national levels. However, on the other hand, such rules are not rules, standards, or codes of behaviour comparable to state ones, that is, with a claim to be universally valid within the nation-state. They are at first specialized rules for a small range of specific institutes, based on a functional differentiation.

From the point of view of the state, the traditional legislative function centred towards the state is losing significance. The classical hierarchy of norms is collapsing in the face of alternative forms of regulation. Standards are defined by transnational networks. At the same time, regulation is getting increasingly specialized and interdisciplinary.[32] To exercise their influence at the global level, states need to cooperate with each other and coordinate the policies they apply. Consequently, the role played by networks can be interpreted as causing a hollowing out of the state. There is a dislocation of state power and this process leads to a change of the nature of state power. Civil society, transnational and transgovernmental activities become more influential. However, besides the development of rules based on non-state and private initiative, it should not be overlooked that states enshrine all their capacities. In particular, the 2007–2009 financial crisis enhanced the role of the state, not least as a lender of last resort at the national level, when financing or taking over distressed banks. It underscored the importance of international coordination between states both in responding to the crisis and especially deciding on the implementation of future policies. The need to cooperate has been repeatedly reaffirmed by states representatives and is considered an essential measure to surmount that crisis. For example, the Declaration of the Summit on Financial Markets and the World Economy of the G20 states that:

> 'We are determined to enhance our cooperation and work together to restore global growth and achieve needed reforms in the world's financial systems.'[33]

Then, NGOs provide mediation work. They help creating a reasonable link between international organizations of states and civil society. Thus, they add to

---

[32] R. A. Posner, The Decline of Law as an Autonomous Discipline: 1962–1987 (1986–1987) 761–780, discussing the reasons leading to the lost of significance of state regulation; National Intelligence Council, Global Trends, supra note 6, x–xiii, 81–87.

[33] Declaration of the Summit on Financial Markets and the World Economy of the G20, 15 November 2008; see also: G-20, Communiqué, Meeting of Ministers and Governors, Sao Paulo, Brazil (8–9 November 2008); Letter of the International Monetary Fund and FSF (November 13, 2008).

the changing role of the state.[34] It is also possible to see responsible authorities or states encouraging private associations to enact rules. The ISO is a case in point where a private solution proves to be more adequate.[35] In some cases, states can remain or become even more influential when they support an institutional decentralization in their favour. Moreover, private rules are not isolated from public policies, but dependent on them. However, as far as state agencies are concerned, their role is ambivalent. They can apply their policies independently from the state and develop their activities in collaboration with the SROs, affording them considerable powers or conversely restraining their power.[36] In effect, with a view to the unlimited number of possible constellations and interdependencies between the public and private order, it is often not possible to draw a rigorous line between these regimes, public and private actors or networks.

Public–private relations evolve and change or rather can interchange. Public sector activities can be privatized and vice versa. A differentiation can also be made in relation to the regulatory role: information gathering, standard setting, or behaviour modification. Depending on the role, a regulatory regime can be both public and private. In the field of finance there is a large variety of bodies engaged in the regulatory process as well at the national level as beyond national governments and regulatory agencies. These bodies set standards which are then adopted and must be transposed into national regulatory frameworks. Prima facie, it is assumed that their activities are essentially part of a public sector process, albeit in a way they are influenced by the private sector. On the other hand, they could nonetheless be subsumed to the private sector because they are only partly acting as representative of their governments. They are experts, not accountable as such. Moreover, the political process is not directly involved in the formulation of standards and rules and states will not take position unless they adopt these new, highly specialized, and technical rules defined by experts.[37]

Besides the mechanisms leading to the specific workings of these regimes, how should one qualify their rules? Are these entirely different from state legal rules, or are they based on a sectoral approach (un-)related to state rules? Originally, private standards or rules are different from state statutes, because they emerge endogenously from prevailing industry practices, while state rules stem from exogenous public intervention.[38] State rules are laid down in the course of a political process while private standards and rules are solely motivated by practical, functional, and

[34] R. Wedgwood, Legal Personality and the Role of Non-Governmental Organizations and Non-State Political Entities in the United Nations System (1999) 21–36, 31.

[35] Chapter 3, point 6 Global Networks, 6.2 Technological Standard Setting Networks.

[36] M. Thatcher, Independent Regulatory Agencies in Europe (Summer 2005) 6–7; see also the discussion regarding the FSA by Page, supra note 30, 127–149.

[37] J. Freeman, The Private Role in Public Governance (June 2000) 543–675; Hutter, supra note 29, 3; J. Black and D. Rouch, The development of the global markets as rule-makers: engagement and legitimacy (May 2008) 226; V. Schreiber, International Standards, Neues Recht für die Weltmärkte? (2005) 137–149; Chapter 3, point 6 Global Networks.

[38] T. Padoa-Schioppa, Regulating Finance: Balancing Freedom and Risk (2004) 41–42.

technical rationales. In some sense, they actually stand for modern, dynamic, fast-track decision-making structures while state regulation could be said to be staunchly traditional and heralding stability. Although private rules may adopt different forms from a formal point of view, this aspect is not decisive. In particular, standards as a form of governance may be more significant and even more compelling than precisely defined public rules, even constitutional ones. In fact, public rules should not always be associated with hardness and private standards with softness. Both the substantive coverage and the responsible actors play a determining role. At the global level, standards may be a preferable way of regulating, because they offer flexibility and are an efficient tool to coordinate the activities of national authorities. On their part, state rule-based approaches may be mechanical formulas, unadapted to changing practical circumstances. They should be applied uniformly and are less flexible. Changes occur in the course of lengthy processes. Nevertheless, they present the considerable advantage of being enforceable.

The intent of this passage has been to point to aspects of the transformation toward private regulation. Although states keep their authority and play a determining role within the economy, their ability to deal with new, global issues is eroding. NGOs and SROs are influential. As a result, the shape public–private relations and cooperation take changes depending on the issue. At the transnational level, the role of non-state – both governmental and private – regulatory regimes is significant.[39]

3 A Process of Transformation into State Regulation

As observed, non-state, private autonomous regimes and alternative forms of regulation regularly represent a global law without the state. However, these regimes rarely appear in their pure form only. In reality, there are numerous modes of interactions, and cooperation between private and public actors and hybrid solutions frequently occur. Not that cooperation cushions the fact that these regimes also exist as such, but rather it raises questions about their relationship to the state regulatory regime. The process of constitution of autonomous regimes, their relation to state regulation, or the 'seeking of relationships', as discussed by Koskenniemi in relation to international law, highlight structural conflicts between various regimes, that is, basically between state regulation and private rules, and among private rules themselves. Fragmentation creates the danger of conflicting and incompatible rules, standards, regimes of rules and institutional practices. It reflects the rapid expansion of international and global legal activity into various new fields and the diversification of its objects and techniques. In order for the new law to be efficient, it often includes new types of treaty clauses or practices that may not be compatible

[39] National Intelligence Council, Global Trends, supra note 6, x–xiii, 81–87; P. Nobel, Gesetz, oder private Selbstregulierung? (1987) 457.

with old general rules of law or the law of some other specialized sector or branch. New rules or regimes of rules develop and deviate from what was earlier provided by the general law. When such deviations become general and frequent, the unity of law suffers.[40] For example, in the case of international law, the number of specialized tribunals simply makes for greater fragmentation. Such tribunals work against the national legal unity of application of the legal order defined at the national level. The same applies to arbitrage as a private autonomous regime. The standard proceedings can be best adapted to the economic rationality and needs of the parties concerned. Conflict arises, however, with official state rules applying to the same issues or hinders their full implementation.[41]

Here, transnationalism certainly plays a key role. However, the transnational dimension is new and unique as a regulatory concept. Transnational regimes break the hierarchy of state law and tribunals. States appear to be without appropriate instruments at that level. Transnational standards and rules, mostly private ones, are not determined in the course of a political process, but guided by economic considerations.[42] They are made valid by privately organized decision-making processes. The conceptual bonds with states rules are loosened. The implications of the appearing porosity of the national and transnational regulatory regimes are not clear. There is no official global authority; accordingly, no global political constitution in the world society exists,[43] and states are in a position to choose to support and admit hybrid or alternative regulatory measures or not. State regulation appears to be one regulatory sphere among others. This is also the case of public international law hovering between technical specialization and a need to tackle issues worldwide. International law disposes of a range of specialized regimes, like trade law or investment law, which should apply at the global level. All these orders of rules are de-politicized, bear an utilitarianist character, and are based on a law and economics approach. Efficiency is the decisive factor.[44]

One important discrepancy between rules defined by private and public regimes concerns the scope of their application. Classical state regulation reflects the developments within civil society, translating them into rules. While state statutes are declared to cover the public interest, private regulatory regimes are first shaped and destined to apply to directly interested and involved actors. They are specialized regimes. Although they may be generally recognized, they do not assert

---

[40] Koskenniemi, supra note 16, 14.

[41] M. Senn, Decentralisation of Economic Law – An Oxymoron? (October 2005) 435–437, with further references.

[42] Chapter 4, point 1 Fragmentation, 1.3 The transnational Dimension; K.-H. Ladeur, Towards a Legal Theory of Supranationality – The Viability of the Network Concept (March 1997) 33–54.

[43] N. Luhmann, Das Recht der Gesellschaft (1993) 582.

[44] Chapter 1, point 3 Public Theories of Regulation.

their claim to be universally valid.[45] For a broader public, private regulatory regimes lack transparency as far as their formation, internal procedures, and rule-making function are concerned. They face the reproach that their operations do not follow a democratic process, as stated. However, these shortcomings could be overcome through increased disclosure as a means of countering these reproaches and the challenges arising from globalization.

In relation to the state, the question is how to harness this variety of regimes. Rather than being isolated, interactions and exchanges are unavoidable. Two aspects can be distinguished: the substantive one and the technical-institutional one, meaning the question of formal linkage of the regimes. The substantive issue does not change as such. It is submitted to formalization and concretization within a regulatory regime. States are free to decide to regulate on these issues themselves or integrate existing international or global standards into their regulatory regime. In practice, this will regularly be the case. Transformation into state rules and juridification are common. However, measures taken at the national level may not be satisfactory in case a global approach would impose itself under an effectiveness point of view as indicated by the Yahoo! case discussed above.

Under a technical-institutional point of view. one resultant difficulty is the linkage between regimes and their coherence. The regimes develop different attitudes. They make legitimacy claims which are linked to their proper accountability appraisal. Furthermore, the role of the state must be redefined insofar as the concept of a state-centred approach remains the determining parameter. Institutional power is a key issue in this respect. How can states attempt to develop an approach to these multiple, divergent regimes? State law can neither simply map network structures into its concepts nor integrate all standards into a state legal regime. The rules should be reconceptualized to include a wider variety of actors and modes of governing. The state should adopt a role of broad regulatory governance. There is a challenge of meta-regulation. As discussed by Koskenniemi in relation to public international law:

> Neither of the principal legal responses to regime-formation – constitutionalism and pluralism – is adequate, however. The emergence of regimes resembles the rise of nation States in the late nineteenth century. But if nations are 'imagined communities', so are regimes. Reducing international law to a mechanism to advance functional objectives is vulnerable to the criticisms raised against thinking about it as an instrument for state policy: neither regimes nor states have a fixed nature or self-evident objectives. They are the stories we tell about them. The task for international lawyers is not to learn new managerial

[45] For instance: article 5 paragraphs 1 and 2 of the Federal Constitution of the Swiss Confederation of 18 April 1999 (SR 101), on the Rule of law states that:

1. All activities of the state shall be based on and limited by law.

2. State activities must be conducted in the public interest and be proportionate to the ends sought.

See also: M. P. Wyss, Öffentliche Interessen – Interessen der Öffentlichkeit?: das öffentliche Interesse im schweizerischen Staats- und Verwaltungsrecht (2001) 1–196; Tamanaha, supra note 21, 68–72.

vocabularies but to use the language of international law to articulate the politics of critical universalism.[46]

In relation to international law, states opt for the method of adopting international law rules based on the well-known theories.[47] A different track to link non-state regulation to state regulatory regimes is applied and encountered in specialized statutes. It consists in declaring that non-national regulatory developments have to be taken into account when regulating. This is the case of article 7 Finmasa, as stated in Chap. 4, expressly requiring that 'international minimal standards' must be observed by the supervisory authority. This implies that regulation laid down at levels other than the statute, regulation enacted by the supervisory authority, or also practices will have to take these standards into account and integrate or apply them. Indirectly, this means that these standards are implicitly recognized as being part of the body of state regulation.

A further track to link private, non-state and state regimes is to examine whether jurisprudence is able to accommodate privately written rules according to the status of publicly enforceable law. The former could be recognized through the judicial review of norms. Juridical decisions could declare them applicable; they would subsequently assume the character of state rules or be recognized as belonging to the state regulatory regime. However, they regulate relationships between non-state actors and may also represent non-state, private regulatory regimes either at the national or global level, that is, transnational law. For example, the Swiss Federal Court has already taken position by declaring that self-regulatory norms are not binding on the judge in a judgment rendered regarding the application of rules of conduct, enacted by the Swiss Bankers Association. It designed them as an 'instrument of the ethical self-regulation' whose primary role is to preserve the repute of the banking profession (article 1 CDB) and, consequently, the interest of the banks, that is, not the public interest. So, it did not recognize them.[48] Now, it remains interesting to see how the courts will deal with the issue in a future case due to the fact that self-regulation has been expressly recognized by the supervisory authority in the meantime and declared binding for all financial institutes concerned.[49] Will it review the rules of bodies whose source of power derives neither from statute nor

---

[46] M. Koskenniemi, The Fate of Public International Law: Between Technique and Politics (January 2007) 1.

[47] Chapter 4, point 2 Standardization, 2.3 Gradual Transformation, 2.3.1 From Standards to Rules.

[48] Case 125 IV 139 of 30 April 1999; see also: Case 109 Ib 146 of 3 June 1983 and Case 117 II 315 of 15 August 1991; Chapter 3, point 1 Self-Regulation, 1.3 Voluntary Codes of Conduct; on the interpretation of regulation: R. Zäch, Tendenzen der juristischen Auslegungslehre (1977) 313 et seqq.; R. Baldwin and M. Cave, Understanding Regulation, Theory, Strategy, and Practice (1999) 130–131; Black, supra note 28, 54–56.

[49] Circular of the FINMA: Self-regulation recognized as a minimum standard by the Swiss Financial Market Supervisory Authority of 20 November 2008, FINMA-Circ. 08/10 Self-regulation as minimum standard.

the prerogative where they exercise public law functions? Is there a public law element or a 'state interest'?[50]

On its side, Koskenniemi's analysis pleads for the unity of law, similarly to Dupuy. His approach focuses on 'seeking relationships' to link the different regimes centred towards the state or international law.[51] It could include examining whether jurisprudence is able to accommodate privately written rules according to the status of publicly enforceable law. However, this approach applies to regimes which deviate from the state legal system. Regimes emerging autonomously, that is, without state participation, or outside the state are not covered by his study.

Another track is soft law. The concept has been explored in detail in Chap. 2. It was concluded that such law serves as an umbrella concept, rendering self-regulation a sub- or pre-form.[52] Besides soft law, customary law represents another possibility, as discussed briefly in the same chapter. The main argument was that private autonomous regimes do not belong to the category of customary law, because they are determined by functional differentiation and are distinctive, targeted regimes applying to specific issues. In addition, the velocity of their emergence cannot be compared to the one to customary law.[53]

Yet another track is to enlarge the focus of international law. The relationship between non-state, private autonomous regimes and the state can be characterized as an interpretative conflict and a return to a coordinating form of international law could be postulated. Hence, the point is whether an approach based on the application of interpretation rules is a viable solution. In concreto, the Vienna Convention on the Law of Treaties, in particular its 'General Rule of Interpretation' could be a workable approach.[54] It may apply to hybrid forms of regulation as far as it can be linked to the state rules, but it will not be applicable to purely private autonomous regimes. The VCLT does not give any developed articulation to special kinds of regimes.

With their concept of 'Responsive Regulation', Ayres and Braithwaite develop another approach to assess regulation. They argue that neither the best regulation strategy nor the best regulation can be defined either by a uniform method nor standard assessment procedures. Instead, they adopt an attitude of responsiveness, claiming that governmental or state regulation should support the self-governance of private markets through more delegation of regulatory functions. This attitude implies that the best regulatory response to an issue depends on the context, particularities, regulatory culture, and history of a sector or subject to be

---

[50] Baldwin and Cave, supra note 48, 135.

[51] P. Marie Dupuy, L'unité de l'ordre juridique international (2002) 9–489; Koskenniemi, supra note 16, 20–25, 245.

[52] Chapter 2, point 3 Institutional Structure, 3.3 Private Regulation: From Association to Self-regulation.

[53] Chapter 2, point 1 Embedding Autonomous Regulatory Regimes, 1.3 Civil Society Approach; Koskenniemi, supra note 16, 248; Braithwaite and Drahos, supra note 28, 475–485; see also: A.-M. Slaughter, Sovereignty and Power in a Networked World Order (2004) 304; Held and Mc Grew, Goldblatt and Perraton, supra note 2, 70 et seqq.

[54] Article 31 VCLT, Section 3, Interpretation of treaties; Koskenniemi, supra note 16, 250–253.

regulated.[55] It also implies that the state recognizes alternative regulatory regimes as such. It does not try to integrate or adapt them to its rules, but rather fosters their configuration and implementation.

Not least with view to this situation, no claim is made here to a proper, definitive alternative solution to regime linkage.[56] However, it is advocated that autonomous regimes and alternative forms of regulation are not completely estranged regimes. While they rest upon a (mostly cosmopolitan) ethos, the values they represent and promote are basically similar to those represented by states and expressed in the form of rules. There is a basic consistency as far as fundamental (ethical) values are concerned. In addition, these regimes and their rules are not static, but dynamic. They evolve and adapt themselves to prevailing circumstances and due to the necessity to identify a common denominator, it can be reasonably admitted that they will converge in the course of time. A similar view is shared by Sassen, arguing that there is a move 'toward cross-border convergence of particular denationalized components' of nation-states involved.[57] Moreover, competitive pressures encourage organizations to become more similar. They will function more efficiently if they are more alike.[58] On the other hand, it should not be overlooked that even more fragmentation is to be expected of actors, regimes, rules, and approaches to regulation, due to the structural gap left by state regulatory regimes. It adds to institutional transformation. Thus, it can be advocated that another way of solving the issues of seizing and integrating regimes, will be to rethink not only the national concept of regulation, but in particular the international legal order and if possible deliberately create institutions able to cope with contemporary developments in the long run.

4 Conclusion

This chapter has represented an attempt to assess autonomous regulatory regimes and alternatives forms of regulation. The approach has focused on the following selected aspects: institutionalization, as the core issue, and the process of transformation into private and state regulation. There is an idea of governance and of shifting the balance between key institutions: the private market actors within civil society, their own representative organizations and the state. Non-state, private autonomous regimes are assessed as regimes best adapted to the challenges of transnationalism and capable of producing efficient self-regulatory solutions,

[55] I. Ayres and J. Braithwaite, Responsive Regulation, Transcending the Deregulation Debate (1992) 4–5, 17.

[56] National Intelligence Council, Global Trends, supra note 6, x-xiii, 81 et seqq.

[57] Berman also supports the convergence approach. Berman, supra note 15, 518–526; Sassen, supra note 2, 390.

[58] S. D. Krasner, Power politics, institutions, and transnational relations (1995) 261.

operating in the vacuum of state intervention. In practice, a great number of regulatory arrangements exist, often involving both the state and private industry.

While there is no general dichotomy between state or international law and regulation defined by private autonomous regulatory regimes or networks, given the fact that they are based on the same ethos, there are varying degrees of legal characteristics, varying degrees of impact, varying degrees of legitimate power. The question of linkage of these regimes or networks to the state regulatory regime needs to be solved. It is assumed that these various regimes will tend towards some alignment in the long run. At the same time, the institutional structure will have to be rethought.

Conclusion

The study has intended to explore the concept of regulation in a broad sense. The main task has been to identify regulation amid various regulatory orders. Regulation has been identified not only as the domain of the state, but also covering non-state regulation and regulation defined by civil society actors. Discussion has focused on both public and private ordering. The features of non-state and private autonomous regulatory regimes and alternative forms of regulation have been analyzed with a view to elucidating these regimes. The approach was interdisciplinary, including legal, economic, political, international relations, and sociological perspectives. Building on a theoretical framework, the characteristics of a broader concept of state regulation were introduced, before delineating a hypothetical path to explain the emergence of these regimes. From enlarging the concept of state regulation – based on the traditional approach to regulation and state strategies – through the decentred analysis of regulation, discussion subsequently moved to civil society and non-state regulation. The institutional structure of these alternative forms of regulation was considered. Various practical cases served to illustrate the theoretical debate, each representing another form of non-state regulation, co-opted regulation, or state regulation.

Based on the findings of the preliminary discussion, which delineated the concept of autonomous regulatory regimes and alternative forms of regulation, analysis has focused on two main features: fragmentation and the mechanisms of standardization. Addressing these features poses diverse challenges, in particular regarding the nature of autonomous regulatory regimes and their relation to the state. It has also been noted that in reality a number of hybrid forms of state and private regulation exist. The regulatory framework is a complex conglomerate of rules at the national, international, transnational, and global level. What distinguishes non-state and private autonomous regulatory regimes from traditional forms of regulation is their transnational character, their origin in civil society, and their focus on efficiency. Contrary to state regulation, politics is not directly determining. Although such regimes present an issue of enforcement, they have a history of working effectively. Their impact is significant. One important challenge is to determine a path or mechanisms to link them to state regulation to ensure coexistence. Besides states increasingly assuming a role of governance, these regimes can be expected to adjust to each other in the course of time.

M. Senn, *Non-State Regulatory Regimes*,
DOI 10.1007/978-3-642-14974-0, © Springer-Verlag Berlin Heidelberg 2011

In summary, this study concludes that the diverse regulatory regimes are not completely estranged. Adopting a holistic approach allows for establishing more reliable means to assess the issue. It helps embed and link them to other forms of regulation, in particular state regulation. This study thus contributes to an existing mosaic of essays exploring regulatory issues. It has highlighted key avenues for future research on non-state, autonomous regulatory regimes. The challenge will be to continue to refine this integrative, all-embracing concept of regulation. It enhances institutional changes occurring in the course of the process of gradual refinement and transformation of regulatory regimes.

Bibliography

ABBOTT Kenneth W., Toward a Richer Institutionalism for International Law and Policy, in: Journal of International Law & International Relations, Volume 1 (2005) 9–34.
ABBOTT Kenneth W., SNIDAL Duncan, The International Standards Process: Setting and Applying Global Business Norms, in: Nobel Peter, ed., International Standards and the Law (Stämpfli Verlag AG, Bern, 2005) 105–142.
ABEGG Andreas, Regulierung hybrider Netzwerke im Schnittpunkt von Wirtschaft und Politik in: Kritische Vierteljahresschrift (KritV) Nr. 2–3, 89. Jahrgang (2006) 266–290.
ADLER Matthew D., Beyond Efficiency and Procedure: A Welfarist Theory of Regulation, in: 28 Florida State University Law Review (Fall 2000) 241–338.
ALBERT Mathias, LEHMKUHL Dirk, Einleitung: Transnationales Recht, in: Zeitschrift für Rechtssoziologie, Schwerpunktheft Transnationales Recht, Jahrgang 23, Heft 2 (2002) 159–164.
ALBERT Mathias, STICHWEH Rudolf, eds, Weltstaat und Weltstaatlichkeit, Beobachtungen globaler politischer Strukturbildung nach der Globalisierung (VS Verlag für Sozialwissenschaften, Wiesbaden, 2007).
Alternatives to State Regulation, Better Regulation Task Force (July 2000).
AMSTUTZ Marc, The Constitution of Contractual Networks, in: AMSTUTZ Marc, TEUBNER Gunther, Networks, Legal Issues of Multilateral Co-operation (Hart Publishing, Oxford and Portland, 2009), 309–346.
AMSTUTZ Marc, TEUBNER Gunther, Networks, Legal Issues of Multilateral Co-operation (Hart Publishing, Oxford and Portland, 2009).
ARNER Douglas W., Financial Stability, Economic Growth, and the Role of Law (Cambridge: Cambridge University Press, 2007).
AUBRY Jean-Bernard, La globalisation, le droit et l'Etat (Montchrestien, collection Clefs Politique, Paris, 2003).
AVIRAM Amitai, A Network Effects Analysis of Private Ordering, Berkeley Program in Law & Economics, Working Paper Series, Paper 80 (2003).
AXELROD Robert and KEOHANE Robert O., Achieving Cooperation under Anarchy: Strategies and Institutions, in: Oye Kenneth A., ed., Cooperation under Anarchy (Princeton: Princeton University Press, 1986) 226–254.
AYRES Ian and BRAITHWAITE John, Responsive Regulation: Transcending the Deregulation Debate (Oxford Socio-Legal Studies, Oxford, 1992).
BALDWIN Robert, Rules and Government (Clarendon Press Oxford, 1995).
BALDWIN, Robert Why Rules Don't Work, in: The Modern Law Review, Volume 53, No 3, (1990) 321–337.
BALDWIN Robert and CAVE Martin, Understanding Regulation, Theory, Strategy, and Practice (Oxford: Oxford University Press, 1999).
BARNHOORN L.A.N.M. and WELLENS Karel, eds, Diversity in Secondary Rules and the Unity of International Law (T.M.C. Asser Institute, The Hague, Nijhoff, 1995).

BARRETT Scott, Creating Incentives for Cooperation: Strategic Choices, in: Kaul Inge, Conceicao Pedro, Goulven Katell Le, Mendoza Ronald U., eds, Providing Global Public Goods, Managing Globalization (Oxford: Oxford University Press, 2003) 308–328.

BARTELT Guido, Regulatorische Marktinterventionen – Ansätze zu einer Theorie regulatorischer Marktintervention als Grundlage zur Beurteilung ihrer Effizienz, Diss. No. 1061 (St.Gallen, 1989).

Basel Committee on Banking Supervision, BCBS, International Convergence of Capital Measurement and Capital Standards, A Revised Framework, Basel Committee on Banking Supervision (BCBS), Bank for International Settlements (BIS) (June 2004).

BAUDENBACHER Carl, Globalisierung und Regionalisierung des Wirtschaftsrechts, in: Internationales und Europäisches Wirtschaftsrecht, Band I, St.Gallen, 2004.

BAUDENBACHER Carl and HIGGINS Imelda, Decentralisation of EC competition law enforcement and arbitration, in: 8 Columbia Journal of European Law (Winter 2002) 1–18.

BAYNE Nicholas, Hard and Soft Law in International Institutions: Complements, Not Alternatives, in: Kirton John J., Trebilcock Michael J., eds, Hard Choices, Soft Law, Voluntary Standards in Global Trade, Environment and Social Governance (Ashgate, Aldershot, 2004) 336–352.

BECK Ulrich, Was ist Globalisierung (Suhrkamp, Frankfurt am Main, 2007).

BECKERT Jens, EBBINGHAUS Bernhard, HASSEL Anke, MANOW Philip, ed., Transformationen des Kapitalismus, Festschrift für Wolfgang Streeck zum sechzigsten Geburtstag (Campus Verlag, Frankfurt/New York, 2006).

BENJAMIN Joanna, Financial Law (Oxford: Oxford University Press, 2007).

BENJAMIN Joanna, Sources of legal risk for financial institutions, in: Journal of International Banking and Financial Law Special Supplement (April 2004) Appendix 1, 18–29.

BENJAMIN Joanna and ROUCH David, The International Financial Markets as a Source of Global Law: The Privatisation of Rule-making?, in: Law and Financial Markets Review, Volume 2, No. 2 (March 2008) 78–86.

BENTHAM Jeremy, An Introduction to the Principles of Morals and Legislation, ed. J.H Burns and H.L.A. Hart (Clarendon Press, Oxford, 1996).

BENZ Arthur and PAPADOPOULOS Yannis, eds, Governance and Democracy, Comparing national European and international experiences (Routledge, London, 2006).

BERG Albert Jan, van den, The New York Arbitration Convention of 1958, Deventer/Boston, 1994; Guide to ICC arbitration (ICC Publishing, ICC Publication No. 448, 1994).

BERLE Adolph A. and MEANS Gardiner C., The Modern Corporation and Private Property (Transaction Publisher, 1991).

BERMAN Paul Schiff, From International Law to Law and Globalization, in: Columbia Journal of Transnational Law, Volume 43 (2005) 485–556.

BERMAN Paul Schiff, Globalization of Jurisdiction, in: University of Pennsylvania Law Review, Volume 151, No. 2 (2002) 311–529.

BERNSTEIN Steven and CASHORE Benjamin, Can Non-State Global Governance be Legitimate? An Analytical Framework, in: Regulation & Governance, no. 1 (2007) 347–371.

BEYERLIN Ulrich, BOTHE Michael, HOFMANN Rainer, PETERSMANN Ernst-Ulrich, eds, Recht zwischen Umbruch und Bewahrung: Völkerrecht – Europarecht – Staatsrecht, Festschrift für Rudolf Bernhardt (Band 120 Springer, Heidelberg, 1995).

BIERSTEKER Thomas J. and HALL Rodney Bruce, Private authority as global governance, in: Hall Rodney Bruce and Biersteker Thomas J., eds, The Emergence of Private Authority in Global Governance (Cambridge Studies in International Relations, No. 85, Cambridge University Press, 2002) 203–222.

BIGNAMI Francesca E., Transgovernmental Networks vs. Democracy: The Case of the European Information Privacy Network, in: Michigan Journal of International Law 26 (2005) 807–868.

BLACK Antony, Guild & State, European Political Thought from the Twelfth Century to the Present (Transaction Publishers, New Brunswick and London, 2003).

Black Antony, Individuals, Groups and States: A Comparative Overview, in: The Individual in Political Theory and Practice, Janet Coleman, ed., European Science Foundation (Clarendon Press, 1996) 329–340.

Black Julia, Constitutionalising Self-Regulation, in: The Modern Law Review, Volume 59, (1996) 24–55.

Black Julia, Constructing and contesting legitimacy and accountability in polycentric regulatory regimes, in: Regulation & Governance, Volume 2, Issue 2 (June 2008) 137–164.

Black Julia, Critical Reflections on Regulation, Discussion Paper No: 4, ESRC Centre for Analysis of Risk and Regulation, London School of Economics and Political Science (January 2002).

Black Julia, Decentring Regulation: Understanding the Role of Regulation and Self-Regulation in a 'Post-regulatory' World, in: Current Legal Problems, Volume 54 (2001) 103–146.

Black Julia, Law and Regulation: The Case of Finance, in: Parker Christine, Colin Scott, Nicola Lacey, and John Braithwaite, eds, Regulating Law (Oxford University Press, 2004) 33–59.

Black Julia, Rules and Regulators (Clarendon Press, Oxford, 1997).

Black Julia, The Decentred Regulatory State?, in: Peter Vass, ed., 2006–7, in: CRI Regulatory Review (Centre for Regulated Industries, University of Bath, 2007) 249–290.

Black Julia, The development of risk-based regulation in financial services: just 'modelling through'?, in: Julia Black, Martin Lodge, and Mark Thatcher, eds, Regulatory Innovation, A Comparative Analysis (Edward Elgar, Cheltenham, Northampton, 2005) 156–180.

Black Julia, Lodge Martin, and Thatcher Mark, eds, Regulatory Innovation, A Comparative Analysis (Edward Elgar, Cheltenham, Northampton, 2005).

Black Julia, Rouch David, The development of the global markets as rule-makers: engagement and legitimacy, in: Law and Financial Markets Review, Volume 2, Issue 3 (May 2008) 218–233.

Blair Michael QC and Walker George, eds., Financial Markets and Exchanges Law (Oxford: Oxford University Press, 2007).

Blair William, Interference of Public Law in the Performance of International Monetary Obligations, in: Giovanoli Mario, ed., International Monetary Law, Issues for the New Millennium (Oxford: Oxford University Press, 2000) 395–412.

Böckli Peter, Harte Stellen im Soft Law, Zum Swiss Code of Best Practice for Corporate Governance, in: Der Schweizer Treuhänder, Nr. 11 (2002) 981–996.

Böckli Peter, Neun Regeln der "Best Practice" für den Rückkauf nichtkotierter eigener Aktien, in: Der Schweizer Treuhänder, Nr. 6–7 (2001) 575–586.

Böckli Peter, Zum Börsengesetz von 1995: neue Rechtsinstitute und neue Probleme, in: Basler Juristische Mitteilungen, Nr. 5 (1998) 225–271.

Boddewyn J. J., Advertising self-regulation: organization structures in Belgium, Canada, France and the United Kingdom, in: Wolfgang Streeck and Philippe C. Schmitter, eds, Private Interest Government, Beyond Market and State (Sage Series in Neo-Corporatism, London, 1985) 30–43.

Born Gary, International commercial arbitration in the United States: commentary and materials (Deventer/Boston, 1994).

Borrie Gordon, The Regulation of Public and Private Power, in: Public Law (1989) 552–567.

Botschaft des Bundesrates an die Bundesversammlung betreffend den Entwurf eines Bundesgesetzes über die Banken und Sparkassen vom 2. Februar 1934, BBl 1934 I 179.

Botschaft über eine neue Bundesverfassung vom 20. November 1996 und Verfassungsentwurf 1996, Bundesblatt 149. Jahrgang, BBl 1997 I 1-642.

Botschaft zur Änderung des Obligationenrechts (Transparenz betreffend Vergütungen an Mitglieder des Verwaltungsrates und der Geschäftsleitung) vom 23. Juni 2004, BBl Nr. 30, 3 August 2004, 4471–4493.

Botschaft zur Änderung des Obligationenrechts (Aktienrecht und Rechnungslegungsrecht sowie Anpassungen im Recht der Kollektiv- und der Kommanditgesellschaft, im GmbH-Recht,

Genossenschafts-, Handelsregister- sowie Firmenrecht) vom 21. Dezember 2007, BBl Nr. 11 (18 March 2008) 1589–1750.

BOVENS Mark, Analysing and Assessing Accountability: A Conceptual Framework, in: European Law Journal, Volume 13, No. 4 (July 2007) 447–468.

BOYER Robert and SAILLARD Yves, eds, Théorie de la régulation, l'état des savoirs (La Découverte, Paris, 2002).

BOYLE Alan, Soft Law in International Law-Making, in: Evans Malcolm D., International Law, (2nd ed., Oxford: Oxford University Press, 2006) 141–158.

BRAITHWAITE John, Enforced self-regulation: A new strategy for corporate crime control, in: Michigan Law Review, Volume 80 (June 1982) 1466–1507.

BRAITHWAITE John, Neoliberalism or Regulatory Capitalism, Occasional Paper 5, Regulatory Institutions Network, ANU (October 2005).

BRAITHWAITE John, Regulatory Capitalism, How it works, ideas for making it work better (Edward Elgar, Cheltenham, Northampton, 2008).

BRAITHWAITE John, and Drahos Peter, Global Business Regulation (Cambridge: Cambridge University Press, 2000).

BREYER Stephen, Regulation and Its Reform (Harvard University Press, Cambridge MA, 1982).

BRÖLMANN Catherine, Deterritorialization in International Law: Moving Away from the Divide Between National and International Law, in: Nijman Janne and Nollkaemper André, eds, New Perspectives on the Divide Between National and International Law (Oxford: Oxford University Press, 2007) 84–109.

BRUNSSON Nils and JACOBSSON Bengt and Associates, A World of Standards (Oxford: Oxford University Press, 2000).

BUCHANAN M. James and GORDON Tullock, The Calculus of Consent: Logical Foundations of Constitutional Democracy (Ann Arbor Paperbacks, 1962).

BURCHELL Graham, GORDON Colin and MILLER Peter, eds, The Foucault Effect, Studies in Governmentality, with two lectures by and an interview with Michel Foucault, Gordon (The University of Chicago Press, Chicago, 1991).

BURKE-WHITE William W., International Legal Pluralism, in: Michigan Journal of International Law, Volume 25 (2004) 963–979.

BUTLER Henry N. and RIBSTEIN Larry E., The Sarbanes-Oxley Debacle, What We've Learned; How to Fix It (The AEI Press, Washington, D.C., 2006).

BYERS Michael, ed., The Role of Law in International Politics, Essays in International Relations and International Law (Oxford: Oxford University Press, 2000).

CAFAGGI Fabrizio, ed., Reframing Self-Regulation in European Private Law (Kluwer Law International, Alphen aan den Rijn, The Netherlands, 2006).

CALLIESS Gralf-Peter, FREILING Jörg, and RENNER Moritz, Law, the State, and Private Ordering: Evolutionary Explanations of Institutional Change, in: German Law Journal, Volume 9, No. 4 (2008) 397–410.

CANE Peter, Self-Regulation and Judicial Review, in: 6 Civil Justice Quarterly (1987) 324–347.

CARLSNAES Walter, RISSE Thomas, and SIMMONS Beth A., eds, Handbook of International Relations (Thousand Oaks, CA: Sage Publications, 2002).

CASSESE Sabino, Administrative Law without the State? The Challenge of Global Regulation, in: New York University Journal of International Law and Politics, Volume 37, Number 4 (2005) 663–694.

CASSESE Sabino, The Globalization of Law, in: Journal of International Law and Politics, Volume 37, Number 4 (2005) 973–993.

CAWSON Alan, ed., Organized Interests and the State, Studies in Meso-Corporatism (Sage Publications, London, 1985).

CHAYES Abram and HANDLER CHAYES Antonia, Compliance Without Enforcement: State Behavior Under Regulatory Treaties, in: Negotiation Journal, Volume 7, Number 1 (January 1991) 311–330.

CHAYES Abram and HANDLER CHAYES Antonia, The New Sovereignty, Compliance with International Regulatory Agreements (Harvard University Press, Cambridge, London, 1995).

CHEMILLIER-GENDREAU Monique and MOULIER-BOUTANG Yann, Le droit dans la mondialisation, Une perspective critique (Presses Universitaires de France, Paris, 2001).

CHEY Hyoung-Kyu, Do markets enhance convergence on international standards? The case of financial regulation, in: Regulation & Governance (2007) no. 1, 295–311.

CHINKIN Christine, A Critique of the Public/Private Dimension, in: European Journal of International Law, Volume 10 (1999) 387–395.

CHINKIN Christine, Monism and Dualism: The Impact of Private Authority on the Dichotomy Between National and International Law, in: Nijman Janne and Nollkaemper André, eds, New Perspectives on the Divide Between National and International Law (Oxford: Oxford University Press, 2007) 134–162.

CLOGHESY Michael E., A Corporate Perspective on Globalisation, Sustainable Development, and Soft Law, in: John J. Kirton, Michael J. Trebilcock, eds, Hard Choices Soft Law, Voluntary Standards in Global Trade, Environment and Social Governance (Ashgate, Aldershot, 2004) 323–328.

COASE Ronald H., The Nature of the Firm, in: Economica, Volume 4 (1937) 386–405.

COFFEE John C., Gatekeepers, The Role of the Professions in Corporate Governance (Oxford: Oxford University Press, 2006).

COFFEE John C., Law and the Market: The Impact of Enforcement, in: University of Pennsylvania Law Review, Volume 156, No. 2 (December 2007) 229–311.

COGLIANESE Cary and KAGAN Robert A., eds, Regulation and Regulatory Processes (The International Library of Essays in Law and Society, Aldershot, Ashgate, 2007).

COGLIANESE Cary and LAZER David, Management-Based Regulation: Prescribing Private Management to Achieve Public Goals; in: Coglianese Cary and Kagan Robert A., eds, Regulation and Regulatory Processes (The International Library of Essays in Law and Society, Aldershot, Ashgate, 2007) 423–462.

COGLIANESE Cary, NASH Jennifer, and OLMSTEAD Todd, Performance-Based Regulation: Prospects and Limitations in Health, Safety and Environmental Protection, RWP02-050 (John F. Kennedy School of Government, Harvard University, Faculty Research Working Papers Series, December 2002).

COLEMAN Janet, ed., The Individual in Political Theory and Practice (European Science Foundation, Clarendon Press, 1996).

Commission on Global Governance, Our Global Neighborhood: The Report of the Commission on Global Governance (Oxford: Oxford University Press, 1995).

Committee on the Global Financial System (CGFS), The role of ratings in structured finance: issues and implications in 2005 (CGFS Publications, No 23, January 2005).

Conclusions of the work of the Study Group on the Fragmentation of International Law: Difficulties arising from the Diversification and Expansion of International Law (United Nations, 2006).

COTRAN Eugene and AMISSAH Austin, eds, Arbitration in Africa (The Hague and Boston, Kluwer Law International, 1996).

CRAGG Wesley, Multinational Corporations, Globalisation, and the Challenge of Self-Regulation, in: Hard Choices, Soft Law, Voluntary Standards in Global Trade, Environment and Social Governance, John J. Kirton, Michael J. Trebilcock, eds (Ashgate, Aldershot, 2004) 213–227.

CUTLER Claire A., Private international regimes and interfirm cooperation, in: Rodney Bruce Hall and Thomas J. Biersteker, eds, The Emergence of Private Authority in Global Governance, Cambridge Studies in International Relations, No. 85 (Cambridge: Cambridge University Press, 2002) 23–40.

CUTLER Claire A., HAUFLER Virginia, and PORTER Tony, eds, Private Authority and International Affairs (State University of New York Press, 1999).

CUTLER Claire A., HAUFLER Virginia, and PORTER Tony, Private Authority and International Affairs, in: Cutler Claire A., Haufler Virginia, and Tony Porter, eds, Private Authority and International Affairs (State University of New York Press, 1999) 3–28.

CUTLER Claire A., HAUFLER Virginia, and PORTER Tony, The Contours and Significance of Private Authority in International Affairs, in: Cutler Claire A., Haufler Virginia, and Tony Porter, eds, Private Authority and International Affairs (State University of New York Press, 1999) 333–376.

DAVIES Howard, Designing a system of financial regulation, Peking University, Beijing, Lecture (20 June 2006).

DAVIES Howard, Reforming Financial Regulation: Progress and Priorities, in: Ferran Eilis and Goodhart Charles A. E., eds, Regulating Financial Services and Markets in the Twenty First Century (Hart Publishing, Oxford, 2001) 17–24.

DAVIES Howard and Green David, Global Financial Regulation, The Essential Guide (Polity, Cambridge, Malden, 2008).

Declaration of the Summit on Financial Markets and the World Economy of the G20 (15 November 2008).

DEAKIN Simon, The Return of The Guild? Network Relations in Historical Perspective, in: AMSTUTZ Marc, TEUBNER Gunther, Networks, Legal Issues of Multilateral Co-operation (Hart Publishing, Oxford and Portland, 2009), 53–73.

DELBRÜCK Jost, Exercising Public Authority Beyond the State: Transnational Democracy and/or Alternative Legitimation Strategies?, in: Indiana Journal of Global Legal Studies, Volume 10 (2003) 29–43.

DELBRÜCK Jost, The Role of the United Nations in Dealing with Global Problems, in: Indiana Journal of Global Legal Studies, Volume 4 (1997) 277–296.

DE MINICO Giovanna, A Hard Look at Self-Regulation in the UK, in: European Business Law Review, Volume 17, No. 1 (2006) 183–211.

DIMAGGIO Paul J. and POWELL Walter W., Introduction, in: Powell Walter W. and DiMaggio Paul J., The New Institutionalism in Organizational Analysis (The University of Chicago Press, Chicago and London, 1991) 1–38.

DJELIC Marie-Laure and SAHLIN-ANDERSSON Kerstin, eds, Transnational Governance, Institutional Dynamics of Regulation (Cambridge: Cambridge University Press, 2006).

DJELIC Marie-Laure and SAHLIN-ANDERSSON Kerstin, Introduction: A world of governance: The rise of transnational regulation, in: Djelic Marie-Laure and Sahlin-Andersson Kerstin, eds, Transnational Governance, Institutional Dynamics of Regulation (Cambridge: Cambridge University Press, 2006) 1–28.

DRAHOS Peter, The regulation of public goods, in: Journal of International Economic Law, Volume 7, Issue 2 (2004) 321–339.

DUPUY Pierre Marie, L'unité de l'ordre juridique international, Cours général de droit international public (2000) Recueil des cours, Volume 297 (2002) 9–489.

Economist, The, Hungry tiger, dancing elephant, How India is changing IBM's world (April 7th 2007) 65–67.

Economist, The, Regulating business, The trial of Sarbanes-Oxley (April 22nd 2006) 59–60.

Economist, The, Regulating the professions, Taking care of their own (December 18th, 2004) 62, 64.

ENGWALL Lars, Global enterprises in fields of governance, in: Djelic Marie-Laure and Sahlin-Andersson Kerstin, eds, Transnational Governance, Institutional Dynamics of Regulation (Cambridge: Cambridge University Press, 2006) 161–179.

ERRASS Christoph, Kooperative Rechtssetzung (Dike Verlag AG, Zürich/St.Gallen, 2010).

EVANS Malcolm D., International Law, 2nd ed. (Oxford University Press, Oxford, 2006).

Federal Finance Administration FFA, Federal Banking Commission, Federal Office of Private Insurance FOPI, Guidelines for Financial Market Regulation (Bern, September 2005).

FEHR Ernst, FISCHBACHER Urs, Social norms and human cooperation, in: Trends in Cognitive Sciences, Volume 8, No. 4 (April 2004) 185–190.

FEINTUCK Mike, 'The Public Interest' in Regulation (Oxford: Oxford University Press, 2004).

FERGUSON Adam, An Essay on the History of Civil Society (1767) http://www.constitution.org/af/civil.htm.

FERRAN Eilis and GOODHART Charles A. E., eds, Regulating Financial Services and Markets in the Twenty First Century (Hart Publishing, Oxford, 2001).

FERRARINI Guido A., Origins of Limited Liability Companies and Company Law Modernisation in Italy: A Historical Outline, in: Gepken-Jager Ella, van Solinge Gerard, Timmerman Levinus, eds, VOC 1602-2002 400 Years of Company Law, Law of Business and Finance, Volume 6 (Kluwer Legal Publishers, 2005) 189–215.

Financial Services Authority, Newsletter of the FSA (January 2006) FSA, Reviewing our Money Laundering Regime PS06/1.

Financial Services Authority, Principles-based regulation, Focusing on the outcomes that matter, FSA (April 2007).

Financial Stability Forum, Report of the Financial Stability Forum on Enhancing Market and Institutional Resilience (7 April 2008).

FISCHER-LESCANO Andreas and TEUBNER Gunther, Fragmentierung des Weltrechts: Vernetzung globaler Regimes statt etatistischer Rechtseinheit, in: Mathias Albert, Rudolf Stichweh, eds, Weltstaat und Weltstaatlichkeit, Beobachtungen globaler politischer Strukturbildung nach der Globalisierung (VS Verlag für Sozialwissenschaften, Wiesbaden, 2007) 37–61.

FISCHER-LESCANO Andreas and TEUBNER Gunther, Regime-collisions: The vain search for legal unity in the fragmentation of global law, in: Michigan Journal of International Law, Volume 25 (Summer 2004) 999–1046.

FISCHER-LESCANO Andreas and TEUBNER Gunther, Regime-Kollisionen, Zur Fragmentierung des globalen Rechts (Suhrkamp, Frankfurt am Main, 2006).

FLETCHER George P., Basic Concepts of Legal Thought (Oxford: Oxford University Press, 1996).

FLORINI Ann M., Who does what? Collective action and the changing nature of authority, in: Higgott Richard A., Underhill Geoffrey R. D., and Bieler Andreas, eds, Non-State Actors and Authority in the Global System (Routledge, London and New York, 2000) 15–31.

FÖGEN Marie Theres, Geschichte der Evolution eines sozialen Systems, in: Jusletter (24 March 2003).

FOLLAK Klaus Peter, International Harmonization of Regulatory and Supervisory Frameworks, in: Giovanoli Mario, ed., International Monetary Law, Issues for the New Millennium (Oxford: Oxford University Press, 2000) 291–322.

FOUCAULT Michel, Naissance de la biopolitique, Cours au Collège de France (1978–1979), Ewald François, Fontana Alessandro, Michel Senellart, eds, Hautes Etudes (Gallimard, Seuil, Lonrai, 2004).

FRANCK Thomas M., Fairness in International Law and Institutions (Clarendon Press, Oxford, 1995).

FREEMAN Jody, The Private Role in Public Governance, in: New York University Law Review, Volume 75, Number 3 (June 2000) 543–675.

FRIEDLAND Roger and ALFORD Robert R., Bringing Society Back In: Symbols, Practices, and Institutional Contradictions, in: Walter W. Powell and Paul J. DiMaggio, The New Institutionalism in Organizational Analysis, The University of Chicago Press, Chicago and London, 1991, 232–263.

FRIEDLI Georg, Übersicht über die Praxis der Aufsichtskommission zur Sorgfaltspflicht der Banken 1998–2001, in: Swiss Review of Business Law, no. 3, 2002, 165–184.

FRIEDMANN Wolfgang, HENKIN Louis and LISSITZYN Oliver, ed., Transnational Law in a Changing Society, Essays in Honor of Philip C. Jessup (Columbia University Press, New York and London, 1972).

G-20, Communiqué, Meeting of Ministers and Governors (Sao Paulo, Brazil, 8–9 November 2008).

GASSER Urs, Regulating Search Engines: Taking Stock and Looking Ahead, in: Yale Journal of Law & Technology (Spring 2006) 124–157.

GEISS Robin, Non-State Actors: Their Role and Impact on the Fragmentation of International Law, in: Zimmermann Andreas and Hofmann Rainer, eds, Unity and Diversity in International Law, Proceeding of an International Symposium of the Kiel Walther Schücking Institute of International Law November 4–7, 2004 (Duncker & Humblot, Berlin, 2006) 303–327.

GEPKEN-JAGER Ella, VAN SOLINGE Gerard, TIMMERMAN Levinus, eds, VOC 1602-2002 400 Years of Company Law, Law of Business and Finance, Volume 6 (Kluwer Legal Publishers, 2005).

GEPKEN-JAGER Ella, VAN SOLINGE Gerard, TIMMERMAN Levinus, Verenigde Oost-Indische Compagnie (VOC), The Dutch East India Company, in: Gepken-Jager Ella, van Solinge Gerard, Timmerman Levinus, eds, VOC 1602-2002 400 Years of Company Law, Law of Business and Finance, Volume 6 (Kluwer Legal Publishers, 2005) 41–81.

GHARAVI Hamid G., The proper scope of arbitration in European Community competition law, Tulane European and Civil Law Forum (Winter 1996) 185–205.

GIDDENS Anthony, The Consequences of Modernity (Stanford: Stanford University Press, 1990).

GIDDENS Anthony, The Constitution of Society, Outline of the Theory of Structuration (Polity, Press, 1984).

GIERKE Otto von, Das Deutsche Genossenschaftsrecht, Akademische Druck, Band I-IV, 1. Auflage Berlin 1868 (Neudruck Verlagsanstalt, Graz, 1954).

GIERKE Otto von, Die Grundbegriffe des Staatsrechts, Naturrecht und deutsches Recht, Die historische Rechtsschule und die Germanisten (1903, Scientia Verlag Aalen, Berlin, Neudruck 1973).

GIOVANOLI Mario, A new architecture for the global financial market: legal aspects of international financial standard setting, in: Mario Giovanoli, ed., International Monetary Law, Issues for the New Millennium (Oxford: Oxford University Press, 2000) 3–59.

GIOVANOLI Mario, ed., International Monetary Law, Issues for the New Millennium (Oxford: Oxford University Press, 2000).

GORDON Colin, Governmental rationality: an introduction, in: Burchell Graham, Gordon Colin and Miller Peter, eds, The Foucault Effect, Studies in Governmentality, with two lectures by and an interview with Michel Foucault, Gordon (The University of Chicago Press, Chicago, 1991) 1–51.

GOSEWINKEL Dieter, MERKEL Wolfgang and SIMON Dagmar, ed., Unternehmen, Staat, Globalisierung: Festschrift für Jürgen Kocka (2007).

GRABOSKY Peter N., Using Non-Governmental Resources to Foster Regulatory Compliance, in: Governance: An International Journal of Policy and Administration, Volume 8, No. 4 (October 1995) 527–550.

GRANOVETTER Mark, Economic Action and Social Structure: The Problem of Embeddedness, in: American Journal of Sociology, Volume 91, Issue 3 (1985) 481–510.

GREIF Avner, Institutions and the Path to the Modern Economy, Lessons from Medieval Trade (Cambridge: Cambridge University Press, 2006).

GRIFFITHS John, What is Legal Pluralism?, in: Journal of Legal Pluralism, Nr. 24 (1986) 1–55.

GRUNER Erich, Der Einbau der organisierten Interessen in den Staat, in: Schweizerische Zeitschrift für Volkswirtschaft und Statistik, Volume 95 (1959) 59–79.

GRUNER Erich, Die Wirtschaftsverbände in der Demokratie, Vom Wachstum der Wirtschaftsorganisationen im schweizerischen Staat (Eugen Rentsch Verlag, Erlenbach-Zurich und Stuttgart, 1956).

GRUNER Erich, Wirtschaftsverbände und Staat, Das Problem der wirtschaftlichen Interessenvertretung in historischer Sicht, in: Schweizerische Zeitschrift für Volkswirtschaft und Statistik, Volume 90 (1954) 1–27.

GUNNINGHAM Neil, Environment, Self-Regulation, and the Chemical Industry: Assessing Responsible Care, in: Law and Policy, Volume 17, Issue 1 (1995) 57–109.

GUNNINGHAM Neil and REES Joseph, Industry Self-Regulation: An Institutional Perspective, in: Law & Policy, Volume 19, Issue 4 (1997) 363–414.

HAAS Peter M., Introduction: Epistemic Communities and International Policy Coordination, in: International Organization, Volume 46, No. 1 (Winter 1992) 1–35.

HAGGARD Stephan and SIMMONS Beth A., Theories of International Regimes, in: International Organization, Volume 41, No. 3 (Summer 1987) 491–517.

HALL Rodney Bruce and BIERSTEKER Thomas J., eds, The Emergence of Private Authority in Global Governance, Cambridge Studies in International Relations, No. 85 (Cambridge: Cambridge University Press, 2002).

HALL Rodney Bruce and BIERSTEKER Thomas J., The emergence of private authority in the international system, in: Hall Rodney Bruce and Biersteker Thomas J., eds, The Emergence of Private Authority in Global Governance, Cambridge Studies in International Relations, No. 85 (Cambridge: Cambridge University Press, 2002) 3–22.

HAMANN Andrea, RUIZ FABRI Hélène, Transnational networks and constitutionalism, in: International Journal of Constitutional Law, Volume 6, No 3–4 (2008) 481–508.

HANCHER Leigh and MORAN Michael, eds, Capitalism, Culture, and Economic Regulation (Oxford: Oxford University Press, 1989).

HANCHER Leigh and MORAN Michael, Organizing Regulatory Space, in: Hancher and Moran, eds, Capitalism, Culture, and Economic Regulation (Oxford: Oxford University Press, 1989) 271–299.

HARRISON Jeffrey L., MORGAN Thomas D., VERKUIL Paul R., Regulation and Deregulation, Cases and Materials, American Casebook Series (West Publishing Co., St.Paul, Minnesota, 2nd ed., 2004).

HART H. L. A., Herbert Lionel Adolphus, The Concept of Law, 2nd ed., Clarendon Law Series (Oxford: Oxford University Press, 1997).

HAUFLER Virginia, Private sector international regimes, in: Higgott Richard A., Underhill Geoffrey R. D., and Bieler Andreas, eds, Non-State Actors and Authority in the Global System (Routledge, London and New York, 2000) 121–137.

HAUFLER Virginia, Self-Regulation and Business Norms: Political Risk, Political Activism, in: Cutler Claire A., Haufler Virginia, and Tony Porter, eds, Private Authority and International Affairs (State University of New York Press, 1999) 199–221.

HELD David, Democracy and the Global Order: From the Modern State to Cosmopolitan Governance (Cambridge, Polity Press, 1995).

HELD David, Reframing Global Governance: Apocalypse Soon or Reform!, in: Held David & McGrew Anthony, eds, Globalization Theory, Approaches and Controversies (Polity Press, Cambridge, 2007).

HELD David & MCGREW Anthony, eds, Globalization Theory, Approaches and Controversies (Polity Press, Cambridge, 2007).

HELD David and MCGREW Anthony, Political Globalization: Trends and Choices, in: Kaul Inge, Conceicao Pedro, Goulven Katell Le, Mendoza Ronald U., eds, Providing Global Public Goods, Managing Globalization (Oxford: Oxford University Press, 2003) 185–199.

HELD David and MCGREW Anthony, GOLDBLATT David and PERRATON Jonathan, Global Transformations, Politics, Economics and Culture (Polity, Cambridge, 2008).

HESTERMEYER Holger, Where Unity Is at Risk: When International Tribunals Proliferate, in: König Doris, Stoll Peter-Tobias, Röben Volker, Matz-Lück Nele, eds, International Law Today: New Challenges and the Need for Reform?, Beiträge zum ausländischen öffentlichen Recht und Völkerrecht, Band 193 (Springer, Berlin, Heidelberg, New York, 2008) 123–140.

HICKS John Richard, The Foundations of Welfare Economics, in: 49, Economic Journal (1939) 696–712.

HIGGOTT Richard A., Underhill Geoffrey R. D., and Bieler Andreas, eds, Non-State Actors and Authority in the Global System (Routledge, London and New York, 2000).

HILLEMANNS Carolin, UN Norms on the Responsibilities of Transnational Corporations and Other Business Enterprises with regard to Human Rights, in: German Law Journal, Volume 4, No. 10 (1 October 2003) 1065–1080.

HOBBES Thomas, Leviathan or the Matter, Forme and Power of a Commonwealth Ecclesiastical and Civil, Part I, Ch. 13.

HOFMANN Rainer, GEISSLER Nils, eds, Non-State Actors as New Subjects of International Law (Veröffentlichungen des Walther-Schücking-Instituts für Internationales Recht an der Universität Kiel, Band 125, Berlin, 1999).

HOLSTI K.J., Governance without Government: Polyarchy in Nineteenth-Century European International Politics, in: Rosenau James N. and Czempiel Ernst-Otto, Governance without Government: Order and Change in World Politics (Oxford: Oxford University Press, 2000) 30–57.

HOOD Christopher, Administrative Analysis (Wheatsheaf, Brighton, 1986).

HOOD Christopher, The Tools of Government in the Information Age, in: Moran Michael, Rein Martin and Goodin Robert E., eds, The Oxford Handbook of Public Policy (Oxford: Oxford University Press, 2006) 469–481.

HOOD Christopher, ROTHSTEIN Henry, and Baldwin Robert, The Government of Risk, Understanding Risk Regulation Regimes (Oxford: Oxford University Press, 2004).

HOPFE Cathleen, The Rise of International Commercial Arbitration and the Demise of Judicial Recourse: Whatever Happened to "Public Policy"?, in: 9 World Arbitration & Mediation Report (1998) 263.

HOPT Klaus J., Comparative Company Law, The Oxford Handbook of Comparative law, Chapter 36 (Oxford: Oxford University Press, 2006) 1161–1191.

HUNT Benjamin, The Timid Corporation, Why Business is Terrified of Taking Risk (John Wiley & Sons Ltd., Chichester, 2003).

HUTTER Bridget M., Is Enforced Self-regulation a Form of Risk Taking?: The Case of Railway Health and Safety, in: International Journal of the Sociology of Law (2001) 29, 379–400.

HUTTER Bridget M., Regulation and Risk: Occupational Health and Safety on the Railways (New York: Oxford University Press, 2001).

HUTTER Bridget M., The Attractions of Risk-based Regulation: accounting for the emergence of risk ideas in regulation, Discussion Paper No: 33, ESRC Centre for Analysis of Risk and Regulation, London School of Economics and Political Science (March 2005) 1–14.

HUTTER Bridget M., The Role of Non-State Actors in Regulation, Discussion Paper No: 37, ESRC Centre for Analysis of Risk and Regulation, London School of Economics and Political Science (April 2006) 1–19.

HUTTER Bridget M.,and JONES J. Clive, From government to governance: External influences on business risk management, in: Regulation & Governance, no. 1 (2007) 27–45.

ILO Tripartite Declaration of Principles concerning Multinational Enterprises and Social Policy (International Labour Office, Geneva, 3rd ed., 2001).

Institute of International Finance, Final Report of the IIF Committee on Market Best Practices: Principles of Conduct and Best Practice Recommendations, Financial Services Industry Response to the Market Turmoil of 2007–2008 (July 2008).

Institute of International Finance, Proposal for a Strategic Dialogue on Effective Regulation (December 2006).

IOSCO Report on the Activities of Credit Rating Agencies, Report of the Technical Committee of IOSCO (September 2003).

IOSCO Report of the SRO Consultative Committee of the International Organization of Securities Commissions, Model for Effective Self-Regulation (May 2000).

IOSCO Statement of Principles regarding the Activities of Credit Rating Agencies, Statement of the Technical Committee of IOSCO (September 2003).

JACKSON Howell E., Variation in the Intensity of Financial Regulation: Preliminary Evidence and Potential Implications, John M. Olin Center for Law Economics, and Business Discussion Paper No. 521 (August 2005).

JACOBSSON Bengt and SAHLIN-ANDERSSON Kerstin, Dynamics of soft regulations, in: Djelic Marie-Laure and Sahlin-Andersson Kerstin, eds, Transnational Governance, Institutional Dynamics of Regulation (Cambridge: Cambridge University Press, 2006) 247–265.

JACOT-GUILLARMOD Olivier and PESCATORE Pierre, eds, L'avenir du libre-échange en Europe: Vers un Espace économique européen? (Schulthess Polygraphisher Verlag, Zurich, 1990).

JENKS Wilfred C., Multinational Entities in the Law of Nations, in: Wolfgang Friedmann, Louis Henkin and Oliver Lissitzyn, ed., Transnational Law in a Changing Society, Essays in Honor of Philip C. Jessup (Columbia University Press, New York and London, 1972) 70–83.

JENKS Wilfred C., The Conflict of Law-Making Treaties (BYBIL volume 30, 1953) 401–453.

JEPPERSON Ronald L. and MEYER John W., The Public Order and the Construction of Formal Organizations, in: Walter W. Powell and Paul J. DiMaggio, The New Institutionalism in Organizational Analysis (The University of Chicago Press, Chicago and London, 1991) 204–231.

JESSUP Philip C., Transnational Law, Storrs Lectures on Jurisprudence (Yale University Press, New Haven, 1956).

JORDANA Jacint and LEVI-FAUR David, eds, The Politics of Regulation: Examining Regulatory Institutions and Instruments in the Governance Age (Cheltenham: Edward Elgar, 2004).

KALDOR Mary, Global Civil Society, An Answer to War (Ppolity, Cambridge, 2003).

KALDOR Nicholas, Welfare Propositions of Economics and Interpersonal Comparisons of Utility, in: 49, Economic Journal (1939) 549–552.

KAUFMANN Christine, Globalisation and Labour Rights, The Conflict between Core Labour Rights and International Economic Law (Hart Publishing, Oxford and Portland, Oregon, 2007).

KAUL Inge, CONCEICAO Pedro, GOULVEN Katell Le, MENDOZA Ronald U., eds, Providing Global Public Goods, Managing Globalization (Oxford: Oxford University Press, 2003).

KAUL Inge, GRUNBERG Isabelle, STERN Marc A., eds, Global Public Goods, International Cooperation in the 21st Century (New York: Oxford University Press, 1999).

KAUL Inge and MENDOZA Ronald U., Advancing the Concept of Public Goods, in: Kaul Inge, Conceicao Pedro, Goulven Katell Le, Mendoza Ronald U., eds, Providing Global Public Goods, Managing Globalization (Oxford: Oxford University Press, 2003) 78–111.

KEOHANE Robert O., Governance in a Partially Globalized World: Presidential Address, American Political Science Association, in: American Political Science Review. Volume 95, No. 1 (March 2001) 1–13.

KEOHANE Robert O., Power and Governance in a Partially Globalized World (Routledge, London and New York, 2002).

KEOHANE Robert O., The Demand for international regimes, in: International Regimes, Stephen D. Krasner, ed. (Cornell University Press, New York, 1983) 141–172.

KEOHANE Robert O., and NYE Joseph S. Jr., Between Centralization and Fragmentation: The Club Model of Multilateral Cooperation and Problems of Democratic Legitimacy, RWP01-004, John F. Kennedy School of Government, Harvard University, Faculty Research Working Papers Series (February 2001).

KEOHANE Robert O., and NYE Joseph S. Jr., Governance in a globalizing world, in: Keohane Robert O., Power and Governance in a Partially Globalized World (Routledge, London and New York, 2002).

KEOHANE Robert O., and NYE Joseph S. Jr., The club model of multilateral cooperation and problems of democratic legitimacy, reprinted in: Robert O. Keohane, Power and Governance in a Partially Globalized World (Routledge, London and New York, 2002) 219–244.

KERN Alexander, DHUMALE Rahul, EATWELL John, Global governance of financial systems – The International Regulation of Systemic Risk (Oxford University Press, Oxford, New York, 2006).

KERWER Dieter, Rules that Many Use: Standards and Global Regulation, in: Governance, Volume 18, No. 4 (2005) 611–632.

KILGUS Sabine, Effektivität von Regulierung im Finanzmarktrecht (Dike Verlag AG, Zurich, St. Gallen, 2007).

KINGSBURY Benedict, The Concept of 'Law' in Global Administrative Law, in: European Journal of International Law, Volume 20, no. 1 (2009) 23–57.

KINGSBURY Benedict, KIRSCH Nico, & STEWART Richard B., The Emergence of Global Administrative Law, in: Law and Contemporary Problems, Volume 68, Numbers 3 & 4 (Summer/Autumn 2005) 15–61.

KINGSBURY Benedict, KIRSCH Nico, STEWART Richard B., & WIENER Jonathan B., Foreword: Global Governance as Administration – National and Transnational Approaches to Global Administrative Law, in: Law and Contemporary Problems, Volume 68, Numbers 3 & 4 (Summer/Autumn 2005) 1–13.

KIRTON John J., TREBILCOCK Michael J., eds, Hard Choices, Soft Law, Voluntary Standards in Global Trade, Environment and Social Governance (Ashgate, Aldershot, 2004).

KIRTON John J., TREBILCOCK Michael J., Introduction: Hard Choices and Soft Law in Sustainable Global Governance, in: Kirton John J., Trebilcock Michael J., eds, Hard Choices, Soft Law, Voluntary Standards in Global Trade, Environment and Social Governance (Ashgate, Aldershot, 2004) 3–29.

KNILL Christoph, LEHMKUHL Dirk, Private Actors and the State: Internationalization and Changing Patterns of Governance, in: Governance, An International Journal of Policy, Administration and Institutions, Volume 15, No. 1 (January 2002) 41–63.

KNOWLES Robert, Comment, Starbucks and the New Federalism: The Court's Answer to Globalization, in: Northwestern University Law Review, Volume 95, No. 2 (2001) 735–778.

KÖNIG Doris, STOLL Peter-Tobias, RÖBEN Volker, MATZ-LÜCK Nele, eds, International Law Today: New Challenges and the Need for Reform?, Beiträge zum ausländischen öffentlichen Recht und Völkerrecht, Band 193 (Springer, Berlin, Heidelberg, New York, 2008).

KORKUT Umut, Participatory policy-making, participatory civil society: A key for dissolving elite rule in new democracies in the era of globalization, in: World Futures, Journal of General Evolution, Volume 63, Issue 5 & 6 (2007) 340–352.

KOSKENNIEMI Martti, Carl Schmitt, Hans Morgenthau, and the Image of Law in International Relations, in: Michael Byers, ed., The Role of Law in International Politics, Essays in International Relations and International Law (Oxford: Oxford University Press, 2000) 17–34.

KOSKENNIEMI Martti, Fragmentation of International Law: Difficulties Arising from the Diversification and Expansion of International Law, Report of the Study Group of the International Law Commission, United Nations, A/CN.4/L.682 (13 April 2006).

KOSKENNIEMI Martti, From Apology to Utopia: The Structure of International Legal Argument, Reissue with a New Epilogue (Cambridge: Cambridge University Press, 2005).

KOSKENNIEMI Martti, Global Legal Pluralism: Multiple Regimes and Multiple Modes of Thought (Harvard, 5 March 2005).

KOSKENNIEMI Martti, Power politics, institutions, and transnational relations, in: Risse-Kappen Thomas, ed., Bringing Transnational Relations Back In, Non-State Actors, Domestic Structures and International Institutions, Cambridge Studies in International Relations (Cambridge: Cambridge University Press, 1995) 257–279.

KOSKENNIEMI Martti, Structural causes and regime consequences: regimes as intervening variables, in: International Organization, Volume 36, No. 2, Spring (1982) 185–205.

KOSKENNIEMI Martti, The Fate of Public International Law: Between Technique and Politics, in: The Modern Law Review, Volume 70, No 1 (January 2007) 1–30.

KOSKENNIEMI Martti, The Gentle Civilizer of Nations – The Rise and Fall of International Law 1870–1960 (Cambridge: Cambridge University Press, 2002).

KRASNER Stephen D., International Regimes (Cornell University Press, Ithaca, NY, 1983).

KUNREUTHER Howard C., MCNULTY Patrick J., and KANG Yong, Third-Party Inspection as an Alternative to Command and Control Regulation, in: Risk Analysis, Volume 22, No. 2 (2002) 309–318.

LADEUR Karl-Heinz, ed., Public Governance in the Age of Globalization (Ashgate, Aldershot 2004).

LADEUR Karl-Heinz, Towards a Legal Theory of Supranationality – The Viability of the Network Concept, in: European Law Journal, Volume 3, No. 1 (March 1997) 33–54.

LEHMKUHL Dirk, The Resolution of Domain Names vs. Trademark Conflicts: A Case Study on Regulation Beyond the Nation-State, and Related Problems, in: Zeitschrift für Rechtssoziologie, Jahrgang 23, Heft 1 (2002) 61–78.

Letter of the International Monetary Fund and Financial Stability Forum (November 13, 2008).

Levi-Faur David, The Global Diffusion of Regulatory Capitalism, The Annals of the American Academy of Political and Social Science, Volume 598 (2005) 12–32.

Lipschutz Ronnie D. and Fogel Cathleen, "Regulation for the rest of us?" Global civil society and the privatization of transnational regulation, in: Hall Rodney Bruce and Biersteker Thomas J., eds, The Emergence of Private Authority in Global Governance, Cambridge Studies in International Relations, No. 85 (Cambridge: Cambridge University Press, 2002).

Loquin Eric and Kessedjian Catherine, eds, La mondialisation du droit (Litec, Paris, 2000).

Luhmann Niklas, Das Recht der Gesellschaft (Suhrkamp, Frankfurt am Main, 1993).

Luhmann Niklas, Law as a Social System, in: Northwestern University Law Review, Volume 83, Nos. 1 & 2 (1989) 136–150.

Luhmann Niklas, Soziale Systeme (Frankfurt am Main, 1985).

Luhmann Niklas, The World Society as a Social System, in: International Journal of General Systems, 8 (1982) 131–138.

Luna Martinez José de and Rose Thomas A., International Survey of Integrated Financial Sector Supervision, World Bank Policy Research Working Paper 3096 (July 2003).

Macalister-Smith Peter, Non-Governmental Organizations, Humanitarian Action and Human Rights, in: Beyerlin Ulrich, Bothe Michael, Hofmann Rainer, Petersmann Ernst-Ulrich, eds, Recht zwischen Umbruch und Bewahrung: Völkerrecht, Europarecht, Staatsrecht, Festschrift für Rudolf Bernhardt, Band 120, (Springer, Heidelberg, 1995).

Macaulay Stuart, Non-Contractual Relationships in Business: A Preliminary Study, in: American Sociological Review, Volume 28, No. 1 (February 1963) 1–19.

Maitland Ian, The Limits of Business Self-Regulation, in: California Management Review, Volume XXVII, No. 3 (1985) 132–146.

Majone Giandomenico, Delegation of Regulatory Powers in a Mixed Polity, in: European Law Journal, Volume 8, No. 3 (September 2002) 319–339.

Majone Giandomenico, The European Commission: The Limits of Centralization and the Perils of Parliamentarization, in: Governance: An International Journal of Policy, Administration and Institutions, Volume 15, no 3 (July 2002) 375–392.

Majone Giandomenico, The New European Agencies: Regulation by Information, in: Journal of European Public Policy, Volume 4, no 2 (1997) 262–275.

Majone Giandomenico, The Rise of the Regulatory State in Europe, in: West European Politics, Volume 17, no 3 (July 1994) 77–101.

Marcussen Martin, The transnational governance network of central bankers, in: Djelic Marie-Laure and Sahlin-Andersson Kerstin, eds, Transnational Governance, Institutional Dynamics of Regulation (Cambridge: Cambridge University Press, 2006) 180–204.

Martens Kerstin, Examining the (Non-)Status of NGOs in International Law, in: 10 Indiana Journal of Global Legal Studies, 1 (2003) 1–24.

Marti Arnold, Selbstregulierung anstelle staatlicher Gesetzgebung, in: Schweizerisches Zentralblatt für Staats- und Verwaltungsrecht, 101, Heft 11 (2000) 561–586.

Martin Lisa L., The Political Economy of International Cooperation, in: Kaul Inge, Grunberg Isabelle, Stern Marc A., eds, Global Public Goods, International Cooperation in the 21st Century (New York: Oxford University Press, 1999) 51–64.

Mathis Klaus, Effizienz statt Gerechtigkeit, auf der Suche nach den philosophischen Grundlagen der Ökonomischen Analyse des Rechts, Schriften zur Rechtstheorie, Heft 223 (Duncker & Humblot, Berlin, 2004).

Matz-Lück Nele, Promoting the Unity of International Law: Standard-Setting by International Tribunals, in: König Doris, Stoll Peter-Tobias, Röben Volker, Matz-Lück Nele, eds, International Law Today: New Challenges and the Need for Reform?, Beiträge zum ausländischen öffentlichen Recht und Völkerrecht, Band 193 (Springer, Berlin, Heidelberg, New York, 2008) 99–121.

McCormick Roger, Legal Risk in the Financial Markets (Oxford: Oxford University Press, 2006).

McCrudden Christopher, ed., Regulation and Deregulation, Policy and Practice in the Utilities and Financial Services Industries (Clarendon Press, Oxford, 1999).

McCrudden Christopher, Regulation and Deregulation: An Introduction, in: McCrudden Christopher, ed., Regulation and Deregulation, Policy and Practice in the Utilities and Financial Services Industries (Clarendon Press, Oxford, 1999) 3–14.

McGill Ross K. and Sheppey Terence A., The New Global Regulatory Landscape, Impacts on Finance and Investment (Palgrave Macmillan, Basingstoke and New York, 2005).

Mearsheimer John, J., The False Promise of International Institutions, in: International Security, volume 19, no. 3 (1994/95) 5–49.

Meidinger Errol, Competitive Supragovernmental Regulation: How Could It Be Democratic?, in: Chicago Journal of International Law, Volume 8, No. 2 (Winter 2008) 513–534.

Meidinger Errol, Look Who's Making the Rules: International Environmental Standard Setting by Non-Governmental Organizations, in: Human Ecology Review, Volume 4, No. 1 (1997) 52–54.

Meier Richard T., Sigrist Tobias, Der helvetische Big Bang, Die Geschichte der SWX Swiss Exchange (Verlag Neue Zürcher Zeitung, Zurich, 2006).

Merry Sally Engle, Legal Pluralism, in: Law & Society Review, Volume 22, No. 5 (1988) 869–896.

Mertens Hans-Joachim, Lex Mercatoria: A Self-applying System Beyond National Law?, in: Gunther Teubner, ed., Global Law Without a State (Ashgate, Dartmouth, 2006) 31–43.

Michael Douglas C., Cooperative Implementation of Federal Regulations, in: Yale Journal on Regulation, Volume 13 (1996) 535–601.

Michael Douglas C., Federal Agency Use of Audited Self-Regulation as a Regulatory Technique, in: Administrative Law Review, Volume 47 (Spring 1995) 171–253.

Michaels Ralf, The Re-State-ment of Non-State Law: The State, Choice of Law, and the Challenge from Global Legal Pluralism, in: 51 Wayne Law Review (2005) 1209–1259.

Michelman Frank I., Traces of Self-Government, in: Harvard Law Review Volume 100 (1986) 4–77.

Miller Geoffrey P., An Interest Group Theory of Central Bank Independence, in: Journal of Legal Studies, Volume 27, Issue 2 (1998) 433–453.

Moloney Niamh, New frontiers in EC capital markets law: from market construction to market regulation, in: Common Market Law Review, Volume 40, No. 4 (2003) 809–843.

Montesquieu Charles Louis de Secondat, Baron de La Brède et de Montesquieu, De l'esprit des lois (Genève, 1748).

Moody's Bank Credit Report, Crédit Suisse, October 1989, p. 4 and Moody's Corporate Credit Report, CS First Boston, Inc., Financière Crédit Suisse – First Boston (April 1990).

Moran Michael, Rein Martin and Goodin Robert E., eds, The Oxford Handbook of Public Policy (Oxford: Oxford University Press, 2006).

Morand Charles-Albert, Le droit néo-moderne des politiques publiques, Droit et société 26 (L.G. D.J., Paris 1999).

Morgan Bronwen, The Economization of Politics: Meta-Regulation as a Form of Nonjudicial Legality, in: Social & Legal Studies, Volume 12, No. 4 (2003) 489–523.

Morgan Bronwen and Yeung Karen, An Introduction to Law and Regulation, Texts and Materials (Cambridge: Cambridge University Press, 2007).

Morgenthau Hans, La réalité des normes, En particulier des normes du droit international, Fondements d'une théorie des normes (Alcan, Paris, 1934).

Mulgan Richard, Accountability: An Ever-Expanding Concept?, in: Public Administration, Volume 78, Number 3 (Autumn 2000) 555–573.

Nagel Jürgen G., The Company and the Port City: Trading centres of the Malay Archipelago and their role in commercial networks during the seventeenth and eighteenth centuries, in: Schulte Beerbühl Margrit, Vögele Jörg, eds, Spinning the Commercial Web, International Trade, Merchants, and Commercial Cities, c. 1640–1939 (Peter Lang, Frankfurt am Main, 2004) 249–273.

National Intelligence Council, Global Trends 2025: A Transformed World, NIC 2008-003 (November 2008).

NIJMAN Janne and NOLLKAEMPER André, Beyond the Divide, in: Nijman Janne and Nollkaemper André, eds, New Perspectives on the Divide Between National and International Law (Oxford: Oxford University Press, 2007) 341–360.

NIJMAN Janne and NOLLKAEMPER André, eds, New Perspectives on the Divide Between National and International Law (Oxford: Oxford University Press, 2007).

NOBEL Peter, Die neuen Standesregeln zur Sorgfaltspflicht der Banken, in: Wirtschaft und Recht, Volume 39, Issue 3/4 (1987) 149–166.

NOBEL Peter, Die Sorgfaltspflicht des Bankiers, in: 50 Jahre eidgenössische Bankenaufsicht: Jubiläumsschrift (Schulthess Verlag, Zurich, 1985) 205–226.

NOBEL Peter, ed., International Standards and the Law (Stämpfli Publishers Ltd., Berne, 2005).

NOBEL Peter, Gesetz oder private Selbstregulierung?, in: Kolloquium Schweizerisches Kapitalmarktrecht, Schweizerische Beiträge zum Europarecht, Band 31 (Geneva, 1987) 441–463.

NOBEL Peter, Globalization and International Standards with an emphasis on Finance Law, in: Nobel Peter, ed., International Standards and the Law (Stämpfli Publishers Ltd., Berne, 2005) 43–66.

NOBEL Peter, Schweizerisches Finanzmarktrecht, Einführung und Überblick, 2., vollständig neu bearbeitete und erweiterte Auflage (Stämpfli Verlag AG, Bern, 2004).

NOBEL Peter, Selbstregulierung, in: Freiheit und Ordnung im Kapitalmarktrecht, Festgabe für Jean-Paul Chapuis (Zurich, 1998) 119–134.

NOBEL Peter, Transnationales und Europäisches Aktienrecht (Stämpfli Verlag AG, Bern, 2006).

NOBEL Peter, Zur Regulierungsarchitektur im Finanzmarktbereich, in: Aktuelle Fragen des Bank- und Finanzmarktrechts, Festschrift für Dieter Zobl zum 60. Geburtstag (Schulthess, Zurich, 2004) 106–128.

NOBEL Peter and STIRNIMANN Isabel, Zur Behandlung von Entschädigungen im Vertrieb von Anlagefonds- und strukturierten Produkten durch Banken Eine Untersuchung im Lichte des Bundesgerichtsentscheids BGE 132 III 460, in: Swiss Review of Business and Financial Markets Law, no. 5 (2007) 343–356.

NOLL Roger G., ed., Regulatory Policy and the Social Sciences (University of California Press, Berkeley, 1985).

NORTH Douglass C., Institutions, Institutional Change and Economic Performance (Cambridge University Press, Cambridge, 1990).

NORTH Douglass C., Understanding the Process of Economic Change (Princeton University Press, Princeton and Oxford, 2005).

NOTTAGE Luke R., The Procedural Lex Mercatoria: The Past, Present and Future of International Commercial Arbitration, CDAMS Discussion Paper No. 03/1E (December 2006).

NOWROT Karsten, Die UN-Norms on the Responsibility of Transnational Corporations and Other Business Enterprises with Regard to Human Rights – Gelungener Beitrag zur transnationalen Rechtsverwirklichung oder das Ende des Global Compact?, in: Beiträge zum Transnationalen Wirtschaftsrecht, Heft 21, (Halle-Wittenberg, 2003).

NOWROT Karsten, Legal Consequences of Globalization: The Status of Non-Governmental Organizations Under International Law, in: Indiana Journal of Global Legal Studies, Volume 6 (1998–1999) 579–645.

O'BRIEN John, International Law (Cavendish Publishing Limited, London, Sydney, 2001).

OECD, From Red Tape to Smart Tape, Administrative Simplification in OECD Countries (Paris, 2003).

OECD Guidelines for Multinational Enterprises, which were revised in the year 2000 (Paris, 2000).

OECD Guiding Principles for Regulatory Quality and Performance (2005).

OECD Informal Institutions, How social norms help or hinder development, Johannes Jütting, Denis Drechsler, Sebastian Bartsch, and Indra de Soysa, ed., Development Centre Studies (2007).

OECD Meeting on Alternatives to Traditional Regulation, OECD (Paris, 1994).

OECD Recommendation of the Council of the OECD on Improving the Quality of Government Regulation, OECD/GD(95)95.

OECD Report on Regulatory Reform: Synthesis, The (Paris, 1997).

OECD Reviews of Regulatory Reform, Regulatory Polices in OECD Countries, From Interventionism to Regulatory Governance (Paris, 2002).

OGUS Anthony I., Regulation: Legal Form and Economic Theory (Hart Publishing, Oxford, 2004).

OGUS Anthony I., Rethinking Self-Regulation, in: Oxford Journal of Legal Studies, Volume 15, No 1 (Spring 1995) 97–108.

OLSON Mancur, The Logic of Collective Action: Public Goods and the Theory of Groups (Harvard Economic Studies, 1965).

ÖRÜCÜ Esin, The enigma of Comparative Law, Variations on a Theme for the Twenty-First Century (M. Nijhoff Publishers, Leiden / Boston, 2004).

OSBORNE David and GAEBLER Ted, Reinventing Government (Reading, MA Addison Wesley, 1992).

Oxford, The English Dictionary, 2nd ed., Complete Text (Clarendon Press, Oxford, 1996).

OYE Kenneth A., ed., Cooperation under Anarchy (Princeton: Princeton University Press, 1986).

OYE Kenneth A., Explaining Cooperation under Anarchy: Hypotheses and Strategies, in: Oye Kenneth A., ed., Cooperation under Anarchy (Princeton: Princeton University Press, 1986) 1–24.

PADOA-SCHIOPPA Tommaso, Regulating Finance – Balancing Freedom and Risk (Oxford: Oxford University Press, 2004).

PAGE Alan C., Regulating the Regulator – A Lawyer's Perspective on Accountability and Control, in: Eilis Ferran and Charles Goodhart, eds, Regulating Financial Services and Markets in the 21st Century (Hart Publishing, Oxford, 2001) 127–149.

PAGE Alan C., Self-Regulation: The Constitutional Dimension, in: The Modern Law Review, Volume 49, No 2 (March 1986) 141–167.

PALMISANO Samuel J., The Globally Integrated Enterprise, in: Foreign Affairs, Volume 85, no. 3 (May/June 2006) 127–136.

PATERSON John and TEUBNER Gunther, Changing Maps: Empirical Legal Autopoiesis, in: Social & Legal Studies, Volume 7, Issue 4 (1998) 451–486.

PARKER Christine, The Open Corporation, Effective Self-Regulation and Democracy (Cambridge: Cambridge University Press, 2002).

PARKER Christine, SCOTT Colin, LACEY Nicola, and BRAITHWAITE John, eds, Regulating law (Oxford: Oxford University Press, 2004).

PAULSSON Jan, International Handbook on Commercial Arbitration, Paulsson Gen ed., International Council for Commercial Arbitration, Volumes 1–4.

PELTZMAN Sam, The Economic Theory of Regulation after a Decade of Deregulation, Brookings Papers on Economic Activity (Washington, D.C., Brookings, 1989) 1–41.

PELTZMAN Sam, Toward a More General Theory of Regulation, in: Journal of Law and Economics, Volume 19, no 2 (1976) 211–240.

PETERS Anne, The Globalization of State Constitutions, in: Nijman Janne and Nollkaemper André, eds, New Perspectives on the Divide Between National and International Law (Oxford: Oxford University Press, 2007) 251–308.

PETERSMANN Ernst-Ulrich, Justice as Conflict Resolution: Proliferation, Fragmentation and Decentralization of Dispute Settlement in International Trade (EUI Working Papers LAW No. 2004/10, San Domenico).

PETERSMANN Ernst-Ulrich, State Sovereignty, Popular Sovereignty and Individual Sovereignty: from Constitutional Nationalism to Multilevel Constitutionalism in International Economic Law? (EUI Working Papers, LAW No. 2006/45, San Domenico).

PICCIOTTO Sol, Constitutionalizing multilevel governance?, in: International Journal of Constitutional Law, Volume 6, No. 3–4 (2008) 457–479.

PICCIOTTO Sol, Networks in International Economic Integration: Fragmented States and the Dilemmas of Neo-liberalism, in: Northwestern Journal of International Law and Business, Volume 17 (1996) 1014–1056.

PISTOR Katharina, The Standardization of Law and Its Effect on Developing Economies, in: The American Journal of Comparative Law, Volume 50, No. 1 (Winter 2002) 97–130.

PORTER Tony, States, Markets and Regimes in Global Finance (St.Martin's Press, New York, 1993).

POSNER Eric A., Law and Social Norms (Harvard University Press, Cambridge, London, 2000).

POSNER Richard A., Overcoming Law (Harvard University Press, Cambridge, 1995).

POSNER Richard A., The Decline of Law as an Autonomous Discipline: 1962–1987, in: Harvard Law Review, Volume 100 (1986–1987) 761–780.

POSNER Richard A., Theories of Economic Regulation, in: The Bell Journal of Economics and Management Science, Volume 5, No. 2 (Autumn 1974) 335–358.

POWELL Walter W., Expanding the Scope of Institutional Analysis, in: Powell Walter W. and DiMaggio Paul J., The New Institutionalism in Organizational Analysis (The University of Chicago Press, Chicago and London, 1991) 183–203.

POWELL Walter W. and DIMAGGIO Paul J., The New Institutionalism in Organizational Analysis (The University of Chicago Press, Chicago and London, 1991).

POWER Michael, The Audit Society, Rituals of Verification (Oxford: Oxford University Press, 1997).

PRIEST Margot, The Privatization of Regulation: Five Models of Self-Regulation, in: Ottawa Law Review, Volume 29 (1997–1998) 233–302.

PRYLES Michael, Dispute Resolution in Asia (Hague, Kluwer International, 2nd ed., 2002).

RAUSTIALA Kal, The Architecture of International Cooperation: Transgovernmental Networks and the Future of International Law, in: 43 Virginia Journal of International Law (2002) 1–92.

RAWLS John, A Theory of Justice, The Belknap Press of Harvard University Press, 1971, revised edition (Oxford: Oxford University Press, 1999).

REDFERN Alan and HUNTER Martin, Law and Practice of International Commercial Arbitration, 3rd ed., (London, Sweet & Maxwell, 1999).

REINICKE Wolfgang H., Global Public Policy: Governing Without Government? (Brookings Institution Press, Washington, DC, 1998).

RHINOW René, Wirtschafts-, Sozial- und Arbeitsverfassung, in: Ulrich Zimmerli, ed., Die neue Bundesverfassung, Konsequenzen für Praxis und Wirtschaft, BTJP 1999 (Stämpfli Verlag AG, Bern, 2000) 157–182.

RHODES R.A.W., Understanding Governance, Policy Networks, Governance, Reflexivity and Accountability (Open University Press, Buckingham / Philadelphia, 2001).

RICHERSON Peter J. and BOYD Robert, Not by Genes Alone, How Culture Transformed Human Evolution (The University of Chicago Press, Chicago and London, 2005).

RIEMER Hans Michael, Nicht Staatliche Normensysteme und andere Gesetze und ihr Verhältnis zum System der staatlichen Rechtsnormen – ein Überblick, in: recht, Heft 3 (2007) 114–122.

RISSE Thomas, Transnational Governance and Legitimacy, in: Arthur Benz and Yannis Papadopoulos, eds, Governance and Democracy, Comparing national European and international experiences (Routledge, London, 2006) 179–199.

RISSE-KAPPEN Thomas, Bringing transnational relations back in: introduction, in: Risse-Kappen Thomas, ed., Bringing Transnational Relations Back In, Non-State Actors, Domestic Structures and International Institutions (Cambridge Studies in International Relations, Cambridge University Press, 1995) 3–33.

RISSE-KAPPEN Thomas, ed., Bringing Transnational Relations Back In, Non-State Actors, Domestic Structures and International Institutions (Cambridge Studies in International Relations, Cambridge University Press, 1995).

ROBÉ Jean-Philippe, Multinational Enterprises: The Constitution of a Pluralistic Legal Order, in: Teubner Gunther, ed., Global Law Without a State (Ashgate, Dartmouth, 2006) 52–53.

Robert, Le Nouveau Petit, Dictionnaire de la Langue Française (Paris, 2003).

ROBERTS Simon, After Government? On Representing Law Without the State, in: The Modern Law Review, Volume 68, No 1 (January 2005) 1–24.

ROBERTS Simon, Against a Systemic Legal History, in: Jusletter (7 April 2003).

ROCK Edward B. and WACHTER Michael L., Islands of Conscious Power: Law, Norms, and the Self-Governing Corporation, in: University of Pennsylvania Law Review, Volume 149, No. 6 (June 2001) 1619–1700.

ROSENAU James N., Governance, Order, and Change in World Politics, in: James N. Rosenau and Ernst-Otto Czempiel, Governance without Government: Order and Change in World Politics (Oxford: Oxford University Press, 2000) 1–29.

ROSENAU James N., Governing the ungovernable: The challenge of a global disaggregation of authority, in: Regulation and Governance, no. 1 (2007) 88–97.

ROSENAU James N. and CZEMPIEL Ernst-Otto, Governance without Government: Order and Change in World Politics (Cambridge: Cambridge University Press, 2000).

RUBINO-SAMMARTANO Mauro, International Arbitration Law and Practice, 2nd ed. (Kluwer Law International, Hague, 2001).

RUCH Alexander, Informalisierung und Deregulierung nach schweizerischem Verfassungsrecht, in: Schweizerisches Zentralblatt für Staats- und Verwaltungsrecht, Band 103, Nr. 10 (2002) 505–528.

RUFFNER Markus, Die ökonomischen Grundlagen eines Rechts der Publikumsgesellschaft, Ein Beitrag zur Theorie der Corporate Governance (Schulthess Verlag, Zurich, 2000).

SAJÓ András, Transnational Networks and Constitutionalism, in: Acta Juridica Hungarica, Hungarian Journal of Legal Studies, Volume 47, Nr. 3 (2006) 209–225.

SANTOS Boaventura de Sousa, Toward a New Common Sense: Law, Science and Politics in the Paradigmatic Transition (Routledge, New York, 1995).

SANTOS Boaventura de Sousa, Toward a New Legal Common Sense: Law, Globalization, and Emancipation, 2nd ed. (Butterworths, London, 2004).

SASSEN Saskia, Territory, Authority, Rights: From Medieval to Global Assemblages (Princeton: Princeton University Press, 2006).

SASSEN Saskia, The Places and Spaces of the Global: An Expanded Analytic Terrain, in: Held David & McGrew Anthony, eds, Globalization Theory, Approaches and Controversies (Polity Press, Cambridge, 2007) 79–105.

SASSEN Saskia, The state and globalization, in: Hall Rodney Bruce and Biersteker Thomas J., eds, The Emergence of Private Authority in Global Governance, Cambridge Studies in International Relations, No. 85 (Cambridge: Cambridge University Press, 2002) 91–112.

SCHAEDE Ulrike, Cooperative Capitalism: Self-Regulation, Trade Associations and the Antimonopoly Law in Japan (Oxford: Oxford University Press, 2000).

SCHAUER Frederick, Playing by the Rules: A Philosophical Examination of Rule-Based Decision-Making in Law and in Life (Oxford: Oxford University Press, 1991).

SCHAUER Frederick, The Tyranny of Choice and the Rulification of Standards, in: Journal of Contemporary Legal Issues, Volume 14 (2005) 803–814.

SCHIFF David and NOBLES Richard, eds, Jurisprudence (Butterworth, London, 2003).

SCHMITTER Philippe C., A Prolegomenon to a Theory of Interest Politics, in: Jens Beckert, Bernhard Ebbinghaus, Anke Hassel, Philip Manow, ed., Transformationen des Kapitalismus, Festschrift für Wolfgang Streeck zum sechzigsten Geburtstag (Campus Verlag, Frankfurt/New York, 2006) 297–313.

SCHMITTER Philippe C., Still the Century of Corporatism?, in: The Review of Politics (1974) 36:1, 85–131.

SCHREIBER Vera, International Standards, Neues Recht für die Weltmärkte?, St.Galler Studien zum Privat-, Handels- und Wirtschaftsrecht, Band 75 (Haupt Verlag, Bern, 2005).

SCHULTE BEERBüHL Margrit, VÖGELE Jörg, eds, Spinning the Commercial Web, International Trade, Merchants, and Commercial Cities, c. 1640–1939 (Peter Lang, Frankfurt am Main, 2004).

SCHULTE BEERBüHL Margrit and VÖGELE Jörg, Spinning the Commercial Web, International Trade, Merchants, and Commercial Cities, c. 1640-1939 Centuries. An Introduction, in: Schulte

Beerbühl Margrit, Vögele Jörg, eds, Spinning the Commercial Web, International Trade, Merchants, and Commercial Cities, c. 1640–1939 (Peter Lang, Frankfurt am Main, 2004) 11–23.

Schwander Ivo, Der contrat sans loi und das nichtstaatliche Recht im Internationalen Privatrecht, in: Swiss Reports presented at the XVII Congress of the International Academy of Comparative Law, 16- 22 July 2006, Utrecht, The Netherlands (Schulthess Verlag, Zurich, 2006) 117–134.

Schwarcz Steven L., Private Ordering, in: Northwestern University Law Review, Volume 97 (Fall 2002) 319–350.

Schwarcz Steven L., Private Ordering of Public Markets: The Rating Agency Paradox, in: University of Illinois Law Review, Volume 2002, No. 1 (2002) 1–27.

Schwarcz Steven L., The Role of Rating Agencies in Global Market Regulation, in: Ferran Eilis and Goodhart Charles A. E., eds, Regulating Financial Services and Markets in the Twenty First Century (Hart Publishing, Oxford, 2001) 297–310.

Scott Colin, Analysing Regulatory Space: Fragmented Resources and Institutional Design, in: Public Law (Summer 2001) 283–305.

Scott Colin, Private Regulation of the Public Sector: A Neglected Facet of Contemporary Governance, in: Journal of Law and Society, Volume 29, No. 1 (March 2002) 56–76.

Scott Colin, Privatization and Regulatory Regimes, in: Moran Michael, Rein Martin and Goodin Robert E., eds, The Oxford Handbook of Public Policy (Oxford: Oxford University Press, 2006) 651–668.

Scott Colin, Regulating Constitutions, in: Christine Parker, Colin Scott, Nicola Lacey, and John Braithwaite, eds, Regulating Law (Oxford: Oxford University Press, 2004).

Scott Colin, Regulating Private Legislation (CLPE Research Paper 22/2007, Volume 03, No. 4, Toronto).

Scott Colin, Self-Regulation and the Meta-Regulatory State, in: Cafaggi Fabrizio, ed., Reframing Self-Regulation in European Private Law (Kluwer Law International, Alphen aan den Rijn, The Netherlands, 2006) 131–145.

Scott Richard W., Institutions and Organizations, 2nd ed., Foundations for Organizational Science (Sage Publications Series, 2001).

Scott Richard W. and Meyer John W., The Organization of Societal Sectors: Propositions and Early Evidence, in: Walter W. Powell and Paul J. DiMaggio, The New Institutionalism in Organizational Analysis (The University of Chicago Press, Chicago and London, 1991) 108–140.

Securities and Exchange Commission, Annual Report on Nationally Recognized Statistical Rating Organizations, As Required by Section 6 of the Credit Rating Agency Reform Act of 2006 (June 2008).

Securities and Exchange Commission, Concept Release Concerning Self-Regulation (November 18, 2004) 17 CFR Part 240 – Release no 34-50700; File No. S7-40-04.

Securities and Exchange Commission, Oversight of Credit Rating Agencies Registered as Nationally Recognized Statistical Rating Organizations; Final Rule (June 18, 2007) 17 CFR Parts 240 and 249b.

Seidl-Hohenveldern Ignaz und Loibl Gerhard, Das Recht der Internationalen Organisationen einschliesslich der Supranationalen Gemeinschaften (7., ü. A., Carl Heymanns Verlag KG, Köln, 2000).

Seligman Joel, The Transformation of Wall Street: A History of the Securities and Exchange Commission and Modern Corporate Finance (Aspen Pub. N.Y., 3rd ed., 2003).

Selznick P., Focusing Organisational Research on Regulation, in: Roger G. Noll, ed., Regulatory Policy and the Social Sciences (University of California Press, Berkeley, 1985) 363–368.

Sen Amartya K., Collective Choice and Social Welfare (Holden-Day, San Francisco, 1970).

Sen Amartya K., Global Justice: Beyond International Equity, in: Kaul Inge, Grunberg Isabelle, Stern Marc A., eds, Global Public Goods, International Cooperation in the 21st Century (New York: Oxford University Press, 1999) 116–125.

SEN Amartya K., The Discipline of Cost-Benefit Analysis, in: The Journal of Legal Studies, Volume 29, No. 2 (June 2000) 931–952.

SENDEN Linda, Soft Law, Self-Regulation and Co-Regulation in European Law: Where Do They Meet?, in: Electronic Journal of Comparative Law, volume 9.1 (January 2005) http://www.ejcl.org/91/art91-3.html.

SENN Myriam, Decentralisation of Economic Law – An Oxymoron?, in: Journal of Corporate Law Studies, Volume 4, Issue 2 (October 2005) 427–464.

SHAPIRO Martin, Judicial Delegation Doctrines: The US, Britain, and France, in: West European Politics, Volume 25, Issue 1, Special Issue, The Politics of Delegation: Non-Majoritarian Institutions in Europe (January 2002) 173–199.

SHAPIRO Sidney A., TOMAIN Joseph P., Regulatory Law and Policy: Cases and Materials, 3rd ed. (LexisNexis, Newark NJ, 2003).

SHLEIFER Andrei, A theory of yardstick competition, in: Rand Journal of Economics, Volume 16, No. 3 (Autumn 1985) 319–327.

SIMMA Bruno, Self-Contained Regimes, in: Netherlands Yearbook of International Law, Volume XVI (Martinus Nijhoff Publishers, 1985) 111–136.

SIMMONS Beth A., International Law and State Behavior: Commitment and Compliance in International Monetary Affairs, in: American Political Science Review, Volume 94, No. 4 (December 2000) 819–835.

SIMMONS Beth A., The Legalization of International Monetary Affairs, in: International Organization, Volume 54, No. 3 (Summer 2000) 573–602.

SIMMONS Beth A. and MARTIN Lisa L., International Organizations and Institutions, in: Handbook of International Relations, Walter Carlsnaes, Thomas Risse, and Beth A Simmons, eds (Thousand Oaks, CA: Sage Publications, 2002) 192–211.

SINCLAIR Darren, Self-Regulation Versus Command and Control? Beyond False Dichotomies, in: Law and Policy, Volume 19, No. 4 (October 1997) 529–559.

SKELCHER Chris, Jurisdictional Integrity, Polycentrism and the Design of Democratic Governance, in: Governance, Volume 18, No. 1 (2005) 89–110.

SLAUGHTER Anne-Marie, A New World Order (Princeton: Princeton University Press, 2004).

SLAUGHTER Anne-Marie, Global Government Networks, Global Information Agencies, and Disaggregated Democracy (Harvard Law School Public Law, Working Paper No 18, 2001).

SLAUGHTER Anne-Marie, Governing the Global Economy through Government Networks, in: Michael Byers, ed., The Role of Law in International Politics, Essays in International Relations and International Law (Oxford: Oxford University Press, 2000) 177–205.

SLAUGHTER Anne-Marie, Sovereignty and Power in a Networked World Order, in: 40 Stanford Journal of International Law (2004) 283–327.

SLAUGHTER Anne-Marie, The Power and Legitimacy of Government Networks, in: The Partnership Principle, New Forms of Governance in the 21st Century, ed. by the Alfred Herrhausen Society for International Dialogue (Archetype Publications, London, 2004) offprint.

SLAUGHTER Anne-Marie, ZARING David, Networking Goes International: An Update, in: Annual Review of Law and Social Science, Volume 2 (2006) 211–229.

SLOAN John and FITZPATRICK Gerard, The Structure of International Markets Regulation, in: Blair Michael QC and Walker George, eds., Financial Markets and Exchanges Law (Oxford: Oxford University Press, 2007) 455–500.

SMITH Adam, An Inquiry into the Nature and Causes of the Wealth of Nations, 1776, Glasgow Edition (Clarendon Press, Oxford, 1976).

SOBEL Robert, The Big Board, A History of the New York Stock Market (The Free Press 1965).

SPAR Debora L., Lost in (Cyber)space: The Private Rules of Online Commerce, in: Cutler Claire A., Haufler Virginia, and Tony Porter, eds, Private Authority and International Affairs (State University of New York Press, 1999) 31–51.

SPAR Debora L., Ruling the Waves, Cycles of Discovery, Chaos, and Wealth from the Compass to the Internet (Harcourt, Inc., New York, San Diego, London, 2001).

SPAR Debora L., The Public Face of Cyberspace, in: Kaul Inge, Grunberg Isabelle, Stern Marc A., eds, Global Public Goods, International Cooperation in the 21st Century (New York: Oxford University Press, 1999) 344–362.

STEINER Henry J., Vagts Detlev F., Koh Harold Hongju, Transnational Legal Problems, 4th ed. (Foundation Press, New York, 1994).

STEPHAN Paul B., International Governance and American Democracy, in: Chicago Journal of International Law, Volume 1, no. 2 (2000) 237–256.

STEPHAN Paul B., The Futility of Unification and Harmonization in International Commercial Law, in: Virginia Journal of International Law, Volume 39 (2000) 743–797.

STERN Brigitte, How to Regulate Globalization?, in: Michael Byers, ed., The Role of Law in International Politics, Essays in International Relations and International Law (Oxford: Oxford University Press, 2000) 247–268.

STIGLER George J., The Theory of Economic Regulation, in: The Bell Journal of Economics and Management Science, Volume 2, No. 1 (Spring 1971) 3–21.

STIGLITZ Joseph E., Globalization and Its Discontents (W. W. Norton & Company, New York, London, 2003).

STOLL Tobias, Responsibility, Sovereignty and Cooperation – Reflections on the "Responsibility to Protect", in: König Doris, Stoll Peter-Tobias, Röben Volker, Matz-Lück Nele, eds, International Law Today: New Challenges and the Need for Reform?, Beiträge zum ausländischen öffentlichen Recht und Völkerrecht, Band 193 (Springer, Berlin, Heidelberg, New York, 2008) 1–16.

STREBEL-AERNI Brigitte, ed., Standards für nachhaltige Finanzmärkte (Schulthess Juristische Medien AG, Zurich, 2008).

STREECK Wolfgang and SCHMITTER Philippe C., Community, market, state – and associations? The prospective contribution of interest governance to social order, in: Wolfgang Streeck and Philippe C. Schmitter, eds, Private Interest Government, Beyond Market and State (Sage Series in Neo-Corporatism, London, 1985) 1–29.

STREECK Wolfgang and SCHMITTER Philippe C., eds, Private Interest Government, Beyond Market and State (Sage Series in Neo-Corporatism, London, 1985).

STUPP Eric, DUBS Dieter, Verhaltensregeln, in: Watter Rolf, Vogt Nedim Peter, eds, Börsengesetz, Art. 161, 161bis, 305bis und 305ter Strafgesetzbuch, Basler Kommentar (Helbing Lichtenhahn Verlag, Basel, 2007) 150–166.

SUNSTEIN Cass R., After the Rights Revolution: Reconceiving the Regulatory State (Harvard: Harvard University Press, 1990).

SUNSTEIN Cass R., Paradoxes of the Regulatory State, in: 57 University of Chicago Law Review, Volume 57 (1990) 407–441.

TAMANAHA Brian Z., A General Jurisprudence of Law and Society (Oxford: Oxford University Press, 2001).

TAMANAHA Brian Z., A Non-Essentialist Version of Legal Pluralism, in: Journal of Law and Society, Volume 27, no. 2 (June 2000) 296–321.

TAMANAHA Brian Z., On the Rule of Law, History, Politics, Theory (Cambridge: Cambridge University Press, 2004).

TECT, The Evolution of Cooperation and Trading, Tect – Eurocores (2005) unpublished paper on file with author.

TEUBNER Gunther, Codes of Conduct multinationaler Unternehmen: Unternehmensverfassung jenseits von Corporate Governance und gesetzlicher Mitbestimmung, in: Dieter Gosewinkel, Wolfgang Merkel and Dagmar Simon, ed., Unternehmen, Staat, Globalisierung, Festschrift für Jürgen Kocka zum 65. Geburtstag, WZB-Vorlesungen (Verlag des Wissenschaftszentrums Berlin, 2007) 36–51.

TEUBNER Gunther, ed., Dilemmas of Law in the Welfare State, De Gruyter, Berlin/New York, 1986

TEUBNER Gunther, Global Bukowina: Legal Pluralism in the World Society, in: Gunther Teubner, ed., Global Law Without a State (Dartmouth, 2006) 3–28.

TEUBNER Gunther, Globale Bukowina: Zur Emergenz eines transnationalen Rechtspluralismus, in: Rechtshistorisches Journal 15 (1996) 255–290.

TEUBNER Gunther, ed., Global Law Without a State (Ashgate, Dartmouth, 2006).

TEUBNER Gunther, Global Private Regimes: Neo-Spontaneous Law and Dual Constitution of Autonomous Sectors? in: Karl-Heinz Ladeur ed., Public Governance in the Age of Globalization (Ashgate, Aldershot 2004) 71–87.

TEUBNER Gunther, Juridification: Concepts, Aspects, Limits, Solution, in: Gunther Teubner, ed., Juridification of Social Spheres: A Comparative Analysis in the Areas of Labor, Corporate, Antitrust, and Social Welfare Law, Schriftenreihe des Europäischen Hochschulinstituts, Florence (De Gruyter, 1987).

TEUBNER Gunther, Law as an Autopoietic System (Oxford: Oxford University Press, 1993).

TEUBNER Gunther, Recht als autopoietisches System (Frankfurt am Main, 1989).

TEUBNER Gunther, Self-Constitutionalizing TNCs? On the Linkage of "Private" and "Public" Corporate Codes of Conduct, in: Gralf-Peter Callies (ed.) Governing Transnational Corporations – Public and Private Perspectives, Indiana Journal of Global Legal Studies 17 (2010) 1–20

TEUBNER Gunther, NOBLES Richard, SCHIFF David, The Autonomy of Law: An Introduction to Legal Autopoiesis, in: Schiff David and Richard Nobles, eds, Jurisprudence (Butterworth, London, 2003).

THATCHER Mark, Delegation to Independent Regulatory Agencies: Pressures, Functions and Contextual Mediation, in: West European Politics, Volume 25, no. 1, Special Issue, The Politics of Delegation: Non-Majoritarian Institutions in Europe (January 2002) 125–147.

THATCHER Mark, Internationalisation and Economic Institutions, Comparing European Experiences (Oxford: Oxford University Press, 2007).

THATCHER Mark, Regulation after Delegation: Independent Regulatory Agencies in Europe, in: Journal of European Public Policy, Volume 9, No. 6 (2002) 954–972.

THATCHER Mark and STONE SWEET Alec, Theory and Practice of Delegation to Non-Majoritarian Institutions, in: West European Politics, Volume 25, no. 1, Special Issue, The Politics of Delegation: Non-Majoritarian Institutions in Europe (January 2002) 1–22.

THÜRER Daniel, Globalisierung der Wirtschaft: Herausforderung zur 'Konstitutionalisierung' von Macht und Globalisierung von Verantwortlichkeit – Oder: Unterwegs zur 'Citizen Corporation', in: 119, Zeitschrift für Schweizerisches Recht, NF (2000) 107–122.

THÜRER Daniel, Soft Law, in: Rudolf Bernhard, ed., Encyclopedia of Public International Law, Volume IV (North-Holland, Amsterdam / London / New York / Oxford / Paris / Shannon / Tokyo, 2000) 452–460.

THÜRER Daniel, 'Soft Law' – eine neue Form von Völkerrecht?, in: Zeitschrift für Schweizerisches Recht, Band 104 I, Heft 4 (1985) 429–453.

THÜRER Daniel, The Emergence of Non-Governmental Organizations and Transnational Enterprises in International Law and the Changing Role of the State, in: Rainer Hofmann, Nils Geissler, eds, Non-State Actors as New Subjects of International Law (Veröffentlichungen des Walther-Schücking-Instituts für Internationales Recht an der Universität Kiel, Band 125, Berlin, 1999) 37–58.

TÕKÉS Rudolf L., Institution-Building in Hungary, Analytical Issues and Constitutional Models, 1989–1990, Discussion Paper Series, no. 64 (Collegium Budapest Institute for Advanced Study, October 2001).

TRIGO TRINDADE Rita and SENN Myriam, Control and Responsibility of Rating Agencies in Switzerland, in: Swiss Reports presented at the XVII Congress of the International Academy of Comparative Law, 16- 22 July 2006, Utrecht, The Netherlands (Schulthess Verlag, Zurich, Geneva, 2006) 137–161.

ULRICH Hans, Das Unternehmen als soziales produktives System, 2nd ed. (Bern, 1970).

UNGER Jonathan and CHAN Anita, China, Corporatism, and the East Asian Model, in: The Australian Journal of Chinese Affairs, No. 33 (January 1995).

VAN AAKEN Anne, Effectuating Public International Law Through Market Mechanisms? (CLPE Research Paper 34/2008, Volume 04, No. 7, Toronto).

VASS Peter, ed., 2006-7, CRI Regulatory Review (Centre for Regulated Industries, University of Bath, 2007).

VIBERT Frank, Models of Regulation, The Single Market and the Financial Services Action Plan (European Policy Forum, London, 2002).

VISSCHER Charles de, Stages in the Codification of International Law, The Hague 1930 – Geneva 1958 – Vienna 1969, in: Wolfgang Friedmann, Louis Henkin and Oliver Lissitzyn, ed., Transnational Law in a Changing Society, Essays in Honor of Philip C. Jessup (Columbia University Press, New York and London, 1972) 17–33.

WATTER Rolf, VOGT Nedim Peter, eds, Börsengesetz, Art. 161, 161bis, 305bis und 305ter Strafgesetzbuch, Basler Kommentar (Helbing Lichtenhahn Verlag, Basel, 2007).

WEBER Max, Grundriss der Sozialökonomik, III. Abteilung: Wirtschaft und Gesellschaft (Tübingen, 1947).

WEBER Max, Wirtschaft und Gesellschaft, 5th rev. ed., Johannes Winckelmann, ed. (Mohr Siebeck, Tübingen, 2002).

WEBER Rolf H. and ARNER Douglas W., Toward a New Design for International Financial Regulation, in: University of Pennsylvania Journal of International Law, volume 29, no. 2 (Winter 2007) 391–453.

WEDGWOOD Ruth, Legal Personality and the Role of Non-Governmental Organizations and Non-State Political Entities in the United Nations System, in: Rainer Hofmann, Nils Geissler, eds, Non-State Actors as New Subjects of International Law (Veröffentlichungen des Walther-Schücking-Instituts für Internationales Recht an der Universität Kiel, Band 125, Berlin, 1999) 21–36.

WEINBERGER David, Everything is Miscellaneous, The Power of the New Digital Disorder (Times Books, New York, 2007).

WIEGAND Wolfgang, WICHTERMANN Jürg, Die Standesregeln der Banken als "blosse" Auslegungshilfe – zur (Un-)Verbindlichkeit von Selbstregulierungen, BGE 125 IV 139, in: recht (2000) 28–36.

WIENER Norbert, Cybernetics, or control and communication in the animal and the machine (New York: John Wiley & sons, Inc., 1948).

WILLKE Helmut, Entzauberung des Staates, Überlegungen zu einer sozietalen Steuerungstheorie (Königstein/Taunus 1983).

WILLKE Helmut, Systemtheorie III: Steuerungstheorie, 2nd ed. (Lucius & Lucius, Stuttgart, 1998).

WOLFRUM Rüdiger, International Law of Cooperation, in: Rudolf Bernhard, ed., Encyclopedia of Public International Law, Volume II (North-Holland, Amsterdam/Lausanne/New York/ Oxford/Shannon/Tokyo, 1995) 1242–1247.

World Trade Organization, WTO Panel Report on United States Import Prohibition of Certain Shrimp and Shrimp Products, WT/DS 58/AB/R (15 May 1998).

WYMEERSCH Eddy, The reforms of the European Financial Supervisory System - An Overview, in: European Company and Financial Law Review, Volume 7, Issue 2 (July 2010) 240–265.

WYSS Martin Philipp, Öffentliche Interessen – Interessen der Öffentlichkeit?: das öffentliche Interesse im schweizerischen Staats- und Verwaltungsrecht (Stämpfli Verlag, Bern, 2001).

YABLOKOVA Oksana, Amended NGO Bill Quickly Approved, in: Moscow Times (22 December 2005).

YOUNG R. Oran, The Effectiveness of International Institutions: Hard Cases and Critical Variables, in: Rosenau James N. and Czempiel Ernst-Otto, Governance without Government: Order and Change in World Politics (Oxford: Oxford University Press, 2000) 160–194.

ZÄCH Roger, Tendenzen der juristischen Auslegungslehre, in: Zeitschrift für Schweizerisches Recht, Band 96, I. Halbband (1977) 313–343.

ZARING David, International Institutional Performance in Crisis, in: Chicago Journal of International Law, Volume 10, No. 2 (Winter 2010) 475–504.

ZARING David, International Law by Other Means: The Twilight Existence of International Financial Regulatory Organizations, in: Texas International Law Journal, Volume 33 (1998) 281–330.

ZIMMERLI Ulrich, ed., Die neue Bundesverfassung, Konsequenzen für Praxis und Wirtschaft, BTJP 1999 (Stämpfli Verlag AG, Bern, 2000).

ZIMMERMANN Andreas and HOFMANN Rainer, eds, Unity and Diversity in International Law, Proceeding of an International Symposium of the Kiel Walther Schücking Institute of International Law November 4–7, 2004 (Duncker & Humblot, Berlin, 2006).

ZIMMERMANN Heinz, Risiko und Repräsentation: Über Krisen des Finanzsystems, in: Strebel-Aerni Brigitte, ed., Standards für nachhaltige Finanzmärkte (Schulthess Juristische Medien AG, Zurich, 2008) 19–39.

Index